MARIA MAVROMATAKI

GREEK
MYTHOLOGY
AND RELIGION

COSMOGONY

THE GODS

RELIGIOUS CUSTOMS

THE HEROES

editions HAÏTALIS

CONTENTS

PUBLISHED BY: HAÏTALIS
TEXTS: MARIA MAVROMATAKI
(Archaeologist - Tour guide)
EDITING & DTP: BARRAGE LTD
ART EDITING: FOTINI SVARNA
COLOUR SEPARATIONS: COLOUR CENTER LTD
PRINTING: A. PETROULAKIS S.A.

Copyright © 1997
EDITIONS: HAÏTALI
ASTROUS 13, 13121 ATHENS
TEL.: 5766.883

INTRODUCTION 4

A. COSMOGONY

1. THE CREATION OF THE WORLD 6
2. URANUS - GE - CRONUS 8
3. CRONUS - RHEA - ZEUS 8
4. THE BATTLE OF THE TITANS 9
5. ATLAS 10
6. THE BATTLE OF THE GIANTS 13
7. THE CREATION OF MAN 16
8. DEUCALION'S FLOOD 19

B. THE GODS 20

1. THE TWELVE GODS OF OLYMPUS 24
Zeus 28
Hera 35
Athena 38
Poseidon 48
Apollo 52
Artemis 62
Demeter - (Persephone) 69
Hermes 76
Aphrodite 82
Ares 90
Hephaestus 95
Hestia 98
2. THE OTHER GODS
Dionysus, Asclepius 100
Helius - Eos - Selene 113
Iris- the Harpies-Winds, The Pleiades-the Hyades .. 116
Hades - Charon, Pan, The Nymphs 118
Eros, The Graces - Hebe, The Muses 123

Themis - the Hours, Nemesis - the Furies ... 128
The Cabeiri - the Telchines 130
Nereus - the Neraids, Proteus 132
Triton, The Sirens - Scylla - Charybdis ... 134

C. RELIGIOUS CUSTOMS — 136

1. THE PANHELLENIC GAMES 138
The Olympic Games 138
The Pythian Games, The Isthmian Games ... 140

2. THE ORACLES 145

D. THE HEROES — 148

1. HERACLES 151

2. MYTHS OF ATTICA
Aegeus - Theseus 172
Daedalus and Icarus 186

3. THE THEBAN MYTHS
Europa - Cadmus 188
Laius - Oedipus 191
Oedipus' children 195

4. THE VOYAGE OF THE ARGO
Phrixus and Helle 198
Jason - Medea 200

5. PELEUS - THETIS - ACHILLES 206

6. THRACE - Orpheus and Eurydice 210

7. MYTHS OF THE ARGOLID
Inachus - Phoroneus - Io 212
Danaus - Nauplius - Palamedes 214
Danae - Perseus 214
Oenomaus - Pelops 219
The house of Atreus 222

8. THE TROJAN WAR 230

9. ODYSSEUS - The voyage home 244

INTEX 254

INTRODUCTION

T he myths were the first creations of the human mind, and they were formed out of a profound need to provide an allegorical explanation for all the phenomena of life. The awe man felt when faced by the uncontrollable forces of nature, his metaphysical anxieties, his awareness both of his weakness and of his uniqueness, and even the moral rules on which he based his own life and his communication with other human beings - all these were expressed in magical narratives of symbolic content. Taken as a whole, these mythical traditions make up what we call mythology, in which we see reflected man's original feelings towards the way in which life manifested itself. In addition, the myths also provide us with a clear picture of the indivdualities of each people, of their mental composition, of the areas into which their mental quests carried them, of their achievements and of their course through history.

The Greeks were among the earliest peoples to create myths, which they used as a way of understanding and interpreting anything which transcended the human scale and struck them as inexplicable and impossible to control. Their narratives were passed down orally from generation to generation, changing and becoming richer in accordance with the needs and the stage of development of each era. The Greeks combined their mythological traditions with their wealth of moral concepts in order to produce, in their fertile imaginations, a series of supreme beings, the gods, who commanded the universe and ordered human destiny. These gods were the object of their worship, and divine conduct was their guide in deciding how to live the virtuous life. The feats of the gods and heroes were a source of inspiration and creation for the Greeks, leading them on to the upward path that led to the conquest of ambitious goals. Mythology stimulated the restless minds of

the Greeks, and was the force that led to the creation of what today we call Greek civilisation.

The first consideration to which the Greeks - like all the other peoples of the world - gave their attention was that of how the world was created and of the powers that controlled its operation. The earliest inhabitants of the country later called Greece seemed to have identified the universe with the earth itself, which yielded up its fruits and enabled life to survive. The fertility of nature and the fruitfulness both of the earth and of mankind were seen as the ultimate mysteries, and deified. The earth, with its life-endowing powers, took the form of a female deity who was responsible for fertility and reproduction. The prehistoric inhabitants of Greece worshipped this goddess in sacred places and honoured her with offerings and depictions in art.

In the Mycenean period (16th-12th century BC), the great earth goddess Ge was flanked by a whole host of new deities, most of them male. Thanks to the deciphering of Linear B script, dating from the Mycenean period, we know that this was the time that saw the birth of the cults of gods who survived for centuries in the ancient Greek religion and mythology. The names of Zeus, Ares, Hermes, Dionysus and Poseidon have been read inscribed in Linear B on clay tablets found in the Mycenean palaces, and they were the most important deities of the historic period. The Greek pantheon took its final form after the Dorian invasion of Greece, and apart from the purely Doric deities it included elements from pre-Greek religion, from the pantheon of the Myceneans and from the religious beliefs of the Near East. The new gods became the regulators of the universe and guardians of the cosmic order. Stories of their doings were told in a vast number of widely-varying myths which interpreted all the concerns of human beings and explained all the functions of nature and living creatures.

p. 4
The famous Sphinx of the Naxians, a votive offering by the people of Naxos at the sanctuary of Delphi (570 BC, Delphi Museum).

p. 5
A Melian relief showing Scylla. This terrible monster had a female body and the head and tail of a dragon. Dog's heads sprouted from around her waist (fifth century BC, British Museum).

COSMOGONY

p.6

Above: Zeus hurling a thunderbolt at the Titan Iapetus (section of the pediment from the temple of Artemis-Medusa in Corfu, 585 BC, Corfu Archaeological Museum).

Below: The Giant Cantharus in a scene from theBattle of the Giants (detail from the north frieze of the Treasury of the Siphnians, Delphi, 525 BC, Delphi Archaeological Museum).

p.7

Rhea, instead of the new-born Zeus, gives Cronus a stone wrapped in swaddling-clothes (red-figure pelike 460 BC, Metropolitan Museum, New York).

1. THE CREATION OF THE WORLD

The earliest account of how the world came about is to be found in Homer, who in the *Iliad* twice refers to **Oceanus** as the originator and father of all things. For the ancient Greeks, Oceanus was an enormous river that encircled the entire world, giving life from its rushing flood to the sea, the springs and the smaller rivers. The wife of Oceanus, and primordial mother, was called **Tithys**. From their union sprang three thousand rivers and three thousand nymphs, the **Oceanids**. With their brothers the **Rivers**, the Oceanids were responsible for bringing up children and preserving youth. Among them, human thought distinguished some of the most important figures in mythology, such as Europa, Calypso, Tyche and Eurynome. Oceanus and Tithys were also the parents of the Greek **gods,** who later came to rule the world.

A different version of the creation of the world and of the gods themselves is given us by the ancient writer Hesiod in his *Theogony*. "The very first of all **Chaos** came into being", he tells us, followed by **Ge** with her broad embrace, the eternal and steadfast couch of the immortals who dwell on Olympus; then came **Eros**, the most beautiful of the immortals, who sprinkles gods and men alike with his sweet passion, taming the heart and overcoming all prudent counsel. Chaos gave birth to **Erebus** and **Night**, who in turn generated the **Air** and the **Day**. Ge gave birth to the star-studded **Sky (Uranus)**, the **Mountains** and the **Sea**. Later, she formed a bond with Uranus and brought the Titans, the Cyclopes and the Hundred-Handed Ones into being.

2. URANUS - GE - CRONUS

Relations between Uranus and his children were far from friendly. The great god's rage fell chiefly upon the Titans, whom he imprisoned and left incarcerated in the bowels of the earth. Their mother, outraged by this injustice, forged a sickle and summoned her sons to put an end to the source of their woes. Cronus, the youngest of the sons, was the boldest of all: he hid in his parents' bed, and when Uranus laid himself down and turned to embrace Ge, Cronus castrated him with the sickle, casting his genitals into the sea. Aphrodite was born out of those organs in the foam of the sea, while the drops of blood that fell upon the earth gave birth to the three Erinyes (Fates), the Melian Nymphs (nymphs of the ash-tree) and the Giants.

3. CRONUS - RHEA - ZEUS

After the castration of Uranus, power passed to Cronus. He immediately set free his brothers and married the Titaness Rhea. From their union sprang Demeter, Hestia, Hera, Hades and Poseidon. But Cronus' children fared little better than their father: fearing that one of his descendants would dethrone him, he swallowed each of his offspring as soon as they were born.

Rhea found this catastrophic situation more than she could bear, and before giving birth to Zeus, her last child, she consulted Uranus and Ge. With their help, she managed to conceal Zeus in a cave on Crete, giving Cronus a stone wrapped in swaddling-clothes to swallow. In order to drown the baby's wailing, the **Curetes**, Rhea's sons, clashed their bronze shields together and danced outside his hiding-place. The baby Zeus was nurtured on the milk of the goat

Amaltheia, whom he later honoured highly by naming a constellation after her. Today, the Greek expression for the cornucopia, the 'horn of plenty', is still the '**horn of Amaltheia**'.

4. THE BATTLE OF THE TITANS

When Zeus grew up, he encountered his father, vied with him in strength and wisdom, and was victorious. He used an emetic potion to force Cronus to disgorge all the children in his belly - along with the stone he had swallowed instead of Zeus. Zeus himself took the stone to the Oracle at Delphi and set it up there as an eternal symbol of his superiority.

However, the children of Cronus resolved to punish their father, and rallied round the leadership of Zeus to wage war on him. Cronus took as his allies the majority of his brothers the Titans, and so fought the famous Battle of the Titans against the future gods of Olympus. The Titan Oceanus and his daughter Styx, her children Kratos (Power), Bia (Violence), Zelus (Zeal) and Nike (Victory), and Prometheus, son of the Titan Iapetus, took the side of the gods. Even Ge, the mother of the Titans, aided the gods, prophesying that they would be victorious only if they liberated the Cyclopes and the Hundred-Handed Ones, whom Cronus had imprisoned in Tartarus. Zeus liberated them, and they did indeed play a decisive part in his victory. The Cyclopes gave Zeus his thunderbolt, Poseidon his trident, and Hades the 'Hat of Darkness', a dog-skin helmet which made him invisible.

The Titans made their camp on Mt Orthrys, while the gods occupied Olympus. The war lasted ten years, culminating in some highly dramatic battles. Hades, made invisible by his helmet, crept up on Cronus and stole his weapons, and while Poseidon menaced Cronus with his trident Zeus finished him off with the thunderbolt. The three Hundred-Handed Ones bombarded the other Titans with rocks, but a sudden yell from the god Pan made them turn on their heels and flee (hence the concept of 'panic').

Such Titans as survived the war were imprisoned in Tartarus, where the Hundred-Handed Ones stood guard over them. Thus the old divine order was chained up in the bowels of the earth, while the victorious Olympian gods ascended into the bright sky, bringing new values and new concepts into the world.

5. ATLAS

Zeus reserved one of his harshest punishments for Atlas, whom Cronus had placed at the head of the Titans during the war. Altas was exiled to the ends of the earth, in the west, where the Garden of the Hesperides lay, and was condemned to hold the earth and the sky up on his shoulders. Nonetheless, this arduous task allowed Atlas to learn the secrets of the earth, the sky and the depths of the sea, and he was the first to discover that the universe was spherical in shape. According to the traditions, Atlas had various children: the seven Pleiades, after whom the stars of the constellation by that name were called (Alcyone, Electra, Celaeno, Maea, Merope, Taygete and Sterope), the Hesperides (often identified with the Pleiades), Hesperus, Hyas, Calypso and Pasiphae.

p.10
Altas was only once able to take the globe off his shoulders: when he had to help Heracles by fetching him the Apples of the Hesperides (see pp. 163-164). One of the metopes of the temple of Zeus at Olympia shows Heracles carrying the sky and the earth, with the support of Athena, while Atlas holds out the precious Apples of the Hesperides to him (460 BC, Olympia Archaeological Museum).

p.11
Atlas engaged in his arduous task of supporting the globe on his shoulders (Roman statue, Naples National Museum).

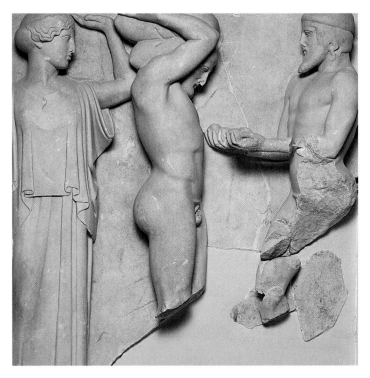

6. THE BATTLE OF THE GIANTS

A ccording to one story, the Giants sprang from the drops of blood that fell to earth when Cronus castrated Uranus. They were huge and monstrous creatures with snakes for hair and tails ending in dragons. Another version relates that Ge gave birth to these monsters immediately after the Battle of the Titans, as a way of avenging herself on the gods for incarcerating her children in Tartarus and ceasing to honour her. Urged on by Ge, the Giants launched a surprise attack on the gods, hurling rocks and burning tree-trunks at them. This was the start of the famous Battle of the Giants, which caused turmoil all over the earth: the Giants demolished mountains, caused the ground to tremble, moved rivers and made the sea engulf the land. The doings of the Giants - which may reflect a series of changes in the geology of Greece - naturally led to a reaction from the gods.

Zeus gathered his allies, ready for war: Poseidon, Ares, Hephaistus, Hermes, Apollo, Dionysus with the Sileni and the Satyrs, the Fates, Hera, Aphrodite, Artemis, Cybele, Styx and her daughter Nike, Hecate - and the goddess Athena, who sprang, fully-armed, from the head of Zeus during the course of the Battle of the Giants. Although the gods

p.12
Apollo, Artemis, and the Giants Cantharus during the Battle of the Giants (part of the north frieze of the Treasury of the Siphnians at Delphi, 525 BC, Delphi Archaeological Museum).

p.13
Athena, in her aegis fringed with snakes, strikes terror into her foes during the Battle of the Giants (from the pedimental sculptures of the Battle of the Giants belonging to the Archaic temple of Athena on the Acropolis, late sixth century BC, Acropolis Museum).

fought bravely, the Giants withstood all the blows dealt them. At that point, the gods remembered a prophecy which had advised them to enlist the help of a mortal if they wished to be victualable, and they summoned Heracles to the battle. His assistance proved to be invaluable, and in desperation Ge set out in search of a magic herb to save her sons. Zeus, learning this, forbade Auge (the dawn), Helius (the sun) and Selene (the moon) from appearing until he himself had discovered the herb and destroyed it.

The result was that the Giants fell dead, one after the other. Athena slew Pallas and skinned him, making a shield out of his hide. She also dealt the death blow to Enceladus, at whose head she cast Sicily. Dionysus turned himself into a lion and devoured Erytius (or Rhoetus), and a touch of his staff was enough to dispose of most other opponents. Heracles killed Alcyoneus and, with Apollo, Ephialtes; Zeus slew Eurymedon and Porphyrion; and Poseidon accounted for Polybotes. After the Giants had been wiped out, the gods were left as sole masters of the earth and of all the creatures that lived there.

*p.15
Sections of the north frieze of the Treasury of the Siphnians at Delphi, showing the Battle of the Giants. From left to right, above: Cybele's lion attacking a Giant, Apollo, Artemis, and the Giants Cantharus, Ephialtus and Hypertus; below, Athena, the Giants Berectus, Laertus and Astartus, Ares, and the Giants Biatus and Enaphus (525 BC, Delphi Archaeological Museum).*

7. THE CREATION OF MAN

THE FIVE GENERATIONS OF MAN

According to Hesiod, the first human beings were the children of Ge, and they were subjects of Cronus. These men lived in peace and without cares, and with no need to labour to survive. They shared amongst themselves all the good things that nature bestowed upon them and were forever young. They were the *golden race* of mankind. Next came the *silver race*, whose society was one of extreme matriarchy and who lived - in misery - in ignorance of the gods. Zeus punished this race of man with annihilation, and they were succeeded by the *bronze race*. This new tribe of men believed in the gods, but they were warlike and pitiless. As a result, their time upon the earth was short, and they were followed by another *bronze race* - though its members were noble in the soul and inspired by heroic feelings. They took part in the voyage of the *Argo* and fought the Trojan War, and now they dwell forever in the Elysian Fields. The last generation of man is the *iron race*, unjust and cruel creatures who inhabit the earth down to the present day and have never experienced happiness.

p.17
Atlas and Prometheus were exiled to the western and eastern extremities of the world, where they patiently underwent the punishments that Zeus had decreed for them. Altas, on the left, bears the world on his shoulders, while on the right Prometheus, lashed to a pillar in the Caucasus mountains, bleeds under the merciless talons of an eagle. The snake behind Atlas is a symbol of the world, which is supported by a large column (Laconian cylix, 550 BC, Rome, Vatican Museum).

EPIMETHEUS - PROMETHEUS - PANDORA

A different version of the origins of the human race is to be found in many other ancient writers. In the time of the Titans, they say, there were no mortal beings on the earth: only the deathless gods. The gods then decided to create a new order of being, and shaped its likeness in earth and fire. Next they ordered Epimetheus and Prometheus, sons of the Titan Iapetus, to arrange the details of the new creatures and endow them with powers and gifts. Epimetheus undertook this task, and equipped all the creatures of the earth, the sea and the sky with the things they would need to survive and perpetuate their species. The good things that the gods had given were shared out fairly, so that although the

new creatures differed from each other, none was more or less virtuous than the others, and none possessed all the gifts of nature.

However, Epimetheus made a significant mistake. He was so absorbed by his care for the other animals that he forgot to give man any qualities at all, leaving him bare and lacking in any special abilities. Prometheus, when he saw man's state, decided to help him. He stole wisdom from Athena and fire from Hephaestus and gave them both to the human race, whom he also taught the arts and sciences and endowed with hope as a weapon in the face of the adversities of life. Some ancient writers emphasise the contribution made by Prometheus still more, stating that it was he, with the help of Athena, who shaped man out of clay and fire and gave him an appearance similar to that of the gods.

The initiatives taken by Prometheus sent Zeus into a rage - and they were not the only reason for the god's wrath. There is a tradition which tells of another occasion on which Prometheus had outwitted Zeus. Once, after sacrificing an ox, Prometheus had wrapped the meat in one piece of the animal's skin and the fat and bones in another, offering both to Zeus to choose between. Although Zeus knew of Prometheus' cunning, he chose the bones and allowed Prometheus to give the meat to man. This was the origin, it was said, of the human custom of eating the meat of the sacrificial animal and offering the fat and bones to the gods.

Yet the punishment that Zeus had in store for Prometheus was a cruel one. He exiled him to the eastern extremity of the earth - just as he had sent Atlas to the west - and tied him to a stake in the Caucasus mountains. Each morning, an eagle swooped down, tore him with its talons and ate his liver; but each evening his liver grew back again, and so Prometheus was condemned to a life of perpetual agony. He suffered this torture for thirty years, until Heracles released him by shooting the eagle with his arrows.

Prometheus was not alone in his sufferings, for Zeus also punished mankind for having accepted the fire and the knowledge that were the property of the gods. Zeus ordered Hephaestus to make a mixture of earth and water and from it to create a woman as beautiful as a goddess.

When she was ready, Athena adorned her and taught her how to weave, while Aphrodite endowed her with grace and passion, the Graces and Peitho garlanded her with gold ribbons and the Hours decorated her with spring flowers. Hermes, on the other hand, put malicious and lying words into her heart. Zeus called her Pandora, because she had received gifts (*dora*) from all the gods, and sent her off to Epimetheus. Bewitched by her beauty, he fell in love with her and took her out for mankind to see. Pandora's fate was to be the cause of all human misfortune, because she opened the lid of a jar from which evils of all kinds immediately spilled out to fill the world. Only hope was left in the jar, because Pandora closed the lid again at the last moment. As a result, mankind - who until that time had known no pain, sickness or death - was doomed to everlasting unhappiness.

8. DEUCALION'S FLOOD

Punished thus by the gods, man lived in misery and had become so evil that Zeus made up his mind to wipe the entire human race from the face of the earth. He thus unleashed a terrible flood, which he thougt no one would survive. But Prometheus, knowing Zeus's plan, managed to warn his son Deucalion, who with his wife Pyrrha (the daughter of Epimetheus and Pandora) built an ark and fitted it out with everything he might need. Then he entered the ark and shut the hatches. Suddenly a gale sprang up and torrential rain began, and before long all the rivers and seas had risen until the whole of the land was flooded except for the peaks of the highest mountains. For nine days, the storm swept Deucalion and Pyrrha across the sea at its will, until at last the weather cleared and the ark grounded on a mountain peak (Parnassus, Orthrys, Athos or Etna). No other human beings had survived the flood. Deucalion and Pyrrha stepped out of the ark and offered sacrifices to Zeus in thanksgiving for their salvation - not forgetting to beg him to create more human beings. He heard their plea, and told them to cover their faces, pick up stones and throw them over their shoulders without looking behind them. All the stones thrown by Deucalion turned into men, and all Pyrrha's became women. Thus, before long the earth was populated again and the species had survived. Pyrrha and Deucalion also had children of their own: Hellen, Amphyction, Protogenia, Melanthia, Thyia and Pandora, the eldest of whom (in some accounts, the son of Zeus) was to become the father of the Greeks (or *Hellenes*).

p.18
The myth of Pandora was interpreted by the poet Hesiod as a punishment imposed by the gods on the entire human race, since the box she opened released evil into the world. However, according to one school of thought the fact that Pandora was made out of earth and water and that all the gods gave her gifts reflects the generative powers of the earth, generously offering its fruits to mankind. The interior of this cylix shows Athena and Hephaestus adorning Pandora, here referred to as Anesidora (470-460 BC, British Museum).

THE GODS

P olytheism was one of the principal features of ancient Greek religion. For the ancient Greeks, the gods, taken as a whole, represented a single concept: nature, in all its manifestations, and each god or goddess was associated with one or more of the powers of nature. The role of the gods was not so much that of creating the world as of maintaining order and harmony in it. As a result, each was assigned specific properties which had a more profound symbolic meaning: they were capable of interpreting each apparently inexplicable natural phenomenon and functioned as the guardians of balance in nature and in human society alike.

To the Greek mind, the gods were immortal, omnipotent and magnificent. They could control all mortal beings in every sphere of their lives, determining their fortunes, their relationships, and when they came into the world and left it. Yet the gods were not distant, inaccessible beings: man could approach them easily, seeing them, hearing them and even touching them. As contradictory and mutually complementary beings, they constituted the incarnation of the perfect human - but a human who was free of the deprivations and prohibitions of life, who could take pleasure in whatever presented itself to him, who could injure himself without suffering pain or death, could fall in love without being subject to the barriers applicable to mankind, who could experience anger or jealousy without having to suppress his feelings, who could carouse and get drunk, who could live and enjoy himself with his creatures as if he were both creator and creation. The ancient Greeks assigned to their gods all the properties that they themselves would have liked to possess, but

p.21
Part of a votive relief from the sanctuary of Artemis at Brauron, known as the 'relief of the gods'. Zeus, seated, was probably depicted holding his sceptre, and Leto and Apollo stand in front of him (fifth-fourth century BC, Brauron Museum).

which their human nature prevented them from obtaining.

This is the light in which we have to view the anthropomorphism of the ancient Greek gods. The human properties of the gods in no way detracted from their status as divine beings. In fact, the characteristics which men attributed to them functioned as models for human behaviour, and constituted the targets which ordinary mortals set themselves. The physical similarity between the gods and men served a similar purpose. The idealised divine forms which took shape in the ancient Greek mind were neither more nor less than the image to which human beings themselves would have liked to approximate. On the other hand, the gods actually assumed human form when they were to appear to mortals, and so their bodies were not necessarily corporeal: they might better be described as fields of energy from which supernatural powers could emanate.

Each of the ancient Greek city-states had its own pantheon. However, the whole of Greece shared the same main divine fig-

ures, which had been created out of the common needs of members of the same race. The first written references to the ancient Greek gods date from the Mycenean period. The names of Zeus, Poseidon, Ares, Hermes and Dionysus have been read on clay tablets with inscriptions in Linear B script found in the Mycenean palaces of Mycenae itself, Pylos and Cnossus and dating from about 1400-1200 BC. The Olympian pantheon took its final form in the tenth or ninth centuries BC (the Geometric period), and established itself in the Greek mind thanks to the epics of Homer, which were tremendously popular throughout antiquity.

When the city-states came into being in the eighth century BC, the religious concepts of the Greeks were renewed and enhanced with fresh elements, and the first 'official' locations for worship of the gods appeared. The ancient Greek religious system reached completion in the Archaic and Classical periods (6th-5th centuries BC), which was also the time when Greek civilisation was at its zenith.

pp.22-23
Part of the east frieze of the Treasury of the Siphnians at Delphi, showing an assembly of the gods on Olympus. From left to right: Ares, Aphrodite, Artemis, Apollo and Zeus (525 BC, Delphi Archaeological Museum).

THE TWELVE
GODS OF OLYMPUS

A mong all the gods worshipped by the Greeks, the twelve deities who dwelt on Mt Olympus, the highest mountain in Greece, formed a special category of their own. The gods of Olympus were usually taken to be Zeus, Hera, Athena, Poseidon, Apollo, Artemis, Demeter, Hermes, Aphrodite, Ares, Hephaestus and Hestia. In certain local variations, positions among the 'twelve' were occupied by Pluto, Dionysus, Heracles or other local cult heroes. The twelve gods - six male and six female - were divided in accordance with their properties and activities into six couples united by bonds of friendship or kinship: Zeus/Hera, Poseidon/Demeter, Apollo/Artemis, Hermes/Athena, Ares /Aphrodite, Hephaestus/Hestia.

The gods of Olympus lived mostly in peace, in a home which was both idyllic and imposingly majestic. In choosing to dwell on Olympus, they were on the borderline between earth and sky, and could thus supervise everything that the creatures of the world were doing. Their main object of interest was man, whom they sometimes showered with gifts and sometimes persecuted. Their attitude to one another was somewhat similar: terrible crises might break out in

p.25
Part of the east frieze of the Parthenon. Poseidon, Apollo and Artemis, with the other gods of Olympus, have gathered to greet the Athenians on the Acropolis at the Panathenaic Festival (440 BC, Acropolis Museum).

their relations, but there were many occasions on which as loving companions they caroused together at sumptuous banquets,
eating ambrosia and drinking nectar - the sole sustenance of the
gods. The leader of the gods was Zeus the omnipotent, followed
by the others in a rudimentary hierarchy in which each deity had
a sphere of influence of his or her own.

Whatever the powers of the twelve gods might be, none of
them had the right to break the sacred oath they had given by
the waters of the Styx. **Styx**, the daughter of Oceanus and
Tithys, personified the sacred river of the Underworld and had
been specially honoured by Zeus for the part she had played in
the Battle of the Giants. The gods thus swore by the waters of
the Styx, and if they happened to break a promise they had

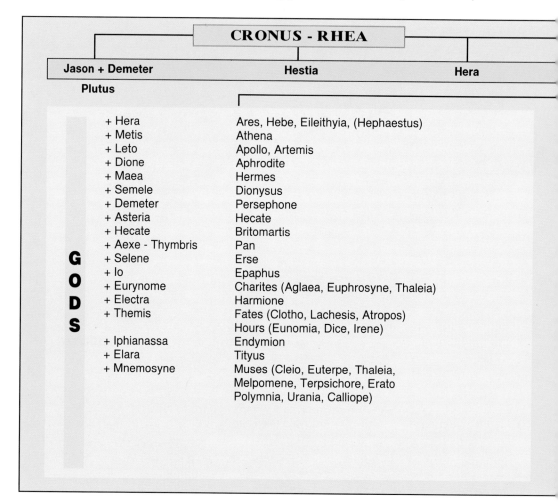

CRONUS - RHEA

Jason + Demeter **Hestia** **Hera**

Plutus

G O D S

+ Hera	Ares, Hebe, Eileithyia, (Hephaestus)
+ Metis	Athena
+ Leto	Apollo, Artemis
+ Dione	Aphrodite
+ Maea	Hermes
+ Semele	Dionysus
+ Demeter	Persephone
+ Asteria	Hecate
+ Hecate	Britomartis
+ Aexe - Thymbris	Pan
+ Selene	Erse
+ Io	Epaphus
+ Eurynome	Charites (Aglaea, Euphrosyne, Thaleia)
+ Electra	Harmione
+ Themis	Fates (Clotho, Lachesis, Atropos)
	Hours (Eunomia, Dice, Irene)
+ Iphianassa	Endymion
+ Elara	Tityus
+ Mnemosyne	Muses (Cleio, Euterpe, Thaleia, Melpomene, Terpsichore, Erato Polymnia, Urania, Calliope)

made, their punishment was to spend a year in a kind of coma, after which they were banned from the meetings of the other deities for a further nine years.

If the gods swore by the Styx, the gravest oath for mankind was 'by the twelve gods'. The penalty for breaking this oath was particularly severe, since apart from anything else the gods of Olympus were a kind of supreme court for human offences - one which had to be treated with absolute respect and unflagging care to ensure that the proper honours were paid to it. The ancient Greeks worshipped each god separately, and also set up altars to all the Twelve Gods in the very centres of their cities. The Altar of the Twelve Gods in Athens, in particular, was the exact centre of the city, and all distances were measured from it.

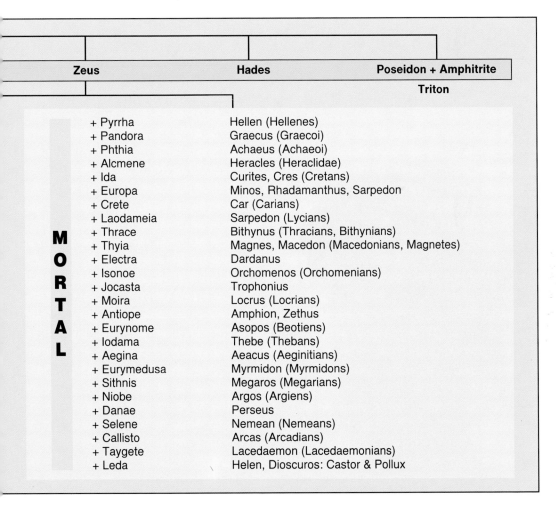

Zeus — **Hades** — **Poseidon + Amphitrite** — **Triton**

MORTAL

+ Pyrrha	Hellen (Hellenes)
+ Pandora	Graecus (Graecoi)
+ Phthia	Achaeus (Achaeoi)
+ Alcmene	Heracles (Heraclidae)
+ Ida	Curites, Cres (Cretans)
+ Europa	Minos, Rhadamanthus, Sarpedon
+ Crete	Car (Carians)
+ Laodameia	Sarpedon (Lycians)
+ Thrace	Bithynus (Thracians, Bithynians)
+ Thyia	Magnes, Macedon (Macedonians, Magnetes)
+ Electra	Dardanus
+ Isonoe	Orchomenos (Orchomenians)
+ Jocasta	Trophonius
+ Moira	Locrus (Locrians)
+ Antiope	Amphion, Zethus
+ Eurynome	Asopos (Beotiens)
+ Iodama	Thebe (Thebans)
+ Aegina	Aeacus (Aeginitians)
+ Eurymedusa	Myrmidon (Myrmidons)
+ Sithnis	Megaros (Megarians)
+ Niobe	Argos (Argiens)
+ Danae	Perseus
+ Selene	Nemean (Nemeans)
+ Callisto	Arcas (Arcadians)
+ Taygete	Lacedaemon (Lacedaemonians)
+ Leda	Helen, Dioscuros: Castor & Pollux

ZEUS

p.28
The head of a bronze statue of Zeus. The god is depicted as a stern, imposing figure - appropriately enough, for the chief deity among the Olympian gods (from the sanctuary of Zeus at Olympia, 520-510 BC, Athens Archaeological Museum).

p.29
A majestic figure of Zeus holding his sceptre and the thunderbolt which is his principal symbol (detail of a Panathenaic amphora, 480-470 BC, Berlin State Museum).

Z eus, the most senior of the Olympian gods, was the son of Rhea and Cronus, the cruel Titan who devoured his newborn children out of the fear than one of him might usurp his throne. Zeus had the good fortune to avoid that fate, because his mother gave Cronus a stone wrapped in swaddling-clothes to eat and hid her son in a cave on Mt Aegeum at Lycnus in Crete (see Cronus - Rhea - Zeus). When he grew up, Zeus overthrew Cronus in battle and after liberating his brothers fought the Titans because they refused to acknowledge him as their leader (see Battle of the Titans). After this fresh victory, Zeus had to face the terrible Giants, whom he overcame with the help of many other gods (see Battle of the Giants). Yet more trouble was in store for him: **Typhon**, the monstrous son of Tartarus and Ge, sought to destroy the world. Zeus attempted to prevent him, but Typhon cast him, unconscious, into a ravine. The help of Hermes and Pan was needed before the god could come to his senses and overcome the horrible monster.

After these exploits, Zeus was now justly recognised as the ruler of all the world. Yet his power was not without its restrictions, and he was not omnipotent. His role was primarily to co-ordinate the activities of the other gods and make sure that they were not exceeding their powers. He was, in any case, the guarantor of order in the sphere of divine as well as human affairs. The kings of the earth were seen as his descendants, and they were often described as *born of Zeus* and *nurtured by Zeus*. When the Greek cities ceased to have kings, Zeus was called *Polieus* and *Poliouchos* - the patron of the city. The defence of the Greek cities was among his responsibilities, which is why he was worshipped, with Athena (the goddess of martial prowess) as *Promachus*, leader in battle, and *Soter*, saviour. Another of his epithets

was *Eleutherius*, liberator, because he granted freedom to those under his protection.

When the ancient Greeks referred to *Olympian Zeus*, as they often did, they meant the father of the gods and men who ruled the world from his palace on Mt Olympus or in the sky. He was the origin of heavenly light (hence his epithets *Uranius*, heavenly, and *Aetherius*, of the air) and he regulated meteorological phenomena. He sent the wind, the clouds, the rain and the thunder and lightning, in each of which roles he had a separate epithet. His symbols were connected with these powers, too: not only the thunderbolt, but the eagle, too, the sacred bird which flies higher in the sky than any other and faster than everything but lightning. The Greeks worshipped Zeus on mountain-tops, where the earth met the sky, the source of the epithet *Acraeus*. The phenomena, controlled by Zeus, which occurred in the heavens were taken as signs from the gods and capable of providing people with information about things which were destined to happen. The oracle at Dodona, one of the most important in Greece (see Oracles), was dedicated to Zeus.

The father of the gods also exercised close control over earthly things. His rain made the fields fertile, and he was worshipped as *Genethlius*, the life-giver, and *Georgus*, the farmer. Here there was a connection between Zeus and the Underworld, the place where all the fruits of the earth lay in store, and so he was called *Chthonius* (subterranean), *Plusius* (rich) and *Meilichius* (he who sweetens the weather). In honour of Zeus Meilichius, the festival called the *Diasia* was held, with whole pigs being burned a a symbol of fertility and productiveness.

Apart from his power over heaven and earth, Zeus protected the dwellings of human beings. In each house there was an altar to *Zeus Herceius* (*hercus* = the courtyard around the house), and he was the protector of peace in the household (*Zeus Ephestius*), of the family's possessions (*Zeus Ctesius*) and of the institution of marriage (*Zeus Gamelius*). Furthermore, he safeguarded friendship among men (*Zeus Philius*) and assisted those in need of it, especially supplicants (for whom

p.30
Europa, daughter of King Agenor of Phoenicia (see p. 188), was one of the mortals who inspired passion in the heart of Zeus. The god transformed himself into a bull and approached the pretty girl, who courageously climbed on to the animal's back. Zeus abducted her, taking her to Crete and lying with her under a plane-tree (Rome, Villa Giulia).

he was *Zeus Hicesius*) and strangers (*Zeus Xenius*, from the root which develops into the concept of hospitality). This list of the gods powers concludes with his supervision over the oaths sworn by human beings (*Zeus Horceius*) and his responsibility for administering justice if those oaths were broken. His punishments could be harsh in the extreme, but he was always willing to forgive if mortals demonstrated their remorse and prayed to him. For all these reasons, the Greeks never omitted to honour the chief of the gods with magnificent sanctuaries, festivals and sporting contests: two of the four major Panhellenic festivals - the Olympics and the Nemean Games - were dedicated to Zeus (see Panhellenic Games).

p.31

Zeus and Hera, on their thrones in the palace on Olympus and attended by Athena, accept the offerings of Iris, messenger of the gods. Zeus is holding his thunderbolt and his sceptre, and he is crowned with an eagle. His throne is magnificently ornamented with Sphinxes and athletes (red-figure amphora, 500 BC, Munich Archaeological Collection).

p.32
A terracotta group of Zeus abducting Ganymede. Zeus fell in love with the handsome lad and bore him off to Olympus, where he was cup-bearer to the gods at their banquets. In order to appease King Troas, Ganymede's father, Zeus gave him a vine with gold leaves and grapes which Hephaestus had made (480 BC, Olympia Archaeological Museum).

There are countless myths associated with Zeus, and many of them are particularly striking. They include, notably, the narratives about his love affairs, which inspire wonder mixed, when seen in the light of modern morals, with certain questions. However, it is easy to understand these mythological traditions if we can identify their symbolic content. In describing the erotic encounters of their primary deity, what the ancient Greeks were doing was to attribute to some higher being the generation of all the elements of nature, of all laws and intellectual or spiritual poweres, of the rules which govern society, and even of the origins of mankind itself. Thus, according to these traditions, Zeus lay with Metis, the personification of wisdom or learning, and Athena was born. Then he contracted a union with Themis, who symbolised law and the moral order, and brought into the world the Hours (in the ancient

Greek scheme of things, these corresponded to the seasons of the year) and the Fates, which govern the destiny of all human beings. His union with Mnemosyne produced the nine Muses, source of all poetic inspiration, and on Demeter he fathered Persephone, who symbolised the regeneration and fertility of the earth. He and Leto were the parents of Apollo and Artemis - that is, of the light of the sun and the moon - and from his union with Eurynome were born the Graces, who brought a touch of beauty into the lives of mortals. Zeus also lay with many of the nymphs and hero-ines, thus becoming the father of the patriarchs of the Greek tribes. With Pyrrha, he fathered Hellen, father of the Hellenes; with Taygete, Lacedaemon (the Lacedaemonians or Spartans); with Niobe, Argus (the Argives), with Thyia, Macedon (the Macedo-nians), and with Ida, Cres, father of the Cretans (see Table II). Apart from any other factors which may have been involved, the formation of such myths satisfied the need felt by the aristocrats of the early historical period to trace their descent back to the great-est god worshipped by their nation, thus allowing them to feel themselves genuine successors to his powers.

p.33
A bronze statuette from the sanctuary at Dodona showing Zeus about to hurl his thunderbolt (470 BC, Athens Archaeological Museum).

The symbolic meaning of the mythological traditions was often hidden behind an amusing facade, and in many of these stories we can detect the ingenuity of the Greeks. In the texts of the ancient writers, Zeus is always coupled with Hera as his partner (though she was also his sister), and the life of the divine spouses is depicted as very similar to that of the ordinary patriarchal family. Zeus was systematically unfaithful to his wife, and thought up thou-sands of tricks to give himself opportunities to be with his lovers. Transformation was his favourite device: he ap-peared to Europa as a bull, to Leda as a swan, to Danae as a golden shower of rain, and to Antiope as a satyr. And once, when he fell passionately in love with the boy **Ganymede**, he turned himself into an eagle in order to snatch the lad and bear him off to Olympus, where he became cup-bearer at the banquets of the gods. Hera, distraught with jealousy, did everything in her power to frustrate Zeus in his amours, or to take revenge when he was unfaithful to her. But although the great god was the lord of all creation, he could not withstand his Fate, which was to bestow upon mankind the rich fruits of his amorous exploits.

HERA

era alone among the goddesses of Olympus enjoyed the status of lawful wife and official partner to Zeus. She, like Zeus, was the child of Cronus and Rhea. According to one tradition, she was born in Samos: the people of that island believed she first saw the light of day beneath a chaste-tree by the banks of the river Imbrassus, where her sanctuary - the famous Heraeum of Samos - was later built.

There was another Heraeum at Argos. This was the goddess's most important cult centre, and it was associated with the love between her and Zeus. The brother and sister, so the story went, loved each other long before they became rulers on Olympus, and even in childhood were in the habit of meeting as lovers unbeknownst to their parents. According to one version of the myth, Zeus first lay with Hera on Mt Coccygas (the name means 'cuckoo'), not far from Argos. There, he saw her for one day only but conceived a passion for her; he thus immediately caused there to be a violent rainstorm, transformed himself into a cuckoo and sought shelter from the rain in her bosom. Hera felt sorry for the poor bird and covered it with her dress. Zeus then returned to his actual form and made love to her - after first promising to marry her. The people of Argos built a temple to Hera on the spot, and on the sceptre carried by her cult statue they fashioned the figure of a cuckoo, the sacred bird which heralds the coming of spring and the burgeoning of nature.

The sacred marriage between the two deities has been interpreted as a symbol of the fertility of the earth, and this ties in with the description given by Homer in the *Iliad* (XIV, 388ff in the translation by Lord Derby): *"Thus saying, in his arms he clasped his wife; the teeming earth beneath them caused to spring the tender grass, and lotus dew-besprent, crocus and hy-*

p.34
Hera attacking the Giants (detail from the north frieze of the Treasury of the Siphnians at Delphi, 525 BC, Delphi Archaeological Museum).

p.35
The head of a statue of Hera found in the Heraeum at Argos and attributed to the school of sculpture of Polyclitus (420 BC, Athens Archaeological Museum).

acinth, a fragrant couch, profuse and soft, up-springing from the earth". Through her union with the greatest of the Olympian gods, Hera acquired all his properties, though in a feminine version of them. Thus, in antiquity she was worshipped as *Acraea* and *Gamelia*, that is, as the patroness of marriage and married life. And since for the ancient Greeks woman's supreme destiny in life was to bring legitimate children into the world, Hera was often referred to as *Teleia* ('the complete one'), since by fulfilling her mission she had reached completion as an entity. It was the custom for young couples, before marriage, to sacrifice to Hera Teleia and Zeus Teleius. But Hera also represented all the other stages in the lives of women: young girls honoured her as *Parthenos* (the 'virgin' or 'maiden'), married women as *Teleia* and widows as *Chera* (meaning 'widow'): there was a myth that at some point Zeus and Hera separated, and while their dispute lasted she was in a state of virtual widowhood.

The legitimate children of Zeus and Hera were Ares, Hebe and **Eileithyia**. Some authors add Hephaestus to the list as their son, while according to others Hephaestus was born to Hera without male intervention at the same time as Athena sprang from the head of Zeus. It is no coincidence, however, that both deities were the parents of Hebe, the goddess who symbolises eternal youth, and of Eileithyia, the protector and helper of women in childbirth and thus the guarantor of the renewal of life. Apart from bringing up her own children, Hera also supervised the rearing of Thetis, of the Lernaean Hydra, of the Lion of Nemea and of the dragon that guarded the Apples of the Hesperides. Heracles suckled her against her wishes, and according to one myth the Milky Way originated in the drops of milk that were shed when Hera thrust him violently away from her breast.

Hera possessed more majesty than any other goddess on Olympus. Seated on her golden throne, she inspired the respect of the other deities, who rose to their feet as soon as they saw her and treated her as if she were their queen. As was also the case with Zeus, all Olympus shook when the goddess revealed her rage. Her power dimmed only in the face of that of her almost omnipotent husband, al-

p.36
A colossal head, probably from the cult statue of Hera at the Heraeum in Olympia (600 BC, Olympia Archaeological Museum).

though she never forgave him for his infidelities. The quarrels between the divine couple very often ended in extremely violent clashes. Hera's wrath was capable of creating turmoil throughout the universe, which according to one interpretation indicates a martial dimension to her cult. This perhaps explains why the war-god Ares was said to be the son of Hera and Zeus.

Apart from her desire to avenge herself on her husband, Hera mercilessly persecuted his lovers and his illegitimate children. Many of the mythical heroes were the targets of her vindictiveness, including Heracles, Leto, Io, Semele, Ino and Dionysus. But she was just as steadfast in protecting those who were loyal to her and those who had been unjustly treated - including personalities such as Thetis, Jason and Achilles. She was especially fond of the city of Argos, which in one version of the myth was her birthplace, and during the Trojan War her wholehearted support for the Greek cause often put her own existence in danger.

p.37
A red-figure cylix showing a scene from the Battle of the Giants. On the right, Hera - dressed as a priestess and with a crown on her hair - is launching an attack with a javelin and has cast down a Giant. Behind her, Apollo is fighting nude and crowned, holding a sword and a bow, while on the left Ares, with a helmet and a shield, is hurling his spear at an opponent (420-400 BC, Berlin).

ATHENA

p.38
A bronze shield from Olympia ornamented with the figure of Medusa the Gorgon. Medusa was a terrible monster whom Perseus beheaded (see p. 216) or whom Athena herself disposed of during the Battle of the Giants. The goddess then fixed the monstrous head to her shield, striking terror into the hearts of all her opponents (sixth century BC, Olympia Museum).

p.39
Zeus is depicted seated on an elaborate throne as Athena, fully-armed, springs from his head. Behind Zeus is Poseidon, with an unidentified goddess, and in front are Eileithyia, goddess of childbirth, and Ares. The ornamentation of the throne includes a depiction of an owl, the bird which symbolised the wisdom of Athena (black-figure amphora, 550-540 BC, the Louvre).

F or the ancient Greeks, Athena, one of the most important Olympian deities, was the goddess of wisdom and skill. This aspect of her character is clear in the descriptions of her birth. According to the tradition, during the Battle of the Giants Zeus lay with Metis, daughter of Oceanus and Tithys, who bore concealed within herself all the world's wisdom. When it became known that Metis was pregnant, a prophecy was uttered that the daughter she bore would in turn give birth to a son who would be a threat to Zeus because he would deprive him of his power. Zeus, overcome with fear, swallowed Metis whole, and after nine months developed an unbearable pain in his head. He begged Hephaestus (or in some writers, Prometheus) to split his head with an axe, and Athena immediately sprang out fully-armed, uttering warlike cries. She threw herself straightaway into the battle with the giants and made a significant contribution to her father's victory by slaying the Giants Pallas and Enceladus.

The fact that Athena was born from the head of Zeus and never received a mother's care meant that her powers were more masculine than feminine. Above all, she was a martial goddess, one who had entered life dressed for war and uttering battle-cries. Her military accoutrements included a helmet, a spear and the *aegis*, a goat-skin shield which Amaltheia had given Zeus and which only Athena was entitled to use. To the shield was fastened the *gorgoneum*, the head of Gorgo the Medusa which turned to stone anyone who set eyes upon it. (Gorgo had been beheaded by Athena herself, or by Perseus with the goddess's assistance, see Danae - Perseus.). Athena was also alone in being allowed to enter her father's armoury, and could even use his thunderbolt.

Athena's warlike nature, in which she was worshipped as *Areia*, differed from the character of Ares himself, the god of war. Ares represented disorderly conflict, the violence of war, while Athena was believed to have taught mankind the techniques and rules of war - that is, of pitched battle. As a result, the two half-siblings were often described by ancient writers in a state of conflict, and this was particularly true during the Trojan War. The fierce god Ares, who had taken the Trojan side, was frequently wounded by Athena as she strove to defend the Greeks. Athena and Hera brought boldness and courage to their protection of their favourites the Achaeans, and at crucial moments Athena is seen aiding Menelaus, Diomedes, Achilles, Agamemnon and Odysseus. It was she who gave Odysseus the idea of the Trojan Horse, and she had no hesitation in declaring him to be her equal in intelligence and ingenuity. On his difficult voyage back to Ithaca, Athena stood by Odysseus and served him loyally in every adversity. She was also particularly fond of the descendants of Agamemnon: when Agamemnon's son Orestes slew his mother so as to be avenged for the murder of his father, Athena defended him in court and saved him from the Furies who had been pursuing him for the crime of matricide. Many of the heroes, too, received her support, including Perseus, the Argonauts, Bellerophon, Tydeus and, of course, her absolute favourite, Heracles. Thanks to the assistance she generously granted to individual human beings and to entire cities, Athena was worshipped by the ancient Greeks as *Soteira*, 'saviour'.

Another of her cult epithets was *Promachus*, which derived from the protection she was believed to provide in battles. Indeed, the Athenians were convinced that during the Persian Wars of the early fifth century BC it was she who had given them the victory. They thus named her *Athena Nike* ('victory') and built a temple by that name on the Acropolis. They also set up an enormous statue of Athena Promachus - made by the great sculptor Phidias - on the sacred rock. A tradition tells us that the tip of her spear and the crest of her helmet could be seen from out at sea off Cape Sunium, and so the statue truly dominated the whole of Attica.

The frequently-used epithet *Athena Hippia* ('of the horses') is also associated with the military prowess of the goddess. According to the relevant

p.40
Athena, clad in a Doric robe, barefoot, and helmeted, rests thoughtfully on her spear, in front of a column (the 'Mourning Athena' relief, 460 BC, Acropolis Museum).

p.41
Bronze statuette of Athena Promachus, dedicated on the Acropolis by Meleso, lady of Athens. The goddess is wearing a tunic which partly covers her aegis, and the tall crest on her helmet rests on the neck of a swan. She would have had a shield in her left hand, and would have been preparing to cast her javelin with the right (470 BC, Athens Archaeological Museum).

myth, it was Athena who taught mankind how to tame the horse, and she gave Bellerophon a golden bridle to enable him to break in the winged horse Pegasus (for which she was known as *Athena Chalinites*, 'of the bridle'). There is a connection here between Athena and Poseidon, another important Olympian god, who was also called *Hippius* (see Poseidon).

When Athena Hippia tamed the wild horse, she acquired a fresh dimension in the minds of the Greeks: now she became the goddess of ingenuity and skill, representing the concept of the superiority of the mind over physical power and the violence of war. She was responsible for the development of all the crafts and techniques that made it easier for man to live in peace. For that reason, she acquired the cult epithet *Ergane*, 'the worker', and architects, sculptors and painters honoured her as their patron. Musicians credited her with the invention of the flute and believed that she was the first to perform the war-dance called the *pyrrhiche*, after the victory of the gods in the Battle of the Giants. It was Athena, too, who made man's first weapons and tools, and she who taught the arts of ship-building (to the Argonauts), ploughing the fields with oxen, making pottery on the wheel, working bronze, and creating objects in gold. Her involvement with the crafts of the fire brought her close to the god Hephaestus, with whom she was worshipped in the Hephaesteum in the Agora of Athens.

Her greatest invention of all, however, was the art of weaving. Throughout antiquity she was renowned as possessing the highest skills in this field, and it was she who wove and embroidered the superb garments worn by the gods and heroes. Her first pupil at the loom was Pandora, who passed on the knowledge to the other women. This attribute of Athena's was the source of the myth of **Arachne**, another skilful weaver who dared to compare herself to the goddess and challenge her to a competition. The goddess turned Arachne into a spider (still known by that name in Greek today) and condemned her to spin in perpetuity but to have all her works destroyed by man.

The peaceful side of Athena's character was symbolised by the olive, the tree which she gave to the Athenians and

p.42
During the Trojan War, Athena was an invaluable helper of the Greeks, whose best-loved heroes she protected from Trojan arrows. Here she is seen supporting Ajax during his duel with Hector (red-figure cylix, 480 BC, the Louvre).

p.43
The head of a terracotta statue of Athena found at Olympia. The goddess must have been wearing a helmet, which has not survived. Note the careful depiction of the hair, and the great spirituality of the goddess's expression (490 BC, Olympia Archaeological Museum).

taught them how to cultivate. According to the myth, it came about that there was a contest between Athena and Poseidon over which of them should be the patron of the city of Athens. The other gods advised Athena and Poseidon to offer the city one gift each, and the winner of the contest would be he or she whose gift was the better. Both ascended to the Acropolis, and Poseidon struck the ground with his trident: a spring of salt water immediately welled up. Athena stamped her foot, and an olive, the first in the world, sprouted on the spot. In the end, the city was awarded to Athena, and took its name from her. The divine olive tree continued to adorn the sacred rock, and when the Persians burned the Acropolis in 480 BC it immediately put out fresh leaves. In commemoration of this, an olive tree has been planted on the Acropolis and can be seen today on the west side of the Erechtheum.

After the dispute with Poseidon, Athena was forever the patron goddess of the city. Indeed, it was said that **Erechtheus**, the legendary first king of Athens, was reared by Athena, which is why he was worshipped with her in the Erechtheum, one of the most important temples on the Acropolis. The temple was dedicated first and foremost to Athena Polias - that is, the patron of the city. In the temple was kept the famous wooden cult statue (*xoanon*) called the *Palladium*, which according to tradition had fallen from the sky. Athena also brought up another of the early kings of Athens, Erichthonius. **Erichthonius** was born out of the seed of Hephaestus, which spilled out to fertilise the soil of Attica when Athena refused his amorous advances and managed to escape from his embrace. Athena gave the king who was in a manner of speaking her son the blood of Gorgo, which he could use either to make medicaments to heal the sick or poisons to take life.

The cult of Athena was thus of the greatest importance in Athens. The citizens dedicated to her the most marvellous monument built before or since, the Parthenon, which still dominates the landscape of Athens even today. This magnificent temple, designed by the architects Ictinus and Callicrates and ornamented by the great sculptor Phidias, was dedicated to *Athena Parthenos* - 'the virgin'. This epithet was attached to Athena because, as the Homeric Hymn tells us, she "avoided the marriage bed and was untouched by amorous desires". Since in effect she had no mother, there is no connection between Athena and the concepts of love, marriage and maternity, and she maintained her perpetual virginity. It was in this capacity that she acquired the epithet *Pallas*, which expresses her unchanging youthfulness and is derived

p.44
Statuette of the 'Varvakeio Athena', a replica in miniature of the chryselephantine statue of Athena Parthenos created by Phidias for the Parthenon. The statue seems to have been about 11.5 metres in height, and the goddess was shown standing, wearing her aegis with its head of a Gorgon and a helmet ornamented with griffons and a sphinx in the centre. In one hand, she held a small Nike (victory) and in the other her spear. At her feet was her shield, around which was entwined a snake. On the base of the state was a scene showing the birth of Pandora, while Athena's shield was decorated with scenes from the Battle of the Amazons and the Battle of the Giants (second or third century AD, Athens Archaeological Museum).

from the word *pallax*, meaning a young girl or boy.

Another of the ways in which the Athenians honoured the patron goddess of their city was to hold its most splendid festival, the **Panathenaea**, in her honour. The festival was traditionally held to have been founded by Erichthonius, and in 566/5 BC the tyrant Pisistratus reorganised it and divided it into two feasts, the Greater and the Lesser Panathenaea. The Greater Panathenaea were held every four years in the month of Hecatombion (late July), and were of notable splendour. Athletic contests were held on the first days of the festival, with competitions for horse and chariot racing, wrestling, boxing, the *pancratium*, the high and long jump, throwing the javelin and the discus, foot races and torch races. Next came the contests for recitation, music - and dance, including the famous *pyrrhiche* which Athena herself had first performed. The winners received as prizes what were known as Panathenaic amphorae: these were large and highly-decorated vessels filled with a considerable quantity of olive oil which would mean a major financial gain for their holder.

The last day of the Panathenaea was the most splendid of all, as the entire population of Athens took part in the magnificent Panathenaic procession, which wound its way up to the Acropolis in order to present the cult statue of Athena with a fresh garment, called the *peplos*. The procession started out from the Keramaikos area, at the building called the *Pompeum* (the 'procession house'), in the courtyard of which a portable ship had been set up. Each time the Panathenaea came round, the new *peplos* for the statue - decorated with scenes from the Battle of the Giants - was hung on the mast of this ship. Then, accompanied by all the Athenians, it was carried through the Agora along the Panathenaic Way and then up to the Acropolis. At last, in the presence of all the city's officials and notables, the people of Athens would deliver the *peplos* to cover the statue of Athena in the Erechtheum. The ceremony ended with the sacrificing of numerous animals, while the Athenians celebrated with sumptuous banquets as a way of conveying their gratitude to their beloved goddess. The Panathenaic procession was such an important event in the life of Athens that the sculptor Phidias chose to depict it, with unsurpassed skill, on the Ionicn frieze of the Parthenon. It was Phidias, too, who created the masterly gold and ivory statue of Athena Parthenos which adorned the interior of the temple and was among the greatest art-works of antiquity.

p.47
Part of the Ionic north frieze of the Parthenon, with a scene from the Panathenaic Procession: young men carry pitchers of water needed for the ceremony (440 BC, Acropolis Museum).

POSEIDON

Poseidon, like Zeus, was the son of Cronus and Rhea. According to one version of the tale, when he was born Rhea hid him in a stable and presented Cronus with a mule, which he swallowed thinking it was his son. The newborn baby thus escaped his father's cruel habits and grew to maturity - according to some myths, in Rhodes, where he was reared by the Telchines, first inhabitants of the island. When he grew up, Poseidon helped Zeus in the Battle of the Titans and received his famous trident as a gift from the Cyclopes. At the end of the war, it was Poseidon who shut the Titans up in Tartarus, and he thus became the god who guaranteed order in the affairs of the universe. He also made a decisive contribution to the victory of the gods in the Battle of the Giants.

As soon as all the obstacles were out of the way and the new gods had supplanted their predecessors, Zeus, Poseidon and Hades - the sons of Cronus - shared out power over the cosmos. Zeus was given the sky, Poseidon the sea, and Hades the underworld, while all three had stakes in the earth itself. Poseidon thus possessed two palaces, one on Mt Olympus and the other in the depths of the sea. Homer tells us that his sea-bed palace was near Aigae and that it was an imposing structure made of gold where the god lived with Amphitrite, his legal wife. According to the myths, Amphitrite tried at first to repulse Poseidon's advances, and hid in the sea in the land of the mythical Atlas. Poseidon was inconsolable at his loss, and dispatched a dolphin to find Amphitrite and talk her into coming back. After that time, the dolphin became a sacred animal, and its name - *Delphinus* - was given to the consellation still so-called today.

Poseidon, then, came to be above all, for the Greeks, the god of the sea, who was capable of calming the waves or of summoning up terrible storms and so taking the lives of those who displayed disrespect for him. Artists often depicted him voyaging across the waves in his gold chariot, surrounded by dolphins and the other creatures of the deep. Equally frequently, he was shown in his fiercer aspect, whipping up the sea with his trident and dis-

p.49
A bronze statue of Poseidon (or Zeus, according to some scholars) found in the sea off Cape Artemesium. The god is shown as a dominant figure, with a grim expression of complete concentration as he prepares to hurl his trident (460 BC, Athens Archaeological Museum).

playing no mercy. It was Poseidon who relentlessly pursued Odysseus after the Trojan War was over and prolonged his wanderings over the troubled seas, because Odysseus had had the effrontery to blind the Cyclops Polyphemus, son of the god. Equally rough treatment was meted out to many of the other Greeks who fought at Troy. During the hostilities, Poseidon had been among the passionate supporters of the Greek side, because the Trojans had treated him badly despite the fact that he had founded their city. Yet he was unable to bear the sight of the Greeks devastating Troy and committing acts of violence against its citizens, and so he cast them adrift on stormy seas to make sure that their joy in victory was far from complete.

Poseidon's power to command anything to do with the marine world caused him to be called by the epithets *Enalius, Thalassius, Pelagius, Pontius, Pontocrator, Isthmius* and *Porthmius* - all of which mean, roughly, 'of the sea'. His most important sanctuaries were on headlands (such as Capes Sunium and Taenarus) or close to the sea, as at the Isthmus of Corinth. The Isthmus was the venue for the Isthmian Games, one of the most important Panhellenic festivals (see Panhellenic Games).

In earlier stages of the development of Greek religion, however, Poseidon's powers had been much wider. He was responsible for controlling activities related to the earth and its forces. The Greeks attributed the violent and destructive earthquakes that so often wrecked their country to his wrath (which is why he was known as *Gaeochus* or *Seisichthon*, 'he who rocks the earth'). On the other hand, the god who caused earthquakes would also be capable of stopping them and of ensuring the stability of the earth and the safety of buildings, which is why he was also known as *Asphalius* ('the safe one') and *Themelius* ('he of the foundations').

Poseidon was responsible for a number of other geological phenomena as well as earthquakes. He had the power to bring into being mountains, islands, valleys and channels, and also to cause clefts to appear in the earth or whole areas to sink beneath the waves. Nisyros was created when Poseidon trapped the giant Polybotes beneath a rock he had picked up on Cos. Euboea, Cyprus and Sardinia were said to have been created in a similar manner, while Rhodes was born out of the union between the god and Aphrodite (or Halia, sister of the Telchines). The mythical island of **Atlantis** was traditionally said to have been first inhabited on his initiative, when he lay with Cleito and fathered five pairs of twin boys. Poseidon appointed Atlas, the first-born, as king of the island, and endowed his brothers with wealth and respect for good

p.51
A marble statue of Poseidon from a sanctuary on the island of Melos. The sea-god has his right hand - holding the trident - raised, while leaning to the right to rest on a dolphin-shaped support (130 BC, Athens Archaeological Museum).

order. He was also the founder of Orchomenus: his union with Chrysogone (or Tritogeneia), daughter of Aeolus, gave life to Minyas. His other children included Boeotus, Delphus, Pelias the king of Iolcus, Neleus who founded Pylus, Taenarus, Eleius, Nauplius, Phaeax who was the father of the Phaeaceans, Chius who gave his name to the island of Chios, Abderus, and Paeon from whom the tribe of the Paeonians were descended. His almost uncontrollable powers and the disasters he could cause were expressed in a whole series of myths, in which he appears as the father of numerous monsters and other wild beasts with an inclination towards torture, rapine, robbery and murder (see Aegeus - Theseus). On the other hand, Poseidon was also the father of some of the most important heroes in the Greek myths, apart from the primogenitors of tribes and founders of cities we have noted above. Proteus, Orion, Theseus, Despoena (a deity worshipped in Arcadia, held to be the daughter of Demeter) and even Athena are mentioned among his children.

According to a tradition from Thessaly, it was Poseidon who breathed life into the first horse in the world. His connection with horses was familiar throughout the Greek world, which is why one of his cult epithets was *Hippius*. The myths tell us that he was overcome with lust for Demeter, who transformed herself into a mare to avoid him. Poseidon therefore became a stallion, and the fruit of their union was Arion, who had the form of a horse. The winged horse Pegasus was another of his sons, by Medusa. The bull, too, was closely linked with Poseidon, and played a central part in another set of myths. When Minos became king of Crete, the story goes, Poseidon caused a beautiful white bull to appear from the waves of the sea as a sign of his favour. But Minos refused to sacrifice the bull, and so Poseidon caused Pasiphae, Minos' wife, to fall in love with it, the fruit of their union being the Minotaur. After coupling with Pasiphae, the bull became unmanagably wild and terrorised Crete and Attica until Theseus killed it. The link between Poseidon and these two animals is further evidence of the impulsive, violent powers which the Greeks attributed to him, at least in the early stages of his cult and before he became confined to his role as sea-god.

APOLLO

p. 52

A white cylix from the sanctuary of Delphi showing Apollo making a libation. Seated, and wearing a wreath of bay or myrtle, the god is holding his lyre and pouring the wine on to the ground from a bottle.

(490 BC, Delphi Museum).

p. 53

A detail of the west pediment of the temple of Zeus at Olympia, showing scenes from the Battle of the Centaurs (see p. 183). Apollo is depicted at the centre of the composition, ready to assist the Lapiths and in rage over the impious behaviour of the Centaurs (460 BC, Olympia Archaeological Museum).

Apollo, the god who more than any other represented the values of Greek civilisation, was the son of Zeus and Leto. When Leto was with child and the time for her to give birth was approaching, she had to face up to the wrath of Hera, insulted by her husband's infidelity. In an attempt to prevent Leto's children from being born, Hera decreed that all the places in Greece should drive her out. Leto was forced to wander from Crete to Samothrace and from Troy as far as Carpathos and the Cyclades, never finding a place of peace to bring her children into the world. In the end, she reached the island of Delos, which according to the myths had once been a nymph. Out of respect for Hera, the nymph had rejected the advances of Zeus and flung herself into the sea, falling like a star. Zeus punished Asteria, as she was then called, by turning her into a barren island which did not even have a single fixed position in the sea, being blown hither and thither by the wind. The sailors who caught sight of the island on their travels called it Ortygia. As soon as Leto set foot on Ortygia, four columns rose from the bed of the sea and held the island firm. This was where one of Zeus' most important sons was to be born: this arid, deserted place had nothing to fear from the ire of Hera, and in any case it had been for Hera's sake that Asteria suffered as she had.

Nonetheless, Hera prevented her daughter Eileithyia, protector of childbirth, from coming to Leto's aid,

and so the poor woman was afflicted with birth pangs for nine fruitless days and nights. Some of the important goddesses (Rhea, Amphitrite, Dione and Themis) gathered on Delos, and succeeded in conveying Eileithyia there without her mother's knowledge. Leto knelt down, leant against a rock on Mt Cynthus, put her arms around a palm tree that stood next to the river Inopus, and give birth first to Artemis and then to Apollo. As the children were born, swans flew across the sky and Nymphs sang songs of praise, while the island was flooded with gold and took the name Delos, which means 'a place visible and known to all'. After that time, Delos was always in the same place, at the centre of a circle of islands called the Cyclades (from *cyclos*, 'circle'). Delos was also to be the site of the first and the most celebrated of all the Greek sanctuaries of Apollo.

Immediately after being born, Apollo ascended Mt Olympus, where he was ceremoniously greeted and offered the nectar and ambrosia that would make him immortal. His first concern was to found an oracle so that he could convey to mankind the deci-

sions and desires of his father. So, leaving Olympus, he travelled through many parts of Greece before coming to the place called Delphi, on the wild and wooded mountain of Parnassus near the city of Crisa. There Apollo marked out the boundaries of his sanctuary, which was to develop into one of the most important sacred places of the Greeks. According to the tradition, the area had previously belonged to the goddess Ge, who also possessed oracular powers. Her oracle was guarded by a terrible dragon called Python. In order to gain control over the oracle, Apollo had to kill the dragon, which is why he was known as *Pythian Apollo* and the priestess of his oracles was the *Pythia*. The Panhellenic festival held at Delphi in honour of Apollo was called the *Pythia* or the *Pythian Games* (see Panhellenic Games). After killing Python, Apollo made his way to the Vale of Tempe in Thessaly to be purified. In commemoration of the event, a festival called the *Septeria* (meaning 'feast of the purification') was held at Delphi every eight years. However, there is also a tradition that Ge was succeeded at the Delphic oracle by Themis, who passed it on to her sister Phoebe. It was Phoebe who then gave it to Apollo, thus explaining why the god was called *Phoebus Apollo*.

As soon as Apollo had gained control at Delphi, he looked around for people who were suitable to administer his sanctuary. From his vantage point high up on Parnassus, he spied out at sea a ship bearing Cretan merchants who were carrying products from their island to Pylus in the Peloponnese. He decided that they be his priests, immediately turning himself into a dolphin

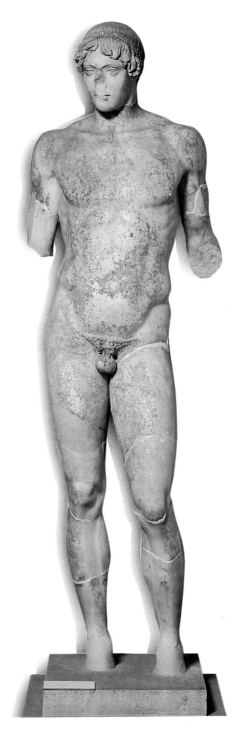

and going on board the ship. The sailors, aghast, allowed their vessel to be swept along by the wind, which bore them into the port of Crisa. There Apollo transformed himself into a star and then into a handsome man, ordering the Cretans to climb up the mountain to his temple, sacrifice, and vow to serve the sanctuary and the oracle. After that time, the oracle functioned without interruption and Apollo was worshipped with the epithet *Delphinius* (see Oracles).

Of all the Olympian gods, Apollo was most closely associated with oracles. He taught mankind the art of prophecy, and this is reflected in the numerous myths in which he is the father of some of the most important seers (Melambus, Amphiaraus, Calchas, Tiresias, Manto and Cassandra). His prophetic powers are associated with the original image the Greeks had of him: Apollo was the god of light and of the sun, the deity who emitted solar energy and thus overcame the darkness. He was thus able, in the light of day, to reveal to men what lay in store for them, and to make plain everything that was hidden. Many very ancient traditions are associated with the first light of dawn that the Greeks called *lycauges*, the 'wolf-light', and Apollo was worshipped as *Lycius*, 'of the wolves'. In his oracles, which were conveyed by the Pythia, he gave mortals the advice they required either about their personal lives or on the political level. The Greek cities and many other states around the known world avoided taking decisions before consulting the Delphic Oracle. The god played an important part, too, in guiding the colonial activities of the Greeks. Apollo, known in this instance as *Archegetes*, 'chief leader', would determine in an oracle who was to be the leader of the colonising party,

p.56

A bronze statue found at Piraeus and probably depicting Apollo. The god is nude, in the kouros type, and would have been holding a bow and a phial (530 BC, Piraeus Archaeological Museum).

p.57

A large head, probably from a chryselephantine statue of Apollo. It was found in the sanctuary at Delphi, along with two other heads which can be presumed to be of Leto and Artemis (550 BC, Delphi Archaeological Museum).

would recommend a destination, and would supervise the construction of the temples and buildings in the new city.

According to the myths, Apollo left his sacred island and his oracle each winter and travelled to the far north, the land of the Hyperboreans. In that mythical place, the sun always shone and night never fell. While Apollo was away, the god Dionysus looked after the oracle, and when spring came Apollo would be back in Greece, bringing the sun and the light with him. People would celebrate to welcome him home as he appeared, wreathed in myrtle leaves, on his chariot drawn by snow-white swans.

The swan and the dolphin were the sacred creatures of Apollo, and his favourite plant was the hyacinth. For the ancient Greeks, **Hyacinth** was originally a youth of great beauty whom the god loved, but one day, as they played at archery, Apollo's shot missed and killed his friend. The story of the god's love for the beautiful **Daphne**, daughter of the river Peneus, came to an equally unhappy end. Daphne spent her time hunting in the forests, and had no desire either to marry or to lie with a man. As soon as Apollo saw her, he was wild with lust and set off in pursuit of her. Daphne ran as fast as she could, but her attempts to escape were in vain. In despair, she called upon her father to save her, and Peneus transformed her into a bay tree (*daphne*, in Greek). Although Apollo was bitter never to have tasted her love, he made her his symbol, and he was often depicted by the writers and artists of antiquity wearing a crown of laurel leaves.

A laurel crown was the prize for the victors in the Pythian Games, and the Pythia herself munched laurel leaves before uttering the oracle. The first temple to Apollo at Delphi was supposed to have been built of laurel boughs, as was another temple to the god, that at Eretria (*Apollo Daphnophorus*).

In art, Apollo is often shown with his bow and arrow, weapons which had been constantly with him since birth. Cleverly-placed arrow shots were his way of protecting the heroes he loved and punishing those who were disrespectful of him. It was thus that he took the lives of **Tityus**, who attempted to ravish Leto, of **Eurytus**, who had the affrontery to challenge Apollo to a contest of archery, and of the **children of Niobe**, who had dared to question the beauty of Leto's children. In the Trojan War, it was the arrows of Apollo that killed Patroclus, because the god, co-founder with Poseidon of the city, was on the Trojan side. The Greek camp often smarted under his lash, and he was

p.58

A Melian amphora showing Apollo playing the lyre as he returns, on his winged chariot, from the legendary land of the Hyperboreans. Behind him are his escorts, two Hyperborean maidens, while Artemis and her favourite deer await him (seventh century BC, Athens Archaeological Museum).

the cause of death of many of the great warriors, including even Achilles himself. As a result, the ancient mind came to attribute sudden deaths to 'the arrows of Apollo', who was given the epithet *Moiragetes*, leader of the Fates (*Moires*) and was seen as the deity who shaped the human destiny.

However, even when the god of light caused human death, he made sure that it was instantaneous, thus releasing the body from intolerable pain. Apollo was also able to alleviate all human anguish: he was a helper in sickness, and he bestowed health. He may have punished impeity by sending down plagues and epidemics, but it was he, too, who found the cure and purified infections of all kinds once the moral order had been restored. For that reason, he was worshipped as *Iatrus* (physician) and *Epicurius* (helper). Asclepius, the Greek god most closely associated with medicine, was the son of Apollo and Coronis, and it was from his father that he first learned the skill of making medicaments (see Asclepius).

Apollo was capable not only of curing human beings but also of restoring the health of nature itself. He was responsible for ensuring that the fields bore fruit, and he protected them against insects and rodents. In the month of Thargelion (May), the Greeks celebrated the festival called the *Thargelia* in which they called upon him to protect their crops from being shrivelled up by the rays of the sun. He was equally alert to threats to the health of animals, and he himself was often shown pasturing the flocks. According to one tradition, Apollo killed the Cyclopes and Zeus, as a punishment, sent him to Pherrae in Thessaly as cow-herd to king Admetus. A similar punishment found him pasturing the flocks of Laomedon, king of Troy. Yet another myth features Apollo as the guardian of the flocks: this time, Hermes was said to have stolen Apollo's cattle, but in order to expiate his crime gave him the lyre made of the shell of a tortoise that was to become another of his symbols (see Hermes).

p.59
A small ivory statue of Apollo Lyceus found in the Agora of Athens; it is a Roman copy of the marble statue by Praxiteles which stood in the Lyceum (third century AD, Museum of the Agora of Athens).

In this way, the god of shepherds became the god of music, and ever afterwards was to be seen making the magical sounds that accompanied the dancing of the Graces, the Hours, Harmony, Hebe, Aphrodite and the Muses. Apollo used his first lyre to defeat the god Pan and the Silenus Marsyas in a contest of music, after which he gave it to Orpheus, a celebrated musician who was his own son by the Muse Calliope. The song sung by women at weddings (the *hymenaeus*) was also associated with Apollo: in the minds of the ancient Greeks, **Hymenaeus** had been a beautiful youth who was either the god's lover or his son by Calliope. By another muse, Thaleia, Apollo was the father of the **Corybants**, who surpassed all other creatures in their skill in the dance. Yet when Apollo played his lyre for them, the nine Muses could enchant like no other beings. With the Muses, who were never far from his side, Apollo *Musagetes* ('leader of the Muses') became the patron of poetry and all the other arts, endowing mortals with inspiration and creative imagination.

p.60

A bronze panel from the sanctuary of Zeus at Olympia, with an incised scene showing Zeus and Apollo playing his lyre between two gods and two female figures who may be Muses or Hyperborean maidens (650-625 BC, Olympia Archaeological Museum).

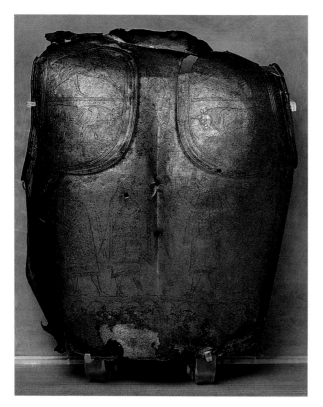

Apollo was for the Greeks a perpetual adolescent, the representative of eternal youth, and for that reason artists tended to depict him with an adolescent body and long blonde tresses which emitted a glowing light. Apollo thus became the patron of god of adolescents, and he attended the rites of initiation at which the *ephebes* became adult men. In the Dorian cities, the festival called the *Carneia* was held in his honour: it consisted of special ceremonies during which the young men were admitted to the body of full citizens (see also Artemis).

Apollo fathered many other children apart from Asclepius, the Corybants, Orpheus and all the famous seers. Most of them were kings of cities or the legendary fathers of the tribes: Chaeron who built Chaeronia, Lycoreus who founded a city named after him; Anius king of Delos; Troilus; Tenes king of Tenedus; Miletus who founded the race of the Milesians; Epidaurus who gave his name to the ancient city; and Ion, the father of all the Ionians. **Ion** was born after Apollo ravished Creusa, daughter of king Erechtheus of Athens. Creusa neglected the newborn baby, and so Apollo gave it to the Pythia to bring up in Delphi. When Ion grew to maturity, he returned to his birthplace and became king. This was the myth by which the ancient Greeks explained the Ionian origins of Apollo and linked him to the city of Athens.

p.61

During the Trojan War, Apollo took the side of the Trojans because he himself had founded their city. Here he is shown with his bow, supporting Hector during the duel with Ajax (red-figure cylix, 480 BC, the Louvre).

ARTEMIS

p.62

Artemis, who for the ancient Greeks was the goddess of the hunt, from a relief found in the sanctuary of Brauron (fifth-fourth century BC, Brauron Museum).

p.63

Artemis seated on rock, with her beloved deer, accepts the offerings of supplicants to her (fourth century BC, Brauron Museum).

Artemis was also the daughter of Zeus and Leto and was born on Delos with her brother Apollo. She shared many of Apollo's characteristics, and could to some extent be described as his female side. She, too, was connected with light in the heavens: not that of the sun, but the moonlight, whose spreading rays keep the darkness at bay. It is no coincidence that in quite a number of myths the moon-goddess Selene and Artemis are identified, and there is also confusion between Artemis and a number of other characters in the Greek myths who personified the powers of the moon (Aphaea, Britomartis, Hecate, Iphigenia and others). The goddess's lunar attributes were manifest in the way she was depicted by artists: surrounded by the moon and stars, or holding a lighted taper.

There was a tradition that Artemis had been born before her brother and helped Leto bring Apollo into the world. Here she took the place of Eileithyia, the goddess of childbirth, and for that reason she was worshipped as *Artemis Lochia*, the patron of pregnant women. At her sanctuary at Brauron in Attica (where she was *Artemis Brauronia*), women who had successfully given birth would make sacrifices and offerings to Artemis, and the clothes of women who had died in childbirth were also dedicated to her.

Artemis was often worshipped as *Kourotrophos* because she was believed to watch over the upbringing of young children. This cult was particularly strong in Ephesus, where her important temple was one of the Seven Wonders of the World. Artemis' assistance continued to be just as significant as children

grew to maturity. At the time of the difficult transition from ado-lescence to adulthood, the ancient Greeks used to invoke the support of Artemis and held special rites dedicated to her. At Brauron, young girls spent some time in the goddess's sanctuary, where they learned all they would need to know about woman-hood. These young girls were called *arctoi* (= bears), and the time they spent in the sanctuary was their *arcteia*. At another im-portant sanctuary, that of *Artemis Orthia* in Sparta, youths were whipped before the goddess's altar in a ceremony which has been interpreted as a means of toughening them in preparation for their inclusion in the army of adult citizens.

In the minds of the ancient Greeks, Artemis was a pure virgin who had never known the joys of love and marriage. Her virgin-ity was most clearly expressed in the myth of Hippolytus, a handsome, chaste youth who - like the goddess - was unmoved by physical passions and spent his life hunting amid the moun-tains and trackless forests. Hippolytus - who was the son of The-seus - came to a tragic end when he rejected the love of Phae-dra, but Artemis rewarded him by compelling the people of his birthplace, Troezen, to worship him as a god. Actaeon, on the other hand, who happened to see Artemis bathing naked, was transformed into a stag and killed by his own hunting-dogs. With Apollo, Artemis killed the children of Niobe and disposed of Tityus, who had attempted to ravish Leto. Her bow also loosed the arrow which killed **Callisto**, who had broken her oath of virginity and lain with Zeus. **Orion**, son of Poseidon, met a similar fate, either be-cause he had lain with Io or because he ravished Opis, one of the Hyperborean Maidens.

Artemis' greatest joy was to run through the dense forests hunting with her golden bow, accompanied by her dogs and her favourite animal, the deer. The swift, nim-ble deer was closely associated with the goddess, both in depictions of her and in the traditions of mythology. Indeed, Artemis often transformed herself into a deer, as she did in the story of the twin Gi-

p.64
Artemis, the goddess of hunting, was worshipped as 'mistress of the beasts' because she enjoyed complete rule over wild nature and the animals. Here, on what is called the François krater, she is shown winged, taming two lions (570 BC, Florence Archaeological Museum).

p.65
The head of a colossal chryselephantine statue which according to some scholars shows Artemis (see the illustration on p. 57). The goddess is wearing a crown and ear-rings and has a hieratic cast of countenance (550 BC, Delphi Archaeological Museum).

ants called the **Aloides**, who wished to kill the gods and lie with Artemis. The goddess turned herself into a deer and ran very swiftly betweeen the two Giants, who in their endeavours to kill her slew each other.

The hunting-goddess was renowned for her skill at archery. No god or mortal could best her for accuracy, and those who dared to compete with her were usually severely punished. Agamemnon, for instance, killed one of her deer and then boasted of being a better marksman than Artemis herself: as a result, Artemis demanded that he sacrifice his daughter Iphigenia at Aulis, since only then would she allow the wind to blow and carry the Greek ships over the Aegean to Troy. At the last moment, however, she took pity on the girl and sacrificed a deer in her place. Iphigenia became a priestess in the famous sanctuary of Artemis in the country of the Tauri. Much later, she was brought back to Greece by her brother Orestes, together with a cult statue of Artemis. This *xoano* was set up in the sanctuary at

p.66

Left, a bronze statue of Artemis (fourth century BC, Piraeus Museum).

Right, a terracotta statuette of Artemis holding a deer (from the goddess's little sanctuary at Kanoni, Corfu, 500-480 BC, Corfu Archaeological Museum).

Brauron and Iphigenia became the founder of the special cult of *Artemis Tauropolos*.

As the goddess of the hunt, Artemis was closely associated with the beasts and was worshipped as *Potnia theron* - that is, as the mistress and queen of nature and animals. She lived among nature and in the fields, thus giving rise to her epithet *Agrotera* (from *agros*, a field), and she also bore a close relationship to rivers and lakes, where she would stop to rest and where she would dance and sing with the Nymphs, the Muses and the Graces. Her affinity with rivers was reflected in an amusing myth involving the river Alpheius. Once, **Alpheius** was overcome with passion for the goddess and hid himself where she was dancing with her friends, with the intention of bearing her off by force. But Artemis had realised that something was amiss, and she smeared mud all over her face and that of her companions, making it impossible for Alpheius to recognise her. In the area she was afterwards worshipped as *Artemis Alphaea*.

p.67

During the Trojan War, Artemis helped the Trojan side, and although she avoided becoming directly embroiled in the hostilities, she was forced to fight Hera, by whom she was wounded. Yet even as they were engaged in combat Hera praised her for her strength and accuracy with the bow. In the illustration, Artemis assisting Paris during his duel with Menelaus (red-figure cylix, 480 BC, the Louvre).

DEMETER
(Pesephone)

Demeter, daughter of Cronus and Rhea, was for the ancient Greeks the great goddess of agriculture. As can be deduced from her name (*De* = earth, *meter* = mother), she was responsible for the fruitfulness of the earth, and she protected the crops - in particular wheat, one of man's basic foodstuffs. Her cult would seem to have had its roots in the very ancient fertility goddess, and Demeter is one of the oldest of the gods in the Greek pantheon despite the fact that Homer, who devotes much space to the heroic deeds of the deities, hardly mentions her at all.

The goddess of the soil was worshipped, as one would expect, by the very earliest of the tribes of farming people who settled in Greece, and her oldest shrines were to be found in isolated agricultural areas. In upland Arcadia, she was called *Deo* and her bronze statue, made by the sculptor Onatas, showed her with a female body and a horse's head. There must have been some connection between this statue and the myth which tells of Demeter's love affair with Poseidon. In order to avoid the god's advances, Demeter turned herself into a mare, but Poseidon took the form of a stallion and mated with her. The fruit of their union was the horse Areion. According to another version of the story, they became the parents of **Despoena**, a chthonic (underworld) deity who was worshipped at an important sanctuary on Mt Lycosura in Arcadia. Demeter's connection with Poseidon, god of the waters, has been interpreted as a symbolic reference to the earth being made fertile by the life-giving rain.

p.68

A relief from Eleusis showing Demeter, seated, greeting Kore, who is holding torches (480 BC, Elefsina Museum).

p.69

The Ninnius panel, dedicated at the sanctuary of Eleusis, shows a scene from the Eleusinian Mysteries. In the upper section is Demeter, seated, with Kore in front of her and accompanied by initiates, while below Demeter once more, seated and surrounded by the sacred objects of the Mysteries, greets Iacchus (second half of the fourth century BC, Athens Archaeological Museum).

Symbolism of a similar kind should probably be detected in the myth which tells of Demeter's love for the hero Jason. The couple lay together - in a ploughed field - three times, bringing into the world **Plutus**, the good who represented earthly wealth and especially that which was produced by tilling the soil. It was Demeter, then, who endowed mankind with the gifts of the earth and protected all farm-work. The feasts held to honour her always coincided with the most important events in the agricultural calendar. In spring, when green plants sprouted on the earth, mortals called her *Chloe* (= fresh, green). At harvest time, the *Thalysia* was celebrated and Demeter was honoured above all other deities, while when the corn was threshed the feast was called the *Aloön* (from the word for a threshing-floor). However, Demeter's greatest festival was the *Thesmophoria*, held throughout Greece in autumn, when the winter wheat was planted. During the Thesmophoria, the women conducted secret rites which were supposed to guarantee a good harvest. Early in the summer, at the time of the feast called the Scirophoria, the women had buried some piglets in pits dug in the earth. At the time of the Thesmophoria, the decomposing meat of these animals was disinterred and, mixed with wheat, was placed on Demeter's altar amid supplications to grant fertility to the fields.

Demeter's greatest contribution to mankind was, of course, the fact that she had taught humans to cultivate grain crops. According to the myth, she had assigned the task of teaching all the world about these crops to **Triptolemus**, a hero of Attica (the name means 'he who ploughs three times'). He mounted his chariot,

p.71

An Apulian krater showing the Rape of Persephone. Hades and Persephone are speeding on a chariot towards the dark Kingdom of the Dead. The moon goddess Selene is lighting their way with a torch, while Hermes keeps them company on their journey (360-350 BC, British Museum).

which was drawn by winged snakes, and taught farmers how to plant, harvest and thresh wheat, showing them also the tools they would need for the task.

The phenomena of the annual flowering and withering away of the plants of the earth were very closely connected with the goddess of agriculture, and were explained by one of the finest myths in the Greek cycle, preserved in the Homeric Hymn to Demeter. Demeter, the myth tells us, had borne Zeus a beautiful daughter called Persephone. Her beauty bewitched Pluton (Hades), the god of the underworld, who decided to abduct her and take her to live

p.72

A view of the Telesterium at Eleusis, where the most important ceremonies in the Eleusinian Mysteries took place. As far back as 1200 BC, there had been a Mycenean megaron on the site of the Telesterium, and rites in honour of Demeter were held there. In the sixth century BC, the megaron was replaced by a new building for celebration of the goddess's mystical cult. Over the centuries, the Telesterium was reconstructed a number of times: by the Pisistratids (525 BC), by Cimon (478-461 BC), by Ictinus in the time of Pericles, and by numerous later architects.

in his dark kingdom. One day, as Persephone was at play with the Oceanids in a meadow full of flowers, she spied a narcissus of incomparable beauty. Persephone bent down to pick it, but as she did so the earth opened up and Kore (as Persephone is also called; the word simply means 'girl' or 'daughter') was snatched away by Pluton. In her terror, the girl began to shriek - so loudly that her cries reached the ears of her mother. Demeter, shocked by her daughter's disappearance, set off in pursuit of her. She searched for nine days and nights, but in vain. No one knew where Persephone had gone, and only Hecate had heard her cries. But the sun-god Helius, who sees everything, told Demeter that Hades had stolen her daughter and the goddess, embittered by the indifference of Zeus to her plight, came down into the world from Mt Olympus. Transformed in her grief into an old woman, she travelled unceasingly through towns and villages.

One day, Demeter came to Eleusis in Attica, and she sat down to rest (on a stone afterwards called 'the Unsmiling Stone') in the shade of an olive tree next to an undefiled well. Just at that moment, along came four girls with pitchers to draw water: their names were Demo, Callidice, Callithoe and Cleisidice, and they were the daughters of king Celeus of Eleusis and his wife Metaneira. In surprise, they asked the old woman what was the matter, and she replied that she had escaped from captivity among pirates. Now she was exhausted, though, and she begged the girls to take her back to the palace, where she could work as a nurse. The girls brought her before their parents, who put her in charge of Demophon, their youngest son.

The goddess dwelt in the palace, never smiling, never eating and never sleeping. But Iambe, one of the slave-girls, managed to make her laugh by telling jokes, and all she would put in her mouth was

a little *cyceon* - that is, flavoured barley-water. In gratitude for the hospitality she had received, Demeter decided that she would make Demophon immortal. Each day, she smeared his body with ambrosia, and each night she held him over the fire. But one evening Metaneira caught sight of Demeter roasting her son (as she thought) and let out an angry cry. Demeter then revealed her identity and commanded Celeus to build a temple in her honour, with an altar, near the well called Callichorus, and to order the Eleusinians to hold special ceremonies in her honour. According to the tradition, that was the origin of the famous Eleusinian Mysteries, in which Demeter and Kore were honoured.

However, Demeter continued to be both sad and angry. As soon as her temple was ready, she shut herself up inside it and refused to return to Olympus. As she mourned, so did the whole of nature: the fields lay bare, flowers withered, and the fruit rotted on the branch. People began to die of hunger, and the gods were alarmed lest all humanity be wiped out. Zeus was now seriously worried, and he instructed Iris to talk Demeter round: but her efforts were in vain. Then he sent Hermes to Pluton, to ask him to release Persephone. Pluton agreed, but as Persephone was getting ready to depart, he gave her to eat a pomegranate seed. By this trick to make her eat in the underworld, Pluton had made sure that he would not lose her for ever: she would be his for four months every year.

Persephone returned to her mother, and immediately all the flowers bloomed. Before long, the fields were full once more of wheat-stalks and fruit. Green things covered the earth once more, and continued to do so for eight months - as long as Demeter had her daughter by her. For the remaining four months, Persephone would be in the underworld with Hades, creating - with him - the underground powers that prepared the fertility of the earth. The pomegranate which Hades had given her, with its thousands of seeds, was a symbol of fertility in the fields, of

p.73

A relief from Eleusis showing Demeter, Kore and Triptolemus. Demeter is holding a sceptre in her left hand and Kore a lighted torch, both symbols of the Eleusinian Mysteries, which took place by night. The two deities would also have been carrying ears of wheat as offerings to the young Triptolemus, depicted standing between them (440-430 BC, Athens Archaeological Museum).

the union between the seed and the earth, of Persephone's bond with the god of the underworld.

Before retiring into the heavens once more, Demeter taught the kings her divine craft and the manner in which she herself was to be worshipped. The rituals that were to be held in Demeter's honour - the Mysteries - were open to all, but there was an absolute ban on any revelations as to what happened during the rites. This was the beginning of the **Eleusinian Mysteries**, which were praised by the ancient writers as representing a unique moment of happiness in the human existence. Although the ban on disclosure of the content of the rituals has been effective, we do know something about the stages in the festival and some of the rites. The Great Mysteries were held in the month of Boedromion (late September), and they celebrated the return of Kore to earth. After the seventh century BC, Eleusis was part of the Athenian realm, and the Mysteries were among the most important religious events in the lives of the Athenians - and indeed of all Greeks.

Six months before the Great Mysteries, the Lesser Mysteries took place on the banks of the river Ilissus in Athens, as a kind of preliminary stage for what was to follow. The start of the Great Mysteries was held in Athens, too: on the previous day, the sacred objects used in the Mysteries were brought to Athens, where they were housed in Demeter's sanctuary beneath the Acropolis. On the first day of the festival, the faithful gathered in the Poikile ('painted') Stoa in the Agora, where the *prorrhesis* (the official announcement that the Mysteries had begun) was issued.

On the next four days, sacrifices were made and all the initiates washed and purified themselves by the sea at Phaleron Bay. On the morning of the fifth day, a splendid procession set out from the Dipylon Gate and headed for Eleusis along the Sacred Way. The procession was made up of the faithful, called *mystes* ('initiates'), the priests, and the two most important religious figures in the Mysteries: the *hierophant* ('he who shows the sacred things'), who was always a member of the Eleusinian family of the Eumolpidae, and the *daduch* or torch-bearer, who belonged to the Athenian family of the Cyreces. The initiates wore laurel wreaths and bore branches of the same plant, while the procession was headed by an image of Iacchus, a deity who displayed affinities to Persephone and may well have represented her male side. At certain points along the route, the procession halted to perform brief rites at the shrines on the Sacred Way (the sanctuary of Apollo Daphneius, the sanctuary of Aphrodite, etc.). At the bridge over the river Cephissus, it was the custom for mocking jokes to be exchanged among the initiates, and there was much merriment. In the evening, the procession finally reached Eleusis. On the next day, the most important part of the Mysteries began. The initiates sacrificed to the two gods, fasted, and drank barley-water as Demeter had done when searching for her daughter. Then they entered the *Telesterium* ('hall of rituals'), which was Demeter's temple, and took part in an initiation ceremony of which we know almost nothing. It seems certain, however, that the rites took place by night, to torchlight, and that there were three parts: the *legomena* (that which was said), the *dromena* (that which was done) and the *deiknyomena* (that which was shown). The *legomena* seems to have consisted of a recital of the Demeter and Persephone myth and the *dromena* of a 'dramatic' reconstruction of the story. During the *deiknyomena* the hierophant entered the *anactorum* ('the palace'), which was the inner sanctum of the Telesterium, and revealed to the initiates the sacred things of the Mysteries, which until that time had remained hidden. In the course of this process, and in a highly evocative atmosphere, the initiates gradually reached a state of mental and spiritual elevation, communing with the divine drama and ultimately attaining what was called *epopteia* - redemption and the purification of their souls.

p. 74

A relief from Eleusis showing Demeter, Kore and Triptolemus. Demeter is holding a sceptre in her left hand and Kore a lighted torch, both symbols of the Eleusinian Mysteries, which took place by night. The two deities would also have been carrying ears of wheat as offerings to the young Triptolemus, depicted standing between them (440-430 BC, Athens Archaeological Museum).

HERMES

p.76

Hermes, with winged feet and hat, taking the infant Dionysus to the Nymphs , 440 BC, Vatican Museum.

p.77

This superb statue of Hermes by the sculptor Praxiteles shows the god taking his young brother Dionysus to the Nymphs. Leaning against a tree-trunk over which his cloak is skilfully arranged, Hermes is offering something to Dionyus - probably a bunch of grapes (330 BC, Olympia Museum).

ermes was born in Arcadia, in a cave on Mt Cyllene, out of the union between Zeus and Maea, one of the daughters of Atlas called the Pleiades. While still a babe in arms, he made up his mind to run away from his mother, and happily left the cave and entered the world. The first creature he encountered was a tortoise: without hesitating, Hermes killed it and removed its shell, which he covered with ox leather and strings made from the intestines of a lamb stretched across a wooden frame. He had made a lyre, the first there ever was in the world, and with it he played music and sang.

Before long, however, Hermes grew hungry, and so he ran off to find the herds of cattle which Apollo was grazing in the mountains of Pieria, far to the north. He was there by nightfall, and immediately stole five of Apollo's cows, Once he had separated them from the herd, he forced them to walk backwards so that Apollo would be unable to make sense of their tracks. Hermes took the cows to 'ylos, and by the banks of the Alpheius he found a shed to keep them. He then singled out two cows to cook - but fire was not yet known in the world, so the god took a pointed laurel twig and rubbed it against a thicker branch until a spark leaped up. Thus it was he who invented fire. Hermes then set about skinning and jointing the two beasts. After offering twelve pieces to the gods (amongst whom he included himself!) he spit-roasted and ate the remainder. At dawn, he made his way back to the cave in which he had been born, and silently lay down to sleep in his cot.

In the meantime, Apollo had noticed that five of his cows were missing. With his oracular skills, he had no trouble in finding out who was responsible, and he hurried to Mt Cyllene. Hermes was asleep, rolled up in his blankets, so Apollo woke him and angrily demanded his cattle. Hermes innocent-

ly drew Apollo's attention to his infancy and denied having anything to do with the theft. So Apollo made the young god follow him to Olympus, to give an account of himself before Zeus, father of both of them. Hermes employed all his eloquence and verbal wiles in swearing to the most powerful of the gods that he had never taken any cows anywhere near his home. His skill in lying and his persuasiveness caused Zeus to laugh, and to command Hermes to show Apollo where he had hidden the cattle. The two brothers were reconciled, and Hermes gave Apollo his lyre, making a *syrinx* (shepherd's pipe) so that he, too, could continue to make music. In exchange, Apollo promised to love Hermes more than any other child of Zeus and appointed him as protector of herds and flocks. He also gave Hermes a *ceryceium*, a gold staff which was his symbol of office as the messenger of Zeus and the bearer of his decisions to gods and mortals alike.

Hermes, the beloved messenger of the gods, was depicted by artists holding his staff, with winged sandals on his feet and the *petasus*, the hat worn by travellers, on his head. For the ancient Greeks, he was also the lord of the winds and all the other phenomena associated with the air. There was a tradition that Hermes had been the first to observe the stars in the sky and understand how the world changes and the seasons revolve. That was why his name, in its Latin version, was given to one of the planets (Mercury).

As the god of the winds, Hermes was associated with journeys, becoming the patron of all travellers, and he was also responsible for the street doors of houses and the outer gates of cities. The milestones and signposts placed at crossroads were called Herms

and consisted of oblong pillars surmounted by a bust of the god.

It was natural for the traveller god to become the patron of commerce (*Hermes Agoraeus*), and statues of him stood in the Agora of almost every ancient Greek city. Hermes was credited with having invented weights and measures and the scales, and the profits made in trade were regarded as gifts from him (in which case he was *Hermes Cerdoös*). The god was thought of as an indefatigable runner, and he was the ideal taken by youths for their training in the gymnasium. It was he who endowed the bodies of athletes with strength and elegance, and there were statues to him wherever sporting activities took place.

Yet his principal capacity was that of messenger. Running faster than the wind, the winged god crossed land and sea to convey messages from the gods. In addition, he was capable of going beyond the bounds of the earth and entering the Underworld. He was *Hermes Psychopompus* or *Psychagogus*, the god who led the souls of the dead into Hades. On the last day of the festival called the Anthesteria and dedicated to Dionysus, the Athenians honoured their dead by sacrificing to *Hermes Chthonius*. His connection with the dead ought to be seen in conjunction with the belief that the human soul was like a breath of wind, which left the body at the moment of death. This was a sign that the god of the wind was about to take the soul to the Underworld. According to similar ancient beliefs, ghosts and dreams were also made of air, and Hermes was responsible for making them appear to human beings.

As the herald of the gods and interpreter of their words, Hermes was presented as eloquent and persuasive. Here he was *Hermes Logius*, the patron of orators,

p. 78
The funerary lecythus of Myrrhine. Hermes Psychopompus is shown leading the dead Myrrhine down to the Underworld, while her relatives sadly bid her farewell (430-420 BC, Athens Archaeological Museum).

p. 79
Above, a detail from the Français krater, showing Hermes, with his winged sandals and his caduceus in his hand, running to perform some mission (570 BC, Florence Archaeological Museum). Below, a silver coin depicting Hermes carrying the newborn Dionysus (Athens Numismatic Museum).

philosophers and writers. It is no coincidence that the Greek verb meaning to interpret (h*ermeneuo*) is derived from the name of the god. According to one myth, Zeus once wished to lie with Io at Argos, so he asked Hermes to find some way of diverting the Argives and preserving his secrecy. Hermes thus embarked upon a speech, and his words, like the wind, caressed the ears of the townspeople and kept them close to him for many hours. When the gods created Pandora, it was Hermes who gave her the gift of human speech: but he also endowed her with malice, the power to lie and deceive. The Greeks returned the compliment, often telling stories like the one about his infancy, in which he is wily and fraudulent. Yet behind all his machinations was tremendous ingenuity and perspicacity, as we can see in the traditions about all the things he invented.

The myth in which Hermes steals the cattle of Apollo also reveals another side of the god's character. He was the thief that comes in the night, who would bear off anything not properly protected, just as a strong gust of wind will carry away things which are not safely tied down. Here Hermes had the benefit of the incredible speed at which he could move and his ability to conceal himself - as he did during the Battle of the Giants, when his dogskin helmet made him as invisible as the wind itself.

Yet another aspect of Hermes is evident in the myth of Apollo's cattle: the fact that Apollo made him a gift of the cows and appointed him as the protector of the flocks. Hermes thus became a pastoral god and was worshipped as *Hermes Nomius* ('of the flocks'). One of his principal symbols was the ram, the sheep that leads the flock, the animal whose generative power causes

pp.80-81
The infant Hermes, in his cradle between his parents - Zeus and Maea - listening as Apollo accuses him of stealing his cattle. On the left are the cattle, hidden in a cave, while a hare in a tree symbolises Hermes (Caeretean hydria, 520 BC, the Louvre).

the species to multiply. In the traditions of Arcadia, Hermes was the father of the pastoral god *par excellence*, Pan the goat-footed. Like his son, Hermes was capable of being overcome by irresistible physical passion and he is often depicted in pursuit of maidens and Nymphs, who ran to hide from him in caves and forests. Among the fruits of his amours were Myrtilus the servant of king Oenomaus of Pisa, Polybus king of Sicyon, Bunus king of Corinth, Autolycus the wily ancestor of the still more cunning Odysseus, Harpalacus, Abderus who gave his name to the city of Abdera, Aethalides the herald, Eudorus who distinguished himself in the Trojan War, and the brothers Eurytus and Echion, who were among Jason's companions on the *Argo*.

APHRODITE

p.82
Aphrodite of the Roses, a marble statue from Rhodes showing the goddess bathing (first century AD, Rhodes Archaeological Museum).

p.83
Aphrodite, the most erotic of the ancient Greek goddesses, dazzled gods and mortals with her beauty and inspired love and passion in all the creatures of the earth (the Venus de Milo, second century BC, the Louvre).

Aphrodite, the symbol of female beauty and love, was praised as no other deity in antiquity - and even in modern times. The myth of her birth has been a source of inspiration for great artists in every period of human history. Some ancient writers describe her as the daughter of Zeus and Dione, but according to the majority she was the offspring of Uranus (making her *Aphrodite Urania*).

When Cronus sliced off the genitals of Uranus, he cast them into the sea, where they floated among the waves, covered in blood. But as they drifted, a coat of white foam covered them, growing little by little and ultimately taking the shape of a woman. The foam floated past Cythera and came at last to Cyprus, where the slender-bodied goddess *Aphrodite Anadyomene* rose out of the sea (or from a sea-shell, in some versions). As soon as she stepped ashore, she was greeted by the Hours, who placed a bracelet on her arm and a garland on her head. Then they led her to Olympus and presented her to the gods, who were stunned by her beauty.

On Cythera, Aphrodite's cult was particularly popular, and the goddess was worshipped as *Cytheria*. In Cyprus, she took the name *Cypris* and became the patron of the island. Her cult was especially important in the city of Paphos on Cyprus and became associated with that of the local hero Pygmalion. **Pygmalion** was supposed to have fallen in love with a statue of Aphrodite, and in order to heal his passion Aphrodite brought the statue to life. The fruit of Pygmalion's amours was Paphos, and the city took its name from him.

Aphrodite, the most beautiful of all the women in the world, inspired lust

in all the humans and other creatures on the planet. No one could escape the traps she set to amuse herself with the doings of love-crazed men and women: *"Even the animals of the mountain follow her, wagging their tails. The goddess is gladdened by this sight, fills their hearts with love and causes them to sleep two by two in the shady dells"* (Homeric Hymn to Aphrodite). And when Hera decided, according to the myths, to drive Zeus wild with love, she borrowed Aphrodite's girdle, which had the power to bewitch and deceive. It was Aphrodite who lit the flame of love for Jason in Medea's heart, and who endowed Pandora with her charms.

However, she often used her erotic powers to punish the impious. Helen of Troy and her sister Clytemnestra were both unfaithful to their husbands in response to the goddess's wish because their father Tyndarus had failed to honour Aphrodite as was his duty. The women of Lemnos were punished for the same reason, and made to smell so repulsive that their husbands would not come near them. In their wrath, the women slew all the male population of the island and were forced to live alone for a while, until Aphrodite, in answer to the entreaties of Hephaestus, sent the crew of the *Argo* to Lemnos to mate with the women. And Diomedes, who had had the temerity to wound Aphrodite during the Trojan War, paid a high price for his effrontery: the goddess caused his wife to fall in love with Cometes son of Sthenelus, Diomedes' friend and companion in battle. Her severest punishment of all was reserved for Hippolytus, who stubbornly refused to take pleasure in her gift of love. To avenge herself on him, Aphrodite filled with passion the heart of Hippolytus' step-mother Phaedra, and his denial of her was the cause of his meeting a terrible end.

Aphrodite did not restrict herself to sending her darts of love into the hearts of mankind: the immortals were no less vulnerable to her. Most of the amorous adventures in which Zeus became embroiled were her doing. The greatest of the gods once resolved to pay her back in her own coin, planting in her soul a seed of passion for **Anchises**, a handsome youth who belonged to the famous race of the Dardani of Troy. One evening, after Anchises had returned from a day of grazing his sheep on the slopes of Mt Ida, Aphrodite appeared to him in mortal form, visiting his hut as a beautiful, splendidly-dressed woman. As soon as Achises saw her in her magnificence, he realised she must be one of the goddesses, but Aphrodite deceived him, claiming to be the daughter

p.85
A group of Aphrodite and Pan, from Delos. Aphrodite, nude and probably fresh from her bath, is raising her sandal to drive away Pan, who is incapable of resisting her beauty. Between them, a little winged Cupid is stirring up the passions of goat-footed Pan (100 BC, Athens Archaeological Museum).

of king Otreus of Phrygia and that Hermes had sent her to Anchises to be his wife. Blinded with love, Anchises lay with her on a bed strewn with the hides of bears and lions. Just before dawn, she told him who she really was and promised to make him a king as long as he never disclosed what had taken place between them. The fruit of their union was **Aeneas**, who was brought up by the Nymphs and fought in the Trojan War when he was grown. That was why Aphrodite took the Trojan side, and even sustained a wound in her efforts to save her son. In fact, she was partly responsible for the war, since she had driven Helen into the arms of Paris as his prize for judging that she was more beautiful than Hera and Athena (see the House of Atreus).

Anchises was not Aphrodite's only mortal lover: there was also **Adonis**, son of Cinyras and Smyrna. Aphrodite first noticed Adonis when he was still in infancy. She hid him in a chest and gave him to Persephone to look after, but when the boy grew up Persephone was unable to resist his charms and refused to return him. Zeus decided that Adonis would stay with Persephone, in the Underworld, four months in every year. Aphrodite was to have him for a further four, and for the remainder of the year the youth could go where he pleased. He chose Aphrodite, and spent eight months of the year with her. But one day a wild boar killed Adonis while he was out hunting, and from the drops of his blood the first roses in the world sprouted. Aphrodite wept bitterly at the loss of her darling, and her tears were transformed into another new flower, the anemone. In her grief, she implored Persephone to send Adonis back to her, even if only for six months of every year. Persephone agreed, and so Adonis became the symbol of nature as it bloomed and withered away again, a cycle of which Aphrodite was the protector.

It is precisely this facet of the goddess's nature that lies behind her role in affairs of the heart. The passion which she planted in the human soul was the force that propelled fertilisation and reproduction (*Aphrodite Genetyllis* or *Genetrix*). Her beneficial influence extended to the fruits and flowers of the earth as well as to men, and the animals of land, sky and sea were equally at her mercy. Her symbols were the laurel, the pomegranate, the dove, the swan, the hare and the ram, all of them connected with physical love and reproduction. Aphrodite's connection with fertility is manifest not only in the Adonis myth, but also in the tradition according to which her union with Dionysus led to the birth of Priapus, a misshapen child with monstrous genitalia.

p.86
Aphrodite was very often depicted flying through the sky on the back of a swan or goose. In this cylix she is shown, against a white ground, travelling on the back of a goose and holding a white flower (470-460 BC, British Museum).

Even the myth of Hermaphroditus, who was the son of Hermes and Aphrodite, can be explained in a similar manner. One day as he was bathing, the Nymph Salmacis saw him and fell in love with him. Hermaphroditus returned her feelings, and the two young people locked together in an embrace so tight that they became one, generating a creature with characteristics of both genders.

The myth of Aphrodite's birth out of the sea is very probably a reflection of the close connection between water and physical love, sexuality and fertility. There was a tradition that the goddess had lain with Poseidon himself, the master of the seas, to whom she bore Eryx and Rhodes. She was

often depicted by ancient artists seated on a sea-horse and accompanied by Tritons and Nereids. In some sanctuaries, especially those by the coast, she was worshipped with the epithets *Pelagia, Pontia* and *Limenia,* all of which referred to her power to calm the sea and ensure that ships voyaged safely. It was as *Aphrodite Euploea* (= 'of the good voyage') that she was worshipped at her important sanctuary in Cnidus.

It would seem that Aphrodite's activities were not confined to love and physical passion, but also extended into other areas connected with reproduction. With Hera, she was the patron of marriage - given that love is a fundamental condition for harmony between the spouses. Aphrodite herself was married to Hephaestus, the god of fire - a marriage which was not her own choice, but that of Hera, who managed in this way to join the fire of Hephaestus with the generative power of Aphrodite, the beauty of art with the beauty of nature.

The myths tell us that Aphrodite was once unfaithful to her lame husband with Ares, the powerful god of war. Helios the all-seeing told Hephaestus of his wife's trysts in the fire-god's own palace, and he decided that she deserved to be caught in the act.

p.87
According to a later tradition, Aphrodite emerged from the sea in a shell. Here she is shown seated, in a wet garment, appearing out of an open sea-shell (fourth century BC, Athens Archaeological Museum).

Skilled craftsman that he was, he made nets of metal hammered so thin that they were as invisible as spider's webs, and spread them on the bed he shared with Aphrodite. Then he pretended to be called away to his forge on Lemnos - and when Ares and Aphrodite lay together, becoming entangled in the net, he suddenly reappeared in the palace and made fools of the illicit couple in front of all the gods. Apollo, watching the scene, craftily asked Hermes whether he would like to be in Ares' place. Hermes replied that he would take Aphrodite to bed even if it meant being shackled in three times as many chains and being exposed to the view not only of the gods but of all the goddesses as well! In the end, Hephaestus released the lovers - but only after Poseidon promised to compensate him for his own humiliation.

Ares and Aphrodite had four children: Harmony, Deimus, Phobus ('fear') and Eros. Eros, who rarely left his mother's side and was her constant companion (with the Graces and the Hours), was the littled winged god who ruthlessly shot his darts into the heart, causing both joy and pain. The fact that Eros was the son of Ares as well as Aphrodite gave a rather military cast to the concept of love and, of course, to the goddess herself as its patron. Aphrodite was indeed frequently portrayed with weapons, and she was worshipped with the epithet *Panoplus* ('fully-armed'). The Greeks endowed her with the idea of war in the sphere of the feelings. There was also a connection with the world of the dead, since both sex and death are essential for rebirth and the perpetuation of the species. Thus, Aphrodite was worshipped (with Hermes) as *Aphrodite Chthonia* ('of the underworld') and in some cemeteries as *Aphrodite Melaena* or *Scotia* ('dark').

Of course, even in these gloomier sides of the goddess mortals perceived the ultimately inevitable triumph of love in all its forms. As well as the non-physical side of love (*agape*), Aphrodite also represented its purely sexual aspect (*eros*), and was even connected with prostitution (*Aphrodite Pandemus* = common, vulgar). At her sanctuary on the Acrocorinth worked a large number of *hetaerae* (concubines) who were thought of as sacred. The *hetaerae* held splendid ceremonies in honour of Aphrodite and often posed half-(or fully)naked as models for statues of Aphrodite. According to the traditions, the great sculptor Praxiteles was the first to be inspired by a *hetaera*, called Phryne, in the creation of a masterly statue of the goddess (the 'Aphrodite of Cnidus').

p.88
A wall-painting from Pompeii showing a tender embrace between the illicit lovers, Aphrodite and Ares. Behind them is a Cupid, firing a dart into the hearts of the two lovers (first century BC, Naples National Museum).

ARES

For the ancient Greeks, Ares was the god of war, the figure behind all violence, battles and other conflicts among men. The son of Zeus and Hera, he had inherited his mother's difficult, mercurial temperament, which made him unpopular with mankind and even among the gods. Zeus himself tells Ares, in the *Iliad*, that *"I do not fight other gods, as you do, because you always want to see quarrelling, pain and war. You have your mother's unbending and intolerable obstinacy!"* As a result, Ares was never worshipped to any great extent, and no Greek city had him as its patron.

The god's cult, such as it was, seems to have begun in Thrace, where - according to Homer - Ares lived. From there, knowledge of him spread to Boeotia and then throughout Greece, ultimately leading to his establishment as one of the twelve gods of Olympus. Ares' properties are partly connected with his origins, since for the ancient Greeks Thrace was a place of rough people and crude customs. Furthermore, it was from Thrace that the storms of winter came to lash the south of Greece. Ares was often compared to a storm, thundering down across the field of battle and causing the clanging of weapons that shook earth and heaven alike. Even when supine on the earth he inspired terror in the human heart, for his body occupied two acres of ground.

In the human imagination, this vast warrior, armed to the teeth, spread death wherever he went, whether flames were bursting out of his chest or whether he was simply racing by in his chariot drawn by golden horses. Unlike Athena, who had devised methodical and

orderly ways of waging war, Ares loved bloodshed and chaotic fighting. In the Trojan War, however, he was seriously wounded by Athena as he strove to help the Trojan side, thus proving that technique was capable of overcoming brute force.

Ares was the father of many children, most of whom were cruel, violent kings. Among his sons were Diomedes of Thrace, who bred man-eating horses, Oenomaus of Pisa, and the dragon which devastated Thebes and its surroundings until slain by Cadmus. Another son called **Cycnus** set up house in the temple of Apollo Pagasaeus and defiled that sacred place with his weapons. After a fierce fight, Heracles killed him, upon which his father transformed him into a swan (*cycnus* in Greek, then as now). **Flegyas**, son of Ares by Chryse, also tried to burn down a temple of Apollo, but the god of light shot him with an arrow. Penthesilea, queen of the Amazons, was the daughter of Ares, as was **Alcippe**, daughter of Agraula and born in Athens. According to the tradition, Halirrhothius, the brutal son of Poseidon, tried to ravish Alcippe, but Ares was lying in wait for him and killed him just at the crucial moment. Poseidon demanded that the gods try Ares for murder, the first instance in which the twelve gods of Olympus were recognised as a supreme court in capital cases. Ares was tried - and acquitted - on a rocky outcrop to the west of the Acropolis in Athens, which was later called the *Areopagus* (= 'rock of Ares') and became the court of Athens (the name is still used for the modern Greek supreme court).

Ares' union with Aphrodite resulted in the birth of Eros, Harmony, Deimus and Phobus (see Aphrodite). Attribution of the parenthood of Harmony to the god of war and the goddess of love could be seen as a symbol of the need for balance and order to be produced from a blend between opposing powers. Harmony, who later became the wife of king Cadmus of Thebes, thus bestowed upon the world the concept behind her name after the violence of Ares had first been united with the serenity and tenderness of Aphrodite. Two of the other children of that union, however, inherited the properties of their father and became his faithful acolytes: Deimus and Phobus, who represented the awe and fear of mankind. Also among the companions of the god were **Eris** (= strife), who caused quarrels, Enyo, the terrible goddess of battle, and Cera, a monster with the teeth and talons of a wild beast.

p.93
A red-figure pelike from Tanagra bearing a scene from the Battle of the Giants. In the upper band, Ares - flanked by Castor and Pollux - is attacking the Giants, who are in the lower part of the painting (fourth century BC, Athens Archaeological Museum).

HEPHAESTUS

wo different traditions were preserved in the ancient world about the birth of Hephaestus, the god of fire. According to the first, he was the son of Zeus and Hera and he grew up on Olympus with the gods. But one day, when his parents became embroiled in yet another of their frequent quarrels, Hephaestus took Hera's side and Zeus, in anger, flung him from Olympus. He fell, with an injured foot, on the island of Lemnos, where the local people took care of him.

The other myth tells us that Hera gave birth to Hephaestus alone, as the son of no father, because she was so outraged by the infidelities of Zeus. But the boy was born lame, and Hera's feeling of disgrace was so strong that she cast him into the sea. Two of the sea-goddesses, Thetis and Eurynome, took pity on the infant and raised him secretly in the cave of Nereus. When Hephaestus grew to manhood, he decided to avenge himself on his mother and take his rightful seat among the gods of Olympus. So he made a golden throne, enveloped it in invisible nets and sent it to Hera as a gift. As soon as she sat on the throne, her son's trap caught her and no one could set her free. The gods tried to persuade Hephaestus to release her, but it was Dionysus who found the way to do so: he drew Hephaestus into revelry, got him drunk, and hauled him back to Olympus on a mule, accompanied by Satyrs and Nymphs. Once Hera was out of the nets, Hephaestus was welcomed into the company of the gods and was given Aphrodite to be his wife, as a reward.

For the ancient Greeks, Hephaestus was the god who protected fire in all its forms. According to the tradition, it was in his keeping when Prometheus stole it to give to mankind. The myths about Hephaestus' fall from Olympus form part of this tradition, since they are connected with the early belief that fire had come down from the heavens. Nor was it coincidental that Hephaestus was said to have

p.94
Hephaestus, drunk and supported by a Satyr, being led to Olympus by Dionysus. He is still holding the tools of his trade, the pincers and the hammer (red-figure pelike, 435-430 BC, Munich Archaeological Collection).

p.95
Hephaestus was, for the Greeks, the most skilful of all craftsmen, and the finest creations of antiquity came from his hand. In the illustration, we see him giving Thetis the famous weapons he made for Achilles and whose praises Homer sang in the Iliad. Holding his hammer, Hephaestus is examining the helmet he has made for the warrior, while Thetis has already taken up the shield and spear (red-figure cylix, 480 BC, Berlin Museum).

landed on Lemnos, a volcanic island where there was fire in the bowels of the earth. By extension, the god became associated with volcanoes and gave them his name (*hephaestia* in Greek, and of course Hephaestus is Vulcan in Latin). The boulders, fire and lava which volcanoes spewed out when erupting were attributed to him, which is why he was worshipped in the vicinity of Mt Etna and was portrayed by the artists as the faithful guardian of a monster that dwelt at the bottom of a kiln. It was in the head of this monster that Hephaestus had his workshop, where he hammered the iron that came molten from the bowels of the earth. Here we can also find a background to explain the intervention of Dionysus, god of wine and the vineyard, to bring Hephaestus back to Olympus: in Greece and Italy, volcanic soils are the best on which to grow grapes, and so it was only reasonable that the god of the vine should be on good terms with the god of volcanoes.

Homer calls Hephaestus *chalkeas*, the metal-worker, because of all the gods he was the most skilful in that craft. Even as a boy in the sea-kingdom of Nereus he had delighted in making objects of metal. Metal-working was his exclusive dominion because it could not be done without the use of fire. In the imagination of the Greeks, Hephaestus, dressed in a loose tunic, wearing a cap on his head and with the hammer and pincers in hand, spent all his time bent over the anvil producing works of incomparable skill. His arms and hands had been toughened by the constant labour, but his lower limbs were atrophied, and so he worked sitting down. This may be the origin of the myth of his lameness and generally ungainly appearance, which often caused the other gods to laugh at him.

Hephaestus' workshop was traditionally taken to be on Lemnos, where the mythical people of the Sindians dwelt. In honour of the god, the islanders had called their chief town Hephaestias, and they built a temple to him near the volcanic hill

p.96
The superb masterpieces made by Hephaestus established him in the minds of the Greeks as the protector of craftsmen. He and Athena inspired the craftsmen of Athens and endowed them with skill. This red-figure cylix shows a bronze foundry on whose walls the labourers have placed images of Hephaestus and Athena (480 BC, Berlin Museum).

Moschylus where they celebrated an unusual religious custom: once a year, they extinguished all the fires in their house for nine days, then relit them from a flame specially brought from Delos. On Lemnos, Hephaestus and Cabeiro (daughter of Proteus) became the parents of the Cabeiroi, spirits of fire and the metals.

However, Hephaestus' home was on Olympus, where he lived with his wife Aphrodite (see Aphrodite). According to other traditions, he was also married to Charis and to Aglaea, one of the three Graces. He had another workshop on Olympus, where the items he made were the finest in the world. Hephaestus had wrought the palaces of all the gods, the bed and golden disc of Helius the sun-god, the goblets of Dionysus and the arrows used by Apollo and Artemis. Also from his hands came the sceptre of Agamemnon, the gold vine which Zeus sent to Ganymede's father when he took the lad to live on Olympus with him, the bracelet which Zeus gave to Europa, the wreath worn by Ariadne at her wedding to Dionysus, the sickle with which Perseus decapitated Medusa, the weapons of Heracles and the famous shield of Achilles, with its superbly-executed narrative scenes, as described by Homer.

Hephaestus was not only a maker of material things: he was also of importance in the creation of living beings. He it was who made Pandora, the first woman, and he also gave life to the gold watch-dog of Zeus, the gold and silver hounds that guarded the palace of Alcinous in the land of the Phaeaceans, and two bulls with bronze legs who belonged to Aeetes, king of Colchis. Among his other creations were the bronze giant Talos who kept ceaseless watch over the Crete of King Minos, and the two golden maidens who helped the god himself on his travels.

Thanks to his unique skills, Hephaestus became associated with Athena, goddess of wisdom and ingenuity. According to the myth, it was Hephaestus who, with his axe, split Zeus' skull to allow the goddess to be born; later, he fell in love with Athena and attempted to ravish her. But she broke free of his embrace and his sperm fell upon the soil of Attica, fertilising and giving life to Erichthonius, the king of Athens. In Attica it was believed that both deities had taught craftsmen how to make things of beauty, which was why they were worshipped together in a temple in the Agora at Athens, the magnificent structure called the Hephaesteum (and often, mistakenly, the Theseum).

HESTIA

estia was the eldest daughter of Rhea and Cronus, and she was worshipped as the most ancient goddess in the Greek pantheon. Her seniority gave her a special kind of primacy on Olympus, and all the other gods - including Zeus - were careful to respect her. According to one tradition, Zeus gave permission for Hestia to be worshipped in every temple, regardless of the god to which it was dedicated.

Once, it was said, both Apollo and Poseidon desired her and wished to make her their own. The goddess fled them, and when they hastened in pursuit of her she cast herself at the feet of Zeus and then, laying her hand on his head, swore an oath of perpetual virginity. Like Artemis and Athena, Hestia never entered into a physical union with any male, remaining forever pure and undefiled.

In the thought of the Greeks, Hestia was the personification of the security of the household and of peace within the family. As can be seen from her name, she protected the *hestia* - the fire, that is, which burned in the hearth of every home and which had been a kind of sacred altar since prehistoric times. At that altar, the members of every Greek family sacrificed to their personal divinity - and the fire was never allowed to go out, so that the goddess would always be present. Given that the city was seen as analogous to the family on a larger scale, Hestia also had her temple in every Greek city. In the Prytaneum, which was the centre of public life, there would be an altar to Hestia where the common flame of all the citizens burned ceaselessly. The altar was regarded as a sanctuary for suppliants and a sacred place, where sacrifices to the gods were made, inviolable oaths were sworn and foreign visitors and emissaries were received. Fire from the altar of Hestia was given to warriors setting out on campaign and to colonists sailing off to found a new dependency of the mother-city. In addition to her altars and temples in the individual cities, Hestia was also worshipped at the great sanctuary of Delphi, which was for the Greeks the *omphalos* - the navel, or centre, that is - of their country and the whole world. The common altar (*hestia*) of all the Greeks was located next to the *omphalos* itself, the stone which symbolised the centre of the world. Hestia was thus not only the protector of the home, but also seems to have been the guardian of the universe, in which case it was only natural that she should live at its absolute centre.

THE OTHER GODS

p.100
Above, Dionysus and Ariadne in a painting from a calyx krater (380 BC, Athens Archaeological Museum).
Below, an actor's mask of a Satyr, from a mosaic in Rhodes (mid-Hellenistic period, Rhodes Archaeological Museum).

p.101
The superb bronze krater from Derveni, ornamented with relief figures of Dionysus and Ariadne amid a troupe of revellers. On the neck of the vessel are high-relief figures of Dionysus, two Maenads and a Satyr (330-320 BC, Thessaloniki Archaeological Museum).

Dionysus

Although Dionysus (or Bacchus) was not counted among the twelve gods of Olympus, he was one of the most important deities of the ancient Greeks. And although he was the son of Zeus and a mortal woman - Semele, daughter of king Cadmus of Thebes - he was not honoured as a mere demigod or hero, as was usual in such cases. Dionysus belonged firmly in the sphere of the divine, and was worshipped along with the immortals. It was only natural, indeed, that special honours should be reserved for a god of his nature, since his life and adventures were the inspiration for the creation of the dithyramb, the satyr play, the comedy and the tragedy - in a word, of the theatre.

According to the myth, Zeus fell in love with Semele as soon as he set eyes on her, and after lying with her and impregnating her he promised to grant her whatever her heart's desire might be. Hera, who had become aware of her husband's infidelity, made approaches to Semele and persuaded her to ask Zeus one single favour: that he should appear to her in the form in which he married Hera. At first, Zeus refused to grant her wish, but because he could not break the oath that he had sworn he came to her room in his chariot, amid all the effects of a terrible storm and hurling his thunderbolt, which caused Semele's death. But Ge took pity on Semele's unborn child, and ordered an ivy plant to grow over the pillars of the house, protecting the baby from the flames. Zeus immediately cut open his own thigh, put the embryo into his own flesh and nurtured it there until its time came to be born. When that hour arrived, he cut his thigh open again and Dionysus came into the world as *pyrigenes, merorrhaphes* and *diplogennemenos* - 'fire-

born', 'thigh-sewn' and 'twice-born'.

Zeus knew, however, that Hera would not be long in pursuing the child, and so he gave it to Semele's sister Ino, who had married king Athamas of Boeotia, to bring up. But Hera soon found Dionysus, whereupon Zeus changed his son into a goat and entrusted Hermes with the task of taking him to Mount Nysa, where the Nymphs took over his upbringing in a cave with abundant wild vines. Dionysus never escaped from the wrath of Hera, even when he grew to manhood: she drove him mad and caused him to wander aimlessly from place to place. These travels took him to Egypt, Syria and ultimately Phrygia, where Rhea cured him and taught him the rites that would later be performed in his honour. Then Dionysus resumed his journeying, teaching people wherever he went the rites he had learned and spreading knowledge of viticulture.

In his wanderings, Dionysus was often to be seen clad in a deerskin, wearing a wreath of vine-leaves and dancing frenetically with the Nymphs. The turmoil he caused in his passing was the origin of the epithets *Bromius* and *Euoeus*, both of which mean 'noisy'. Those who welcomed him when he came to visit were rewarded with the gift of his sweet wine, to gladden and comfort them. But those who drove him away were severely punished, because his wine was also capable of causing a frenzy in which humans committed various atrocities. In Aetolia, for instance, Dionysus received hospitality at the hands of king **Oeneas** (from *oinos*, wine) to whom he gave a vine to plant. The same gift was also bestowed on **Icarius** from Icaria in Attica, a *deme* which was renamed Dionysus after that time. Icarius resolved to let other people taste the wine of Dionysus, but, inexperienced as they were, they drank it neat (without water) and, believing in their intoxication that Icarius had given them poison, they killed him. However, it was not uncommon for mortals to refuse to take part in the rites of Dionysus. The daughters of king Minyas of Orchomenus stayed indoors and would not join the other women as they ran off to celebrate in the forest. As a punishment, a mania came upon them: they dismembered a child, wandered the world and were eventually changed into birds. And as Euripides tells the story in his *Bacchae*, the mistrustful king **Pentheus** of Thebes went so far as to arrest and imprison Dionysus. Dionysus soon freed himself, and talked the king into climbing the mountain and spying on the women as they danced wildly under the influence of Dionysus' wine. Among them was Agave,

Pentheus' mother, who had no hesitation in tearing her son limb from limb, with the other women, under the mass delusion that he was a wild beast. In these myths, we can see clearly the dual nature of wine, and thus of the god who was its patron. When the wine-drinking is moderate and controlled, man reaches a state of mental elevation unattainable by other means, but when consumption is immoderate it can cause a mania of destruction. The role of Dionysus, then, was to teach men to use his gifts wisely and to punish both those who denied him and those who went beyond the permitted limits.

In the minds of the ancient Greeks, Dionysus was the patron of viticulture, of wine and, more generally, of fertility and vegetation. Through drunkenness and ecstatic dance he offered mankind a feeling of boundless freedom which released them from their everyday worries. For that reason, he was known as *Lysius* ('that liberates us from troubles') and *Catharsius* ('that cleanses our souls'). On his wanderings, Dionysus was accompanied by a large troop of Maenads, Satyrs and Sileni. The **Maenads** or **Bacchae** were the women who took part in the god's orgiastic rites. Holding the *thyrsus*, a staff crowned with a pine-cone and adorned with leaves of ivy and vine, they were overcome by a divine madness and reached a state of ecstasty in which they threw themselves into a frenzied dance. If they came across a wild animal, they would tear and eat its flesh, believing that in this way they made contact with the god, whom Zeus had once transformed into a goat. The **Stayrs and Sileni** were spirits of the woods: these monstrous creatures had the legs and tails of horses, exaggeratedly large genitalia, snub noses, curly hair and long beards. The difference between the Sileni and the Satyrs seems to have been in the greater age of the former.

Their sole occupation was to run through the forests, dancing and chasing the Nymphs and other pretty maidens.

The goat-footed god Pan (see Pan) was also a companion of Dionysus, as was **Priapus**, the son of Dionysus and Aphrodite, who

p.104
The interior of a cylix showing a Maenad with a thyrsus in her hand (500 BC, Museum of the Agora of Athens).

p.105
A mosaic floor showing Dionysus on the back of a panther, his favourite animal. He is wearing a festive robe, holds a thyrsus and a drum, and is crowned with ivy. The collar on the swift-running panther is also made of ivy (second half of the second century BC, House of the Masks, Delos).

p.106

During the orgiastic rites of Dionysus, the female followers of the cult took the place of the Maeanads - that is, they were overcome with a divine mania and believed they were coupling with the god himself. The mania was not necessarily caused by intoxication, but its purpose was always mental and spiritual exhilaration. In their frenzied dance, the women forgot their everyday roles and overturned the existing order of things, to which they later reverted, revitalised. Against the white background of this painting, a Maenad with snakes in her hair, a leopard-skin on her shoulders and a thyrsus in her hand is dancing ecstatically holding a small feline creature (490-485 BC, Munich Archaeological Collection).

with his enormous phallus is an obvious fertility symbol. The cult of Dionysus began in rural areas and then spread to the rest of Greece. The widespread nature of the cult can be seen in the fact that the god had a shrine of his own within the temple of Apollo at Delphi, where it was traditionally believed that he dwelt during the three winter months when Apollo was away in the land of the Hyperboreans. In Athens, the cult of Dionysus was imported from Eleutherae in Boeotia at the time of Pisistratus (6th century BC). It was in that city that the foundations were laid for the development of the theatre, an art-form which could trace its origins back to the dithyramb. The *dithyramb* was a cult song to Dionysus which a small group of men dressed as Satyrs chanted while dancing to the accompaniment of a flute. Within the group, the *exarchon* or leader of the dance soon stood out, giving the lead which the others followed, and this was the first nucleus around which the ancient Greek drama later evolved. In a series of developments, the choral song was enhanced with imitative movements, metre, and then dialogue. In the mid-sixth century BC, Thespes of the Attic *deme* of Icaria was credited with being the first person to include an 'actor' in the performance: this was a character who, while not part of the chorus, interacted with it. By the fifth century BC, the theatre had reached its fullest and finest form, consisting of three genres - tragedy, comedy and the Satyr play. Little by little, the subject-matter of the works ceased to be exclusively confined to the life and doings of Dionysus, although theatrical performances continued to focus on the two major festivals of the god, the Great Dionysia and the Lenea.

The **Great Dionysia** was the most splendid festival dedicated to the god. It took place in the month of Elaphebolion (March-April) and commemorated the introduction in Athens of the cult of Dionysus Eleuthereus (from Eleutherae). Two days before the festival began, the *proagon* was held, during which the poets announced to the public the theatrical works they were going to be presenting. The following day was devoted to a reconstruction of the journey by which Dionysus made his way from Eleutherae to Athens: the worshippers carried the statue of the god outside the city walls and at night, by torch-light, they fetched it back to its temple. On the first day of the festival, all the Athenians took part in a procession to the sanctuary of Dionysus during which the atmosphere was festive. The main feature of this procession was that the celebrants held mock phalluses in honour of the god. Once they arrived at the sanctuary, sacrifices were made and a dithyramb competition got under way. When the names of the victors were announced, the crowds poured out into the streets of the city, celebrating. The remainder of the festival was given over to performances of the theatre: on one day, five comedies by five different poets, and on the last three days a competition between three tragic poets, each of whom presented a tetralogy consisting of three tragedies and a Satyr play.

p.107
A black-figure cylix with a scene probably representing the story of the Tyrrhenian pirates. Dionysus is shown as a carefree voyager drinking wine from a horn. A vine covered with grapes has sprung from the mast of the ship, and there are dolphins - the transformed pirates of the myth - swimming in the sea (540-530 BC, Munich Archaeological Collection).

There were also theatrical performances during the **Lenea**, a festival held in the month of Gamelion (January-February) and constituting a symbolic thanksgiving for the fact that the wine was now ready. The competition at the Lenea involved two tragic poets, each of whom presented two tragedies, and five comic poets with one comedy each. The festival of the **Anthesteria** (= feast of the flowers), held in the month of Anthesterion (February-March), was also dedicated to Dionysus. During it, all the Athenians were invited to a banquet, a wine-drinking contest and a ceremony

in which wreaths were offered to the god being honoured. At the same time, there was a symbolic wedding between the god and the wife of the archon-king during which the entire city was regarded as being in communion with Dionysus, thereby ensuring that the soil of Athens would be fertile during the coming year. The last day of this festival was devoted to the dead, and the worshippers offered up kettles full of seeds to Dionysus and Hermes Chthonius. Another of the Dionysiac festivals was the **Lesser Dionysia**, where the most ancient traditions concerning the cult of Bacchus were preserved. The Lesser Dionysia took place in the month of Poseidaeon (December-January) and there were sacrifices to the god, banquets, contests for the ordinary people, magnificent processions, tumultuous dancing and exchanges of ribaldry among the peasantry in which the comic element was predominant.

p.108
The interior of a cylix showing a Satyr riding a donkey. The Satyrs, demonic creatures with horse's legs and tails, were the constant companions of Dionysus. It seems that during the Dionysiac rites the men dressed as Satyrs, wearing masks with beards and animal ears and tying round their waists a kind of apron with a leather phallus and an animal's tail (520-510 BC, Museum of the Agora of Athens).

Dionysus was not only an Athenian god: he occupied a special place in the festivals and myths of many other parts of Greece and especially of those in which viticulture was highly developed. In Naxos, for example, there was a local myth which associated Dionysus with **Ariadne**, daughter of king Minos of Crete. According to the story, after Theseus killed the Minotaur he fled Crete, taking Ariadne with him so as to marry her in Athens. There are a number of versions of the story, but in most Theseus was forced to run his ship aground on Naxos, and he left Ariadne there, abandoning her while she slept. As soon as she woke, grief at her loneliness overcame her; Dionysus spied her as she wept, fell in love with her and made her his wife. They had two children, Oenopion and Staphylus. This myth is most probably a symbol of the fertility of the earth, since Ariadne is believed to be a survival of the Minoan vegetation goddess.

The islands of the Aegean preserved another fascinating tradition about Dionysus. Once, it was said, the god was standing on the beach gazing out to sea when some **pirates of Tyre** caught sight of him from afar and took him for a local princeling. They abducted him in the hope of extracting a ransom from the king whom they supposed to be his father. Dionysus put up no resistance and boarded their vessel - but suddenly the whole boat flooded

with wine, ivy grew up the masts and the sails were covered with vines bearing grapes, while flowers sprouted to adorn the oars. The god transformed himself into a lion and devoured the chief pirate. The remainder of the crew, horror struck into their hearts by the appearance of a beast amongst them, threw themselves into the sea and were changed into dolphins. Only one pirate survived, because from the start he had been opposed to what the others were planning to do. In this myth, we are struck by the transformations of Dionysus, which once again are a ssociated with the violent effects that wine can have on the human consti-tution. It is no coincidence, furthermore, that in the *Bacchae* of Euripides the chorus calls on Dionysus as follows: *"Reveal yourself as a bull or a many-headed beast, O Bacchus, as a dragon or as a lion wrapped in flames"*.

p.109
Above, Dionysus, holding a cantharus of wine, lies back half-drunk across the back of a donkey (Athens Numismatic Museum). Below, a calyx krater showing Ariadne and Dionysus in a tender embrace and surrounded by Cupids, Maenads and Satyrs. At the wedding of the loving couple, Hephaestus gave the bride a superb wreath and the bridegroom some silver cups. Ariadne's wreath later became a bright star in the heavens (early fourth century BC, Athens Archaeological Museum).

Asclepius

Asclepius was the physician-god *par excellence* for the Greeks, the deity who cured mortals and alleviated their pain. According to the most common story, he was born of the union between Apollo and Coronis, daugher of king Phlegyas of Laceria in Thessaly. But before Apollo got Coronis with child, she had been betrothed to Ischys, son of king Elatus of Arcadia. On the day her wedding to Ischys was to take place, a raven brought the news to Apollo, who in his rage damned the bird to remain for ever as black as the news it had brought, before shooting Ischys dead with an arrow. His sister Artemis then slew Coronis. But Apollo took pity on the child that Coronis was to have borne him, and extracted it from her womb just before she passed away. He taught the child the elements of medicine before putting him in the hands of Chiron, the wise Centaur, who instilled the principles of pharmacology in the young Asclepius.

Thessaly was not, however, the only part of Greece that claimed to be the birthplace of Asclepius. One of the other candidates was Epidaurus, where one of the god's most important sanctuaries was located. The local people believed that it was in their area that Apollo had lain with Coronis, and that she had exposed the newborn baby on Mt Myrtium. Apollo protected his son by sending a dog to watch over him and a she-goat to give him milk. In Messene, on the other hand, the tradition was that Apollo and Arsinoe, daughter of the local king Leucippus, were the parents of Asclepius, and that Coronis had simply been the baby's wet-nurse.

However the case may be, all the versions agree that it was with Chiron, among the wooded peaks of Mt Pelion, that Asclepius gained his great knowledge of medicine, and his fame was not long in spreading throughout Greece. Patients flocked to receive treatment at his hands, including many of the important legendary heroes, for Asclepius was said to have been among the crew of the *Argo* and to have taken part in the hunt for the Calydonian boar. His two sons, Machaon and Podaleirius, accompanied the Greeks on the Trojan expedition and healed many of the wounded warriors. Asclepius and his wife

Epione also had four daughters, Iaso, Aceso, Panacea and Hygeia, all of whose names were associated with medicine and healing.

Asclepius did not, however, confine his activities to merely healing the sick: he also raised the dead, and was so successful in doing so that Hades complained to Zeus. The chief of the gods was so incensed by the presumptuousness of Asclepius that he hurled a thunderbolt at him and slew him. In revenge for the death of his son, Apollo killed the Cyclopes, for which he was punished by being made to serve as the shepherd of king Admetus.

After Asclepius' death, the Greeks worshipped him as a god. His cult focused on a number of well-organised sanctuaries, each of which was called the **Asclepium**. The oldest Asclepium was at Trikke in Thessaly, but those of the greatest importance were at Epidaurus, Cos, Corinth and Pergamum. These sanctuaries saw

p.111
A votive relief of the family of Asclepius. The god, in the centre, is leaning on a staff around which is coiled a snake, while behind him come his sons Machaon and Podaleirius and his daughters Iaso, Aceso and Panacea. Worshippers with gifts are approaching the divine family. The relief was found in the Asclepium of Athens, which was founded in around 413 BC on the south slopes of the Acropolis (fourth century BC, Athens Archaeological Museum).

p.112
Above, a head of Hygeia from the temple of Athena Alea at Tegea. This masterpiece is attributed to the sculptor Scopas and is believed to have belonged to the cult statue of Hygeia (360 BC, Athens Archaeological Museum).

Below, the goddess Hygeia was for the ancient Greeks the most important daughter of Asclepius, personifying human health. Hygeia, like her father, was believed to have therapeutic powers and she was worshipped throughout Greece (marble statue of the third century AD, Rhodes Archaeological Museum).

the Greeks take their first steps forward in the medical science, although their therapeutic methods and treatments were based on signs sent to them by the god. When patients arrived at the sanctuary, they were made to fast, bathe and purify themselves before sacrificing and, at night, lying down either on special couches or on the skins of the animals they had sacrificed. In the dark and amid the quiet of nature, they would have dreams in which Asclepius appeared to them and recommended the medicaments they should take. In the morning, the patient would tell the priests what he had dreamed of, and they would interpret the vision. It was the custom for those who were healed to make votive offerings to Asclepius in the form either of pillars describing their cure or of gold and silver coins. The most famous of the physicians who followed Asclepius were called Asclepiads, and they traced their descent back to the god himself. Among them, the ancient Greeks reserved a special place for the great doctor Hippocrates of Cos.

THE CELESTIAL DIVINITIES

Helius - Eos - Selene

Helius was the light of the sun personified, and he was born from the union of the Titan Hyperion with the Titaness Theia. The Greeks imagined him in the form of a gigantic eye seeing everything from on high, or of a resplendent youth with golden hair and a crown surrounded by rays. Each morning, Helius mounted his winged chariot, drawn by horses of fire, and set off from the land of the dawn - the deep bed of the encircling river Ocean - to pass over the earth into the dome of the heavens. By midday, he was at the highest point in the sky; in the afternoon he descended towards the earth again, finally coming to the land of the evening and plunging into Ocean once more. At night, he took his rest on a golden, winged bed which Hephaestus had made for him and was carried from the land of the Hesperides to that of the Ethiopians, where he had his home and where he grazed his sacred herds of red cattle. There was another tradition to the effect that at night Helius rode on a golden disc which took him back from west to east.

Helius had many wives and children: Selene (who was also his sister), the Oceanid Perse or Perseis (on whom he fathered Haete and Circe), Pasiphae (the wife of Minos), and Rhode (by whom he had seven wise children), Neaera (mother of the maidens called the Heliads, who watched over his cattle and sheep), and Clymene of Ethiopia, the mother of Phaethon. According to the myth, Phaethon once coerced his father into lending him the fiery chariot for just a day; but he was unable to master the horses and, out of control, the chariot swerved far too close to earth and burned the fields. Zeus, concerned lest some more general disaster should occur, hurled his thunderbolt and slew Phaethon. His corpse fell into the river Eridanus in Athens, and was buried by the Nymphs

p.113

The sun's daily course across the heavens was the subject of many ancient poems which convey the awe felt by the Greeks when faced with the life-giving powers of Helius, the sun-god. Part of a Homeric hymn to Helius praises "tireless Helius, who is like the immortals and who shines for mortals and the deathless gods alike as he rides his horse, and who looks with terrible eyes from the gold helmet out of which shine rays full of light..". In this illustration, a copper coin of Rhodes showing Helius (Athens Numismatic Museum).

and the Heliads. Indeed, it was said that the tears of the Heliads for their unfortunate brother were transformed into amber.

Of all the various cities in Greece, the cult of Helius was strongest in Rhodes, which had taken its name from his wife. It was in honour of their beloved god that the Rhodians erected the famous Colossus, a bronze statue 32 metres in height which was one of the Seven Wonders of the World. The Colossus of Rhodes was created by the sculptor Charis of Lindos and was made out of the loot left to the islanders after Demetrius Poliorcetes unsuccessfully laid siege to Rhodes in the late fourth century BC.

Helius' sister was Eos, whom Homer describes as "rosy-fingered": she was the personification of the dawn, which brings the first light of day and heralds the imminent start of Helius' daily journey. The incomparable radiance of the dawn, combined with the freshness of early morning, made Eos the object of much wonder and, in the myths, young men are forever falling in love with her. There is a tradition that Ares once developed a

p.114
A calyx krater showing Helius crowned with golden rays as he completes his daily course on a chariot drawn by winged horses. As he approaches, the stars - in the form of little children - dive into the sea (435 BC, British Museum).

passion for Eos, and because she did not resist his advances Aphrodite, in jealousy, placed on her the curse of falling in love with any handsome young man she might meet. As a result, the shining goddess lay with Astraeus, to whom she bore the winds Zephyrus, Borras and Notus as well as Eosphorus and all the stars in the sky; with Cleitus; with Cephalus, son of Hermes; with Orion; and with **Tithonus**, a youth of unsurpassed beauty. Eos induced Tithonus to enter her fiery chariot, in which she bore him off to her palace, where she married him. So that she might never be parted from him, she begged Zeus to make him immortal - and although Zeus granted her wish, Tithonus was still subject to human ageing. Over the centuries, he shrivelled away to such an extent that only his voice was left. To release him from his suffering, Eos transformed him into a cicada. Of their union were born Emathion and Memnon. **Memnon** became king of Ethiopia, fought in the Trojan War on the losing side, and was slain by Achilles. The Greek artists were fond of portraying the scene of Memnon's death, rendering with vigour the mourning of Eos and the carrying of the corpse down into the Underworld.

The third child of Hyperion and Theia was Selene, who bestowed on mankind the gentle light of the moon. Her brilliance, it was said, had been so great that it caused Zeus to fall in love with her. She lay with him, and Pandias was born of their union. In Arcadia, the goat-footed god Pan was believed to be her lover, although elsewhere Helius was her husband and she bore him the three Hours. Her best-known paramour, however, was **Endymion**, whom she had beseeched Zeus to endow with both perpetual youth and perpetual sleep. Every evening, Selene visited Endymion in a cave on Mt Latmus in Caria and lay with him, and their children included fifty daughters who probably corresponded to the fifty weeks of the lunar year. The Lion of Nemea and Erse, symbol of the cool of evening, were also regarded as being the offspring of Selene.

p.115
A box lid which vividly depicts the cycle of the day: in the lower section, Helius on his chariot sets out across the sky, while Selene (the moon) is disappearing, only the rump of her horse being visible. Further behind, Night, too, is driving away on her chariot (second half of the fifth century BC, Athens Archaeological Museum).

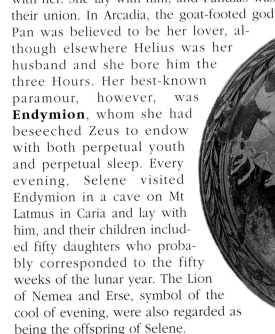

Iris - the Harpies - the Winds

In the personage called Iris, the ancient Greeks brought to life the rainbow with all its bewitching colours, which they imagined to be the goddess's dress or the path along which she walked. Since the rainbow was like a bridge to the sky, Iris was taken to be among the messengers of the gods, capable of running from the heavens down to the world below and conveying divine instructions. Iris was the daughter of Thaumas son of Pontus and of Electra daughter of Oceanus. The artists depicted her as a splendidly-dressed figure with winged sandals and gold wings which allowed her to run like the wind. According to the traditions, her sisters were the storm-birds called the Harpies, and her lover was the wind Zephyrus.

The Harpies - Aello, Ocypete and Celaeno, to give them their names - were voracious winged monsters which made a frightful noise whenever they moved and devastated every place over which they passed. They had the bodies of birds and sharp talons, and they swooped down to devour the fruit of the fields and the foodstuffs man had stored. One of their victims was the blind seer **Phineas** of the Bosporus. The Harpies stole his food and left him starving - nearly to death, in fact, before the Argonauts found him. Jason and his companions discovered where the Harpies had gone and sent after them Zetes and Calais, sons of the wind Boreas, who drove the fierce birds away or, in some versions of the tale, killed them. The Harpies were symbolic of the storm winds, but the Greek myths also had figures to represent the ordinary winds, who were human in form and did much to benefit mortals. The most important winds were Boreas, Notus, Eurus and Zephyrus, all the sons of Eos and Astraeus. Boreas blew wildly from his home among the mountains of Thrace in the north, and he was the strongest of the winds. It was Boreas who snatched **Oreithyia**, daughter of king Erechtheus of Athens, from the banks of the river Ilissus and bore her off to Thrace, where he fathered Zetes, Calais, Chiones and Cleopatra on her. Once, it was said, Boreas had conceived a passion for the mares of Erichthonius of Troy. He transformed himself into a stallion, coupled with them and sired twelve horses capable of striding the winds. Zephyrus, the brisk, fresh west wind, was also the father of two horses: Balius and Xanthus, the famous mounts of Achilles. Zephyrus also fell in love with Hyacinth, Apollo's favourite, and it was he who caused the god's arrow

p.116
Part of a slab from the east frieze of the Parthenon, showing Iris, the messenger of the gods and personification of the rainbow. She is shown with her hair in waves, and is among those waiting to greet the Panathenaic Procession (440 BC, Acropolis Museum).

p.117
Above, an ivory relief from the sanctuary of Delphi showing the myth of Phineas. In the illustration, the Boreads - sons of King Boreas - are pursuing the Harpies (sixth century BC, Delphi Archaeological Museum).

to swerve and slay the boy, who was then transformed into the flower that still preserves his name. Zephyrus and Flora were the parents of all the spring flowers. The two other winds, Notus and Eurus, were personifications of the south and south-east winds, respectively.

The Pleiades - the Hyades

The Pleiades are the constellation still known by that name today. They were the seven daughters of Atlas and the Oceanid Pleione, and they were transformed into stars because they were unable to bear the sight of their father lifting the entire world on his back. The Hyades, who were connected with the constellation Taurus, were the Nymphs who had reared Dionysus at Nysa. There was a tradition that they had had a brother called Hyas, who died of snake-bite, and Zeus transformed them into stars so as to assuage their grief at his loss.

p.117
Below, a relief of one of the Winds from the Tower of Andronicus Cyrrhestes, now usually called the 'Tower of the Winds', near the Roman Agora in Athens (first century BC).

GODS OF
THE EARTH

Hades - Charon

Hades was the son of Cronus and Rhea, and the brother of Zeus and Poseidon. After the conclusion of the Battle of the Giants, the three brothers shared out the universe, and sovereignty over the Underworld fell to Hades' lot. The most characteristic feature of the god of the darkness that lay beneath the earth was his *cynëe*, a helmet given to him by the Cyclopes which made him invisible. And sure enough, Hades was enclosed for ever in an invisible, shadowy country beneath the ground. He only emerged once in the land of the living: to abduct Persephone, whom he took as his wife and who spent one third of each year with him (see Demeter - Persephone). Persephone's stay in the Underworld was a symbol of the processes going on beneath the surface of the soil which enabled the earth to sprout shoots and grow fruit. Hades thus became connected with abundance in agricultural production and acquired the alternative name of Pluton - that is, he who brings wealth (*plutus*).

Even so, in the Greek myths Hades is more closely associated with the concept of death than with that of riches. Immediately after death, the souls of the departed descended into his dark, musty kingdom, which was a kind of perpetual house of imprisonment guarded ceaselessly by **Cerberus**, Hades' fierce, ruthless and loyal hound. The gates of Hades were reached by crossing the river Acheron and the Acherusian Lake or, depending on the local tradition, any one of a large number of other rivers or chasms in the earth. In the Underworld itself, however, there was only one river, the terrible Styx, in whose name the gods swore inviolable oaths.

The task of bringing the dead to Hades was traditionally undertaken by Charon, the indefatigable ferryman who rowed them over the river or lake to the gates of the Underworld. His hire for the trip was one obol, a coin which the dead person's relatives would place in his mouth. Polygnotus, the great painter of the fifth century BC, ornamented the walls of the Treasury of the Cnidians at Delphi with his famous composition called the

p.119
Hades was not only the terrible god of the Underworld who brought death to the souls of men: he was also a life-giving deity whose task it was to prepare the fruits for growth beneath the earth. On the red-figure pelike of this illustration he is holding a horn from which he is scattering seed across a ploughed field. By him stands Demeter, the goddess of farming, holding a plough (430-420 BC, Athens Archaeological Museum).

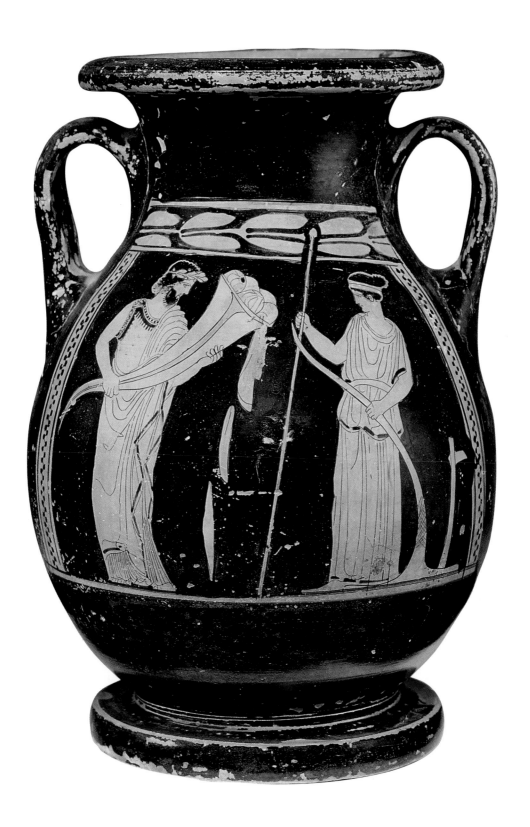

Nekyia (= 'descent into the Underworld'), in which Charon, as an old man, is depicted ferrying a man and a woman across a river. However, it seems likely that the personage of Charon is a later addition to the myth, since in earlier times Hermes alone is mentioned as the guide of dead souls (*Psychopompus*).

Pan

Pan was the important Arcadian pastoral god, and his cult spread to the rest of Greece thanks to the orgiastic festivals in honour of Dionysus, of whose companions he was one. The Greeks portrayed him with goat's feet, a hirsute body, a dense mass of hair, a pointed beard, pointed ears, a crafty smile and the horns of an animal. Pan was the vigorous demon of the mountains and woods, a god whose life was devoted to hunting, singing, dancing and amorous adventures with the Nymphs (not to mention members of the animal kingdom).

Many different traditions have survived as to his origins. Sometimes Ge and Uranus are stated to have been his parents, sometimes Cronus and Rhea, and sometimes even Hermes and a nameless Nymph. In this last version his mother looked on him when he was born and fled, unable to tolerate his ugliness. But Hermes took him to Olympus and presented him to the gods, who became fond of him and de-

p.120
A statuette of Pan from his sanctuary near the river Ilissus in Athens. The pastoral god is shown seated cross-legged on a rock covered with an animal skin. He also has a hide across his shoulders, and in his hands - which have disappeared - there would have been Pan-pipes (Hellenistic period, Athens Archaeological Museum).

lighted in him. Pan was one of Zeus' most faithful helpers: during the Battle of the Giants, he let out wild cries which caused the enemies of the gods to take to their heels, thus originating the concept of *panic*. He was traditionally supposed to have done the same during the Persian Wars, when he spread panic among the foes of the Greeks.

Pan was regarded as the inventor of the Pan-pipe or *Syrinx*, the instrument beloved of shepherds which took its alternative name fom the nymph Syrinx. According to the myth, in her attempt to escape from the unwelcome amorous attentions of Pan, Syrinx transformed herself into a reed, which he cut and from which he made his flute. Pan was also supposed to have challenged Apollo to a contest in music, but only one of the judges, **Midas**, preferred Pan's piping to Apollo's playing of the lyre. As a punishment, Apollo caused Midas to sprout the ears of an ass.

Syrinx was only one of the many pretty maidens whom Pan pursued for amorous purposes; this made him one of the most important gods of fertility and a symbol of the indefatigable human sexual drive. The goat-footed god fell in love with **Pitys** (= pine-tree), who changed herself into a tree of that kind to avoid his attentions; Selene, with whom he managed to lie by donning a sheep-skin when she was out grazing her flocks; and the Nymph **Echo**, who came to an unhappy end.

p.121
A relief from Attica showing Pan with Nymphs. The Nymphs, hand in hand, are dancing in a cave to the sound of Pan's pipes (fourth century BC, Athens Archaeological Museum).

The Nymphs

The Nymphs were goddesses of nature, depicted as pretty young maidens who spent their days dancing in the forests and flower-strewn meadows, at springs and by the banks of rivers. They were regarded as daughters of Zeus, born out of the rain that fell to earth from heaven, gathering in hollow places below the ground from which it welled up in the form of springs. The Nymphs were thus associated with water and vegetation, and they were worshipped at rivers and springs and in damp caves. Their worshippers had a whole host of names for them, in which their properties can be distinguished: thus we have the Crenaean Nymphs (of springs), the Naeads (of the waters), the Meliae and the Dryads (of vegetation and trees), the Alseids (of woods), the Oreiads (of the mountains), the Epimelids (who protected sheep), and the Kourae (who nursed children). A clear connection between the Nymphs and fertility can be distinguished in many myths, in which they appear in the company of Pan, Hermes Chthonius, Persephone, the Satyrs and Dionysus, all of whom are associated in various ways with the production of fruits by the earth. The Nymphs have survived into the modern vernacular tradition of the Greeks, where there are numerous folk tales about the *Neraids*, 'fairies' with all the primordial characteristics of their ancient forebears.

p.122
A votive relief in the form of a miniature temple, from Mt Pentele. Three richly-dressed Nymphs accompany Hermes and goat-footed Pan as they greet three worshippers (360 BC, Athens Archaeological Museum).

EROS

I n the cosmogony of Hesiod, Eros was born out of Chaos and was the most beautiful of all the immortals, the deity who inspired his own sweet passions in all human beings. Physical desire, as personified in the figure of Eros, was thus seen as a primordial element present before the world itself came into being - indeed, as an element which was partly responsible for the world, since its power of attraction gave life to living creatures. There were many other traditions which describe Eros as the son of Uranus and Ge, or of Cronus and Rhea, and even of Iris and Zephyrus. However, the most popular version of all is that in which Eros was the son of Aphrodite, the goddess most closely associated with love, and fierce Ares, god of war.

To the Greeks, Aphrodite's son was a beautiful little boy with

p.123
Relief showing little
Cupids dancing and
playing music.

wings, who flew hither and yon shooting his magic arrows into the hearts of gods as well as men. With **Imerus** and **Pothus**, who symbolised erotic desire, he was Aphrodite's constant companion, and in the spring, when flowers sprang up all over the earth, they all left Cyprus together and visited the human race, spreading reproductive power wherever they went. Eros was a cunning lad, who delighted in tormenting his victims and scorching their souls as if by fire. He was often depicted accompanying **Psyche** (= 'soul'), the personification of human emotion; the Greeks sometimes showed him causing her pain and tears and sometimes tenderly embracing her. The cult of Eros also included **Anteros**, who represented the ability of the heart to withstand erotic passion: Eros loved, and Anteros was the subject of love.

The Graces - Hebe

p.124
In the minds of the ancient Greeks, the winged god Eros took the form of a carefree little boy who filled human hearts with joy, and also with pain.

For the Greeks, the Graces were the deities which bestowed upon men joy, beauty and elegance. According to Pindar, they were responsible for all pleasant, sweet things, and with their intervention individuals could become wise and handsome and could win glory. In the mythical traditions, their parentage was assigned to Helius and Aegle, Zeus and Eurynome, Zeus and Hera, or Dionysus and Aphrodite. The Graces were certainly loyal attendants of Aphrodite, though they took pleasure in revelling, dancing and singing with other goddesses and beautiful mortal women and in decking them with flowers and aromas.

The ancient writers preserve the names of many Graces, but the three who occupied a central position in the minds of the Greeks were Euphrosyne, Thaleia and Aglaea.

Hebe (= 'youth') symbolised perpetual youth and the lasting joys of life. She was the daughter of Zeus and Hera and lived in the palace on Olympus, helping her mother with the housework and serving nectar to the gods. On feast days, she joined the Graces, Harmony, the Hours and Aphrodite as they danced to the music and songs of Apollo and the Muses. When Heracles ascended Olympus, he obtained eternal youth by marrying Hebe.

p.125
A votive relief from the Acropolis of Athens, showing the Graces dancing to the notes of a musician who is probably Hermes (late sixth century BC, Acropolis Museum).

The Muses

According to tradition, when the gods defeated the Titans they asked Zeus to create a group of new divinities whose task would be to sing the praises of that great victory. Zeus therefore lay on nine nights with Mnemosyne, daughter of Uranus and Ge (the name means 'memory'), and the Nine Muses were born. The ancient authors placed the birth of the Muses in the Pieria Mountains, very close to Olympus, and their most important sanctuary was located there. However, there were also other traditions associating them with Olympus itself, with Thrace, with Thespiae

p.126
A floor mosaic from Cos showing the Nine Muses and their symbols (Roman period, Palace of the Grand Master, Rhodes).

in Boeotia and with Mt Helicon. Hesiod tells us that he encountered them on the slopes of Helicon one day and that it was they who bestowed the gift of poetry upon him. In his *Theogony*, he fixed the number and name of the Muses, which were to remain the same throughout antiquity.

Each of the nine Muses who gave poets both memory and the power of expression was responsible for a separate literary or poetic genre. Cleio was the Muse of history, Euterpe of flute-playing, Thaleia of comedy, Melpomene of tragedy, Terpsichore of lyric poetry and dance, Erato of wedding songs (the *hymenaeum*), Polymnia of mime, Urania of astronomy and Calliope of epic poetry. With Apollo *Musagetes* as their companion, they played the lyre to soothe the gods, sang like nightingales (which is why that bird was their symbol), and danced all together, bewitching nature with their grace. Thanks to their artistic capacities, they were said to be the mothers of many of the most famous legendary singers: Calliope, the most respected of the Muses, was the mother of Orpheus and Lenus, Cleio of Hyacinth, Melpomene (in one version of the story) of the Sirens, Thaleia of the Corybants, and Euterpes of Rhesus, king of Thrace.

Tyche - the Fates

Tyche was for the ancient Greeks the deity which gave them good fortune (which is what her name means), wealth and plenty. In most representations, she is depicted holding the Horn of Plenty (the Cornucopia), the baby god Plutus, or a sheaf of corn (symbol of the plenty of the earth). After the Hellenistic period she was regarded as protecting the fortune of the city-states, which explains why, in the famous statue of her he created for Antioch the sculptor Eutychides depicted the goddess wearing a crown in the form of the city walls. Under the Romans, almost every city had a temple dedicated to Tyche alone, who was their guardian and patron goddess.

Hesiod tells us that the Fates were the daughters of Zeus and Themis. The birth, life and death of each mortal were dependent on them, and none of the gods - not even Zeus himself - had the right to intervene and alter their decisions. Of the Fates, it was Clotho who spun the thread of life of every individual, Lachesis who determined the share that was to fall to each, and cruel Atropos who cut the thread of life and brought death.

p.127
The Muse Erato was the patron of love poetry. She is usually depicted with a lyre, as in this statue from the Achilleion in Corfu.

Themis - the Hours

Themis, daughter of Uranus and Ge, dwelt on Olympus and maintained the moral order among gods and men. She was responsible for protecting institutions of all kinds, for ensuring that justice was done, and for sheltering the weak. These properties meant that she was closely associated with Zeus, the lord of the heavens, from whom all justice originated. Thus, in the myths, she was represented as Zeus' second wife, after Metis. Their union resulted in the birth of the Fates and the Hours.

The Hours guarded the gates of heaven, which they could open or close in the secrecy of a dense cloud. They were the loyal companions of Aphrodite, whom they were the first to greet when she rose out of the waves in Cyprus. Their names - Eunomia, Dike and Irene - reveal their properties: they bestowed good laws, justice and peace upon men. In later times, the Hours came to represent the seasons of the year, becoming four in number and acquiring Chronos (= time) as their father.

Nemesis - the Furies

In the Homeric era and down to the time of Herodotus, Nemesis was not a goddess but rather a philosophical context, a moral sense. In their lives, men were constrained by limits and obliged to obey moral laws which the gods had imposed upon them. To oppose these laws or transcend the restrictions of human weakness was for the ancient Greeks to offend against the gods - to commit, in other words, the crime of *hubris*. If a mortal committed hubris, then he could be certain that *nemesis* - the power that punished that which was wrong, divine justice - would soon catch up with him. In the fear which mortals had of the rage and punishment of the gods lay the origins of the cult of the goddess Nemesis. Her most important sanctuary was at Rhamnous in Attica, where the sculptor Agoracritus had created a superb statue of the goddess.

The Furies - Alecto, Megaera and Tisiphone by name - were born out of the blood of Uranus spilled when Cronus cut off his genitalia. They were earth-goddesses, and were associated with Nemesis and Themis in their responsibility for supervising the bal-

p.129
A statue of Themis, from Rhamnous in Attica. The base of the statue gives the name of the sculptor - Chaerestratus - and of the donor, Megacles. Themis was worshipped at Rhamnous, in the sanctuary of Nemesis - a goddess to whom she had a close affinity since both were responsible for supervising the moral order (third century BC, Athens Archaeological Museum).

ance of the universe and maintaining the moral order. In cases of disrespect for parents, of perjury, of injustice against the poor, of arrogance and above all of murder they were relentless in pursuing perpetrators. Their mania for punishment knew no bounds. When Orestes, for example, slew his mother Clytemnestra (who, with her lover Aegisthus, had murdered Orestes' father, Agamemnon), the Furies - with their burning breath, with blood in their eyes and with snakes for hair - pursued him to the temple of Apollo at Delphi. It took the intervention of Athena for them to allow Orestes to be tried by the Areopagus in Athens, after which their substance altered and they became the **Eumenides**, 'the benevolent ones', bestowing their blessing of fertility and fruitfulness upon the earth.

The Cabeiri - the Telchines

The Cabeiri were demonic figures whose cult spread throughout Greece from the coast of the Troad. According to the tradition, they were the three children of Hephaestus with Cabeiro, daughter of Proteus. This would seem to associate them both with fire, of which Hephaestus was the god, and with the sea, since Proteus was a marine deity. The cult of the Cabeiri was particularly highly-developed on Lemnos, the sacred island of Hephaestus where the god had his workshop. There, the Cabeiri were the protectors of metal-workers and also of the vines that grew in abundance on the volcanic soil of the island. The festivals in their honour were celebrated by the local people in a highly-charged Dionysiac atmosphere.

There was also an important sanctuary of the Cabeiri at Thebes, where an aged father called Cabeirus was worshipped with his son. These deities were associated with fire, with fertility and with the vegetation of the earth, and they protected the transition from childhood into adolescence. The Cabeirium in Thebes was the scene of special initiation ceremonies involving the sacrificing of a bull and the drinking of wine. However, the exact content of the Cabeirian Mysteries is now lost, probably for ever.

Samothrace was the scene of another mystical cult, revolving around the worship of the 'Great Gods'. These divinities, whose names were Axierus, Axiocersa, Axiocersus and Casmilus, later became identified with the Cabeiri, who in Samothrace were chthonic deities.

The Telchines, the first inhabitants of Rhodes, were figures who bore similarities to the Cabeiri. They were responsible for bringing up Poseidon on their island, and he later married their sister Halia. The union produced six sons and a daughter called Rhodes. However, a great flood caused the Telchines to leave their island. Only Rhodes remained there, giving her name to the island after she had wed the sun-god Helius, who stopped the cataclysm. But the Telchines were unable to return to Rhodes, which was now ruled by the Heliads, offspring of Helius.

In the minds of the Greeks, the Telchines were frightful demons which bore resemblances to men, snakes and fish alike and could live either on land or in the water. They had magic powers, being capable of parching the land and drying up the sea, of shrivelling up the plants and of causing hailstorms, snow and downpours of rain. These beliefs very probably reflect the geological upheavals which occurred in very early times and from which the island of Rhodes suffered severely.

However, the Telchines were also highly skilled as craftsmen and metal-workers, being the first creatures to work in iron and bronze and to make imposing statues of the gods. Among the artefacts they created were Poseidon's trident and the sickle with which Cronus cut off the genitalia of Uranus. Needless to say, the secrets of their art were very closely guarded, as a result of which mortals viewed them as magicians with supernatural powers.

p.131
A fragment of a red-figure scyphus from the Cabeirium in Thebes. On the right is Cabeirus, seated with a cantharus in his hand (a pose typical of Dionysus), and in front of him is a youth named Pais, serving wine from a krater with an oenochoe. On the left are Crateia and Mitus in an erotic embrace, next to a boy named Pratolaus. These three figures are painted in a 'cartoon' style, as were many of the vases found at the Cabeirium of Thebes (early fourth century BC, Athens Archaeological Museum).

THE MARINE DEITIES

Nereus - the Neraids

Nereus, son of Poseidon and Ge, was one of the marine deities of the ancient Greeks. The writers depict him as an old man with white hair - as white, in fact, as the foam of the waves. His home was in the very depths of the sea, in a magnificent palace built in a cave. From there, he exerted his benevolent powers to protect sailors and keep the sea calm.

Nereus married Doris, daughter of Oceanus, and they produced fifty daughters called the Nereids. The Nereids took after their father in protecting seafarers and assisting all those who travelled the waters, keeping storms at bay and driving away gales. The Nereids were among the most beautiful of the women in the Greek myths; they lived in a silver cave near their father, though they came out to sing on the beaches and dance on the backs of dolphins. The most renowned of the Nereids were Amphitrite, wife of Poseidon, Thetis, mother of Achilles, and Galatea, who married Polyphemus the Cyclops.

Proteus

Proteus, too, was a sea-god, and he was also depicted as a venerable old man. The ancient writers located his kingdom in Chalcidice, or, alternatively, on the island of Pharus (= the lighthouse) in Egypt. Menelaus of Sparta, when in Egypt, wished to meet Proteus and learn about his future, since the old sea-god was famed as a soothsayer. However, he found it impossible to get anywhere near Proteus, so he dressed in the skin of a seal and lay among the real seals on the beach where Proteus was in the habit of taking his mid-day

p.132
A red-figure box showing Poseidon and the Nereid Amphitrite. Poseidon lusted after Amphitrite and wished to make her his own, but she slipped out of his grasp (illustration) and only came back to him when a dolphin, which sought her out in the sea, assured her that she would become the wife of the great god (460 BC, Athens Arch. Museum).

p.133
A statue of a Siren from the top of a funerary monument. The beautiful creature, half-woman, half-bird, is mourning over the tomb, and would have been playing music on a lyre which has disappeared (fourth century BC, Athens Arch.Museum).

p.134
Triton was a huge sea monster whose human body had a fish tail. In the illustration, surrounded by Nereids, he is telling Doris of the abduction of Amphitrite by Poseidon (red-figure box, 460 BC, Athens Archaeological Museum - see p. 132).

p.135
Above, the demonic Sirens: these creatures with women's bodies and the wings and feet of birds were associated with death and could be described as the Muses of the Underworld. Their song reminded men of their lost dreams (funerary Siren, fourth century BC, Athens Archaeological Museum). Below, a Melian relief showing Scylla. This terrible monster had a female body and the head and tail of a dragon. Dog's heads sprouted from around her waist (fifth century BC, British Museum).

rest. When Menelaus rushed impetuously up to him, Proteus transformed himself into a lion, a dragon, a tiger, a wild boar, water, and a tree, but in the end he was forced to submit and to answer Menelaus' questions. There was also a widespread tradition that although the Greeks embarked on the Trojan War in the belief that Helen had been abducted by Paris of Troy, she was in fact the guest of Proteus in Egypt, where Menelaus found her after the war was over and took her back to Sparta. Proteus, with his power to transform himself, has often been interpreted as a personification of the waves, which can assume the most terrifying appearances according to the weather.

Triton

Triton was the son of Poseidon and Amphitrite, and he lived with his parents at the bottom of the sea. He resembled a gigantic monster and he was capable of raising storms, of moving whole islands and of transforming himself with lightning speed so as to spread panic. This primordial image of Triton as a personification of the inexplicable powers of the sea gradually changed, and the Greeks moulded in their imagination a whole tribe of Tritons who made up a kind of chorus of sea-deities similar to the band of Nereids. The Tritons were loyal companions of Poseidon, spending their time swimming in the sea, dancing, falling in love, playing music which they produced by blowing into sea-shells, and pointing out sea-lanes to passing mariners.

The Sirens - Scylla - Charybdis

The Sirens were spirits of the sea with the heads of beautiful women and the bodies of birds. They lived on stretches of rocky coast and on reefs, where they lured ships on to dangerous rocks by enchanting the sailors with their song. As Homer tells us in the *Odyssey*, *"he who draws nigh, in his ignorance, and hears the song of the Sirens will never been seen again returning home by his joyful, tender children and his wife"*. Because of their terrible reputation, the Sirens were associated with death and were depicted seated upon mounds of human skeletons. According to the myths, they once competed with the Muses as singers and, being defeated, threw themselves into the sea and drowned.

The evil spirits of the sea also included Scylla and Charybdis, who lived on either side of the Straits of Sicily. Scylla rolled rocks down to crush passing ships, while Charybdis was the motive power beneath a terrible whirlpool which struck fear into the hearts of sailors and sucked their vessels down to destruction. These monsters, of whom Homer gives us a very vivid picture in the *Odyssey*, were a poetic representation of the dangers that lay in wait for all those who ventured forth upon the waves.

G

RELIGIOUS CUSTOMS

p.136
Above, a wooden panel from Pitsia near Corinth showing a sacrificial scene (540 BC, Athens Archaeological Museum). Below, the temple of Athena Nike on the Acropolis of Athens (424 BC). The Tholos in the sanctuary of Athena Pronaea at Delphi (400-390 BC).

p.137
Statue of a young worshipper carrying a calf for sacrifice (the 'Moschophoros', 530 BC, Acropolis Museum).

The faith of the ancient Greeks in their gods was directly bound up with their cult practices. Their religious beliefs and the mythological traditions that told of the doings of the gods would have meant nothing without the cult customs practised by each individual city-state and by all the Greeks as a nation. In these religious ceremonies, the citizens did honour to the gods that protected them, while at the same time confirming their own national identity and their feeling of belonging to the city-state as a collective body.

The centres of worship in ancient Greece were the sanctuaries, which were clearly-marked areas on the acropolis and in the agora of the city or out in the countryside. The sanctuary contained the **temple** or temples of the gods in question, the **cult statues** inside the temple, the **altars** where ceremonies were held, the numerous **votive offerings**, smaller temple-shaped buildings called **treasuries** where the offerings were kept, and **colonnades** to protect worshippers from adverse weather conditions. The altars were the most important buildings in the sanctuary, since it was there that **animal sacrifices** took place, and these were the culmination of the religious practices of the citizens. Each important event in the life of the city, and festivals of all kinds, would be marked by one or more sacrifices, for which a specific ritual was laid down. After the sacrifices, the flesh of the animals was cooked and served to the worshippers, who concluded the ceremony with a banquet round a common table.

1. THE PANHELLENIC GAMES

p.138
A silver coin from Cos showing a discus-thrower by a sacred tripod. The subject is taken from the games in honour of Apollo, held at the sanctuary of Triopion, close to Cos (460 BC, Athens Numismatic Museum).

p.139
A view of the Stadium at Olympia, where most of the events in the Olympic Games were held.

Cult ceremonies in honour of the gods generally took place during the course of closely-organised religious events known as **festivals**. The festivals of antiquity were held in commemoration of some important mythical tradition, and would involve processions, sacrifices, athletic contests and competitions in various branches of the arts. Each city arranged a whole series of festivals of a purely local nature, but there were four major events during which all the Greeks joined in honouring their greatest gods. These festivals, described as Panhellenic, were the Olympics, the Pythian Games, the Isthmian Games and the Nemean Games.

The Olympic Games

The Olympic Games were dedicated to Zeus, greatest of the gods, and were held every four years at his sanctuary in Olympia. According to tradition, they were founded either by Heracles, by Zeus himself (to commemorate his defeat of Cronus in the contest for sovereignty over the world), or by Pelops when he was victorious in the chariot race against Oenomaus (see Oenomaos - Pelops). Iphitus, king of Elea, was traditionally held to have reorganised the Games and introduced the sacred truce - that is, the ban on fighting among the Greek cities for as long as the Games lasted. Official records of the winners of the Games began in 776 BC, by which time the renown of the festival had spread to the whole of the Peloponnese. Little by little, the event attracted the interest of all the Greeks. All Greek citizens were entitled to attend and compete, but there was a strict ban on women.

To begin with, the festival lasted a single day, later occupying two, three and ultimately five

days. Responsibility for organising the events was in the hands of special officials called Hellanodicae, who supervised the training of the athletes and made sure that the rules of the competition were complied with. On the first day, there were sacrifices to the gods and the athletes took their oaths. The remaining days were given over to the events *per se*, the most important of which were the foot race, the *diaulus* (a foot race two stades in length), the *dolichus* (four stades), the pentathlon (running, wrestling, jumping, the discus and the javelin), boxing, the *pancratium* (a blend of boxing and wrestling), the chariot race, the horse race and the race for armed warriors. On the last day of the Games, the winners were crowned, receiving the prize of the **cotinus** - that is, a wreath made of an olive branch - and of sums of money. The names of the victors were inscribed on stone pillars and poets would write hymns to celebrate their triumphs, while once they returned home their city would receive them as heroes and honour them for the rest of their lives.

pp.140-141
The bases of two kouroi, bearing reliefs of athletic scenes:
Above, two youths playing a game reminiscent of modern hockey (500-490 BC).
Below, the youth on the left is readying himself to jump, two are wrestling and another is resting on his javelin (510-500 BC)
(Athens Archaeological Museum).

The Pythian Games

According to the tradition, the first Pythian Games were held after Apollo killed Python, and,

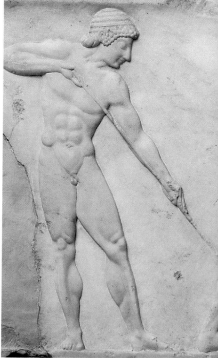

as was fitting for the god of music, they focused in particular on musical contests. To begin with, the Pythian Games were held every eight years, but after the sixth century BC the interval was reduced to four years. In 582 BC athletic events were added to the programme and responsibility for organising the festival was taken over by the Amphictyony of Delphi. All the Greek city-states sent competitors to the Pythian Games, which were particularly popular.

The Pythian Games lasted between six and eight days, and began with processions of worshippers and sacrifices. Next came the artistic events, with competitions for players of the *cithara* and the flute, for the dithyramb and for the drama. The sporting contests were modelled on the similar events at Olympia and followed the same programme. Here, the victors received laurel crowns, though they enjoyed the same honours and privileges.

p.142
The ancient Stadium at Delphi is among the best-preserved in the Greek world. It stood within the boundaries of the precinct of Apollo and was the venue for the events in the Pythian Games.

The Isthmian Games

The Isthmian Games were held every two years in the sanctuary of Poseidon at Isthmia, near Corinth, in the god's honour. There was a tradition that they were founded by the Athenian hero Theseus in emulation of Heracles, who had established the Olympic

Games. According to the traveller Pausanias, however, the Isthmian Games had originally been dedicated to a local hero, Melicertes-Palaemon, son of king Athamas (see The voyage of the Argonauts, Phrixus - Helle). This version of the founding of the Games was promoted by the Corinthians, who were in charge of the sanctuary and wished to have a Corinthian hero in the forefront as the personage of honour during festivals. The myth by which Theseus had initiated the Games, on the other hand, was devised by the Athenians in an attempt to score points over their eternal rivals the Corinthians.

The Games were reorganised in 582 BC along the lines of the Olympics. They were Panhellenic in nature from the start, and during the Games the 'Isthmian libations' were honoured: this was a kind of truce which applied to the cities taking part. After the fifth century BC, there were contests in music, declamation and painting as well as athletic events. The prize for the winners was a wreath of pine twigs, although for a short period - under the influence of the Nemean Games - this was replaced by a chaplet of wild celery.

The Nemean Games

The Games at Nemea were dedicated to Zeus himself. They were originally supervised by the nearby city of Cleonae, and later by Argos; in fact, after the fourth century BC they were celebrated more often in Argos than in the sanctuary of Nemea itself. The founding of the Games was explained by a local myth involving king Lycurgus of Nemea. Lycurgus, ran the story, once received an oracle that his new-born son **Opheltes** would not grow up to be strong and healthy unless he were prevented from touching the ground until he could walk. But one day the princeling's nurse, called Hypsipyle, disobeyed the king's instructions and put the baby down on a clump of wild celery, whereupon an enormous snake slithered up and administered Opheltes a fatal bite. In his honour, funerary games were held, and the Nemead developed out of these.

The Nemean Games became established as a Panhellenic festival in 573 BC, and were held every two years. They, too, followed the model of the Olympic Games and later included musical contests. The judges were dressed in black, as an indication of mourning for Opheltes, and awarded the winners crowns of wild celery.

2. THE ORACLES

T he fear of human beings when faced with the mysteries of life and their weakness by comparison with the vastness of nature created in them a need to communicate with the divine, with the superior powers which they believed regulated the universe and determined their own fates. A knowledge of the wishes of the gods was always a sure guide for human behaviour. In ancient Greece, the precise nature of these wishes was 'decoded' by the art of giving oracles, practised by soothsayers who had the gift of understanding the signs or signals sent by the gods.

The soothsayers uttered their oracles by interpreting flashes of lightning, rolls of thunder, or the flight of certain birds of prey (omens); alternatively, they might observe the direction in which the fire burned when a sacrifice was made, examine the entrails of animals which had just been sacrificed, or base judgements on the sacrificial beast's willingness to approach the altar. The interpretation of dreams was popular, too, and so was palmistry. The most notable soothsayers of ancient Greece were Tiresias, Calchas, Helenus, Amphiaraus and Cassandra.

However, there were abundant instances in which the gods did not manifest themselves to the faithful in the form of signs but spoke directly to an intermediate who for a short time was overcome by a 'divine mania' and transcended his own human essence. Here, the prophet - or more usually the prophetess - entered a state of ecstasy in which he or she delivered the message from the gods to the suppliant.

These practices for foreseeing the future were the basis on which the ancient Greek oracles operated. Each oracle was located within a properly-organised sanctuary and was directly associated with one or other of the gods. Apollo was the archetypal soothsayer for the Greeks, the god who was responsible for conveying to mortals the decisions pronounced by Zeus (see Apollo). The most important of all the oracles, that at Delphi, delivered its messages with the intervention of Apollo, while the oldest, that of Dodona, functioned with the assistance of Zeus.

At Delphi, it was originally the custom for the oracles to be given once a year; later, the oracle spoke once a month. Those

p.144
The temple of Apollo at Delphi, as it is today. The temple was the location of the most important Greek oracle, to which people flocked to consult the god on all manner of issues.

wishing to consult the oracle were required to pay a special tax, to purify themselves, to offer up the fruits of the field and to sacrifice a goat. If the omens attached to this sacrifice were good, then the petitioner could submit his questions. The answers were delivered by the Pythia, the priestess of Apollo, after she and the male priests of the sanctuary had completed a special ritual. This involved them purifying themselves in the water of the Castallian spring, near the sanctuary, and descending into the *adytum* or inner sanctum of the temple, where the sacred vessels were kept with a statue of the god, the navel-stone of the earth, and a bronze tripod over a crack in the ground. The Pythia seated herself on this tripod, inhaled the vapours that emerged from the bowels of the earth and munched laurel leaves to send herself into a trance. Then Apollo would speak through her mouth - though in an incomprehensible tongue which the male priests were trained to interpret. The god's statements were often ambiguous and vague, but the Greeks retained a firm faith in the truth of what the god had said, and the city-states settled many important matters of state by sending to Delphi for an oracle.

At the oracle of Dodona, the messages of the god were delivered by the Selloi, members of the Thesprotian tribe who had dwelt in the area since the earliest times. The Selloi drew their prophetic powers from the earth, which was why they never washed their feet and always slept on the ground. The wishes of Zeus manifested themselves in three different ways, all connected with sound. Initially, the soothsayers interpreted the rustling of the leaves of a sacred oak tree next to the temple, or the flight of the temple doves. After the

pp.146-147
The beautiful valley of Dodona in north-west Greece is the site of the oldest of the Greek oracles, which formed part of a sanctuary dedicated to Zeus. In the illustration, the theatre in the sanctuary of Dodona.

eighth century BC, the oak tree of Zeus was surrounded by a precinct set about with bronze kettles on tripods, which touched each other and emitting a clanking sound when one of them was struck: this noise contained the oracle. By the fourth century BC, only one of the kettles was left at the oracle, and the people of Corcyra (Corfu) dedicated a bronze statuette of a boy with a whip, who produced the noise necessary for the oracle when the wind lashed the whip against the kettle.

Among the other Greek oracles, the most notable were those of Trophonius, a local hero of Lebadea, and the Oracle of the Dead at Ephyra in Epirus, where the oracles were delivered with the help of souls in the Underworld.

D

THE HEROES

pp.148-149
The best-known of the Panhellenic heroes were Heracles, Theseus and the protagonists in the tales about the Trojan War. In the illustrations, Heracles in his lion-skin and carrying his club, Achilles slaying the Amazon Penthesilea (below) and (facing page) Theseus fighting the Minotaur (from a black-figure amphora, sixth century BC, the Louvre).

In later Greek, the word *heros* ('hero') tends to convey a sense of the demi-god, of a being who partook of the divine as well as the human essence since his birth was the result of a union between a god or goddess and a mortal. This, however, was not quite the original meaning of the word.

In Homer, the heroes are the princely leaders of the opposing sides, the most courageous of the warriors, and all those who had cultivated special talents, including the wily Odysseus and the honey-tongued singer Demodocus. By the time of Hesiod, the heroes were no longer entirely mortal, but had entered a higher sphere. In that poet's eyes, the human beings of his own era were far inferior to their robust, bold forebears. Hesiod therefore called these heroes demigods and imagined them living for ever in the Land of the Blessed, in perpetual happiness and far removed from hardships and grief. Later, however, bridges between the demigods and ordinary human beings were built once more, and the heroes were portrayed as the glorious dead of earlier times, who were to be worshipped with special honours.

Although long in their tombs, the heroes were not perceived by the ancient Greeks as lifeless creatures but as powerful forces of the spirit who could manifest themselves to mortals, whether to help them or to persecute them. They very often served as intermediates when humans had to petition the gods. Each city, each tribe and every each separate family could safeguard its unity and well-being by honouring its own special heroes, while together they praised the memory of their common forebears, the great Panhellenic heroes.

HERACLES

H eracles was the most important of the Panhellenic heroes. Nowhere else in the Greek myths is there a hero - or even a god - about whom so many and varied tales were told. Renowned for his heroic achievements and for his supernatural powers, Heracles was the idol of all the Greeks, and at the end of his life he ascended Mount Olympus to take the place among the gods which he so richly deserved.

Heracles was born in Thebes, but he traced his descent to Argos and spent a considerable part of his life there. His mother was called Alcmene, of the line of Perseus; she and her uncle (and future husband) Amphitryon had fled Argos as exiles and taken refuge in Thebes. Shortly before the couple were wed, Amphitryon went away to war, campaigning far from Thebes. During his absence, Zeus spied Alcmene and fell in love with her. Taking the form of Amphitryon, he managed to lie with Alcmene; when the real Amphitryon returned, the couple were married, and in due course twin boys were born: Heracles, son of Zeus, and Iphicles, son of Amphitryon.

While Alcmene was still pregnant, Zeus boasted to the other gods that a man destined for kingship would shortly be coming into the world. Hera, jealous of the advent of yet another of her husband's illegitimate children, managed to hold up the birth of Alcmene's babies, and as a result Eurystheus, son of Sthenelaus king of Mycenae, was born first and became king. Nor did her persecution cease with the birth of Heracles. While he was still in infancy, she dispatched two huge serpents to smother him in his cradle - but the young son of Zeus demonstrated his divinely-inspired bravery by throttling both the snakes. There was a tradition that Heracles managed to trick Hera into letting him suckle her, since it was believed that anyone who drank of the great goddess's milk would become immortal. Hera suckled the babe without recognising it, but when it was too late she realised what she had done and pushed Heracles away - and from the drops of milk that she shed the Milky Way was born.

As Heracles grew up, he had some of the most renowned sages of the ancient world among his tutors. Rhadamanthus taught him wisdom and virtue, Linus was his instructor in letters and the *cithara,* and from Eumolpus he learned music, while Amphitryon was his teacher in riding and chariot-racing, Castor in swordsmanship, Harpalycus son of Hermes in boxing, and Eurotas in archery. The boy soon became both brave and strong, and when he was only eighteen accomplished his first feat, slaying a terrible **lion** which was the scourge of the area around **Mt Cithaeron**. Thespius, king of Cithaeron, wishing to thank Heracles, begged him to lie with all fifty of his daughters so that he could be sure he would have courageous descendants.

In the Theban myths, it was Heracles who freed the city of the

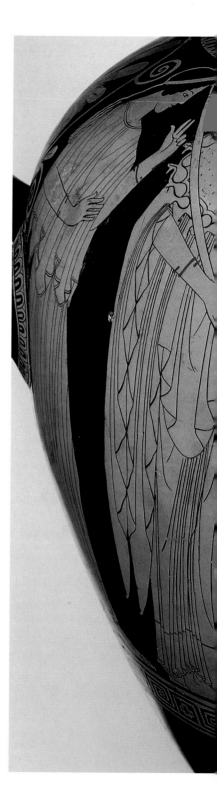

p.153
A red-figure stamnus showing the first feat accomplished by Heracles: as an infant in the cradle, he is receiving the assistance of Athena (left) in disposing of two serpents sent by Hera to kill him, while his brother Iphicles runs in terror to his parents (470 BC, the Louvre).

tribute it had been forced to pay to the **Minyans of Orchomenus**. He campaigned against them, and after defeating them compelled Orchomenus to pay Thebes double the tribute that had earlier gone in the other direction. As his reward, he was given Megara, daughter of the Theban king, as his wife. However, during the fighting Amphitryon was killed, and it was said that Alcmene later married Aeacus.

Heracles' children by Megara had a cruel fate because of Hera's continuing jealousy. The goddess drove Heracles mad and, unaware of what he was doing, he killed the children one by one. When he came to himself and realised what a crime he had committed, he went to the sanctuary of Delphi in search of purification. Apollo ordered him to go to the Argolid and put himself in the service of king Eurytheus. Eurystheus would set him **twelve labours**, which Heracles would have to complete in twelve years. If he succeeded, he would have expiated the murders of his children. Thus it came about that Heracles embarked upon his famous series of labours, which the great hero ultimately achieved successfully.

Heracles' weapons in the face of all these hazards were a club (which he had made himself), a bow and arrows (a gift from Apollo), a sword (the contribution of Hermes), a suit of gold armour (forged by Hephaestus) and the swift horses of Poseidon. His greatest assets of all, of course, were his own physical

p.154
A relief frieze from the proscenium of the theatre at Delphi, showing the Labours of Heracles. In this illustration, Heracles is fighting the Centaurs (left), the Lernaean Hydra (centre) and a Giant (right) (second century BC, Delphi Archaeological Museum).

p.155
Heracles, wearing his lion-skin and carrying an axe, is shown attacking the Lernaean Hydra and grasping its heads in order to strangle it (black-figure amphora, 500 BC, the Louvre).

strength, his bravery and his ingenuity.

The first labour which Eurystheus set Heracles was to kill and skin the terrible **Lion of Nemea**. This beast, which had been bred by Hera or Selene, was in the habit of devouring people and animals in the vicinity of Nemea, and it lived in a cave to which there were two entrances. Heracles tried to kill it with his arrows, his sword and his club, but to no avail. In the end, he blocked one of the mouths to the cave, entered by the other and wrestled with it with his bare hands, finally succeeding in overcoming it. Then he skinned the animal, wearing its hide over his shoulders and using its head as a helmet. Throughout his life, Heracles was never to be seen without his lion-skin.

In the marsh at Lerna, on the shores of the Argolic Gulf, lived a fearsome dragon-like monster with nine serpents' heads. The **Lernaean Hydra**, as the creature was called, fed off the flocks and crops of the surrounding area, while its noxious breath spread death along the local populace. Heracles undertook to slay the beast. With Iolaus, his faithful companion, he went to the spring called Amymone, where the Hydra had its lair. With burning arrows he managed to force it out into the open air, where he set about clubbing it on its multiple heads. But as soon as one head was crushed, two new ones sprang up in its place. Heracles then set Iolaus the task of burning the point on the beast's body where he had just cut off a head, and so, little by little, he succeeded in overcoming the monster. In the end, he disembowelled it and dipped his arrows in its bile, thus making them forever poisoned and deadly.

The third labour of Heracles was to capture the **Hind of Ceryneia**. Although this animal was dedicated to Aphrodite, it had escpaped from its herd and was running free across the world on its brazen hoofs. Heracles pursued the Hind for a whole year, chasing it as far as the land of the Hyperboreans. When the animal began to grow tired, it took refuge on Mt Artemisium and by the river Ladon. There, Heracles shot an arrow at its front legs, immobilising it but being careful not to shed a drop of its blood, for it would have been a crime to injure the sacred animal. Then he hoisted on to his back by its golden horns and carried it all the way back to Mycenae, where he dedicated it to Artemis.

Before long, he was off on his labours again, hunting a huge and dangerous boar on the slopes of Mt Erymanthus in Arcadia. The **Boar of Erymanthus** had been doing widespread damage in the dense forests of Arcadia,

and represented a particular hazard for travellers. On his way to Erymanthus, Heracles was given hospitality by the **Centaur Pholus.** After they had dined, Heracles and Pholus opened a new jar of wine which had been a gift from Dionysus. The other Centaurs of the area were driven wild by the strong smell of the fresh wine and they set about Heracles with rocks and uprooted trees. After a fierce fight, Heracles succeeded in killing some of the Centaurs and driving off the others. But Pholus met his end during this incident: in trying to find out how powerful Heracles' bow was, he accidentally shot himself and perished on the spot. Heracles buried him with full honours, and then continued on his way to Mt Erymanthus. His loud shouts drove the boar out of the forest and up on to the high slopes, where snow still lay. The boar found it hard to run on the snow, allowing Heracles to catch it and strap it on his back before binding it in chains and taking it back to Mycenae. When Eurystheus saw it, he was so terrified that he ran off and hid in a storage jar. Now Heracles was called upon to **clean the Augean**

pp.156-157
A red-figure cylix showing the fourth Labour of Heracles: the hero is depicted returning to Mycenae with the Boar of Erymanthus across his shoulders. Eurystheus, at the sight of the terrible beast, is hiding in panic in a jar (530-520 BC, the Louvre).

stables. Augeas, son of Helius and king of Elis, owned vast numbers of sheep and cattle: his divine father made sure that the animals were safe from all illnesses. But his stables had never been cleaned, and the piles of dung within them caused a frightful stench and poisoned all the surrounding area. Indeed, some of the fields closest to the stables were so deeply covered in dung that they were impossible to cultivate. With the help of Iolaus, Heracles broke down part of the wall around the stable-yard and then diverted the rivers Alpheius and Pineus so that their rushing waters carried away all the filth. Augeas had promised Heracles one tenth of all his flocks if he could accomplish this feat, but he then reneged on his promise, and when Heracles - with Phyleus, Augeas' first-born son - went to the king to demand their fee, he exiled them both. Later, Heracles was able to punish Augeas and install Phyleus as king of Elis in his place.

Eurystheus, too, found it difficult to come to terms with this success, and before long he ordered Heracles off on his travels again, this time to dispose of the **Stymphalian birds**. These creatures lived in the marshy waters of the Stymphalian Lake, and were under the protection of Ares. The monstrous birds were equipped with bronze talons and wings, lived on human flesh and had been

p.158
Heracles fetching the Boar of Erymanthus to Eurystheus, who hides in a jar in fear.

p.159
Athena always stood by Heracles, giving him her help both during his Twelve Labours and at other difficult moments in his life. In this metope from the temple of Zeus at Olympia, Athena is assisting her beloved hero as he strives to clean the Augean Stables (460 BC, Olympia Archaeological Museum).

wreaking havoc in the surrounding fields. Heracles, standing puzzled on a nearby hilltop, soon realised that he would be unable to get close enough to the marsh to shoot the birds with his arrows; then, suddenly, the goddess Athena appeared before him and presented him with two brass rattles which Hephaestus had made. When the rattles were shaken, they made such a did that the birds rose in fright into the sky. Heracles was thus able to shoot most of them down, while those which survived flew so high that they disappeared from sight altogether.

p.160
A red-figure amphora showing Heracles and the Stymphalian Birds (500 BC, the Louvre).

Next on Heracles' list of labours was a trip to Crete to capture a bull and bring it back alive to Mycenae. The **Cretan Bull** was a wondrous creature which Poseidon had caused to emerge from the waves of the sea as a gift to king Minos. But because Minos could not bring himself to sacrifice the animal to the god, Poseidon caused the bull to run amock and spread panic throughout the island. After a tough struggle, Heracles managed to overcome the beast and bore it on his shoulders all the way back to the Argolid. Eurystheus let it loose once more, however, and in its frenzy it did great damage throughout the Peloponnese before seeking refuge at Marathon in Attica, where Theseus later captured it.

The eighth labour of Heracles was to tame the four wild mares belonging to king Diomedes of Thrace. The **Horses of Diomedes** were man-eating, and any traveller arriving on the shores of Thrace was in danger of being devoured. Heracles made his way to the king's stables, slew the grooms and led the horses down to the beach. There he came under attack from the Bistones, one of the tribes of Thrace, whom he defeated, killing king Diomedes. He gave the king's body to the horses to eat, and once they were replete managed to tame them, bringing them home to the Argolid without difficulty.

His next journey was to the land of the Amazons, where he had been instructed to seize the **Girdle of Queen Hippolyta**. The Amazons were a warlike tribe of women who lived by hunting and consuming

the fruit that grew on their trees. They spent much of their time training and in war, marrying only for the purpose of reproduction and assigning the rearing of the children to their menfolk. When a girl-child was born, one of her breasts was amputated so as not to impede her in acquiring military skills; this was the root of their name (which means 'without a breast'). All the boy-children born were destined only for domestic work. The chief town of their country was Themiscura, near the Black Sea, where the main cults were those of Artemis and Ares, the latter being regarded as the father of the first Amazons. Hippolyta, queen of the Amazons, was able to distinguish herself in combat because she wore a girdle which had been given to her by Ares. Admete, daughter of Eurystheus, had conceived a desire for this girdle, which was why Her-

p.161
Above, a metope from the temple of Zeus at Olympia showing Heracles attacking the Cretan Bull. The brave hero is gathering his strength to strike the fierce beast (460 BC, Olympia Museum).

Below, a relief frieze from the proscenium of the theatre at Delphi: Heracles attacking Geryon, the Horses of Diomedes, and Diomedes himself (second century BC, Delphi Museum).

p.162
The bold campaign against the Amazons was one of the favourite themes of ancient Greek artists. Phidias depicted the Battle of the Amazons on the shield of the statue of Athena Parthenos on the Acropolis of Athens. The relief in this illustration is one of a series yielded by a shipwreck at Piraeus with themes from the shield of Athena Parthenos; here, an armed Amazon is being attacked by a Greek warrior (second century BC, Piraeus Archaeological Museum).

acles had been ordered to fetch it. Accompanied by the finest warriors of Argos, Heracles set sail for Themiscura, where Hippolyta received him in friendship and promised to grant him anything he might desire. But Hera appeared to her and, alleging that the foreigners had actually come to the country of the Amazons with the intention of conquering it, managed to persuade Hippolyta to fight against them. After many bloody clashes the Amazons were defeated, and after he had slain Hippolyta Heracles took her girdle and delivered it to Eurystheus as promised.

The king gave the girdle to his daughter and soon had a fresh task for Heracles: now the great hero was to bring home to Mycenae the **Cattle of Geryon**. Geryon was a gigantic creature with three bodies, six arms and three heads who was capable of shouting as loud as a whole army of warriors. He was also the owner of many head of fine red cattle, which grazed in the pastures of the distant island of Erythia, where the shepherd Eurytion and the two-headed dog Orthrus watched over them. Heracles had to cross the whole of Europe to reach Erythia, slaying many wild beasts on his way. To commemorate his feats, he set up two pil-

lars at Tartessus near the Straits of Gibralter, one on the European side and one on the African, and the strait was thereafter known as the Pillars of Heracles. But his journey into the far West soon became still harder, since he had to sail across the windswept wastes of the great Ocean. With the help of Helius, who lent him his gold disc (see Helius), Heracles was able to sail out to Eurythia and approach the cattle of Geryon. He killed Orthrus and Eurytion with his club, and then fought with Geryon himself. One of his arrows pierced all three of the giant's bodies, and, once he was dead, Heracles was able to load the cattle on to Helius' disc and take them back to the Pillars of Heracles. From there, the crossing of Europe was made once more on foot and Heracles finally brought his loot safely home to Eurystheus in Mycenae.

Yet another long journey was in store for Heracles, since his next mission was to bring Eurystheus the **golden apples of the Hesperides**. These apples had been Ge's wedding gift to Zeus and Hera. Hera, enchanted by their beauty, had planted them and before long a tree which bore golden apples had sprung up.

This precious apple-tree was in the land where Atlas lived, holding the earth and the sky on his shoulders (see Atlas).

There were guards on watch around the tree and forever alert: a hundred-headed dragon called Ladon, and the four Nymphs known as the Hesperides, whose names were Aegle, Erytheia, Hesperia and Arethusa. Heracles was at first unable to find the road to the Hesperides, and only succeed-

p.163
A black-figure amphora by the vase-painter Exekias, showing Heracles and Geryon. The giant with three bodies is holding a Gorgon's-head shield and is readying his spear to attack Heracles, who is raising his sword. The shepherd Eurytion lies on the ground (550 BC, the Louvre).

ed in doing so after seizing Nereus (see Nereus), binding him and compelling him to give the right directions. His route took him through North Africa, Arabia and Central Asia, involving a crossing of the Caucasus where Prometheus lay in bondage (see Prometheus). Enraged by the torments that this benefactor of mankind was forced to undergo, Heracles slew the eagle that gnawed at Prometheus' innards and the latter, in gratitude, advised him to sent Atlas to the Hesperides rather than going himself. Following this advice, Heracles approached Atlas and persuaded him to pick the golden apples, after promising that while Atlas was gone he would hold up the earth and the sky. Atlas was back with the apples before long, but now he declared that he would not resume his laborious task. Heracles pretended to agree with him, but tricked him into taking up his burden again by asking him to hold it for a moment while he put a cushion against his neck. Having deceived Atlas, Heracles grabbed hold of the golden apples and took them back to Mycenae. Eurystheus offered them to Athena, who thought it only fair that they should be hung once more on the apple-tree of the Hesperides.

Heracles' last labour was, perhaps, the most difficult of all, since he was the first mortal to attempt to descend into the Underworld and return safe to the land of the living. This time Eurystheus had set his sights on **Cerberus**, the terrible three-headed dog with a mane of snakes and a barbed tail which stood guard over the gates of Hades (see Hades). Heracles' first task was to make his way to Eleusis and be initiated into the Eleusinian Mysteries (see Demeter - Persephone), as a way of obtaining the assistance of the chthonic deities. Then, with Athena and Hermes as his aides, he approached the entrance to Hades and forced Charon to row him across to the shadowy king-

p.164
A metope from the temple of Zeus at Olympia, showing Heracles holding the world on his shoulders and Atlas giving him the Apples of the Hesperides. Behind them is Athena, loyal to Heracles as ever, helping him to lift the heavy burden (460 BC, Olympia Archaeological Museum).

dom of the dead. As soon as he appeared, the souls fled, only the shades of Medusa and Meleager standing their ground. Not far away, however, Heracles came upon Theseus and Peirithus alive, but bound in chains: the two friends had attempted to abduct Persephone, and Hades had punished them with imprisonment. Heracles was able to liberate only Theseus, whom he took back to the land of the living with him. In the meantime, Heracles decided to give thanks to the dead by sacrificing one of Hades' cattle, in order to do which he had to kill the herdsman Menoetius, who challenged him to a wrestling contest. Seeing the visitor's determination, Hades promised to allow Heracles to have Cerberus, on condition that he

p.165
Heracles, after his descent into the Underworld, has brought Cerberus back to Eurystheus, who - once again - is hiding in fear in his jar (hydria from Caerea, 530-525 BC, the Louvre).

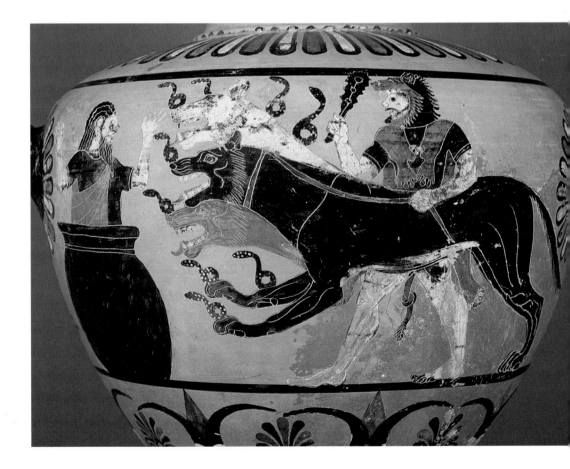

could overcome the dog without using his weapons. Heracles seized Cerberus by the throat, protected by his lion-skin from the poisonous fangs of the animal. In the end, Cerberus had to give up and allow himself to be taken to Mycenae without putting up any further resistance. As soon as Eurystheus saw him, his knees began to tremble and he rushed off in a panic to hide in his jar again. Now Heracles had purified himself of his sins, and he was able to put Cerberus back on his leash and take him home to the Under-world.

The legends associated with Heracles do not, of course, begin and end with the Twelve Labours. The great hero plays a leading role in numerous other adventures, in which he is portrayed not as the servant of some master but as a triumphant warrior and as the avenger of all those who have suffered injustice.

When Heracles returned to Thebes, he gave Megara to Iolaus as his wife and set off in search of a new spouse for himself. On his travels, he learned that Eurytus, king of Oechalia, was prepared to marry his daughter **Iole** to the man who would prove himself the most consummate archer. Although Heracles won the archery contest, Eurytus went back on his promise - and Her-acles later took out his fury on Iphitus, son of Eurytus, whom he threw off the walls of Tiryns, thus committing a breach of the

rules of hospitality.

As soon as Heracles realised he was at fault in this matter, he made his way to Delphi to be purified. But the Pythia refused to give him an oracle - whereupon he threatened to set up an oracle of his own and stole **Apollo's trident** from the sanctuary. Apollo wrestled with Heracles, and the fight went on until Zeus intervened and ordered the two to be reconciled. When they had shaken hands, the Pythia advised Heracles to spend a year as servant to **queen Omphale** in Lydia. In that post, Heracles performed numerous great feats and was soon free of his punishment.

His next adventure was a warlike one. Laomedon, king of Troy, seeing his country being ravaged by a pestilence and by the depredations of a terrible dragon, sent for an oracle which told him to tie his daughter **Hesione** to a rock for the dragon to devour. Heracles travelled to Troy, slew the dragon and released Hesione; in exchange, Laomedon had promised to give Heracles a team of divine horses which were the gift of Zeus. When he broke the agreement, Heracles went back to the Argolid, fitted out a fleet of six ships and campaigned against Troy, which he besieged and laid waste down to its foundations. In other words, we have here an account of a 'Trojan war' which dates from a much earlier period than that described by Homer. Back in Mycenae, Heracles embarked on a whole series of mili-

pp.166-167
Part of the pediment of the Treasury of the Siphnians at Delphi, on the theme of the theft of the Delphic tripod. In the centre is Apollo, dressed in priest's robes, clasping the tripod tightly while Heracles tries to pull it away from him (525 BC, Delphi Archaeological Museum).

p.168
Above, a limestone pediment from a small temple on the Acropolis showing the apotheosis of Heracles on Olympus. Zeus and Hera on their thrones are welcoming Heracles (accompanied by Hermes); Athena, upright, was also present in the composition but has not survived (550-540 BC, Acropolis Museum).
Below, a metope from the temple of Zeus at Olympia: Athena, seated on a rock, is handing Heracles the rattles made by Hephaestus to drive away the Stymphalian Birds (460 BC, Olympia Archaeological Museum).

founded in Olympia a festival in honour of Zeus which was the forerunner of the Olympic Games.

He captured and burned Pylos, slaying the sons of Nereus with the exception of Nestor. He made war on Sparta, killing the sons of Hippocöon, who had fought on the side of Neleus. One evening in Tegea, he had too much wine and, in his drunkenness, ravished **Auge**, daughter of the local king. The fruit of this union was **Telephus**, whom his mother hid in a forest where he was suckled by a deer. Auge herself was sold to king Teuthras of Mysia. When Telephus grew to manhood, he set off for Mysia in response to an oracle from Delphi and met with Teuthras, who promised to give him Auge in marriage. Mother and son were thus set to wed, unaware of the kinship between them. Yet some foreboding had caused them to hate, rather than love each other, and in the nick of time Heracles appeared to them and revealed the truth.

Heracles' last adventure took place in Aetolia. The hero sought the hand in marriage of **Deianeira**, daughter of king Oeneus, as he had agreed with her dead brother Meleager when he visited Hades on the quest for Cerberus. However, the river god Achelous was unwilling to consent to this plan, wanting Deianeira for himself, but Heracles overcame him and Achelous, disgraced, gave him the Horn of Plenty, which he happened to have in his possession at that time. After his marriage to Deineira, Heracles accidentally killed a relative of Oeneus called Eunomus and was forced to flee, with his wife, into exile in Trachina. On their way, they came to the river Euenus, where travellers were carried to the opposite bank by **the Centaur Nessus**. When Nessus took Deianeira on his back, he was overcome by lust and attempted to ravish her, whereupon Heracles shot him with a poisoned arrow. But before dying, Nessus had his revenge: he told Deianeira to draw off some of his blood - by now full of poison - and

p.169
A black-figure amphora, called the 'Nessus amphora' from the scene painted on its neck: Heracles is attacking the Centaur Nessus, who is imploring the hero, with outstretched hands, to spare his life (610 BC, Athens Archaeological Museum).

use it as a magic potion if she ever saw that her husband desired another woman.

Unfortunately, Deianeira very soon had an opportunity to test the efficacy of the potion. After a series of successful campaigns against the Dryopes, the Lapiths and Cycnus, Heracles set out from Trachina in search of Eurytus, in order to punish him for refusing the great hero the hand of Iole. Before long, he had ravaged Oechalia, killed Eurytus and his sons, and abducted pretty Iole, whom he had never ceased to be in love with. On his way home, he stopped at Cape Cenaeum in Euboea in order to make sacrifices as an indication of thanks to Zeus. But because he did not have with him the white tunic it was customary to wear at such ceremonies, he sent his companion Lichas to fetch it from Deianeira. This brought knowledge to Deianeira of the Iole affair, and she de-

cided to use Nessus' potion to win her husband's heart back. And so she saturated the tunic in the blood of Nessus, but as soon as Heracles put it on the poison spread throughout his body and he began to suffer intolerable pain. In trying to tear off the tunic, he ripped away chunks of his own flesh; realising his end was near, he climbed to the summit of Mt Oete and commanded his companions to set fire to him. None of them dared do so except Philoctetes, who received Heracles' bow and arrows as a gesture of gratitude. As soon as the pyre began to blaze fiercely, a cloud of smoke bore Heracles off to Olympus amid thunder and lightning. The gods greeted him warmly and, despite the objections of Hera, he was deified - that is, he became immortal. On Olympus, Heracles married Hebe so as to enjoy eternal youth, and he lived happily with the gods thereafter.

pp.170-171
A black-figure cylix showing Heracles being received on Mt Olympus. Zeus, seated on an elaborate throne and holding a sceptre, is listening carefully to Athena as she leads her beloved hero to the palace of the gods (550 BC, British Museum).

2. MYTHS OF ATTICA

p.172

Theseus and the Amazon Antiope; section of the pediment of the temple of Apollo Daphnephorus at Eretria (500-490 BC, Eretria Museum).

p.173

When Theseus came of age, he found the 'signs' which his father had hidden at Troezen and, with their help, managed to make his way to Aegeus in Athens. Here Theseus, guided by Aethra, is lifting the rock beneath which Aegeus had hidden his weapons and his sandals (terracotta relief, first century AD, British Museum).

Aegeus - Theseus

The vast number of myths originating in Attica focus primarily on the lives and achievements of the famous early kings of the area. According to the traditions, the three first kings - Cecrops, Cranaus and Erichthonius - were born out of the soil of Attica itself, and they then begat a line of princes who brought great honour to the country: Pandion, Erechtheus and his son Cecrops, another Pandion, Aegeus and Theseus.

Theseus, perhaps the greatest king of Athens, was the son of Aegeus. Before his birth, Aegeus - concerned that as yet he had sired no successor - visited the Delphic oracle and received a strange prophecy from the Pythia: until he got back to Athens, he was under no circumstances to open the bags of wine he had with him. On his way, Aegeus stopped at Troezen to ask king Pittheus his opinion of the oracle. When Pittheus heard what the Pythia had said, he opened the wine-bags secretly, got Aegeus drunk on the contents and at night arranged matters so that Aegeus slept with Aethra, daughter of Pittheus, in the hope that the union would produce a child. Not long before, however, Aethra had laid with Poseidon, and so the boy who was to be born would have two fathers and divine origins. Aegeus was pleased to find out that Aethra was pregnant, but he had to return to Athens because his brother Pallas and his fifty sons were forever on the lookout for the slightest opportunity to depose him. Before leaving Troezen, he hid his sandals and his sword under an enormous rock and told Aethra to take their son to that secret spot when he grew up. If he could succeed in lifting the rock, he was to take the hidden items and come secretly to Athens to seek Aegeus out.

Theseus thus grew up in the palace of Pittheus, and became strong and brave. Heracles came on a visit to Pittheus once, wearing the lion-skin that always fright-

ened little children - but Theseus went for it with an axe, thinking it was a real lion! In adolescence, Theseus was taken to Delphi to pray to Apollo. He offered the god some of his hair, cutting off a swathe straight across his forehead, and from that time on he always wore his hair in that manner. When he came of age, Aethra revealed to Theseus who his father was. She showed him the rock, which Theseus lifted and, taking his father's 'signs', set off for Athens. Pittheus advised him to travel by sea, but Theseus chose the land route from Troezen despite all the dangers that lurked along it.

Theseus accomplished a whole series of feats on this journey to Athens, disposing of various criminals who had been ambushing unsuspecting passers-by. The first of these was called **Periphetes**, and he was a son of Hephaestus: his lair was near Epidaurus, where he laid about travellers with a huge club. Theseus wrestled with him and killed him, taking the club, which proved to be of the greatest use in his subsequent adventures.

At the Isthmus of Corinth, another much-feared robber called **Sines** (a son of Poseidon) was in the habit of taking passers-by captive and tying them to two pine trees which he had bent down to ground level. When he released the pine trees, the unfortunate traveller would either be tossed high in the air or torn to pieces. Theseus put Sines to death in exactly the same manner, afterwards lying with his daughter Perigune and fathering Melanippus on her.

A little further on, at Crommyon, Heracles dispatched **Phaea**, a monstrous wild boar which had been laying waste the countryside. Now he entered the area known as the Scironian rocks (still called 'Kakia Skala', the 'bad step', on the Athens-Corinth motorway) and there met **Sciron**. His specialty was to compel travellers to bend and wash his feet, during which process he kicked them into the sea, where they were devoured by a giant turtle. Once again, Theseus disposed of the robber in exactly the same manner, kicking him into the sea from a high cliff.

The next robber to meet his end at the hands of Theseus was **Cercyon**, a son of Poseidon who wrestled with travellers as they came through Eleusis. Last of all, the brave hero Theseus disposed of **Procrustes**, whose lair was on the Sacred Way near the suburb of Daphni at the west entrance to Athens. Procrustes had two beds, a long one and a short one, and he tied short travellers to the long bed and tall ones to the short bed. Then he would 'stretch' the short travellers till they fitted the bed and cut off the extra length of limbs of the tall travellers, leading inevitably to the death of all.

p.175

The interior of a red-figure cylix ornamented with the feats of Theseus. In the centre is the killing of the Minotaur and above, from left to right: Theseus fighting Cercyon, Theseus preparing to strike Procrustes with an axe as he lies on the bed, Theseus threatening Sciron with a basin while the sea monster lies in wait behind a rock for its prey, Theseus capturing the Bull of Marathon, Theseus bending a pine-tree to which Sines is tied, and Theseus attacking the sow Phaea (440-430 BC, British Museum).

After these adventures, Theseus arrived in Athens in triumph. As he passed through the Ilissus area, where the temple of Apollo Delphinius was being built at the time, the building workers began to mock him for looking effeminate and dressing in an effete manner. Theseus' reply to this was to pick up some oxen and toss them high in the sky in an amazing display of strength.

Aegeus, in the meantime, had married Medea and installed her in his palace. In addition, he was still in danger of losing his throne to the Pallantids, the sons of Pallas. Being told of the bravery of

Theseus, the king wished to give him hospitality - without knowing who he was. But Medea possessed the power of prophecy and realised who the young man was; gripped by envy, she talked Aegeus into attempting to poison him as a possible political opponent. Fortunately, what would have been a dreadful act of impeity came to nothing, because when the company sat down to dinner Theseus took out the sword his father had left him, ostensibly to cut up his meat with. Aegeus recognised it at once, and fell upon Theseus' breast. Medea, disgraced by her show of malevolence, immediately took herself off to Asia with her son Medus.

The news that Theseus had arrived soon spread all over Athens and horrified the Pallantids, who now saw that they had no prospect of ever succeeding their uncle on the throne. They plotted to waylay Theseus, but he launched a surprise attack on them and slew them all. Since the dead youths were his own blood relatives, Theseus was brought for trial before the Areopagus, but it acquitted him. His next accomplishment was a major feat of bravery, in which he disposed of a dangerous **Cretan bull** which had fled to the Marathon area (see Heracles, the Cretan bull). On his way to Marathon, Theseus received hospitality from an old woman called Hecale, who treated him kindly and said she would pray for his mission to be successful. But by the time Theseus passed by her house again on his return, Hecale had died; in her honour, Theseus named the surrounding area after her, and it still bears her name today. He brought the Cretan bull back to Athens and sacrificed it in the temple of Apollo Delphinius.

While Theseus was still in Troezen, an attempt to kill the bull of Marathon had been made by Androgeos, son of king Minos of Crete. But the animal gored Androgeos to death and Minos, in his anger, imposed a harsh punishment on the Athenians: every nine years, they were to send him a tribute of seven youths and seven maidens, who would be devoured by the dreadful monster called the **Minotaur** unless any of them could manage to kill it. Theseus, unable to bear the grief of his city over the blood tribute it had to pay, undertook to rid Athens of the obligation: twice the Athenians had wept for the flower of their youth as it sailed off to destruction, and the time for the third tribute was at hand. Theseus took the place of one of the youths who had been selected, said farewell to his father and promised that if he returned victorious he would hoist white sails on his ship rather than the funereal black with which it now was rigged. Theseus offered a branch of the sa-

p.177

A black-figure amphora showing Theseus wrestling with the Minotaur (sixth century BC, the Louvre).

cred olive tree on the Acropolis to Apollo Delphinius, prayed to the god, made his way to Phaleron, sacrificed a she-goat to Aphrodite, and entered the boat for Crete.

Also on board ship was Minos himself, who took personal delivery of the youths and maidens who were to be his victims. During the voyage, Minos attempted to lay amorous hands on Periboea, one of the pretty girls, and was strictly reprimanded by Theseus, who warned Minos that he was the son of Poseidon. Minos questioned this and tossed his ring into the sea, challenging Theseus to seek his father's help in getting it back. Theseus dived into the water forthwith; Zeus hurled a thunderbolt to light his way and Poseidon led him to his palace beneath the waves, where Amphitrite dressed him in a purple tunic and placed a wreath on his head. Before long, Theseus emerged from the waves beside the ship once more, completely dry and with the ring on his finger.

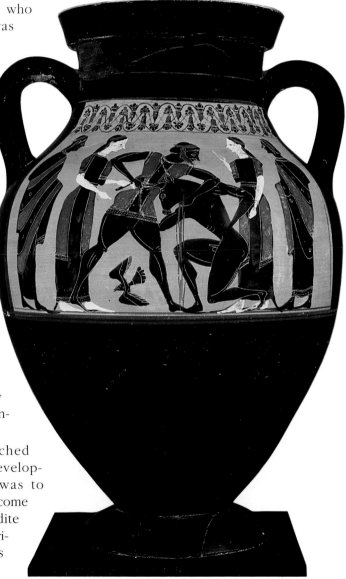

When the party reached Crete, an unexpected development occurred which was to prove decisive for the outcome of the operation. Aphrodite inspired in the heart of Ariadne, daughter of Minos and Pasiphae, a great love for Theseus, and caused the princess to promise to help him in any way she could. Just before Theseus entered the Labyrinth - the name given to the huge and complicated palace of Minos, where the Minotaur lived - Ariadne gave him a ball of thread and helped him to tie the end to the entrance to the maze. As Theseus paid out the thread while walking through the Labyrinth, he would be able to find his way out once he had killed the Minotaur. After searching all the 'labyrinthine' corridors and wandering through the sumptuous chambers of the palace, Theseus did indeed succeed in finding the Minotaur and slaying it after a fierce fight. (The Minotaur was the fruit of the union between Pasiphae, wife of Minos, and the handsome bull which Poseidon had sent to Crete; see Poseidon. It had a human body but the head of a wild bull, and it lived on human flesh.)

Now Theseus was able to find his way back out of the maze, thanks to the thread, and to rush down to the harbour with the

rest of the Athenian youths and maidens - and Ariadne. In order to make sure that the Cretans would not pursue them, Theseus had told his companions to hack holes in the bottoms of all the Cretan ships in the harbour and to kill their watchmen. Thus the Athenians were able to set off for home unmolested, having rid their city of one of its greatest misfortunes.

On the voyage back to Athens, the companions stopped at Naxos, where they left **Ariadne -** either on the initiative of Theseus, in some versions of the tale, or because Dionysus had fallen in love with her and wished to marry her. They also called at Delos, where the Athenians observed the proper rites at the great sanctuary of Apollo. Around the god's altar, the young men and women danced the circle dance called the 'crane', whose complicated movements were a symbolic commemoration of the labyrinthine palace of Minos. Then they sailed rapidly on for Attica. But in his great joy, Theseus forgot to haul down the black sails and raise the white

pp.178-179

A detail from the François krater: after their success against the Minotaur in Crete, Theseus and his young companions have landed in Attica and, in triumph, are dancing the 'crane' (570 BC, Florence Archaeological Museum).

p.180

The west pediment of the temple of Zeus at Olympia was ornamented with uniquely beautiful scenes of the Battle of the Centaurs (west pediment of the temple of Zeus at Olympia, 460 BC, Olympia Archaeological Museum).

ones, as he had promised his father. Aegeus, who climbed the Acropolis every day and gazed out to sea, saw the black ship returning and, in the belief that his son was dead, threw himself off the sacred rock and was killed. The Athenians grieved the tragic fate of their king, though sending up their thanks to the gods for having saved them. Theseus founded the festival called the *Pyanopsia* in commemoration of his triumph, while the ship in which he had travelled to and from Crete, the *Salaminia*, was preserved and could still be seen in the fourth century BC.

The beloved hero of the Athenians immediately took over rule of the city and proceeded to implement what was called *synoecism*

- that is, the unification of all the smaller units of Attica into a single city-state with Athens as its capital. This important event was commemorated each year in a festival called the *Synoicia*, and the *Athenaea*, one of the oldest feasts, was now celebrated as the *Panathenaea* and all the inhabitants of Attica observed it. Theseus as a monarch was remembered for his just law, his charity and his love of the city of Athens.

The rest of his life was full of operations and adventures far from the city, however, in which he was always accompanied by the faithful Peirithus. **Peirithus** came of the Thessalian tribe of the Lapiths, and his friendship with the Athenian king had had rather

p.181

Theseus, on the left, is attacking a Centaur with an axe during the Battle of the Centaurs (west pediment of the Temple of Zeus at Olympia, 460 BC, Olympia Archaeological Museum).

strange beginnings. When Theseus killed the Cretan bull, Peirithus, hearing of his feats, resolved to find out precisely how brave this Athenian was. So he made his way to Attica and stole Theseus' cattle, which were grazing at Marathon. Theseus set off in pursuit of Peirithus, but when the two men finally came face to face they were so overcome with admiration for one another that they shook hands and swore eternal friendship. Theseus was present at the feast to mark Peirithus' wedding, at which the Centaurs of Thessaly were also among the guests. These monstrous animals, rather the worse for wear from drink, attempted to ravish the women of the Lapith tribe. The Lapiths resisted stoutly and ultimately defeated the Centaurs. This, the **battle of the Lapiths and Centaurs**, was among the most popular themes for artists in antiquity, and Theseus was traditionally credited with playing a major part in it.

Theseus and Peirithus were among the company which followed Heracles to the land of the Amazons (see Heracles, the Girdle of Hippolyta). When the company was besieging Themiscyra, the Amazon **Antiope** fell in love with Theseus and when the war was over followed him back to Greece. Hippolytus was born of this union. At some later date, the Amazons launched an attack on Attica; in the end, they were driven off, but not before Antiope had been killed, fighting bravely on the Athenian side.

Theseus' next wife was **Phaedra**, daughter of Minos, who bore her husband two sons, Acamas and Demophon. Hippolytus, in the meantime, had been sent to Troezen, where it was planned that he should be king. Once, when Theseus was on a state visit to Troezen, Phaedra caught sight of the handsome youth in training, immediately fell in love with him, and each day concealed herself in the gymnasium to watch him. Her passion and anxiety were such that one day she spent all the time jabbing her hair-pin into the leaves of a myrtle tree - and since then the leaves of that shrub have always been full of holes. Hippolytus later came to Athens to take part in the Panathenaea, and Phaedra sent him a note in which she declared her passion. But Hippolytus rejected her and, in fear lest he spread the word of what she had

p.182

Theseus attacking an Amazon - probably Antiope - who is falling before him, her strength exhausted (metope from the Treasury of the Athenians at Delphi, 490 BC, Delphi Museum).

p.183

A terracotta statuette of a Centaur from Lefkanti in Evia (Euboea). The Centaurs, monstrous beasts which were half-man and half-horse, lived among wooded mountains, and especially on Mt Pelion, where they spent much of their time pursuing the Nymphs. They were notoriously impulsive and violent, and were also known for their love of raw meat and wine. A special position among them was occupied by the immortal Centaur Chiron, who was famous for his wisdom and his acts of charity (900 BC, Eretria Archaeological Museum).

done, Phaedra committed suicide. Before doing so, however, she wrote a letter to Theseus accusing *Hippolytus* of making amorous advances to *her*. When Theseus read this letter, he invoked his father Poseidon and called on him to punish the young man. So Poseidon sent a wild bull from the sea which cut across Hippolytus' path as he drove in his chariot. The horses, in panic, ran wild, and Hippolytus was thrown from the chariot and killed. Artemis took pity on him and his tragic fate, and she compelled the people of Troezen to worship Hippolytus as a god.

After the death of Phaedra, Theseus and Peirithus decided to find themselves new wives - and to be sure that they came from divine families. The first candidate was **Helen** (later of Troy), then only twelve years old. The two friends travelled to Sparta and found Helen at the sanctuary of Artemis Orthia. Having abducted her, they drew lots and decided that she should become the wife of Theseus. He shut her up in the castle of Aphidnae in Attica and then decided to accompany Peirithus into the Underworld, since he had made up his mind to marry Persephone and that was where she was to be found. Hades, who discovered their plans, was friendly to the two men at first, and then made them sit on the Throne of Lethe ('forgetfulness') where poisonous snakes encircled them and prevented them from getting up. Peirithus stayed there for ever, but Theseus was freed by Heracles when the latter descended into the Underworld to fetch Cerberus.

In the meantime, Helen's brothers Castor and Pollux (the 'Heavenly Twins') came to Athens. After a long search, they found where Theseus had hidden Helen and took her back to Sparta with them - also carrying off Aethra, who had been keeping guard over Helen in Aphidnae, into slavery. Furthermore, the Heavenly Twins also assisted Menestheus, one of Theseus' political opponents, to usurp the throne of Athens. As a result, when Theseus returned from the Underworld he was forced to move to Scyros, where he owned land. There, king Lycomedes took him up to the top of a cliff, pushed him off and killed him.

Despite his tragic end, Theseus always occupied a special place in the hearts of the Athenians, who regarded him as their greatest hero and patron. Indeed, he was seen fighting by their side against the Persians at Marathon in 490 BC, urging them to still greater efforts. In later years, the Athenians sent to Scyros and discovered his tomb, from which they extracted his remains and re-interred them in Athens with full honours.

p.185

Part of the west pediment of the temple of Zeus at Olympia: a Lapith attacking a Centaur during the Battle of the Centaurs (460 BC, Olympia Archaeological Museum).

DAEDALUS - ICARUS

aedalus was the son of king Erechtheus of Athens and Iphinoe. His reputation throughout ancient Greece was the result of his genius, his incredible ingenuity, and his skill in the arts and crafts, especially the making of statues. Daedalus had invented many of the tools used by stone-masons, and he was the first man to create statues so lifelike that it was said they had to be tied down to prevent them from walking away!

Among the apprentices in Daedalus' workshop was his own nephew, called Talos, who in time learned his uncle's craft so well that in some respects he surpassed him. Daedalus, in a fury of envy, hurled the youth down off the Acropolis and killed him - for which he was tried before the Areopagus and sentenced to exile. King Minos of Crete, having heard of Daedalus' talents, offered to give him a home and also entrusted him with the task of constructing a new palace. This was the origin of the famous Minoan palaces of Crete, with their labyrinthine layouts, their sumptuous halls and their superb artistic ornamentation: they were all the work of an Athenian craftsman. Daedalus also thought up and made the hollow wooden cow into which Pasiphae inserted herself in order to mate with the bull sent by Poseidon, a union of which the Minotaur was the issue (see Poseidon).

When Minos discovered that Daedalus had helped his wife to be unfaithful to him, he decided to punish him, and in the meantime set a watch on all ships leaving Crete so that the great craftsman would be unable to escape from the island. Daedalus concentrated all his mental powers on finding a way to flee Crete, and eventually hit upon the idea of imitating the flight of birds. Thus, he made two pairs of wings by using wax to glue feathers together. He gave one pair of wings to Icarus, his son, and kept the other for himself. The wings worked, and father and son soared high above Crete and far from the island. But Icarus, delighted with his achievement, became too bold, flying so high that the sun melted his wax wings, casting him down to drown in what is still called the Icarian Sea. Daedalus flew on and landed in Sicily, where he spent the rest of his life and left a series of wonderful architectural projects.

p.187

A wall-painting from Pompeii showing the fall of Icarus. Daedalus (upper right) is looking in horror at his son, who has fallen into the sea. On the upper left is Helius, who caused the death of Icarus, rushing across the sky in his chariot (10 BC, Naples National Museum).

3. THE THEBAN MYTHS

Europa - Cadmus

Cadmus was the son of king Agenor of Phoenicia and his wife Telephassa. His sister was the pretty princess Europa, whom Zeus fell in love with and adopted the shape of a bull in order to abduct. Europa mounted the back of the bull and they travelled to Crete, where in the shadow of an ancient plane-tree at Gortyn the god took human form and lay with her, Minos, Rhadamanthus and Aeacus being the fruit of their union. When Europa's parents discovered she was missing, they dispatched their sons to find her, Cadmus himself, with Telephassa, undertaking the search in mainland Greece. He travelled widely in the country, making valuable dedications to the gods and founding a number of cities. Eventually, Telephassa died, and Cadmus addressed himself to the Delphic Oracle to see if there was anything he should do. The

Pythia advised him to follow an ox and found a city at the spot to which the beast would lead him. Sure enough, the animal tired and came to a halt at the place which was later to become Thebes. The general area was then called Boeotia (from *bous*, an ox) after the animal that led Cadmus to the spot.

Once he had decided on the site for his city, Cadmus began the preparations for a sacrifice to the gods. On his way to draw water from the spring called Areia, he came across an enormous dragon (who was a son of Ares) which tried to block his way. But he slew the monster by beating its head with a stone, and, following the advice given to him by Athena, drew its teeth and planted them in the soil. Immediately up sprang a tribe of men, the Spartoi (literally, 'sown'), whom Cadmus in fear also struck with a stone. Thinking that one of their number had thrown the stone, the Spartoi began to fight one another until only Echinus, Udaeus, Pelor, Hyperenor and Chthonius were left. These five men were the first inhabitants of Thebes, which was originally called Cadmeia in honour of its founder. However, Cadmus had committed the crime of killing the offspring of a god, and he would have to be punished. Zeus sentenced him to a year as the servant of Ares, after which he would be free to reign as king in Thebes. When he was safety installed on his throne, Cadmus wed Harmony, daughter of Ares and Aphrodite; their children were Semele, Agave (see Dionysus), Ino (see the Voyage of the Argonauts, Phrixus - Helle), Autonoe and Polydorus. In their old age, the royal couple moved away from Thebes and settled in Illyria, after first subduing the people of that area, and had another son, called Illyrius. As the end of their lives approached, Cadmus and Harmony begged Zeus to turn them into harmless snakes, and their request was granted.

When Cadmus left for Illyria, he was succeeded on the throne of Thebes by his son, and then by his grandson Labdacus. The latter came to a tragic end, however: when the cult of Dionysus was first introduced into the area, he displayed unwillingness to believe in it, whereupon the god cursed him and slew him.

p.189
A vase showing the Rape of Europa by Zeus in the form of a bull, against a white ground (fifth century BC, Athens Archaeological Museum).

LAIUS - OEDIPUS

p.191
*The famous Sphinx of the Naxians,
a votive offering by the people of
Naxos at the sanctuary of Delphi
(570 BC, Delphi Museum).*

L aius was the son of king Labdacus of Thebes. He had been only a boy when his father died, and reigned through a regent. Even when he grew to maturity, he had to contend with his kinsfolk Amphion and Zethus, who seized his throne and exiled him. After a brief spell at the court of Pelops in Elis, Laius returned to his homeland and ascended the throne.

Laius chose Jocasta to be his wife, but when the marriage proved childless he sought the advice of the Delphic Oracle. The Pythia recommended that he resign himself to his state, since otherwise any child he might bring into the world would kill him and cause great sorrow to all his house. Laius thus gave up all hope of having a successor - but not so Jocasta. One evening she made her husband drunk, lay with him and got herself with child. When the boy was born, Laius was overcome with terror when he remembered the oracle. So he bound the baby's legs with chains and gave it to a shepherd to expose on the slopes of Mt Cithaeron, in the sacred grove of the goddess Hera, so that it might die as soon as possible.

The fate of this boy, called Oedipus because of his swollen feet, had already been determined and was to be quite different. The shepherd commanded to expose the babe took pity on it, and at the last moment entrusted it to some servants of king Polybus of Corinth who happened to be passing. The servants presented the child to the king, whose wife Merope suggested that since they had no children of their own they should adopt it. And so Oedipus grew up in Corinth, believing Polybus and Merope to be his parents.

One day, during a feast, a drunken youth taunted Oedipus with not being the legitimate son of the king. Since no one in the palace would tell him what the truth of the matter was, Oedipus, too, made his way to Delphi. The oracle the Pythia gave him was a terrible one: he was destined to kill his father, lie with his mother and be the founding father of a terrible house. Bitter and angry, Oedipus left his home and wandered in the surrounding countryside, determined to do everything he could to prevent the prophecy from coming true.

One day, however, as he approached a place where three roads crossed in Phocis - the spot called Schiste - he met a chariot bearing Laius. The Theban king was on his way to Delphi in order to ask what had happened to his son, for he had had a bad dream and was seriously worried. Without recognising each other, the two travellers got into an argument about which of them had right of way, and the argument led to a fight in which Oedipus slew his father, thus fulfilling that part of the prophecy.

The death of Laius was not the only disaster to strike Thebes at that time. The **Sphinx**, a monster with the head of a lion, wings and a female head had settled near the city on a pass that led across Mt Phicium, and was spreading death and destruction among the local people. It was the practice of the Sphinx to ask passers-by a riddle: "What is that which at dawn walks on four legs, at midday with two and in the evening with three?", putting to death all those who failed to find the right answer. For a long time no one had succeeded in answering correctly, and so Jocasta's brother Creon, who was ruling provisionally in Thebes, put up the throne of the city and his sister's hand in marriage to anyone who could solve the riddle and drive away the Sphinx. Oedipus, who happened to be famous for his wisdom, decided to take part in the contest and face the Sphinx. As soon as the monster, sure that Oedipus, too, would fail, had put her question, Oedipus replied confidently, "Why, man: when he is born he crawls on all four feet, then he stands on his own two feet, and at the end of his life he has a stick like a third leg". This was the first time anyone had found the right answer and the Sphinx, mortally disappointed, flung herself off the rock where she sat and was killed. Oedipus was crowned king of Thebes and married Jocasta, without suspecting, needless to say, that she was his own mother. The children of their union were Antigone, Ismene, Polynices and Eteocles.

◄ *p.190*
A black-figure lecythus showing the Sphinx and Oedipus (470 BC, the Louvre).

p.193
Oedipus, seated on a rock, is shown listening to the riddle uttered by the Sphinx on top of an Ionic column. The Sphinx of Thebes came to the city from Asia, and was the daughter of Chimaera and Orthus (interior of a red-figure cylix, 470-460 BC, Vatican Museum).

Some time later, a terrible pestilence struck Thebes and Oedipus, deeply concerned, sent to the oracle of Apollo. The god told the Thebans to find the murderer of Laius and exile him, for otherwise they would not be free of the epidemic. Oedipus personally undertook responsibility for the investigation, but no one in the city could say how Laius had met his end. Eventually, Oedipus called in the soothsayer Tiresias; he was unwilling to speak to begin with, but ultimately revealed that it had been Oedipus who took Laius' life. This was confirmed by what Jocasta could tell about the killing at the Schiste crossroads. Oedipus, crushed by the revelation, was willing to leave the town in order to save its inhabitants, but he did not wish to return to Corinth and run the risk of killing his father Polybus and marrying his mother Merope, as he believed the oracle had forecast.

But his destiny was far beyond his control now. A messenger sent to Thebes to announce the death of Polybus confided to Oedipus that the Corinthian king had not been his real father. He himself, he told Oedipus, had found him with bound feet in the arms of a shepherd on Mt Cithaeron and had taken him to Corinth.

p.194
A marble votive Sphinx from the Acropolis (540-530 BC, Acropolis Museum).

This tragic revelation struck the unfortunate monarch like a thunderbolt, yet he could hardly have imagined that much worse was to come. Now he sought out the shepherd on Cithaeron, to discover whose child he truly was. As soon as the shepherd revealed the truth, Jocasta, unable to shoulder the burden of the sin she had committed, hanged herself from the roof of the palace. Oedipus, gathering together the shattered fragments of his soul, drew the brooches out of his dead mother's (and wife's) dress and with them put out his own eyes, so that he might cease to see the terrible sins he had committed.

After saying farewell to his children, Oedipus prepared to leave Thebes, accompanied on his wanderings only by his daughter Antigone. No land would give him shelter, for now the gods had set their curse upon him. In the end, he came as a suppliant to the sanctuary of the Furies in Attica, and Theseus, taking pity on his sufferings, persuaded the Athenians to let him stay in their city. In the meantime, back in Thebes Polynices and Eteocles were in open confrontation with each other over the question of succession to the throne, causing Creon to seek out Oedipus and try - by imploring him, but also more forcefully - to make him return home. But Oedipus refused to countenance any talk of going back to Thebes, and pronounced heavy curses on his sons for failing to honour him as was their duty.

Exhausted and in despair, Oedipus felt his end was nigh. He called Theseus to him and announced that he himself would choose the spot of his death, somewhere in the Colonus area. Only Theseus would know where he was buried and no other Athenian must ever find the place, so as to make absolutely sure that the curse died with Oedipus. However, shortly before his own death Oedipus was to reveal the secret to his eldest son and it would then pass from generation to generation, with only one Athenian knowing it at any time. In the end, he said farewell to Antigone and Ismene (who had arrived shortly before, as an emissary from Creon) approached the place he had selected and gave up the ghost. A chasm in the earth suddenly opened up, and the tragic hero vanished into it.

Oedipus' children

When Oedipus left Thebes, the throne was first occupied by Creon. But Oedipus' sons, **Polynices and Eteocles**, claimed their rights to the kingship, and decided to rule year and year about. Before long, however, they had quarrelled, and Eteocles exiled his brother and claimed all power for himself. Polynices, feeling he had been hard done-by, took refuge in Argos, where he married Argeia, daughter of king Adrastus. With Adrastus' help, he assembled an army from the surrounding area and set off to make war on Thebes. The campaign was known as that of the 'Seven Against Thebes', since the operation was commanded by seven famous generals. The clashes at the seven gates to the city cost the lives of many warriors, and the Thebans ultimately managed to drive off the invaders. But both the brothers were killed - in fact, they killed each other, thus fulfilling the curse their father had laid upon them shortly before his own death.

After their deaths, Creon became lord of Thebes once more. He saw to it that Eteocles was buried with full honours, because he

had defended his homeland to the death. In the case of Polynices, however, who had become an enemy of Thebes and tried to capture it with the help of a foreign army, Creon declared that the body should not be buried and should be left for the dogs and vultures to pick clean. Only **Antigone**, daughter of Oedipus, opposed this decree. Motivated by sisterly love and determined to obey the divine laws which imposed the interment of all dead bodies, without exception, she disregarded the terrible punishments which Creon had announced and buried her brother, ornamenting his body and mourning him as custom demanded. The penalty for her courage and great-heartedness was a terrible one: the men of the palace guard were ordered to bury her alive. The tragic heroine was locked up in prison, where she hanged herself - and shortly afterwards Haemon, son of Creon, who had loved Antigone and was to have married her, also took his own life. When Creon's wife Eurydice also committed suicide, the hard-hearted Theban king was completely crushed.

According to one version of the story, Oedipus' second daughter **Ismene** met her death during the siege of Thebes. Tydeus, one of the seven Argive generals, came across her in the temple of Athena making love to Periclymenus or Theoclymenus, son of Poseidon. Her timid lover took to his heels to save his skin, and Tydeus slew the girl for having defiled the sacred precinct of the goddess. However, in the accounts given by other writers Ismene survived the attack of Polynices and supported her sister throughout her tribulations.

pp.195-197
A red-figure amphora showing the tomb of Oedipus. Eteocles and Antigone are approaching the memorial to their father in order to leave their offerings there. Behind Eteocles a young woman is carrying a hydria (early fourth century, the Louvre).

4. THE VOYAGE OF THE ARGO

Phrixus and Helle

p.198
Phrixus hanging from the ram with the golden fleece which is carrying him to Colchis, far from his home (fifth century BC, Athens Archaeological Museum).

p.199
A terracotta votive plaque showing the building of the Argo. Athena is urging on the workers carving the bow and raising the mast of the ship (first century AD, British Museum).

Phrixus and Helle were the son and daughter of Nephele and Athamas, king of Boeotia. While the children were still small, Athamas abandoned Nephele for Ino, on whom he fathered two more children, Learchus and Melicertes. Ino was a very bad stepmother, and spent much of her time trying to make life hard for Phrixus and Helle. One of her plots involved the creation of an artificial famine: she persuaded the women to roast the seed corn before planting it, and as a result the crops failed that year. Athamas immediately sent envoys to the Delphic Oracle, as was usual practice in such cases, but Ino bribed the envoys into telling the king Apollo's priestess had advised them that the country could only be saved if Phrixus was sacrificed on the altar of Zeus.

Athamas was prepared to do this for the good of his people, and so he led Phrixus to the altar ready for sacrifice. But at the last moment Nephele managed to snatch him away, and with the mediation of Hermes arranged the escape of both Phrixus and Helle on the back of a ram with a golden fleece. This wonderful animal flew through the air and took the two children far from their enemies. But as they flew over Thrace, Helle leaned over and looked down, lost her balance and fell, which is why that area of the sea has been called the Hellespont (= 'where Helle drowned') ever since.

Phrixus continued on the journey alone. The ram flew to Colchis, where Aeetes, son of Helius and Perseis, was king. After sacrificing the ram to Zeus, Phrixus gave its golden fleece to Aeetes, who offered him hospitali-

ty and wed him to his daughter Chalciope. The precious golden fleece was hung on an oak tree in the sacred grove of Ares, where a fierce dragon kept perpetual guard over it.

In the meantime, Ino's treachery had come to light. Hera sent a madness upon Athamas, causing him to pick up his bow and kill Learchus. Ino, in fear, seized her second son Melicertes and fled, seeking to escape the rage of Hera. When they came to the Saronic Gulf, mother and child plunged into the sea and drowned. The dead boy was brought to shore on the back of a dolphin, beneath a pine tree, and buried by Sisyphus, brother of Athamas. By decree of Zeus, Melicertes was renamed Palaemon after this time, and deified. There was also a tradition that directly after the interment of Palaemon, Sisyphus founded the Isthmian Games, held at the sanctuary of Zeus near Corinth (see the Isthmian Games).

p.200
A terracotta statuette of a Centaur from Lefkanti in Evia (Euboea). A mark painted on the right front leg of the Centaur has led some scholars to the view that this is a depiction of Chiron, since according to the myth the wisest of the Centaurs had been wounded in that spot by the arrows of Heracles (900 BC, Eretria Archaeological Museum).

Jason - Medea

Jason was the son of Polymela and Aeson, the latter being the son of king Cretheus of Iolcus and his wife Tero. But when Cretheus died, he was succeeded not by Aeson but by Pelias, who was the fruit of a union between Tero and Poseidon and thus enjoyed divine origins. Relations between the two half-brothers were poor, and so Aeson left his homeland. Fearing for the fate of his son, he gave him to the wise Centaur Chiron to raise, on the wooded slopes of Mt Pelion. Pelias was thus able to reign peacefully in Iolcus, though at the back of his mind he never forgot an oracle which had once told him he would lose his kingdom to a youth with one sandal.

Jason received an incomparable education from Chiron, and grew up to be intelligent, handsome and courageous. When he reached manhood, he decided to go down the mountain to Iolcus and claim from his uncle the power over the land that was rightfully his. As he crossed the river Anaurus, he lost one of his sandals while carrying a helpless old lady across to the further bank - in fact, the old woman was none other than Hera, who had disguised herself in that way so as to test the young man's generosity. Jason thus came before Pelias wearing only one sandal. Remembering the oracle in terror, Pelias promised to abdicate in Jason's favour, while actually preparing an evil plot to get rid of him. He set Jason a labour which seemed impossible: to make his way to Colchis and bring back the golden fleece from the ram that had borne away Phrixus.

Jason accepted the challenge, however, and embarked on the preparations. With the help of Hera, he assembled the bravest warriors in Greece, and Athena made herself responsible for rapidly constructing a ship called the *Argo*. The ship gave its name to Jason and his companions: the Argonauts (= 'sailors in the *Argo*'). Jason's comrades on this great adventure included some of the most prestigious figures in the Greek myths: Heracles, Theseus, Peleus, the Heavenly Twins, Amphiaraus from Argos, Orpheus, and Acastus, son of Pelias himself.

Shortly after the company set out, they made their first stop at Lemnos, where the Argonauts lay with the women of the island and thus reintroduced a male element into the population (see

p.201
Jason, followed by Medea, presenting himself before Pelius, on his throne, holding the Golden Fleece. A Nike is crowning him in recognition of his triumph, and he is accompanied by Hermes, protector of travellers (calyx krater, 350340 BC, the Louvre).

Aphrodite. Jason himself took queen Hypsipyle as his wife, fathering two children, Euenus and Nebrophonus. The next halt was Samothrace, after which they dropped anchor at Cyzicum in the land of the Dolioni, who welcomed the visitors. When the time came for them to depart, a head wind forced them back into Cyzicum, where this time the Dolioni mistook them for invaders and attacked them. It was not until after a fierce fight that the misunderstanding was resolved and the two sides were reconciled.

Now the *Argo* sailed along the shores of Mysia, coming to the land in which the soothsayer Phineas dwelt. After they had rid him of the Harpies (see Harpies), Phineas was able to give the Argonauts valuable information about the course that lay ahead of them. Before long, they came to the **Symplegades** or 'Clashing Rocks'. These were two huge cliffs, reaching as high as the sky itself and not firmly fixed in the sea. Every so often they clashed together with such terrible speed and power that they were certain to crush any ship foolhardy enough to venture between them. Following Phineas' advice, the Argonauts first released a dove to fly between the rocks, reasoning that if it could pass through unscathed, so could they. The dove flew between the rocks like the wind, and only its tail was slightly harmed. The *Argo* thus got up as much speed as she possibly could and, with the mediation of Athena, managed to pass between the Clashing Rocks losing only a small part of its stern. After that time, the two rocks fused together and never moved again.

When the *Argo* finally reached Colchis, Aeetes promised to give the companions the Golden Fleece, on condition that Jason first accomplished two difficult feats: first he had to yoke two fire-breathing bulls with bronze hooves, and then he was to sow dragon's teeth in a field and deal with the armed warriors who would spring up like plants. In these tasks, the handsome youth had the help of **Medea**, the daughter of Aeetes, who had fallen in love with him. Media talked Jason into taking her back to Greece with him and marrying her. Jason accomplished both the feats he had been set, but Aeetes went back on his word and so the Argonauts were obliged to steal the Golden Fleece: Medea set a charm of sleep on the dragon, Jason seized the Fleece, and they all ran back to the ship and departed. Aeetes set off in pursuit of them, but Medea - determined to make good her escape at any price - slew Apsyrtus her brother and scattered his members one by one over the sea, delaying Aeetes as he stopped to pick them up.

p.202
A helical krater showing the imprisonment by the Argonauts of the Cretan giant Talos. Talos, the bronze creature who guarded the island of Crete, is about to collapse beneath the assault despite the support of Castor and Pollux (400-390 BC, Jatta collection, Ruvo).

The voyage of the *Argo* back to Greece was a favourite subject for narrative among the ancient authors, and its course was variously described. However, most accounts agree that after crossing the Black Sea, the *Argo* sailed up the Danube, entered the Adriatic, and then along the rivers Po and Rhône came to Circe's island off the coast of Tyrrhenia. Circe, who was the sister of Aeetes, immediately recognised her niece Medea and cleansed her of the murder of Apsyrtus. The *Argo* then approached the island of the Sirens, escaping from their bewitching song thanks to Orpheus, who played his lyre and sang of the beauties of his own country so loudly that he drowned out the Sirens (see Sirens). The Argonauts sailed successfully between Scylla and Charybdis (see Scylla and Charybdis) and called at the island of the Phaeacians and at Crete. On Crete, at that time, there was a gigantic bronze creature called **Talos**, whom Hephaestus had made as a guardian for the kingdom of Minos. Each day, Talos ran three times right round the island, tossing huge boulders at ships he conceived to be hostile. When Medea saw Talos, she laid a spell upon him and paralysed him. Then she pulled out the pin that sealed the single vein in Talos' body, drained the *ichor* or divine liquid that kept him alive, and thus caused his death.

After leaving Crete, the Argonauts - clear symbols of the Greek mariners who even in prehistoric times had managed to sail across the Mediterranean and explore new worlds - crossed the Aegean and returned in triumph to Iolcus. Pelias, however, was unwilling to keep the promise he had made, and he refused to abdicate in Jason's favour. Medea hatched an evil plot to deal with the situation: she introduced herself to the king's daughters as a priestess of Artemis and urged them to kill their father, dismember him and boil up the pieces so as to regain their youthfulness. The girls believed her and slew Pelias with their own hands. Jason thus ascended to the throne of Iolcus, and reigned there till his death.

According to a different tradition, after Pelias' death his son Acastus held on to the throne after the death of his father and drove out Jason, who took refuge, with Medea, in Corinth. For ten years, the couple lived there happily with their children - but then Jason fell in love with Glauce, daughter of the king of Corinth, and Medea, rabid with jealousy, poisoned her rival and killed her children as a way of taking revenge. Jason, too, came to a tragic end, falling to his death from the stern of the *Argo*.

p.204
A wall-painting from Pompeii: Media is hiding the knife with which she is about to kill her children at carefree play (first century BC, Naples National Museum).

5. PELEUS - THETIS - ACHILLES

p.206
A black-figure tablet of Achilles preparing for the Trojan War. Thetis is handing the brave warrior his arms, and behind her stands Neoptolemus, still in boyhood (560 BC, Athens Archaeological Museum).

p.207
The young Achilles being taken by Peleas (right) to the wise Centaur Chiron (left), who will undertake his upbringing on Mt Pelion (black-figure lecythus, 530-520 BC, Athens Archaeological Museum).

P eleus was the son of Endeis and Aeacus, king of Aegina. His brother was called Telamon, while Aeacus also had an illegitimate son called Phocus by the Nereid Psamathe. Peleus and Telamon were envious of Phocus and one day killed him, as a punishment from which they were driven out of the kingdom of Aeacus. **Telamon** made his way to Salamis, where he became king and fathered a famous son, Ajax. Peleus, once cleansed of the murder by king Eurytion of Phthias, found his journey's end at Iolcus, where he stayed as the guest of king Acastus.

While he was staying at the palace in Iolcus, Acastus' wife Astydamia fell in love with Peleus, and when he turned down his advances she falsely accused him to her husband of having molested her. Acastus believed his wife and assigned Peleus a difficult hunting task in the hope that he would be killed. But Peleus managed to capture a large number of wild beasts and came through the adventure without harm, so that evening, when he fell asleep on the mountainside, Acastus removed Peleus' knife and set the Centaurs to kill him. Fortunately, Chiron took pity on Peleus, gave him back his knife and sided with him in driving off the other Centaurs. Peleus went on to slay Astydamia and become king of Iolcus.

One evening when the moon was full, Peleus caught sight of the Nereid Thetis dancing on the beach, and fell in love with her. Thetis had already been claimed both by Zeus and by Poseidon, but the Fates had decided that the pretty girl was to be given to a mortal, and the gods had to accede

to their wishes. The mortal in question was, of course, Peleus, but since in his modesty he was unsure how to approach a divinity, he called once more on Chiron for help. Following the Centaur's advice, when next he met Thetis he seized her by the hands and refused to let her go, even when she transformed herself into fire, a snake, a lion and water. In the end, she threw herself into Peleus' arms, and their wedding took place - a little later - with great splendour, in the presence of all the gods of Olympus and accompanied by the music and dancing of the Muses (see the House of Atreus, the Trojan War).

The fruit of the union between Peleus and Thetis was Achilles. When he was still an infant, his mother, who wished to make him immortal, sat him upon the fire each evening and smeared his body with ambrosia during the day. One evening, Peleus caught sight of the boy amid the flames and became so enraged that Thetis abandoned her undertaking, leaving Achilles mortal. Embittered, the Nereid left the palace to return to the depths of the Ocean, and Peleus handed Achilles over to Chiron for his education. As he grew up in the company of the wise Centaur, Achilles learned how to live rough, how to

hunt and ride, and the elements of medicine and music, becoming honest, brave and respectful.

When the Greeks were organising the Trojan War, Thetis became aware by divine insight that her son was going to be killed at Troy, and so she attempted to stop him joining the army. Dressing him in women's clothing, she sent him off to king Lycomedes of Scyros. There, Achilles developed an association with Deidamia, daughter of the king, the fruit of which was Neoptolemus. In the meantime, the leaders of the Greek forces had found out that Achilles was on Scyros, and thanks to a clever trick of Odysseus, they managed to locate him and bring him on board the fleet. What the wily Odysseus did was to enter the women's quarters of the palace pretending to be a merchant of fine cloth. But among his swathes of materials he had hidden a sword and a shield, bait which Achilles would hardly be able to resist; indeed, as soon as the young man saw the weapons, he flung himself on them in delight. He immediately left off his women's dress and, after stopping to greet his father in Iolcus, sailed for Troy with his friend Patroclus (see The Trojan War).

pp.208-209
A detail from the François krater showing the marriage of Peleas and Thetis. All the gods of Olympus were present at the wedding, celebrating the happy event in peaceful friendship. In the illustration, from left to right, Hera, Zeus, the Muses Urania and Calloipe, Dionysus and Hestia (570 BC, Florence Archaeological Museum).

6. THRACE
ORPHEUS - EURYDICE

O rpheus, the great Thracian hero, was the son of king Oeager and the Muse Calliope. His renown spread throughout Greece thanks to his unique skills in music and epic poetry. Almost all the writers of antiquity praised his divinely-inspired talent on the lyre, from which he was able to coax sounds that could tame wild beasts as well as bewitching the human ear. During the voyage of the *Argo*, the melodious song of Orpheus was capable even of drowning out the song of the Sirens, which until then had proved fatal to all the travellers who heard it.

Orpheus the inspired singer was successful in taming Hades. According to the myth, his beloved wife Eurydice died at an early age after being bitten by a snake. Orpheus descended into the Underworld, determined to bring her back. The sound of Orpheus' lyre struck deep into the hearts of all the denizens of the kingdom of darkness: Cerberus lay down at peace for once, the torments of those in punishment were suspended for a while, and even the terrible Furies were reduced to tears. Hades resolved that Orpheus would be allowed to take his wife away with him - but on condition that he did not turn round to look at her until he was safely back in the land of the living. The couple set off in silence, but shortly before they emerged through the gates of the Underworld Orpheus was suddenly struck by doubts as to the honesty of Hades, known to be a wily

character; he turned round to check that Eurydice really was following him, and in a trice she was gone for ever.

Orpheus was shattered by the irretrievable loss of his loved one, and in one version of the myth himself died shortly after. Other traditions blame the Bacchae of Thrace for his demise: they dismembered him and scattered the pieces because Orpheus had shown a lack of respect for the mysteries of Dionysus. A third school of thought held that the tragic hero had been put to death by Zeus himself, for daring to reveal divine mysteries to mankind.

The mysteries of Orpheus, which became a cult celebrated all over Greece and had initiates called Orphists, were directly connected to the cult of Dionysus but differed from it on some points. The Orphists worshipped Dionysus-Zagreus, son of Zeus and Persephone, who was dismembered by the fierce Titans; after they had eaten his flesh and innards, only his heart was left, and this was transplanted into the younger Dionysus, who was the offspring of Zeus and Semele. The Titans were punished by Zeus and burned up by his thunderbolt. Out of the ash of the Titans were born humans, and so they possess both divine elements, originating in Dionysus-Zagreus, and the power of evil they inherited from the Titans. The Orphists thus believed that by means of rites of purification, and with fasting and abstention from meat-eating, men could strengthen the pure sides of their nature and restrict the influence of their animal instincts (cf. Dionysus).

p.211
Orpheus, with his lyre, is attempting to avoid a Maenad attacking him with a sword (red-figure amphora, 450-440 BC, the Louvre).

7. MYTHS OF THE ARGOLID

Inachus - Phoroneus - Io

The tribe of the Argives was traditionally held to have been founded by Inachus, son of Ocean and Tithys. Inachus - after whom a little river in Argos was called - sired many children, who in turn became founders of cities and famous tribal forefathers: Aegialeus, Pelasgus, Argus, Phegeus, Mycene, Io and Phoroneus. Phoroneus, in particular, was famous for his great wisdom and for the contribution he made to human history: it was he who brought fire to earth, who became king of the entire world, who drew up the laws and established the first courts of justice, who made strong weapons and who introduced the worship of the gods.

Inachus' most famous daughter was Io, a beautiful girl who became a priestess of Hera and attracted the amorous attentions of Zeus himself. Zeus lay with her, but Hera, seeing them in each other's arms, flew into a rage with Io and turned her into a cow. Then she tied the cow to an olive-tree in the sacred grove of Mycenae and set Argus the All-Seeing, of the line of Phoroneus - a beast with eyes all over its body and tremendous strength - to keep watch on it. Zeus set Hermes to steal Io, which he did by lulling Argus to sleep with the music of his pipes. But no sooner was this done than Hera sent a gadfly to persecute the unfortunate Io, whom it caused to run madly from one country to another. After crossing the Ionian Sea (and thus giving it its name), Io wandered through Illyria, Aenus, the Bosporus (= 'ox-crossing'), the Crimea and Asia, coming ultimately to Egypt and resuming human form.

p.212
Danae was among the mortal women with whom Zeus fell head-over-heels in love. When her father locked her away in a dark room, Zeus transformed himself into a golden rain in order to enter through a crack in the wall and lie with her. In this bell-shaped krater, Danae is receiving the rain (Zeus) in a hydria (fourth century BC, Athens Archaeological Museum).

p.213
A red-figure hydria on the subject of the slaying of Argus the All-Seeing. Hermes is approaching Argus, who is running away with his club raised. Io, too - transformed into a cow - is running away (460 BC, Boston Museum of Fine Arts).

There she bore Zeus a son, called Epaphus, but her troubles were far from over: Hera now abducted Epaphus, and Io was forced to take to the road again. In the end, she found her son in Syria and fetched him home to Egypt, where she married king Telegonus and, after her death, was worshipped as a goddess under the name Isis. Epaphus ruled in Egypt, married Memphis and fathered Libya.

Danaus - Nauplius - Palamedes

Libya, daughter of Epaphus, lay with Poseidon and became the mother of Agenor, subsequently king of Phoenicia, and Belus, who ruled in Egypt. Belus' sons were Aegyptus and Danaus, who were the fathers of fifty sons and fifty daughters, respectively. Aegyptus and Danaus disagreed violently and the latter, with his daughters (called the Danaids), left Africa, and after stopping briefly in Rhodes settled at Argos and became king there.

One of Danaus' daughters, called Amymone, lay with Poseidon and bore him Nauplius, who gave his name to a city in the Peloponnese (modern Nafplio). Nauplius and Clemene were the parents of Palamedes, who distinguished himself in the Trojan War and was renowned for his wisdom and ingenuity. According to the local traditions, Palamedes completed the system for recording speech in writing, invented counting, weights and measures and coinage, and thought up both the tactics of war and the game of *pessoi* (a forerunner of chess) with which warriors could while away their leisure time. The power of Palamedes' brain inspired envy in Odysseus, who accused him of treason and gave false witness against him. The luckless Palamedes was put on trial and condemned to death.

Danae - Perseus

Acrisius, another king of Argos, was descended from the line of Danaus and had a beautiful daughter called Danae. Since he had once been given an oracle that he would be slain by Danae's son, he shut her up in a dungeon so as to prevent any man from coming near her. But Zeus, who had fallen in love with Danae, transformed himself into a shower of golden rain, penetrated her cell through the cracks in the wall, lay with her and got her with child. Danae brought Zeus' son - Perseus - into the world, whereupon Acrisius, afraid that the prophecy would come true, put Danae and her son in a chest and set them adrift in the sea. The wind

p.215
A box lid showing Perseus with the Graeae (below). The onloookers are Phorkys, father of the Graeae, Hermes, Poseidon (protector of Medusa) and Athena (425 BC, Athens Archaeological Museum).

blew them to Seriphos, where the fisherman Dictys rescued them and took them into his home.

Polydectes, king of the island, conceived a passion for Danae and wished to make her his own. He organised a banquet at which Perseus, now grown to manhood, was among the guests. Perseus boasted that in order to please the king he was willing to perform

any feat, including bringing him the head of Medusa. Polydectes seized the opportunity and challenged Perseus do to precisely that, claiming that otherwise he would take Danae as his wife whether she wished it or not.

Medusa, or **Gorgo,** was a terrible monster with two immortal sisters called Stheno and Euryale. She herself was mortal, but she had the power to turn to stone anyone who looked on her frightful head with its bulging eyes, its broad, flat nose, its boar's teeth and its hair of snakes. With the help of Athena and Hermes, Perseus sought first to find the Graiae, who would put him on the road to the Nymphs, who in turn kept the items he would require to dispose of Medusa. The **Graiae** were three sisters, in the form of old women since their birth, who possessed a total of one eye and one tooth between them. Perseus seized the eye and the tooth in order to compel the Graiae to take him to the Nymphs. The Nymphs gave him a cap which would make him invisible, a pair of winged sandals so that he did not have to stand on the ground, and a magic bag into which he was to put Medusa's head. After crossing Ocean, Perseus found the Gorgons - as Medusa and her sisters were called - asleep. He put on the cap and the sandals, looked at the

reflection of Medusa's face in his shield (as Athena had recommended, so that the monster would not turn him to stone), and cut off her head with a diamond-edged sickle supplied by Hermes. Still without looking at the head, he put it into his bag - while from the stump of Medusa's neck were born Chrysaor and Pegasus, Medusa's two children by her union with Poseidon. Eluding Stheno and Euryale, who set off in pursuit of him, Perseus made his way home. As he passed through Africa, some drops of blood escaped from Medusa's head and wild beasts sprang up all over the continent.

In Ethiopia, Perseus came one day to a coastal place in which was a beautiful girl, called **Andromeda**, tied to a rock. Curious as to what might be going on - and struck by the beauty of the girl - Perseus made inquiries and discovered that a fierce sea-creature was about to emerge from the waves and devour the girl. Cassiope, Andromeda's mother, had boasted that her daughter was more beautiful than the Nymphs themselves, and they prevailed on Poseidon to drown the country in which Andromeda lived and dispatch the monster from the deep. Cepheus, king of the land and husband of Cassiope, consulted an oracle and was told that he

pp.216 - 217
The Gorgon Medusa from the pediment of Artemis-Medusa in Corfu. Medusa is depicted, between two feline creatures, running on her winged sandals. Snakes spring from her head and her waist, and her demonic expression was intended to instil terror. On her right, the nude youth is Chrysaor, while on her left can be seen the winged horse Pegasus: both were her offspring by Poseidon, and were born at the moment of her decapitation (585 BC, Corfu Archaeological Museum).

would have to give up his daughter as food for the monster. Perseus decided that he would slay the creature, but he demanded that he be allowed to marry Andromeda if he was successful. When he had accomplished the task, Cepheus went back on his word - whereupon Perseus produced the head of Medusa from his bag and turned all those present to stone, with the exception of Andromeda, whom he took back to his home island with him.

Back in Seriphos, Polydectes, too, proved to be an oath-breaker, and he was punished in a similar manner, being literally petrified as soon as he set eyes on the accursed head. Dictys became king in the land, and Perseus travelled on to Argos, in the hope of finding his grandfather. But learning of his approach Acrisius had taken refuge in Larisa, afraid that the old oracle might be fulfilled. Tentamides, king of Larisa, organised games in which Perseus was among the competitors. Just as destiny had appointed, during the discus-throwing Perseus missed the target and instead struck Acrisius, wounding him fatally. When he discovered that the dead man had been his grandfather, Perseus wept bitterly for him and buried him with all the appropriate honours.

p.218
A marble antefix from the Acropolis, showing the head of Medusa (530 BC, Acropolis Museum).

P.219
A statue of Pelops from the east pediment of the temple of Zeus at Olympia, showing the chariot-race between Oenomaus and Pelops (460 BC, Olympia Archaeological Museum).

Oenomaus -Pelops

Among the other daughters of Acrisius
was Euarete, who married Oenomaos,
son of Ares and king of Pisa and Elis.
Oenomaus had once received an oracle
that he would meet his end when his
daughter Hippodameia came to wed,
and so he decided to prevent her from
marrying at all costs. He issued a
proclamation to the effect that he
would give Hippodameia to anyone
who could defeat him in a chariot race
- which he believed to be impossible,
since his horses were the gift of Ares
himself and his charioteer was Myrtilus,
most skilled of all men in the chariot
race. Sure enough, all the young men
who had wished to marry Hippodameia
had met their ends at her father's hand,
and he mounted their severed heads
above the door of his palace.

Then Hippodameia met Pelops, son
of king Tantalus of Lydia, and the two
young people fell in love. Before the
inevitable chariot race, Pelops made an
approach to Myrtilus - who was also in
love with Hippodameia - and extracted
a promise of help in defeating Oenomaos in return for half the kingdom
and one night with Hippodameia. Myrtilus took out the axle-pins in Oenomaus' chariot and put wax replicas in
their place, and as a result Oenomaus
was killed during the race. After winning the victory, Pelops, Hippodameia
and Myrtilus left in their chariot. As
they were travelling, Myrtilus attempted to ravish Hippodameia and Pelops
cast him into the ocean in a place
which ever since has been called the
Myrtoan Sea. But at the moment of
death Myrtilus cursed Pelops and all

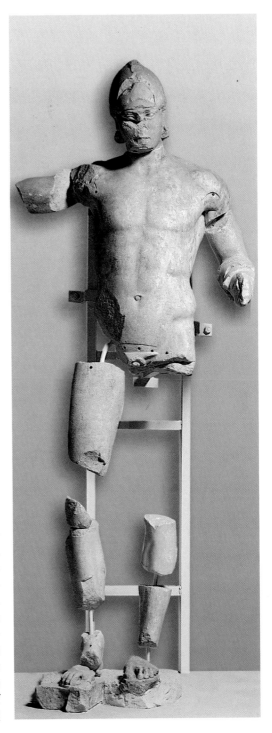

his line, and the curse was to prove most effective.

Nonetheless, Pelops managed to conquer the whole of the Peloponnese, which took his name (= 'the island of Pelops'). He and Hippodameia had many children: Atreus, Thyestes, Alcathous,

Pleisthenes, Hippalcmus, Nicippe and Lysidice among them. He was also the father, by the Nymph Axioche, of an illegitimate son called Chrysippus, whom Atreus and Thyestes killed because they were envious of the obvious affection their father had for him.

Pelops cursed them, and exiled them to Triphyllia. In that country, Thyestes attempted by a stratagem to wrest power from his brother, but - with the intervention of Zeus - Atreus, the first-born son of Pelops, was able to consolidate his rule. When Atreus found out, belatedly, that his brother had attempted to trick him out of his throne and that moreover Thyestes was having an affair with Aerope, his queen, he decided to take revenge. He invited Thyestes to a banquet at which he served up the jointed and roasted bodies of the latter's children. After they had finished, he revealed to his brother what he had been eating, and Thyestes, shocked by the monstrous act, laid his curse upon Atreus, his children and all his line. The *Thyestian feast*, as the awful deed was called, sent a wave of revulsion through both the divine and the human worlds. Thyestes swore revenge for the calamity that had overtaken him, and consulted the Delphic Oracle. There he was told that the only way in which he would succeed in being revenged was to lie with his own daughter. This prophecy was fulfilled when Thyestes lay with Pelopia, his daughter, who gave birth to Aegisthus. Aegisthus later slew Atreus and put his father (Thyestes) on the throne.

p.221
Pelops was the most important mythical hero of the Peloponnese, and he gave his name to it. Among the buildings at Olympia was a sacred area called the Pelopeum where sacrifices in his honour were made. According to one version of the myth, the Olympic Games were initiated in commemoration of Pelops. That brave young man, some said, was loved even by Poseidon, who gave him his famous horses (in the illustration) to ensure that he would defeat Oenomaus in the chariot-race (red-figure hydria, fourth century BC, Metropolitan Museum, New York).

The house of Atreus

p.222

A gold mask from Grave Precinct B at Mycenae (grave V). The stern yet noble expression of the face has led archaeologists to call this 'the mask of Agamemnon'. However, since the mask dates from around 1600 BC and Agamemnon lived about four centuries later, the attribution seems impossible (Athens Archaeological Museum).

p.223

A red-figure pelike of the Judgement of Paris. Paris, seated on a rock next to Hermes, is striving to decide whether Aphrodite, Hera or Athena is the most beautiful goddess (fourth century BC, Athens Archaeological Museum).

When Thyestes became king of Mycenae, the two sons of Atreus, called Agamemnon and Menelaus, were exiled to Sicyon. Later they returned home, drove Thyestes out (to Cythera), and agreed that Agamemnon would rule in Mycenae. He married Clytemnestra, daughter of king Tyndareus of Sparta and his queen, Leda. Clytemnestra was unwilling to marry Agamemnon, who had slain Tantalus, her first husband, but in the end she was compelled to stay with him. The couple had four children, Iphigenia, Electra, Chrysothemis and Orestes.

Menelaus moved from Mycenae to Sparta, where he married Helen, also a daughter of Tyndareus. In fact, however, Helen was the illegitimate daughter of the Spartan king, since Leda had lain on the same night with Tyndareus and also with Zeus, who had transformed himself into a swan to accomplish the seduction. After nine months, Leda gave birth to Clytemnestra, Helen and twin boys, Castor and Pollux (Polydeuces), who went down in legend as the Heavenly Twins. Clytemnestra and Castor were the true children of Tyndareus, while Helen and Pollux were the offspring of Zeus. Even in childhood, Helen was famed for her beauty, and her reputation spread beyond the frontiers of the Greek world (cf. Theseus). When she came of marriageable age, a stream of suitors presented themselves at the palace in Sparta. Tyndareus allowed Helen to choose her own husband, but fearing that the other suitors might, in their jealousy, react with violence when she made her choice, made them swear to respect her decision and stand by the couple should they ever be in need of help. He-

len ultimately chose to marry Menelaus, and they had a single daughter, called Hermione.

p.224

A Laconian relief showing Castor and Pollux, who took part in the Quest for the Golden Fleece and the hunting of the Calydonian Boar and accomplished many brave feats. After death, both became gods and Zeus placed them in the heavens, as the constellation called Gemini. In this role, they helped mortals from on high, and were particularly useful for sailors during storms (sixth century BC, Sparta Museum).

Ten years after the marriage of Helen and Menelaus, Paris (or Alexander), son of king Priam of Troy, made his way to Sparta for the purpose of abducting the beautiful Helen. This move was not the initiative of Paris alone: behind it lay the gods themselves, as the result of an incident which occurred at the wedding of Peleus and Thetis (see Achilles). During the banquet, the goddess Eris, who loved strife and quarrelling, cast into the midst of the feasting gods a golden apple from the garden of the Hesperides on which was written the phrase, "to the most beautiful one".

Hera, Athena and Aphrodite all immediately laid claim to the apple, but Zeus declined to commit himself as to which was the most beautiful of the three. He sent the goddesses, with Hermes, to Mount Ida near Troy, where Paris was herding sheep. He, with his experience in affairs of the heart, was to proclaim which of the three goddesses was the most beautiful. Each of the candidates stated the rewards Paris would receive if his choice fell upon her: Hera offered wealth and sovereignty over all of Asia; Athena intelligence, beauty and victory in whatever contest Paris happened to enter - and Aphrodite offered the heart of the fair Helen of Sparta. Paris' choice eventually fell on the goddess of love, a decision which provoked the fury of both Athena and Hera.

After Paris had given her the golden apple, Aphrodite guided his steps to Sparta, where he was offered hospitality in the palace of the king. But Menelaus had to travel to Crete on affairs of state, and while he was away Paris took the opportunity to abduct Helen. She soon fell madly in love with the handsome prince from Troy, and gladly followed him home to his city. (According to another tradition, their journey took them first to Egypt, where Helen remained, with Proteus, while Paris voyaged on to his own country, alone or with a picture of his loved one.) However the case may be, when Menelaus got home to Sparta and discovered his wife had gone, he and Agamemnon decided that they would raise an expeditionary force to go to Troy and fetch her home. This was the beginning of the Trojan War, in which most of the Greek cities took part, together with those who had been suitors of Helen and

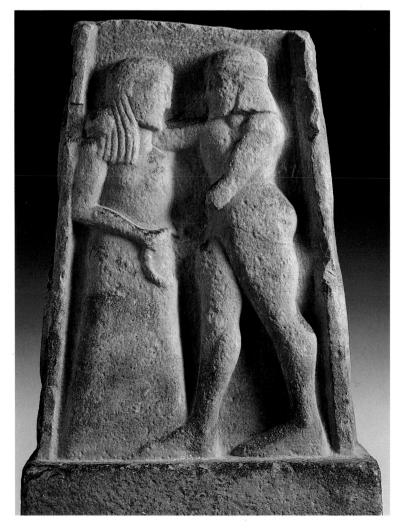

p.225
A Laconian relief, probably showing Menelaus and Helen (sixth century BC, Sparta Archaeological Museum).

p.226
A gilded silver seal show-
ing the slaying of
Clytemnestra. Orestes has
pinioned his mother and
is about to kill her with
his knife (early fourth
century, Ioannina Ar-
chaeological Museum).

p.227
A bronze plate depicting
mythological scenes:
above, Orestes slaying
Clytemnestra and
Aegisthus prostrating
himself as a supplicant at
an altar while Electra, be-
hind them, looks on; be-
low, the abduction of An-
tiope (580 BC, Olympia
Archaeological Museum).

had sworn to give Menelaus their aid (see The Trojan War).

The Trojan War lasted ten years, and ended in a Greek victory over Troy. Menelaus carried off Helen once more, or in the alternative version travelled the world until he came to Egypt and met her near the tomb of Proteus. In the end, the couple came home, married their daughter to Neoptolemus, and lived happily together for many years. When they died, they were buried at Therapne and worshipped by ordinary folk as gods, for Zeus had borne them aloft, into the heavens, and made them immortal along with Helen's twin brothers.

Agamemnon, on the other hand, did not enjoy the honours accorded to his brother, and the fate that lay in store for him was a cruel one. To begin with, before the Greeks set out for Troy he nearly had to sacrifice his daughter Iphigenia, at Aulis, to appease the goddess Artemis and make sure that she would allow their ships to sail (see Trojan War). While Agamemnon was away in Troy, his wife Clytemnestra took Aegisthus to her bed, and the couple lived together in the palace. Agamemnon's son Orestes was exiled from his homeland and his two daughters, Electra and Chrysothemis, though they were allowed to live on at Mycenae did so in unhappiness at the disgrace that had overtaken their family. According to one version of the story, Clytemnestra compelled Electra to marry a shepherd and settle outside the city, so that she would not represent a threat to the illicit couple.

When Agamemnon returned to Mycenae, his wife and her lover murdered him in his bath. Aegisthus ascended to the throne and reigned for seven years. In the end, Orestes came home from exile determined to take

revenge for the death of his father. With the help of Electra and his friend Pylades, he succeeded in killing Aegisthus - but he also slew Clytemnestra. Matricide was one of the crimes which the ancient world found most repellant, and so the tragic hero was hunted down mercilessly by the Furies before he found refuge in the land of the Tauri. This was where his sister Iphigenia was also living, since Artemis had taken pity on her just before the sacrifice was to take place and had put a deer in her place on the altar, removing Iphigenia - out of the sight of all - to her sanctuary in Tauris to serve as a priestess there. The people of Tauris (the Tauri) were in the barbarous habit of sacrificing in the temple of Artemis any strangers who might pass through their land, and Iphigenia, who was obliged to make herself part of this brutal custom, was on the point of sacrificing Orestes when brother and sister recognised each other. After many adventures, they succeeded in escaping from Tauris with the cult statue of Artemis, which they set up in the sanctuary of Artemis Tauropolus they founded at Brauron in Attica. Orestes consulted the Delphic Oracle and then put himself forward for trial before the Areopagus in Athens. In the end, he was acquitted - with the help of Athena, who cast her vote in his favour when the ballot among the other judges was a tie.

pp.228-229
Orestes has captured Aegisthus, his mother's lover, and is preparing to slay him (red-figure amphora, fifth century BC, British Museum).

8. THE TROJAN WAR

The city of Troy stood near the coast of Asia Minor, looking out to the island of Tenedos. The whole area (the Troad) and the inhabitants (the Trojans) had taken their name from a legendary character called Troas, who was the son of king Erichthonius of Athens. Troas married Callirhoe, and the couple had a daughter called Cleopatra and three sons: Assaracus, Ganymede and Ilus. Ilus founded the acropolis of Troy, which was called the Ilium, while the walls of the city, on Mount Ida, were built by Poseidon and Apollo in the time when Laomedon was king. The son of Laomedon was Priam, wife of Hecuba and father of many children: the traditions credit him with numerous daughters and fifty sons, the most famous of whom were Hector, Paris and Hellen.

The Trojan War took place when Priam was king in Troy, and, as archaeological investigations have proved, was not simply a myth or a tradition but an actual historical fact which took place in the twelfth century BC. According to the unsurpassed account given by Homer in the *Iliad*, the Greeks - or Achaeans - set out

p.230
Achilles was one of the brave warriors who took part in the Trojan War. When, in anger, he decided to take no further part in the campaign, the Greek side stumbled from one defeat to another. But it was his destiny to be killed by the Trojans: Paris succeeded in finding the only point on his body where he was vulnerable, the notorious 'Achilles' heel' (red-figure amphora, 445-440 BC, Vatican Museum).

p.231
Below, an Apulian krater showing the sacrifice of Iphigenia at Aulis. The tragic heroine is mournfully approaching the altar, just as a deer, sent by Artemis, is preparing to take her place as the sacrificial victim (370 BC, British Museum).
Above, a detail from the so-called 'Warrior krater', showing armed Myceneans marching as if to war. The vase dates from the late thirteenth century BC, very close to the time that the Trojan War seems likely to have taken place (from Mycenae, Athens Archaeological Museum).

against Troy in order to repossess the fair Helen, whom Paris had stolen from Menelaus of Sparta (see The House of Atreus). In reality, however, the figure of Helen may well conceal the wealth of the fertile Troad, a place which the Greeks knew well given that its inhabitants belonged to the same ethnic group as they did, spoke the same language, worshipped the same gods and had the same customs.

All the Greek kings and princes took part in the campaign against Troy, forming a fleet of between 1,000 and 1,200 ships carrying 100,000 - or perhaps as many as 135,000 - warriors. The flower of Greece gladly fell in behind Agamemnon, commander-in-chief of the operation, with the exception of Achilles (see Peleus - Thetis - Achilles) and Odysseus. Odysseus, king of Ithaca, tried to avoid being enlisted by pretending to be insane: he dressed in the garments of a villager and set out for the fields, which he began to plough and sow with handfuls of salt. The wise Palamedes, who had gone to Ithaca with Agamemnon to enlist Odysseus, eventually managed to show him up for a fraud by putting Telemachus, Odysseus' young son, in front of the plough. Odysseus had to stop his ploughing

p.232-233
A red-figure cylix showing the duel between Menelaus (right) and Paris (left). Seconding the two heroes are Hera and Artemis, respectively (480 BC, the Louvre).

so as not to harm the boy, and thus had to admit that he was perfectly sane. He then added his own small army to that of the Greeks and was to play an important part in the outcome of the war, as were many other famous warriors: Idomeneus of Crete, wise Nestor of Pylos, Ajax Telamonius from Salamis, Diomedes of Argos, Ajax of Locris, Achilles, and Achilles' beloved friend Patroclus.

The Greek fleet assembled in the harbour of Aulis, but strong contrary winds trapped it there. The generals addressed themselves to the soothsayer Calchas, who told them that the ships would be unable to sail unless Agamemnon sacrificed his daughter Iphigenia to Artemis. The goddess, in her rage, was demanding this exchange from the king of Mycenae because he had once shot and killed one of her sacred deer. Agamemnon bowed to his fate and brought Iphigenia to Aulis by pretending that he intended to betroth her to

p.233
Above, a section of a Melian amphora showing a duel between two warriors. It has been interpreted as a depiction of the duel between Achilles and Memnon (fourth century BC, Athens Archaeological Museum).

Achilles. But just before the sacrifice was due to take place, Artemis took pity on the pretty maiden, put a deer in her place on the altar, and whipped her off to her sanctuary in Tauris (see The House of Atreus). A tail wind at once sprang up and the Achaeans set off for Troy.

When the fleet arrived at the Troad, Menelaus sent a deputation to Priam requesting that Helen be returned to her husband, but the answer was negative. The Greeks immediately disembarked from their ships and prepared for battle with the Trojans, whose leader Hector commanded an army which included many notable allies: Lycians, Mysians, Paphlagonians, Maeonians, Phrygians, Thracians, Paeonians, and many others. The first Greek to set foot on Trojan soil was Protesilaus of Thessaly, who met his death at the hands of Hector and was buried with great honours. The Greek assaults concentrated on the most vulnerable section of the walls of Troy, but met with little success. They were thus forced to lay siege to the city and deadlock ensued, since the Trojans, on their part, were reluctant to venture beyond the walls for fear primarily of Achilles. The Greeks were driven by a shortage of provisions to loot the environs of Troy and they captured quite a number of cities in the area.

The siege thus lasted for nine whole years.

Over this period, all the warriors fought with great bravery, but the undoubted protagonists on the Greek side were

p.234
As the war at Troy reached its most crucial point, the Trojans sent out Dolon to spy on the enemy camp. This krater bears a scene showing the capture of Dolon by Odysseus and Diomedes (380 BC, British Museum).

p.235
A black-figure amphora - one of the superb works by the painter Exekias - showing the way in which the warriors lived during lulls in the fighting. Here, Achilles and Ajax are playing draughts (530 BC, Vatican Museum).

Achilles and Agamemnon. Both fought victorious engagements, winning priceless booty and pretty girls from the enemy. One of these maidens was Chryseis, daughter of Chryses, priest of Apollo, whom Agamemnon had taken as his concubine. When Chryses found out what had happened to his daughter, he made his way to the Greek camp and begged to have her back, offering rich gifts in return. Agamemnon spoke roughly to the old man, but in the end was compelled to hand Chryseis over since Apollo, enraged by the insult to his priest, had begun to fire arrows into the Greek army and was decimating it. However, Agamemnon's plunder had to be replaced, and so the commander-in-chief seized Breseis, another prisoner whom Achilles had taken into concubinage. Now Achilles was infuriated too, and he threatened to withdraw from the war altogether, calling his mother Thetis to his aid. She implored Zeus to ensure that her son was avenged, and - sure enough - the Greeks soon began to suffer a constant series of defeats by the Trojans.

Before long, Agamemnon, Odysseus and Diomedes had all been wounded and the Trojans were on the point of overrunning the Greek camp. Agamemnon begged Achilles to return to the fight, promising to give up Breseis. His offer was haughtily rejected, whereupon Patroclus intervened, gaining Achilles' permission to put on his armour - a won-

p.236
Achilles striking the brave Amazon Penthesilea in the neck with his spear; even at the last moment, she is struggling in vain to hit back. Her eye met that of Achilles and, according to the myth, awoke love in him just before she died (black-figure amphora by Exekias, 530 BC, British Museum).

drous suit which had been made by Hephaestus - and take to the field of battle.

This trick worked well to begin with, because the Trojans thought that Achilles had come among them. After a fierce fight, however, Hector succeeded in slaying Patroclus. As soon as Achilles heard this news, he was plunged in despair and anger, reversing all his previous decisions and resolving to go out to fight the Trojans and be avenged for the death of his closest friend. After fierce fighting in which both sides distinguished themselvesAchilles pushed the Trojans back to the Scaean Gates of the city, where Patroclus had fallen. There he fought Hector single-handed and overcame him. Then he tied Hector's corpse to his chariot and drove madly round and round the walls of Troy dragging it behind him. However, when at a later point Priam asked to have the body of his dead son delivered up to him, Achilles did so with all the proper honours. Thus the old king

*pp.236-237
A red-figure cylix showing Ajax, with the help of Athena, striving to overcome Hector, who is being protected by Apollo (480 BC, the Louvre).*

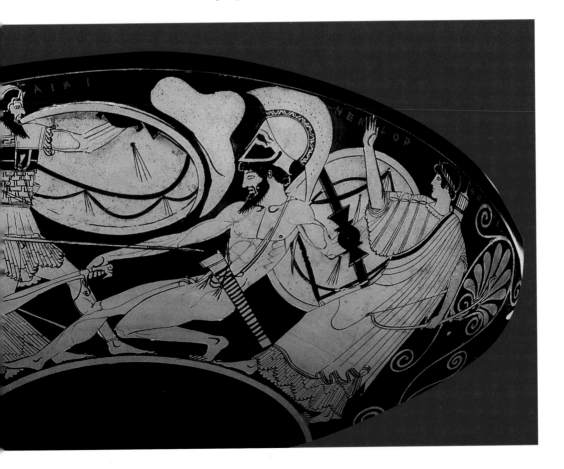

was able to mourn his son, with Hecuba and Hector's wife Andromache, and bury him reverently.

When they lost their leader in this way, the Trojans called for the support of Memnon, son of Io and the king of the Ethiopians, and of the Amazons. Achilles disposed both of Memnon and **Penthesilea**, queen of the Amazons; indeed, according to the tradition, Achilles first shot an arrow at Penthesilea and, having hit her, caught sight of her, whereupon he fell in love with her. She died in his arms. However, his own end was not long in coming. Apollo, still firmly supporting the Trojan side, caused one of Paris' arrows to fly in such a way that it hit Achilles in the heel, the only part of his body where he was vulnerable. The brave warrior fell dead, and immediately a fierce battle broke out above his body, until Ajax and Odysseus succeeded in bringing it back to the Greek camp. There, the Achaeans, with Thetis and the Nereids, mourned their champion for seventeen days and seventeen nights before consigning it to the pyre and then burying the ashes in a tumulus near the beach. Funeral games were held in Achilles' honour. Both Odysseus and Ajax laid claim to the weapons of Achilles, which Agamemnon eventually gave to Odysseus. Ajax, blind with rage, took this as an insult and want-

p.238
A large section of a kettle painted with the theme of the funeral games for Patroclus. The spectators, seated in stands, are watching a horse-race. Among the crowd, the inscription picks out Achilles (580 BC, Athens Archaeological Museum).

ed to seek revenge, but Athena caused him to lose his wits and, in his madness, to begin killing the animals of the camp one by one under the impression that he was slaying warriors. When he came to himself, he stuck his sword in the ground and fell upon it, ending his own life.

Despite the fierce fighting, Troy still held out - and according to a prophecy from the soothsayer Calchas it would continue to do so until Neoptolemus, son of Achilles, and Philoctetes, who possessed the deadly weapons of Heracles (see Heracles), presented themselves on the field of battle. Philoctetes had set out with the Achaean forces, but at one of the stops on the way he had been bitten by a poisonous snake. Agamemnon left him on Lemnos, since his wound could not be healed and from it emanated a fearful stench. During the years of the siege of Troy, Philoctetes managed to stay alive, and ultimately reached Troy with Neoptolemus.

pp.238-239
The Triumphs of Achilles,
by the Austrian painter
Franz Matsch, from the
Achilleio in Corfu.
Achilles, victorious, is
dragging the corpse
of Hector round the
walls of Troy behind
his chariot.

Both men proved to be exceptionally brave: Philoctetes shot the arrow which killed Paris, who had caused the war, and Neoptolemus was the leader of the detachment which captured Troy using the ruse of the wooden horse.

The Trojan Horse was one of Odysseus' most inspired ideas, and thanks to it the conquest of Troy finally occurred after a siege lasting ten years. Implementing the plans of the wily king of Ithaca, the Achaeans constructed an enormous wooden horse, hiding their best warriors in a compartment in the stomach of the animal. Then they pretended to have given up and raised the siege, retreating to Tenedos and leaving the Trojan Horse standing outside the city walls. As soon as the Trojans saw this peculiar object, they were bewildered, and many thought there must be some trick in it. Cassandra, daughter of Priam, who had the power to tell the future, announced to all that disaster was nigh, but no one listened. **Laocöon,** priest of Apollo, also realised that something was afoot, because he threw a javelin at the horse and it struck with a hollow sound. As he was trying to gain the attention of the Trojans and tell them what he had observed, Athena sent two huge serpents out of the sea to kill both Laocöon and his two sons. In the end, the Trojans decided that the horse must be a gift of some kind, and hauled it inside the walls of the city. That night, the Achaean warriors emerged from their hiding-place and, with the troops who had suddenly returned on the ships, captured and looted Troy, killing or taking prisoner its defenders. Neoptolemus slew Priam, Odysseus disposed of Priam's son Diephobus (who had married Helen after the death of Paris),

p.240
A detail from the François krater: Ajax carrying the dead Achilles on his shoulders (570 BC, Florence Archaeological Museum).

p.241
The Dying Achilles, a fine statue by Ernst Hörter which stands in the gardens of the Achilleio, Corfu. As death approaches, Achilles is struggling to remove the deadly arrow of Paris from his foot.

Hecuba was taken prisoner, and Menelaus found Helen (or a picture of her - see The House of Atreus) and took her home to Sparta. The only Trojan to emerge unharmed from the massacre was Aeneas, son of Aphrodite, who ultimately found refuge in Italy and was the forefather of the founders of Rome.

However, the fate of the victors in the Trojan War was little better than that of the losers. The gods, and Poseidon in particular, enraged by the atrocities which the Achaeans committed against the Trojans, swore that terrible disasters would befall them. Some, such as Ajax of Locris, died on the voyage home; others, such as Menelaus, Teucrus (son of Ajax Telamonius) and Odysseus, had to wander far over stormy seas and through hostile lands; and still others, including Agamemnon, met violent deaths as soon as they returned home. Only Nestor, Philoctetes, Diomedes and Idomeneus, who had conducted themselves in a manner that revealed respect for the gods during the war, were allowed to sail home without difficulty.

p.242
Laocöon, who dared to reveal the trick of the Trojan Horse to his fellow-citizens, was cruelly punished by Athena: two huge snakes throttled him and his sons (the Laocöon group, first century AD, Vatican Museum).

p.243
An amphora with reliefs from Mykonos. On the neck is the Trojan Horse, and in the interior are Greek warriors (670 BC, Mykonos Archaeological Museum).

9. ODYSSEUS

The voyage home

Odysseus, the king of Ithaca whose name became a household word, was the son of Laertes and Anticleia. Before setting out for the Trojan War, he married Penelope, daughter of Icarius and niece of king Tyndareus of Sparta, and the couple had a son called Telemachus. Odysseus sailed for Troy knowing full well that an oracle had predicted he would wander for ten whole years before returning home, and it is the adventures of this decade which Homer describes so memorably in the *Odyssey*. Since antiquity, the accomplishments of Odysseus have served as a symbol of the extremes of effort to which man is prepared to go in order to achieve his ideals, and Ithaca encapsulates the idea of the sublime objectives and visions which can be reached only through sacrifice and at great personal cost.

After the fall of Troy, Odysseus' first stop was Ismarus, land of the **Cicones**. Since that people had been allies of the Trojans, Odysseus plundered their land before sailing on across the Aegean. But gales blew his ships south to Cythera and then still further, to the coast of Libya. There dwelt the **Lotus-eaters**, known for the lotus-fruit they produced; anyone who ate of it would forget his home. Some of Odysseus' sailors tried the sweet lotus-fruit and suddenly decided the voyage onward was not worthwhile. Odysseus himself did not taste the fruit, and when he realised what was happening he forced his companions to board the ships and headed out to sea as fast as possible.

The next place that Odysseus and his crew stopped was a wooded island where there were many wild sheep and goats. This was

p.244
A bronze relief from Delphi: Odysseus, lashed beneath the belly of a ram, is escaping from the cave of Polyphemus the Cyclops (605 BC, Delphi Archaeological Museum).

p.245
The famous Eleusis amphora. On the neck is Odysseus, in white, being helped by his comrades to blind the terrified Polyphemus, whom he has succeeded in getting drunk on wine (670-660 BC, Eleusis Archaeological Museum).

the land of the **Cyclopes**, fierce giants with only one eye, fixed in the middle of their foreheads, who lived by breeding sheep and eating human beings. The Greek travellers entered a vast cave, lit a fire, and killed and roasted some sheep. As they were engaged in these tasks, the huge Cyclops Polyphemus, son of Poseidon and Thoosa, suddenly appeared. When he saw the strangers, he devoured two or three of them and then asked Odysseus who he was. "My name is No One", replied Odysseus and offered Polyphemus some wine. Unaccustomed to such drinks, the Cyclops was soon drunk, and told Odysseus that in gratitude for the gift he would eat him last. Before long, however, the drink had sent him to sleep, whereupon Odysseus put out his single eye with a pointed stick and tied the rest of his own companions to the stomachs of some sheep. In the meantime, Polyphemus was yelling in pain; when asked by the other Cyclopes what had happened to him, he said he had been blinded by No One - as a result of which they thought he had gone mad. Polyphemus dragged himself to the mouth of the cave, pushed away the huge boulder he had placed across its mouth, and went outside for the other Cyclopes to see him. While this was going on, Odysseus bound himself beneath the stomach of a ram and, with his companions, made their way back to the ships. When they were safely out at sea, Odysseus called out his real name to Polyphemus, who immediately passed the information on to his father Poseidon, begging the sea-god to avenge him and cause Odysseus as many hardships as possible.

p.247
A black-figure oenochoe showing Odysseus blinding Polyphemus (500 BC, the Louvre).

Next came the **island of Aeolus**. Aeolus, who was the owner of all the winds, proved hospitable to the travellers and

pp.248-249
A black-figure lecythus of the most outstanding workmanship, showing Odysseus' adventures on Circe's island. The witch has already transformed one man of Ithaca ▶

when their visit came to an end gave them a bag in which he had shut up all the winds except Zephyrus. He explained that as long as the bag remained tightly closed they would have a pleasant voyage, since only the gentle Zephyrus, the west wind, would blow them straight back to Ithaca. Odysseus thus set his course for the Ionian Sea and before long was so close to his home island that he could see the smoke from the chimneys of the houses. But then he fell asleep for a short while and Poseidon, who had promised Polyphemus that he should have his revenge, caused Odysseus' companions to open the bag by making them think that it contained wine. All the winds poured out of the bag and began to drive the ships back towards the island of Aeolus. Aeolus, seeing that he was in danger of falling foul of some of the most powerful gods, refused to give them his help for a second time.

Now the sailors had to fight their way forward, without the winds that had favoured them before, and within a few days they came to the **country of the Laestrygonians**, a wild tribe of cannibals who attacked them, captured some of the company, cut them up and cooked them. Odysseus rallied those who were left and they attempted to make their escape amid a hail of rocks. But the Laestrygonians caught up with the Greeks and slaughtered most of the crews, only the ship of Odysseus sailing away undamaged.

After many days of voyaging, Odysseus dropped anchor at Aeaea, Io's island where dwelt **Circe**, daughter of Helius and sister of Aeetes. Circe was a notorious witch whose practice it was to turn anyone who came near her into an animal. Thus, when a detachment of Odysseus' crew, commanded by Eurylochus, visited Circe's palace, they saw everywhere wild beasts which behaved perfectly gently towards the strangers. They were all human beings whom Circe had transformed - as she was soon to do to Eurylochus, squad, touching them with her wand and turning them into swine. Only Eurylochus himself escaped and was able to run back to the ship to warn Odysseus, who had stayed behind on guard. Odysseus set out immediately to rescue his companions, and on his way he met Hermes, who let him smell a magic herb which would protect him against bewitchment. Sure enough, Circe did not succeed in laying any spells on him - indeed, faced with the threat of his sword, she had to lift her spell on his companions. However, she did persuade him to stay for a while on her island, and while he was there the couple had three sons: Agrius, Telegonus and Latinus.

With the help of Circe, Odysseus was able to visit the **Underworld**, where he met the spirit of the soothsayer Tiresias and learned what the future had in store for him: his voyage back to Ithaca would be hard, but his homecoming would be more difficult still. In this part of the *Odyssey*, Homer gives most eloquent descriptions of how the ancients imagined life after death to be and he provides a fascinating narrative of Odysseus' meetings in the Underworld: apart from Anticleia, who gives her son news of Ithaca and the doings of his family, he also encounters the shades of Jocasta, Antiope, Phaedra, Ariadne, Leda, Agamemnon, Achilles, Ajax, Minos, Tantalus and Heracles.

After leaving Circe's island, Odysseus had another terrible danger to deal with: the winds blew his ship close to the island of the **Sirens** (see Sirens), whose sweet song lured passing sailors into a fatal trap. Following Circe's advice, Odysseus blocked up the ears of his companions with wax and commanded them to tie him to the mast and not release him however he might protest. Thus he was able to hear the magic song of the Sirens as they promised eternal happiness, and although he screamed and shouted at his companions to untie him, they did not loose his bonds until the ship was safely clear.

The next obstacle was **Scylla and Charybdis** (see Scylla and Charybdis). In trying to avoid Charybdis, Odysseus steered his ship too close to Scylla, who managed to devour some of his mariners. The survivors also had to pass between the **Symplegades**, which, fortunately for them, had been fixed in place since the time of the voyage of the *Argo* (see The Voyage of the *Argo*).

Now Odysseus and his companions came to the island of Thrinacia, where lived the sacred

into a pig, and is now approaching Odysseus, offering him her magic potion (early fifth century BC, Athens Archaeological Museum).

herds of **Helius** (see Helius). As he had been advised by the soothsayer Tiresias, Odysseus made his companions swear a mighty oath that they would not touch even one of the god's animals. But the weather conditions kept them in Thrinacia for so long that their food ran out, and so they had to kill some of the oxen and roast them. Helius, infuriated by this impeity, waited until they had set sail and then asked Zeus to send a terrible squall down upon them. The ship sank in the ensuing storm and Odysseus, who clung to its mast and then managed to put together a makeshift raft, was the only survivor. The raging gale drove his raft back in the direction of Charybdis. Just as he felt that the whirlpool was about to suck him in, he managed to grab the branch of a fig tree which grew on the rock and hung there until the vortex spewed his raft out once more.

After nine days at the mercy of the wind and waves, Odysseus came to Ogygia, the island of **Calypso**, daughter of Thetis and Oceanus (or Atlas). This beautiful woman lived in a marvellous cavern surrounded by dense groves of trees in which lived sweet-singing birds. As soon as she set eyes on Odysseus she fell in love with him, offering him immortality and perpetual youth if he would stay with her for ever. The charms of Calypso and the magic of the island kept Odysseus there for many years, but nostalgia for Ithaca was always strong in his soul. In the end, Zeus sent Hermes with the message that Calypso was to allow Odysseus to leave. He soon built a new raft, said farewell to Calypso and set sail for home.

Poseidon was not long in spying Odysseus sailing serenely over the ocean. He summoned up a storm which broke up Odysseus' raft and plunged him into the foaming sea. For two days he fought the towering waves before the current cast him ashore, exhausted, on Scheria, the island where the **Phaeacians** lived. Odysseus was too tired even to think where he might be, and fell asleep beneath a tree on the bank of a stream. He was wakened the next morning by the voices of maidens: it was Nausicaa, daughter of king Alcinous and queen Arete, who had come to the river with her friends to wash their clothes and play at ball. Seeing the stranger naked and covered only in leaves, they offered him clothes, allowed him to wash and dress and took him to the palace, enchanted by his almost divine good looks. Alcinous welcomed Odysseus, bestowed precious gifts upon him and after a few days of hospitality fitted out a ship to take him to **Ithaca**. The crew deposited Odysseus, asleep once more, on a lonely beach on his home island, but Poseidon had a severe punishment in store for the gentle Phaeacians: as the ship sailed home, he turned it and its sailors into rocks, and he would have devastated the twin harbours of Scheria, too, if Alcinous had not placated him by sacrificing twelve handsome bulls to him.

When Odysseus awoke, he was not immediately aware that he had come home. But Athena appeared to him, revealed that he was in Ithaca, transformed him into an aged beggar and advised him to go first to the hut of Eumaeus, the faithful swineherd to the palace.

The situation in Ithaca was very different to the way Odysseus had left it. Anticleia had died, Telemachus - now grown to manhood - had set off for Sparta to see if Menelaus could tell him anything about his father's fate, and Laertes, in old age, was a shadow of his former self. Penelope, too, though desperate to see her husband come sailing home, had found herself in a very difficult position. More than a hundred suitors, presuming that Odysseus was dead, had hastened to seek her hand in marriage, hoping to succeed to the throne of Ithaca as well. In order to avoid these suitors,

p.251
A terracotta pillar with reliefs, from Etruria. Odysseus, tied to the mast of his ship, listens in wonder to the song of the Sirens (Roman period, the Louvre).

Penelope had promised that she would choose one of their number to wed as soon as she finished weaving the tapestry she would require for her father-in-law's funeral. For three whole years she had unpicked at night what she had woven during the previous day, deferring the wedding she so little wanted, while the suitors had installed themselves in the palace and were making free with the royal possessions. Not long before Odysseus returned, they had set Penelope what they said was her last time limit for choosing the man she was to marry, and they had also hatched a plot to kill Telemachus.

On receiving Athena's advice, Odysseus hastened to the hut of Eumaeus and there met Telemachus, newly returned from Sparta. Father and son soon recognised one another, fell into each other's arms and set off for the palace with a plan to rid themselves - and Penelope - of the unwelcome suitors. As soon as Odysseus entered the palace, in disguise, his faithful dog Argos spied him; far advanced in years now, after waiting so long for his master, he lay down at Odysseus' feet and died. Then Odysseus entered the banqueting hall, where the suitors treated him with the greatest disrespect in the belief that he was a mere beggar. Only Penelope behaved in a welcoming manner, asking him if he happened to know anything about her husband's fate. Odysseus did not reveal his true identity, but he told Penelope that her husband was alive and would soon be home in Ithaca. Before he laid himself down to sleep, the old woman Eurycleia, who had once been Odysseus' nurse, washed his feet and immediately recognised him by a scar on his leg. Fortunately, Odysseus managed to signal her to silence in good time.

On the following day, the suitors held a banquet and urged Penelope to announce, once and for all, whom she was going to marry. In desperation, she said that she would marry anyone who succeeded in shooting an arrow through the heads of twelve axes driven into the ground. The suitors were to use the bow of Odysseus, who had accomplished the feat himself in earlier years. The suitors began to compete, but they could not even bend the bow. In the end, Odysseus himself announced that he would try, and amid the jeers and insults of the suitors easily managed to send an arrow through the axes. Telemachus, who had earlier hidden the weapons of the suitors, now brought Odysseus a sword and a spear and, after the true identity of the old beggar-man had been revealed, father and son set about slaying the suitors one by one. When Penelope heard the news, she rushed to meet the stranger, but would not be convinced that he was her husband until he had told her of secret marks she bore on her body and described their bridal chamber.

*p.252
A Roman statue of
Penelope, a copy of a
Greek original (Vatican
Museum).*

INTEX

A

Abdera 81
Acastus 201, 205, 206
Aceso 111
Achelous 169
Acheron 118
Achilles 37, 41, 58
.... 97, 115, 113, 208-209
.... 224, 232-238, 249
Acrisious 214, 218
Actaeon 65
Admete 161
Admetus 59, 108
Adonis 85-86
Adrastus 195
Aeacus 154, 206
Aeetes 198-205, 248
Aegeus 172-181
Aegialeus 213
Aegisthus 130, 221, 226-228
Aeneas 85, 242
Aeolus (island of), ... 246-248
Aerope 221
Aeson 200
Aethra 172, 184
Agamemnon 41, 66, 97, 130
.... 222-226, 232-242, 249
Agave 104, 189
Agenor 214
Aglaea 97, 125
Agrius 249
Ajax 233, 238, 242, 248
Ajax of Locris 233, 242
Alcathous 220
Alcinous 97, 250-251
Alcippe 92
Alcmene 151, 154
Amaltheia 9, 38
Amazons 92, 160-162
.... 183, 238
Amphiaraus 56, 145, 201
Amphion 191
Amphitrite 48, 54, 133
.... 134, 177
Amphitryon 151-154
Amymone 214
Anchises 84-85
Andromache 238
Andromeda 217-218
Anius 61
Anthesteria 79, 107
Anticleia 244, 249, 251
Antigone 192-197
Antiope 33, 183, 249

Aphrodite 8, 14, 19, 24, 60
.... 74, 82-89, 92, 95, 97
.... 106, 114, 124, 125, 128
.... 177, 189, 200, 224, 242
Apollo 14, 16, 24, 33, 52-61
.... 62, 65, 74, 76-80, 89, 92, 96
.... 98, 106, 110, 111, 116
.... 121, 125, 127, 130, 140
.... 140, 145-146, 154, 167
.... 174, 175, 176-177,179
.... 231, 236, 238, 241
Apsyrtus 202, 205
Arachne 43
Areopagus 92, 130, 176,
.... 186, 228
Ares 13, 23, 24, 36, 40-41
.... 87-89, 90-93, 114, 124
.... 158, 161, 189, 200, 219
Arete 250
Argeia 195
Argonautes, voyage off 41
.... 43, 116, 189-205
Argos 213, 214, 218, 233
Argus (dog of Odysseus) .33.252
Argus the All-Seeing 213
Ariadne 97, 108, 177-179, 249
Arsinoe 110
Artemis 12, 24, 33, 54, 60
.... 62-67, 97, 98, 110, 156, 161
.... 184, 205, 226-228, 232-234
Asclepius 59, 60, 110-112
Assaracus 231
Asteria 52
Astaerus 115, 116
Athamas 102, 143, 198, 200
Athena 13, 14, 17, 18, 24, 28
.... 32, 36, 38-46, 51, 85, 90, 97
.... 98, 130, 160, 164, 189
.... 197, 201, 20, 22, 16-217, 224
.... 226, 228, 238, 241, 251-252
Atladis 50
Atlas 10, 18, 48, 50, 76, 117
.... 163-164, 250
Atreus 208, 220-222
.... 232, 234, 242
Auge (daughter of the king of
Tegea) 168
Auge (Eos) 14, 65
.... 114-116, 248
Augeus 157-158
Autolycus 81
Autonoe 189
Axioche 221

B

Bacchae (Maenads) 103, 104
.... 109, 211
Belus 214
Bia 9
Bistones 160
Boar of Erymanthus 156
Boetus 51
Boreas 116
Breseis 236

C

Cabeiri 130-131
Cabeirian Mysteries 130
Cabeiro 97, 130
Cadmus 92, 100, 188-189
Calchas 56, 145, 233, 239
Calliope 60, 127, 210
Callirhoe 231
Callisto 65
Calydonian Boar 110
Calypso 6, 10, 250
Carneia 60
Cassandra 56, 145, 241
Cassiope 217
Castor & Pllux 152, 184, 200
.... 222
Castor 152, 184, 222
Cecrops 172
Celeus 72
Centaurs 157, 183, 206
Centaurs, Battle of the 183
Cephalus 115
Cepheus 217, 218
Cera 92
Cerberus 118, 164-169
.... 184, 210
Cercyon 74
Chaeron 60
Chalciope 200
Chaos 6, 123
Charis 97
Charon 118-120, 165
Charybdis 134, 204, 205
.... 249-250
Chione 116
Chios 51
Chiron 110, 200, 206, 208
Chrysogone 51
Cleio 127
Cleito 50
Cleitus 115
Cleopatra (daughter of Boreas)
.... 116
Cleopatra (daughter of Troas)
.... 231
Clytemnestra 84, 130
.... 222, 226-228
Cometes 84

Coronis 59,110
Corybants 60, 127
Cranaus 172
Creon 192-197
Cres 33
Cretan Bull 160, 176, 183
Cretheus 200
Creusa 61
Cronus 8-9, 10, 13, 16, 28
.... 35, 48, 69, 82, 98, 118
.... 120, 122, 128, 131, 138
Curites 8
Cybele 13
Cyclopes 6, 9, 48, 59
.... 111, 118, 244, 246
Cycnus 92, 170

D

Daedalus 186
Danae 33, 214-216
Daphne 57-58
Day 6
Deianeira 168-170
Daimus 89, 92
Delphus 51
Demeter 8, 24, 33, 51, 69-75
Demodocus 148
Demophon (son of Celeus) 72
Demophon (son of Theseus)
.... 183
Deo 69
Despoena 51, 69
Deucalion 19
Dictys 215-218
Diephobus 241
Diomedes 41, 84, 92, 160-161
.... 233, 236, 242
Dione· 54, 82
Dionysia 106-108
Dionysus 5, 13, 14, 23, 24, 37
.... 57, 79, 86, 95, 96, 97
.... 100-109, 117, 120, 123, 125
.... 157, 179, 189, 210, 211
Doris 133

E

Echion 81
Echo 122
Egypt 213, 214, 224, 226
Eileithyia 36, 52, 54, 62
Electra 222, 226-228
Eleusinian Mysteries 73-75
.... 164
Emathion 115
Enceladus 14, 38
Endeis 206
Endymion 115
Enyo 92
Eosphorus 115
Epaphus 214

Ephialtes 14
Epidaurus 61
Epimetheus 16-19
Epione 111
Erato 127
Erebus 6
Erechtheus 44, 61,116
.... 172, 186
Erichthonius 44, 46, 97,
.... 116, 172, 231
Eris 92, 224
Eros 6, 89, 92, 123-124
Erse 115
Eryx 87
Eteocles 192-197
Euarete 219
Eudorus 81
Euenus 201
Eumaeus 251-252
Euphrosyne 125
Europa 6, 33, 97, 188
Eurus 116-117
Euryale 216, 217
Eurycleia 252
Eurydice (wife of Creon) ... 197
Eurydice 210-211
Eurylochus 248
Eurymedon 14
Eurynome 6, 33, 95, 125
Eurystheus 151-166
Euryction (king of Phthia) 206
Euryction (shepherd) 162-163
Eurytus 58, 166, 170
Euterpe 127

F

Fates 8,12, 33, 127
.... 128, 206
Furies 41, 128-130, 194
.... 210, 228

G

Galatea 133
Ganymede 33, 97, 231
Ge 5, 6, 8, 9, 13, 14, 16
.... 28 55, 100, 120, 123
.... 126, 128, 133, 163
Geryon 162-163
Giants 8, 13-14, 26, 28
Giants, Battle of the 13-14
... 26, 28, 38, 46,48, 80, 118, 121
Glauce 205
Graces 18, 33, 60, 67
.... 89, 124-125
Graeae 216

H

Hades (Pluton) 8, 9, 48
.... 71-73, 79, 111-118
.... 164, 165, 169, 184, 210

Halia 131
Halirrhothius 92
Harmony 60, 89, 92
.... 125, 189
Harpies 116, 202
Habe 36, 60, 124-125, 171
Hacale 176
Hecate 13, 62, 72
Hector 231, 234, 237, 238
Hecuba 231, 238, 241
Helen (of Troy) 84, 85, 134
...... 184, 222-226, 232, 234, 241
Helenus 145
Heliads 113, 114, 131
Helius 14, 72, 97
.... 112-115, 125, 131
.... 158, 163, 198, 248, 250
Helle 189, 198
Hellen 19, 33
Hephaestus 17, 18, 24, 36, 38,
... 43, 44, 84, 87-89,95-97, 113,130
.... 154, 160, 174, 205, 237
Hera 8, 13, 24, 32, 33, 35-37,
40, 41, 52, 84, 85, 87, 90, 94, 95,
100, 102, 125, 151-163, 171, 191,
.... 200-201, 213-214, 224
Heracles 14, 18, 24, 36, 37
.... 41, 92, 97, 125, 138
.... 142, 150-171, 172, 174
.... 183, 184, 201, 239, 249
Hermaphroditus 86
Hermes 5, 13, 19, 23, 24, 28
.... 59, 73, 76-89, 102, 108,
115, 120, 121, 123, 152, 154,164,
168,198,213,216-217, 224, 249, 250
Hermione 224
Hesione 167
Hesperides, countryof 10, 36
.... 113, 163-164, 224
Hesperus 10
Hestia 8, 24, 98
Hind of Ceryneia 156
Hippalcmus 221
Hippodameia 219-220
Hippolytus 65, 84, 183-184
Hours 18, 32, 60, 82
.... 89, 115, 125, 128
Hundred-Handed Ones 6, 9
Hyas 10, 117
Hygeia 111
Hymenaeus 60
Hyperboreans, land of the ... 57
.... 160, 156
Hyperion 113, 115
Hypsipyle (nurse of Opheltes) ... 143

I

Iaccus 74
Iambe 72
Iapetus 9, 16

Iaso 111
Icarius (Dionysus 102-103
Icarius (father of Penelipe) 244
Icarus 186
Ida 33
Idomeneus 233, 242
Illyrius 189
Ilus 231
Imerus 124
Inachus 212-213
Ino 37, 102, 189, 198-200
Io 37, 80, 212-214
Iolaus 3155, 158, 166
Iole 166, 170, 171
Ion 61
Iphicles 151
Iphigenia 62, 66, 67, 222
.... 226-228, 232-233
Iphinoe 186
Iris 75, 116, 123
Isis 214
Ismene 192-197
Isthmian Games 50, 138
.... 142-143

J

Jason (Demeter) 70
Jason 37, 81, 84, 200-205
Jocasta 191-194, 249

L

Labdacus 189, 191
Lacedaemon 33
Ladon 156, 163
Laertes 244, 251-252
Laestrygonians 248
Laius 190-194
Laocöon 241
Laomedon 59, 167, 231
Lapiths 110, 224
Latinus 249
Leda 33, 222, 249
Lernaean Hydra 155
Leto 33, 37, 52-54, 58, 62, 64
Libya 214
Lichas 170
Linus 152
Lion of Nemea 36, 115, 155
Lotus-Eaters 244
Lycomedes 184, 209
Lycurgus 143
Lysidice 221

M

Macedon 33
Machaon 110
Maea 10, 76
Manto 56
Marsyas 60
Medea 84, 175, 176, 200-205

Medus 176
Medusa (Gorgon) 38, 51
.... 97, 164, 216-218
Megara 154, 166
Melambus 56
Melanippus 174
Meleager 164, 169
Melicertes (Palaemon) ... 143
.... 198-200
Melpomene 126, 127
Memnon 114, 115, 238
Menelaus 41, 133-134
.... 222-226, 232-234, 241
.... 242, 251
Menestheus 184
Merope 191, 194
Metaneira 72
Metis 32, 38
Midas 121
Miletus 61
Minos 51, 97, 108, 112
.... 160, 176-179, 183
.... 186, 188, 204, 249
Minotaur 108, 176-178, 186
Minyas, Minyans 51, 103, 154
Mnemosyne 33, 126
Moutains 6
Muses 33, 60, 67, 125
.... 126-127, 135, 208
Mycene 213
Myrtilus 81, 219

N

Nauplius 51, 214
Nausicaa 250
Neaera 113
Nebrophon 202
Neleus 51, 169
Nemean Games 31, 138, 143
Nemesis 128, 130
Neoptolemus 209, 226
.... 239-241
Nephele 198
Nereids 87, 133, 134, 238
Nereus 95, 96, 133, 164, 169
Nessus 169-170
Nestor 169, 233, 242
Nicippe 221
Night 6
Nike 9, 13
Niobe 33, 58, 65
Notus 115-117
Nymphs 8, 54, 67, 81, 84
.... 95, 102, 104, 113
.... 117, 120, 122, 123, 216, 217

O

Ocean 6, 9, 26, 38, 113
.... 117, 116. 133. 163. 208

213, 216, 250
Odysseus 41, 50, 81, 148
.... 209, 214, 232, 236, 238
.... 241, 232, 236, 238, 241
.... 242, 244-253
Oeager 210
Oedipus 191-197
Oeneus 169
Oenomaus ...81, 92,138, 219-221
Oenopion 108
Olympic Games 138, 142
.... 143, 169
Omphale 167
Opheltes 143
Oracles of Delphi 9, 56
.....145-157, 172, 189, 191-195
.... 198, 221, 228
Oracles of Dodona 30
.... 145-147
Oreithyia 116
Orestes 41, 66, 130
.... 222, 226-228
Orion 51, 65, 115
Orpheus 60, 127, 201
.... 205, 210-211
Orphic Mysteries 211

P

Paion 51
Palamedes 214, 232
Pallas (Giant) 13, 38
Pallas, Pallantids 172, 174
Pan 9, 60, 81, 106, 115
.... 120-121, 122
Panacea 111
Panathenaea 46, 181, 183
Pandia 115
Pandion 172
Pandora 16-19, 43, 80
.... 84, 97
Paris 85, 134, 24-255
.... 231, 238, 241
Pasiphae .. 10, 51, 113, 178, 186
Patroclus .. 58, 209, 232, 237
Pagasus 43, 51, 217
Peirithus 164, 183-184
Peitho 18
Pelasgus 213
Peleus 201, 206-209, 224
Pelias 51, 200-205
Pelopia 221
Pelops 138, 191, 218-221
Penelope 244, 251-253
Peneus 57-58
Penthesileia 92, 238
Pentheus 103
Periboea 117
Perigune 174
Periphetes 174
Perse (Perses) 138-198

Persephone 33, 70-75, 85-86
.... 118, 122, 165, 184, 211
Perseus 38, 41, 97, 151
.... 214-218
Phaeaceans, land of the 97
.... 205, 250-251
Phaeax 51
Phaedra 65, 84
.... 183-184, 249
Phaethon 113-114
Phegeus 213
Philoctetes 171, 239-241, 242
Phineas 116, 202
Phlegyas 92, 110
Phlora 116
Phocus 206
Phoebe 55
Pholus 157
Phoroneus 213
Phrixus 198-200
Phyleus 158
Pittheus 172-173
Pitys 189
Pleiads 10, 33, 76, 116, 117
Pleione 117
Pleisthenes 221
Plutus ... 70, 127
Podaleirius 110
Polybotes 14, 50
Polybus 81, 191-194
Polydectes 215, 218
Polydeuces 184, 222
Polydorus 189
Polymnia 127
Polyneices 194-197
Polyphemus 50, 136, 246
Pontus 6, 116, 133
Poseidon 8-9, 13-14, 23
24, 43, 44, 48-51, 58, 69, 87, 89,
92, 98, 118, 131, 133, 134, 142,
154, 160,172,174, 177, 184, 186,
.... 197, 206, 214, 217, 231, 242,
.... 246-248, 250-251
Pothos 123
Power 110
Priam ... 224, 231, 234, 237, 241
Priapus 86, 106
Procrustes 174
Prometheus 9, 16-19, 38
.... 95, 164
Protesilaus 234
Proteus 51, 97, 130
.... 133-134, 225-226
Protogenia 19
Psamathe 206
Psyche 123
Pyanopsia 180
Pygmalion 82
Pylades 228
Pyrrha 19, 33

Pythia 55, 56, 58, 62
.... 166-167, 172, 189, 191, 194
Pythian Games 55, 58, 138
.... 140-142, 146
Python 55, 140

R

Rhadamanthus 152, 188
Rhea 8, 28, 35, 48, 54
.... 69, 98, 102, 118, 120, 123
Rhodos (daughter of Deucalion) . 19
Rhodes 50, 87,113
.... 114, 131
Rivers 6

S

Salmacis 86
Sarpedon 188
Satyrs 131, 95, 104, 122
Sciron 174
Scylla 135, 205, 249
Selene 14, 62, 113-115
.... 121, 155
Selli 146
Semele .. 37, 100-102, 189, 211
Septeria 55
Sileni 13, 60, 104, 106
Sines 174
Sinties 92
Sirens 127, 134-135
.... 205, 210, 249
Sisyphus 200
Sparti 189
Sphinx 192
Staphylus 108
Sthenelus 84, 151
Stheno 251
Strength 9
Stymphalian Birds 158-159
Styx 9, 13, 26-27, 118
.... 184, 210, 249
Symplegades 202, 249
Synoecia 181
Syrinx 121

T

Taenarus 51
Talos (nephew of Daedalus) ... 186
Talos 97, 205
Taygete 10, 33
Telamon 206
Telchines 48, 50, 130-131
Telegonus 214
Telemachus .. 233, 244, 251-253
Telephassa 188
Telephus 169
Tenes 60
Tentamides 218
Tero 200
Terpsichore 127
Tethys 6, 27, 38, 213

Teuthras 169
Thaleia 60-127
Thalysia 70
Thargelia 59
Thaumas 116
Theia 113
Themis 32, 54, 55, 127, 128
Theoclymenus (Periclymenus) ..197
Theseus 51, 65, 108
.... 142-143, 160, 164-165
.... 172-185, 194, 201
Thesmophoria 70
Thespes 106
Thespius 152
Thetis 36, 37, 95, 133
.... 206-209, 224, 236, 238, 250
Thoosa 246
Thyestes 220-222
Thyia 19, 33
Tiresias .. 56, 145, 194, 249, 250
Titans 6, 8, 9, 16, 28, 48
.... 48, 126, 211
Titans, Battle of the ... 9, 13, 28
.... 48
Tityus 58, 65
Triptolemus 70
Troilus 60
Trojan Horse 41, 241-242
Trojan War 16, 37, 41, 50,
66, 81, 84, 85,92, 111, 115, 134,
167, 214, 225-226, 231-242
Tydeus 41, 197
Tyndareos 84, 222, 244
Typhon 28
Tyrrhenian pirates 108-109

U

Underworld 26, 30, 71-75
.... 79, 85, 115, 118, 164-165
.... 184, 210, 249
Urania 127
Uranus 6, 8, 13, 82
.... 120, 123, 126, 128, 131

W

Winds 116-117

Z

Zelus 9
Zephyrus .. 115, 116-117,123,248
Zetes 116
Zethus 191
Zeus .. 8, 9, 13, 14, 16,18, 19, 23,
28-33, 33-38, 48, 72-73, 78,
80, 82, 84, 85, 90, 95,97, 98,
100, 102,111,115, 117, 118,
121,122,124-128, 138, 143,
145- 147, 151, 163, 167, 170, 188,
189, 198, 206, 211, 213-215, 224,
.... 236, 250

Creatine ($C_4H_9N_3O_2$)

Creatine is an organic compound that is made in the body from three amino acids: arginine, glycine and methionine. It provides energy to muscle cells for short-burst exercises such as weight lifting and other types of resistance training via phospho-creatine *(see **Chapter 1.1.1.** for more information)*. Creatine supplementation has been well-documented; with several hundred peer-reviewed papers it is perhaps the most researched supplement to date. Furthermore, since a massive 70 per cent of these showed positive results (most of the rest show no significant benefits), creatine is also one of the more used and trusted supplements by athletes today, especially those concerned with strength and muscle mass.

There are many benefits associated with creatine supplementation, which include improvements in high-intensity capacity (including HIIT), repeated sprints, lean muscle mass and a reduction in fatigue. Its supplementation has also shown to help maintain BM in endurance athletes without negatively affecting performance; in general though, athletes gain about one or two kg in the first week of loading, with lower (and slower) gains thereafter.

Creatine has shown to be effective in men and women, and the benefits between vegetarians and non-vegetarians seem to be the same. What is more, creatine has also been well tested on elderly athletes; a recent study showed significant improvements in strength and fatigue in a group of men and women aged between 64 and 86 years.

Supplementation with creatine generally increases the amount of creatine in the muscles by 10-40 per cent; those with a high muscle mass seem to have a lower (but still significant) increase of about 10-20 per cent, and those with a low muscle mass, or those who eat little or no meat or fish, seem to have a higher increase of about 20-40 per cent. Such high increases are often reflected in the results; strength tends to increase by 5-15 percent (though some research has shown far higher gains), and in timed events such as sprints, the finish times are faster by 1-5 per cent.

Creatine monohydrate is the purest and most widely available form of creatine, but there are also many so-called new forms, including those combined with other nutrients. Although there are some that appear to be showing some promise, for the most part there is little or no evidence to suggest that they are more effective or safer.

Commercially available creatine monohydrate is usually sold in tubs of 5g servings, so it is difficult to ingest a specific dose, especially if the servings are in tablet form. A common method for creatine supplementation is to split the intakes into a loading period followed by a maintenance period. The loading period consists of higher daily doses taken several times in the same day for up to a week, with the aim of saturating the muscles with creatine. The maintenance period consists of lower doses that are normally taken once or twice a day for the remainder of the overall time, with the aim of maintaining the elevated levels of creatine caused by loading.

During the loading period, commercial products often suggest intakes of about 20-30g a day in two to six servings for perhaps four to seven days, followed by a maintenance period that consists of 5-15g a day taken in one, two or three servings for the remaining time - perhaps several weeks or months. The intakes suggested among researchers do vary, but their loading intake figures are not usually that dissimilar from the suggested commercial intakes; however, the maintenance intakes seems to be a bit high among the manufacturers. In this text the suggested intakes, taken from a recent and extensive review, are as follows:

- **loading period: 0.3g/kg/BM/day in four equal servings for three to five days**
- **maintenance period: 3-5g/day in two equal servings**
- **cyclic procedure: restart a loading period every three to four weeks of your maintenance period**

The suggested loading intake above means that a 60-kg athlete would be supplementing with 18g of creatine a day, whereas a 100-kg athlete would be loading with 30g a day; these figure compare well with those of the commercial products. As for the cyclic period, this is for those who intend taking creatine supplements for a long time and who might need to give their muscles another creatine saturation-boost. Most research does not exceed 12 weeks, but many athletes use creatine indefinitely, with several creatine-free periods throughout the year. It really depends on what you want. If you reach your desired muscle mass and body mass, and you are happy with your strength gains, then you do not need to continually take creatine; many only retake it, for whatever reason, if they have lost a substantial amount of their previous gains.

If there is anything lacking in research regarding creatine supplementation, then it is suggestions for optimal doses and timings for long-term users. As it is, there are many different suggestions, such as: three months on with one month off, four to six weeks on with three to five weeks off, and eight to 12 weeks on with four to six weeks off. However, such suggestions are normally anecdotal, so you will have to decide what it is that you want from creatine supplementation and then experiment to find the doses and timings that suit you best. For those interested in a simple and short-term method, there is another way that you might prefer; to make the distinction it is referred to as the non-loading method. Many researchers have used the following with good results:

 • **non-loading method: 3-6g/day taken in three to six equal servings over four to 12 weeks**

However much you decide to ingest, keep in mind that the maximum storage capacity of creatine in the body is about 0.3g per kg of body mass, the same as the suggested loading intake above; any more creatine than this will end up in your urine.

When you begin taking creatine your body's synthesis of it will be suppressed, but when you stop, your normal stores will be resumed in about four weeks. After supplement cessation, some athletes experience a small reduction in some of the gains made during the supplementation period, but they are unlikely to return to pre-supplementation levels.

Creatine has been associated with many detrimental side-effects, including weight gain solely through water retention (not muscle mass), cramps, dehydration and altered electrolyte status. Yet none of these claims are supported by scientific evidence, although it has been suggested that any side-effects are probably owing to the impurity of some commercial products. Nonetheless, it is recommended that athletes who previously had, or currently have, renal diseases, diabetes or hypertension, should not exceed 3g of creatine in one day unless under suitably qualified supervision.

Dietary intake might be between one and two grammes a day for those that eat meat and fish; it is considerably less for vegetarians. Some high dietary sources of creatine are beef, pork, salmon, tuna, cod and herring.

Ephedrine ($C_{10}H_{15}NO$)

Ephedra, or *mahuang* in Chinese, commonly refers to the plant, *Ephedra sinica*. Ephedrine is a stimulant that comes from the dried branches of this shrub; its effects are similar to those of amphetamines (speed). Although ephedrine comes from a plant, it has not been categorised under 'herbal supplements' because the vast majority of it is available only in a synthetic form; usually pseudoephedrine, ephedrine hydrochloride (HCL) or ephedrine sulphate.

Since ephedrine stimulates the central nervous system, it keeps you more awake and alert, and also helps with fat loss by raising body temperature. It seems that ephedrine supplementation can promote a loss in fat of nearly 1kg a month - at least in the short term - but it has not shown to reduce fatigue, and its use as a performance enhancer, for either anaerobic or aerobic exercise, is still uncertain. That said, there have been comparatively few trials to test the performance benefits of ephedrine alone (i.e. not in combination with other substances), and the ones that have been carried out used low doses, often in the range of 60-120mg.

However, when higher doses have been used in cycling trials - typically about 180mg - some promising results have emerged, such as finish-time improvements by about 5.1 per cent, and increases in torque and peak power. A trial on 1500-metre runners showed improved finish times by about 2.1 per cent when using a dose of 2.5g per kg of BM. Nonetheless, it must be pointed out that such trials are few, and the subject numbers were very small - usually fewer than 10.

There are so many side-effects associated with ephedrine usage, many of them severe, that it was banned from sale in the USA (including supplements that included it) in 2004 by the Food and Drug Administration. Some of the side-effects reported are palpitations, nausea, heat stroke, gastrointestinal problems, psychosis and sleep disturbances. For those who have used illicit drugs or previously had psychiatric conditions, the side-effects might be even more severe and plentiful. For these reasons, no suggested dose is offered in this text. However, ephedrine is still legal to buy in many countries, including the UK. So if you are tempted to try it, you would be well advised to do so only under the supervision of a qualified sport physician.

Fat burners and appetite suppressers

The term 'fat burner' (also called **thermogenics**) refers to supplements that are claimed to greatly increase energy expenditure, which in turn causes greater fat oxidation, hinder fat absorption, or otherwise encourage the metabolism of fat. Naturally these are of great interest to those wanting to lower their weight via fat loss, and with the obesity problem becoming worse in many parts of the world, the demand for them is high. Those sold commercially usually constitute a combination of ingredients - each with its own claimed fat-burning capability - because it is argued to work better this way.

Fat burners are so much in demand that they are more often considered separately from other combined supplements in sports nutrition, which is why they have a mention here and not under the 'Combined supplements' section. In this chapter, some of the more common supplements used for fat oxidation have already been mentioned as single supplements, such as caffeine and ephedrine, and more will follow in later sections. As it is, most fat burner products seem to be largely made up of any, or a combination of, green tea extract, ephedrine (though not in the USA), caffeine and aspirin.

There are, of course, many other ingredients, some used as a replacement for ephedrine, including many herbal extracts. Some commercial products have shown positive results, but these are usually from small trials, and since such products contain several ingredients, including those already known to work as single supplements, it is difficult to know whether such unique blends are the actual reason for the observed positive effects.

Appetite suppressers normally refer to supplements that are claimed to increase the feeling of fullness, which in turn prevents overeating. Whether such supplements work or not should not be an issue with athletes because athletes need energy, not suppression of appetite, and if overeating is a problem then you would be better advised to see your doctor. No matter, some common appetite suppressors are discussed later in this chapter, and eating disorders are discussed in detail in ***Chapter 10, Women in Training***.

Glutamine ($C_5H_{10}N_2O_3$)

Glutamine is the most abundant amino acid in the muscle cells, and in the body in general (about 60 per cent), and is stored in skeletal muscles, but is also found in the blood. Although glutamine is a DAA, its supplementation becomes essential with certain conditions, such as some gastrointestinal disorders. Glutamine has many biochemical functions, including protein synthesis and increased glycogen production, and is used at a high rate by cells of the immune system. Since prolonged or intense training causes glutamine levels to fall sharply, glutamine supplementation is thought to guard athletes from infection by maintaining the immune system, and is also claimed to increase strength, muscle mass and time to exhaustion.

However, scientific evidence does not generally support such claims; there has been no strong evidence to suggest that glutamine supplementation improves lean body mass, strength in resistance training, or increased glycogen synthesis. Interestingly though, a couple of more recent trials (in 2010 and 2012) found that glutamine supplementation significantly improved time to exhaustion in trained endurance athletes, and visual reaction time and skill performance in basketball players. In the endurance trial the athletes who showed positive results ingested very different amounts of glutamine; 0.05g per kg of BM or 0.2g per kg of BM, so for a 75-kg athlete this is 3.75g and 15g of glutamine, respectively.

In the basketball trial, the athletes who ingested either one or two grammes of glutamine in 500ml of water did significantly better than those who ingested water alone. As it stands, the intakes vary considerably, the positive trials are few and they are way outnumbered by those that do not show any confirmed benefits. For these reasons its usage is not advocated in this text and so no dosage is suggested.

Glutamine comes in two forms: D-glutamine and L-glutamine. They are mirror images of each other but it is L-glutamine that is of use to the body. In commercial products, the terms glutamine and L-glutamine are often used interchangeably (as in this text), so whether they are labelled 'Glutamine' or 'L-Glutamine' makes no difference. However, a closer inspection of the ingredients will often show that the content of L-glutamine is not always 100 per cent, and sometimes it is as low as 60 per cent. The serving suggestions are normally about 5g once or twice a day with fluids.

There are no known side-effects associated with glutamine supplementation. Trials have tested a variety of doses, including 20-30g a day - in one case 28g a day for 14 days, and 0.65g per kg of BM (that is over 50g for an 80-kg athlete). None showed any adverse side-effects, and in blood tests no abnormal levels of glutamine were observed. However, it is not certain whether glutamine supplements are safe if you are pregnant or lactating, so in such cases it is strongly advisable to seek medical advice beforehand.

Animal proteins are the richest source of glutamine - especially beef, chicken, pork, all types of fish, milk and other dairy products - but other good sources include beans, cabbage, spinach and parsley.

Herbal supplements

Herbs in their natural form have been used medicinally for centuries, and extracts of many of these are widely used in modern complementary and alternative medicine. Many of the claims made for them are useful for athletes, especially with regards to weight control and fat loss, and consequently we are seeing more and more appear in sport shops. Even though there are comparatively few herbal sport supplements, there is still a great number available; in this text we concentrate on some of the more popular ones, but no doubt there will be disagreement as to what these should include. The herbal extracts in this section are considered as single supplements, but we shall return to some of them under the *Combined supplements* section.

Capsaicin ($C_{18}H_{27}NO_3$) is the active ingredient of chillies, and **capsinoids** (naturally present in chillies, with a similar molecular structure to capsaicin) are claimed to be especially useful for weight management and fat loss. There is evidence to support this: a 2010 study concluded that capsinoids may be an effective weight-loss aid, in addition to diet and exercise. However, an earlier study showed its potential to deplete glycogen stores during exercise, and even at rest, which may adversely affect an athlete's performance. Therefore, if you need to lose fat and improve your performance, then you can probably choose better than either of capsaicin or capsinoids.

Forskolin ($C_{22}H_{34}O_7$) is a plant that grows in India, and has a long and well-established use in Ayurveda, a traditional Hindu system of medicine. It is theorised that forskolin, or forskolin extract, can stimulate fat metabolism, but studies have been incompatible; some showing improvements in body composition, and some showing no effect whatever. Until more evidence comes to light, the benefits of forskolin regarding weight control and fat loss remain inconclusive.

Glucomannan is the insoluble fibre that comes from konjac, a plant native to eastern Asia, and is known mainly for promoting weight loss. Studies have consistently shown that glucomannan supplementation can induce significant bodyweight reduction via fat loss in overweight and obese (but otherwise healthy) individuals, and seems to be well-tolerated. An eight-week study in 2007 of overweight men and women showed a reduction in fat mass by 1.0-3.9kg and 1.4-6.4kg in men and women, respectively, without exercise; and 1.2-4kg and 2.5-4.7kg in men and women, with exercise. Moreover, LDL cholesterol levels also dropped significantly. Whether it is effective for non-overweight individuals is not certain. The suggested dosages below are those that have produced positive results in fairly recent studies:

- **glucomannan: suggested dosage of between 2g and 4g a day**

Glucomannan is a natural laxative, so it is not advisable to have it just before bedtime, close to exercise time or any time close to an athletic event. Some have also complained that it caused choking and/or blockage of the throat, oesophagus or intestine, so it is better to take it with about 200ml of water.

In general, there is concern by the medical world about the efficacy and safety of most herbal-extract supplements, or even natural forms, be it for medicinal purposes, weight control or as ergogenic aids. Adverse effects are common, and since most herbal supplements come combined with other herbs or chemicals for which no scientific data is available, using them might be an unnecessary risk; the weight loss products are perhaps the ones most associated with adverse side-effects. Moreover, many herbal supplements contain banned substances, so it is best to seek the advice of a sport physician before using them.

Green tea extract is 90-per-cent a chemical compound, known as green tea catchins, from the dried leaves of the tea plant, *Camellia sinensis*. Apart from many medicinal uses, it is often touted for its weight management properties. It is believed that green tea catechins influence the sympathetic nervous system (nerves near the middle part of the spinal cord, supplying the internal organs, blood vessels and glands), such that it increases energy expenditure and fat oxidation. It is still unclear whether green tea catechins help athletic performance, but there is much evidence to support claims that it helps to reduce body fat.

The drop in overall body mass and fat percentage are significant; in one Chinese study in 2008, the subjects lost about 0.7kg and 0.6 per cent, respectively, during a 90-day trial. However, it is unclear for how long, and how much, such benefits will continue. In trials that showed a loss in body fat, the intake dosage varied considerably, but as they seemed to have been well-tolerated the range is given below:

- **green tea extract (catechins): 270mg to 1200mg a day**

Nonetheless, if you have any conditions that are known to be aggravated by caffeine (such as palpitations) then you should not take any green tea supplements without first consulting a doctor. These doses are very high, so even if you have no known intolerance to caffeine you should not start with more than the lowest dose suggested (270mg a day), and this may already be higher than those suggested on commercial products. In one cup of green tea the amount of caffeine is normally between 20g and 50mg, yet there are supplements available that contain five or ten times this amount in one capsule.

Guarana is a climbing plant, native to the Amazon basin, that contains about twice as much caffeine as coffee beans, so its extract is often used as a stimulant in much the same way. However, although Guarana has had some positive results when combined with other extracts and substances there has been little or no positive results when tested in isolation.

Spirulina is a blue-green algae, a simple aquatic plant, that includes many vitamins and minerals, but is particularly rich in protein and iron. It is perhaps one of the more common so-called superfoods (a non-scientific term often used to describe food that contains high levels of nutrients) in supplement form; natural examples are blueberries, broccoli, spinach and tomatoes. The term is often used misleadingly as a marketing tool, even though the health claims made for superfoods are rarely supported by dietitians and nutritional scientists. Many sports people also claim that it improves sporting performance, recovery time and stamina, and some recent studies have shown some positive results in this regard. A small study in 2006 suggested that spirulina intake reduced skeletal muscle damage that perhaps lead to a better time to exhaustion. More recently, a study in 2010 showed several benefits, including a significant increase in exercise performance and fat oxidation, and in 2012 a trial of 41 runners showed a lowering of fat in the blood after meals. However, there are too few studies to make any claims with confidence. Although spirulina contains all eight indispensible amino acids, the US National Library of Medicine views it as no better a source than milk or meat even though it is about 30 times more expensive. Moreover, many suppliers of spirulina advocate its high vitamin B_{12} content, but this is misleading as it is in a form that is biologically dormant in humans. In trials, common doses seem to be 1-10 g day with no apparent side effects, and most commercial recommended doses are well within this range. It seems that spirulina is safe to try, though not recommended for those lactating or with child, and that it may have some benefits. However, owing to its cost and lack of supportive evidence to date, it is not advocated in this text.

Yohimbine ($C_{21}H_{26}N_2O_3$) is a chemical compound extracted from the bark of an African tree called Yohimbe. It is prescribed as a stimulant or aphrodisiac by conventional doctors and herbalists alike, and for these purposes it has been reviewed positively. Further claimed benefits include improvements in stamina, performance, fat burning in general and even losing fat in particular places, but most of these are not supported by scientific evidence. However, one 2009 study concluded that yohimbine might be useful for promoting fat loss in élite athletes, but all other claimed benefits are purely anecdotal. There are several reported side-effects from over-the-counter yohimbine, such as gastrointestinal upset, increased blood pressure, headaches and agitation.

Other herbal extracts such as those from the **gingko biloba** leaves (a unique species of tree), **St John's wort** (a plant species that grows worldwide), **ginseng** (a plant native to N America and Asia) and **kava kava** (a narcotic sedative drink in Polynesia made from crushed roots of a type of pepper plant) have all been tested for various medical conditions, but none has any strong evidence to support supplementation for fat metabolism, weight management, strength, muscle mass, performance or any other benefits expected from a sport supplement for healthy athletes. That said, kava kava may reduce the symptoms of anxiety, which might indirectly help an athlete who is very nervous before an event.

HMB (beta-hydroxy beta-methylbutyrate) ($C_5H_{10}O_3$)

HMB is synthesised by the body from the BCAA, leucine; an indispensible amino acid that must be obtained from the diet. Several studies have shown that HMB supplementation can lead to increased strength and muscle mass, especially in the elderly and those new to training. The muscle mass of previously untrained athletes normally increases by 0.5kg to about 1.0kg over a period of three to six weeks' training, but the effects after this are unclear.

As for trained athletes, the benefits are generally trivial or non-existent, though one recent study did show a notable improvement in lower-body strength. HMB may also be useful for the recovery of damaged muscle cells, so its continued usage by trained and untrained athletes alike may be better for this reason, rather than expecting continual improvement in muscle mass and strength. The effect of HMB on body composition is thought to be negligible.

In many trials the dosage has been taken in one go; often, but not always, near - or even during - training.

- **HMB: suggested dosage is between 1.5g and 3.0g a day**

However, some prefer to take two or three equal servings during the day, especially if their training continues intermittently or for long periods. Nevertheless, if possible, with HMB's suggested benefits regarding muscle cell damage it might be better to take two equal servings either side of your training.

Many body builders take a specific dosage, **38mg per kg of BM**, but this may take the dosage into largely unknown territory. For instance, according to this dosage a 120-kg athlete should take about 4.6g (38mg × 120, then divide by 1000) of HMB a day, but most research has not tested doses exceeding 3g a day, so it is advisable that you do not exceed it either. In any case, as body builders are 'trained' athletes, the muscle-building and strength benefits will be negligible, so any dosage for this purpose may well be a waste of time and money.

No matter, the reason it is thought safe to take high amounts of HMB is because it is water-soluble, so excessive amounts will probably be excreted in the urine, and furthermore, it is believed to have no side-effects. That apart, although some researchers suggest that 3g a day may have better results - in terms of strength and muscle mass - than 1.5g a day, it seems that a jump to 6g a day has no additional benefits. It may turn out that a specific dose will be better in some or all respects, but such a dose is yet to be confirmed.

HMB is found in several foods, including avocado, citrus fruit, alfalfa and catfish, but in very small amounts.

Meal Replacement Products (MRPs)

Meal replacement products (MRPs) are usually bars, or drinks that come in powdered form that need to be mixed with fluid; usually water or milk. They are mostly high in protein, low to moderate in carbohydrates, low in fat and often have high amounts of various vitamins and minerals (and perhaps herbal extracts as well). However, there is such a variety these days it is difficult to be so general. For example, a serving of an MRP might have about 300kcal and include about 40g of protein, 20-30g of carbohydrates, and about 5g of each of fat and fibre. In contrast, a serving of a sport meal (not a powder or bar) might be about 400-500kcal and include about 15g of protein, 50g of carbohydrate, 15-20g of fat and 10g of fibre.

Moreover, a typical powdered MRP will be very low in sodium, perhaps less than a hundredth of a gramme, whereas sport meals are often high in sodium, perhaps half a gramme or more. There are also breakfast and bedtime MRPs. The breakfast MRPs are mostly the same as the usual MRPs, but with a little less of each ingredient, and somewhat cheaper. A bedtime MRP serving might be about 200kcal and include about 40g of protein, and only two or three grammes of carbohydrates and fibre; they often have little or no vitamins and minerals.

The current costs per serving are as follows: about £1 for a usual MRP or a bedtime MRP, about £0.30 for a breakfast MRP, and about £4 for a sport MRP; clearly, they can quickly and easily become an expensive habit. It should be noted that all of the information on MRPs above is extremely vague, and no doubt the ingredients and costs will vary considerably depending on the manufacturer.

The main reason people use MRPs is for fat loss, and this is where most or all of the convincing research for them has come; in trials, MRPs have shown to be very effective supplements for those overweight or obese, but that is not to suggest that they are any better than a wholesome diet. Many such trials have included a large number of subjects - 80 or more is not unusual - and many last for three to ten months. The evidence for fat loss is there, and MRPs have shown to lower fat and LDL cholesterol levels considerably, particularly the high-protein MRPs.

Incidentally, protein powders are often considered to be MRPs, especially since most of the usual type are high in protein, but in this chapter protein supplements have been considered separately. That said, a fairly recent trial found that obese subjects who were on a supervised diet-and-exercise programme lost more weight than those encouraged to be more physically active and who were put on an MRP-diet. Furthermore, the supervised group were better able to maintain their improvements.

As for athletes, there seems to be little or no research of their concern, but MRPs are included here since they might be useful from time to time, but certainly not for general use; an athlete should treat meal 'replacements' as a *supplement* for a rare occasion, if at all. MRPs have no proven benefits over food, and may have unnecessary amounts of nutrients that make it hard to tailor your intakes. Moreover, they can work out to be a needlessly expensive habit, and many find them to be unpalatable with an unpleasant aftertaste.

Pro-hormones

Hormones are produced in the body and transported in tissue fluids, such as blood, to stimulate specific cells and tissues. Testosterone and growth hormones are two of the more important types of hormone that promote strength and muscle anabolism (an increase in muscle mass), whilst also decreasing fat mass and preventing muscle catabolism (the breakdown of muscle mass). **Steroids** are any of a large class of organic compounds that share a distinctive molecular structure containing four rings of carbon atoms; many hormones are steroids, as are many alkaloids and vitamins - an alkaloid is an organic compound of plant origin that has conspicuous physiological actions on humans; morphine, for example.

There are many types of steroids, but perhaps none more familiar than **anabolic steroids**. Steroidal hormones can be separated into five distinct groups according to the receptors to which they bind; a receptor is a molecule in a cell membrane. Anabolic steroids are a class of steroids that interact with androgen receptors to increase muscle and bone synthesis - an **androgen** is a male sex hormone, such as testosterone. Indeed, anabolic steroids are technically referred to as anabolic-androgen steroids (AAS); they mimic the effects of testosterone and dihydro-testosterone in the body.

There seems to be no question that anabolic steroids increase strength and muscle mass, and perhaps even cause the formation of *new* muscle fibres. However, their adverse side-effects are also well established - so much so that they are perhaps better known for these than anything else. Side-effects include liver and hormonal dysfunction, high cholesterol, cardiovascular disease, high blood pressure, deepening of the voice and an increase in body hair; some side-effects are irreversible, especially in women.

There are supplements that block some of the side-effects of anabolic steroids, and they are often prescribed by doctors who are treating patients that *need* steroids, but it would seem more sensible for an athlete to avoid anabolic steroids in the first place. Although they may still be purchased legally in the UK (though banned by sports bodies), they have been illegal to buy in the USA without prescription since 2004.

Pro-hormones are naturally derived precursors to testosterone or other anabolic steroids that increase the strength of hormones already present in the body, but they do not add hormones. Anabolic steroids, on the other hand, do add hormones to the body, and this is an important distinction between them that is often the cause of confusion. There are many pro-hormones, such as dehydroepiandrosterone (DHEA), androstenedione, and 4-androstenediol, and most of them come with the same or similar side-effects as anabolic steroids, but without the potential benefits.

Many finely tuned trials on athletes have repeatedly shown that supplementation with pro-hormones has failed to produce desired effects in body composition, strength, or performance enhancement when compared to placebos. Pro-hormones are legal to buy in the UK, but were banned (along with anabolic steroids) from sale in the USA - with the notable exception of DHEA, which is still widely used in medical trials, especially for the elderly, and is available as an over-the-counter supplement.

The reason DHEA was not banned is that it has been widely used in a large number of medical trials for many years and has consistently shown to have few (and non-severe) side-effects. Manufacturers recommend DHEA in doses of between 50mg and 100mg, and trials have shown that doses far higher have little or no side-effects, but since they do not have any documented benefits (yet the possibility of *some* side-effects) it is a pointless risk and an obvious waste of money.

Protein

The theory in favour of protein supplementation is based largely on its main use by the body as a building material for muscle. In short, and perhaps simplistically put: muscles are largely made from protein, therefore more protein will mean more muscle. Yet there are many other benefits claimed for protein supplementation, such as enhancing muscle recovery, strength and endurance. Most scientists now agree that athletes require a higher amount of protein than the generally recommended intakes, and that such amounts need to be tailored to the type, intensity and duration of the exercise; however, scientists also previously suggested that you should have no problem getting your *higher* requirement from your diet, and therefore supplements were strictly unnecessary.

Moreover, although trials did show improvements with protein supplementation, these were mainly in untrained athletes; the evidence for trained athletes seemed uncertain, especially if the supplement did not contain other nutrients, such as creatine. However, recent trials have shown that the timings were as important as the tailored amounts; protein (and/or amino acids) taken before, during and after exercise may indeed enhance endurance, muscle mass, maintenance of lean body mass, and strength. So, supplementation of protein might be a convenient way to ensure the amounts and timings are better tailored to individual athletes.

Some sources consider the IAA separately from protein, and suggest that 3-6g of just IAA (not protein powders, which normally include all 20 amino acids) should be taken before and after training, as there is some evidence that this will stimulate protein synthesis - and this is where certain supplements overlap and become a little confusing. So, before any further explanation, if you decide to try IAA before and after training, it is probably best to take them with the carbohydrates that you will be ingesting anyway (as part of the carbohydrate cycle - *see* **2.3**).

Protein supplements will normally consist of all the amino acids, both DAA and IAA, but the proportions of each vary considerably. That apart, some of these are treated as supplements in their own right, which we have already mentioned; BCAA, which consists of three IAA, glutamine, which is a DAA, and creatine, which consists of one IAA and two DAA. So the positive results of protein supplementation and/or IAA may well be owing to specific amino acids, rather than IAA or protein (regardless of the form in which it comes) as a whole.

There are many forms of protein available (some have already been mentioned in **Chapter** 3) and each contains all the IAA and most or all of the DAA to a greater or lesser degree, but there is no strong evidence to suggest the superiority of one form over another.

Whey protein (BV = 104) is very good post-exercise because it digests in about 30 minutes, and contains high levels of all the essential amino acids, and hence BCAA. There are two types of whey protein: **whey concentrate**, which is 25 to 89 per cent protein (most are 80-85 %), and **whey isolate (PDCAAS = 1.14)**, which is about 90 to 95 per cent protein. Whey isolate has little or no fat, lactose or minerals, whereas whey concentrate has a little of each of these, but since neither is generally thought to be superior over the other in terms of ergogenic benefits, the cheaper whey concentrate is perhaps the better choice.

However, each of these may be hydrolysed, a process in which a compound is broken down by a chemical reaction with water, which makes the protein easier to mix (far less likely to become lumpy), and is absorbed better and quicker - though it is also the most expensive. Although whey protein has a BV of 104, some manufacturers claim that their whey protein isolate has a BV way over 150.

Casein protein is the main protein present in milk, and has a high concentration (about 20 per cent) of glutamine and a high **BV of 77 (PDCAAS = 1)**. It forms a gel in the stomach, and therefore provides a slow release of amino acids into the bloodstream, sometimes lasting several hours. For this reason, casein is often the favoured protein throughout the day by many athletes, and often last thing at night by bodybuilders because in theory this means more proteins will be absorbed in the body, producing better results.

Soy protein comes from soybeans, but soy supplements contain higher levels of proteins than any of the usual food sources, including soya milk and tofu (bean curd - a soft white substance made from mashed soy beans). It is suitable for vegetarians, contains almost the same amount of IAA as casein, and has a **BV of 74 (PDCASS =1)**.

Albumen (egg-white) protein is a lactose and dairy-free protein. It has a **BV of 100 (PDCAAS = 1)**, the highest natural source, and is considered the best-quality of all the wholefood proteins.

Hemp seed protein (BV = ?; PDCAAS = 46) and **brown rice protein (BV = 83; PDCAAS = 47)** are both complete proteins, but both contain considerably less than the other protein types mentioned above. However, they are particularly easy to digest. **Pea protein (BV = 65; PDCAAS = 69)** is a rich source of amino acids and is comparable to soy protein, but is less allergenic. It is not uncommon to find hemp, rice and pea protein blended as one 'plant protein' powder; this effects a good balance of amino acid contents and digestibility, and is suitable for vegetarians.

If you decide to use protein supplements, and you do not exceed the suggested total daily dose required for your particular needs, then you should not suffer any of the adverse side-effects associated with excessive protein intake, such as diarrhoea, and problems with the liver and kidneys. Refer to ***Chapter 3*** for more details on protein.

Ubiquinone (Q10) ($C_{59}H_{90}O_4$)

Ubiquinone, also known as co-enzyme Q, and commonly referred to as **Q10**, is a chemical compound that plays a vital role in the production of ATP, so it is theorised that supplementing with it will increase exercise capacity. However, whilst there are many well-supported medical uses of ubiquinone, its supplementation for athletic interests seem unclear.

It seems that most studies do not produce positive results for Q10, though one study in 2008 showed favourable results in both trained and untrained athletes, and in both aerobic and anaerobic exercise. However, a very recent study (2012) tested it using doses recommended by manufacturers - since commercial products often suggest very different doses from those used in trials - but it still failed to show any positive effects.

The 2008 trial used 100mg supplements twice a day, and the 2012 trial used 90mg once a day - way below the tolerable levels; in medical trials patients have ingested far higher levels. The most common side-effect with very high doses of ubiquinone (3600mg a day) are gastrointestinal-related, but it seems that levels even as high as 2400mg a day do not produce side-effects. Ubiquinone is not advocated in this text owing to the lack of evidence to support it.

Nonetheless, supplementation with ubiquinone seems very safe at the levels recommended by manufacturers, so it might be worth a try; but if you do not see any results within a few weeks, there would seem little point in persisting with it. Ubiquinone is found in many foods, but is particularly high in heart (beef, pork and chicken), and in the oils of soya beans and olives.

Zinc monomethionine aspartate and magnesium aspartate (ZMA)

ZMA is a combination of two minerals, zinc and magnesium, and one vitamin, vitamin B_6. Zinc is an important player in the structure of protein, and magnesium in energy production; whereas vitamin B_6 is essential for converting some amino acids into other amino acids, but also helps to metabolise fat and carbohydrates. Since some studies have shown that a zinc deficiency may reduce the production of testosterone and insulin-like growth factor 1 (IGF-1) - a protein, similar to insulin, that is important for growth in children and anabolism in adults - it is thought that ZMA will aid and speed up post-exercise recovery, and also improve strength and muscle anabolism.

However, scientific data does not support these ideas; indeed, tests have shown that ZMA supplementation does not enhance training adaptations in resistance-trained athletes, and has no significant effects on serum testosterone levels in those who already intake adequate zinc in their diet - serum is a protein-rich liquid that separates out when blood coagulates (changes to a solid or semi-solid state).

Manufacturers of ZMA supplements include varying amounts of each of the three core ingredients (there are often other added ingredients), but a typical serving might be as follows: zinc (30mg), magnesium (450mg) and vitamin B_6 (10mg). Supplementation with ZMA has no obvious side-effects, but high levels of zinc (more than 50mg a day) may interfere with the metabolism of iron and copper; ingesting 2g or more may well cause nausea, vomiting and fever. ZMA is not advocated in this text.

However, if you still decide on taking ZMA supplements it is important to check the zinc content of any other supplement that you might be taking. (*For more information on zinc, magnesium and vitamin B_6, refer to* **7.4.1**, **7.4.2** *and* **7.3.2**, *respectively.*)

8.2 Other supplements

The supplements in this sub-section have earned themselves a mention, but nothing more, owing to the limited evidence to support the claims made for them and/or unclear information on dosage. No doubt some readers may find the lack of prominence (or the non-appearance) of particular supplements surprising. So if due attention is missing for certain supplements, do not be surprised to see it (or them) elevated in future editions; research is ongoing, and it is research that will change this.

Calcium supplementation may help bone mass in those with premature osteoporosis, and it may also help with body composition, but no confident conclusions can be made at this stage. High supplementation with calcium may cause heart attacks, so to be safe you should only supplement with it as advised by a physician.

Chitosan is a type of polysaccharide that manufacturers derive from shellfish. It is claimed that chitosan will bind fat that will then pass through the body unabsorbed; however, chitosan supplementation has shown to be ineffective at 'binding fat' or improving body composition.

Conjugated linoleic acid (CLA) is a mix of fatty acids that may help to increase muscle and burn fat, but research in these areas have had mixed results so far.

Chromium may have benefits for certain medical conditions, but most studies (200-800 mcg a day for 4-16 weeks) have not suggested it as a useful supplement for athletes.

Hydroxycitric acid (HCA) ($C_6H_8O_8$) is a citric acid derived from a variety of tropical plants, including hibiscus and gambooge, that is claimed to promote fat loss, but research does not support this claim.

Isoflavones, compounds whose derivatives occur in many plants (especially pulses), have not yet shown to be an effective supplement for body composition or performance in exercise, despite the claims.

Nitric oxide (NO) promotes blood and oxygen flow in the body, so some suggest that it may enhance oxygen and nutrient delivery to the muscles, which may in turn provide greater tolerance to exercise, and improve recovery. In studies, untrained and moderately trained athletes have shown better tolerance in aerobic and anaerobic exercise after supplementing with nitric oxide, but highly trained athletes did not gain any positive effects in performance. It is also important to note that most trials have included only young male participants.

L-arginine ($C_6H_{14}N_4O_2$), a DAA, is an amino-acidic precursor to nitric oxide and thus has similar claimed benefits (and for the same reasons) for it. In a 2012-study subjects were given 6g of L-arginine a day but the results were inconclusive; a similar study in 2011 was also inconclusive but it did state that doses less than or equal to 20g were well tolerated and that side-effects were rare in healthy individuals. However, there are a number of serious side-effects associated with high doses, or perhaps even low doses taken long-term, especially for those with diabetes, those who have had a heart attack or those with child; if you decide to try it, seek professional medical advice beforehand.

8.3 Combined supplements

Many supplements are believed to work better in combination with others; indeed, it is often difficult to find research papers on isolated supplements that have the athlete in mind. The supplements most frequently combined with others (or each other) are BCAA, creatine, caffeine, and ephedrine. BCAA taken with carbohydrates as part of the carbohydrate cycle - i.e., before, during and after training, has shown good ergogenic results. Green tea extract with caffeine has shown to be a better fat loss enhancer than when either is taken in isolation.

Creatine has consistently shown to be effective in isolation, but there are data that suggest even better results if combined with carbohydrates or carbohydrate and protein; both combinations increase creatine muscle retention. Creatine has also fared well in ergogenic terms when combined with caffeine or with other supplements. Ephedrine, caffeine and aspirin, known as the ECA stack, is a very popular supplement, and is still legal to buy in the UK. One capsule will normally include 20-30mg of ephedrine (in the form of dried leaves of the ephedra plant) with varying amounts and forms of caffeine and aspirin, and it often includes many other ingredients, including green tea extract, ginger extract and yohimbine. However, this is not uncommon; most combined supplements (and even isolated supplements) are quite different from one manufacturer to another, so it is very difficult for athletes, without professional assistance, to fine-tune supplementation. As already mention in the *Protein* sub-section, it is difficult to tell which ingredients are providing the benefits, and which are the hangers-on. There are seemingly endless way in which supplements can be combined - and certain combinations may prove to be the way forward - but since supplementation in isolation is far from established in most or all cases, it seems that the amounts, timings and precise combinations are somewhat farther away than that.

8.4 Energy drinks

Energy drinks are not used by athletes with even basic sports nutrition knowledge - although research has shown that many athletes have a distinct lack of understanding when it comes to supplementation - because of the ingredients in general, but also because of the abundance of particular ingredients. They consist largely of sugar and caffeine combined with some or all of: guarana, ginseng, ginkgo biloba, vitamins, minerals and anything else that may have the slightest hint of claimed health and/or energy benefits.

Energy drinks are generally unlikely to have any adverse effects on normal, healthy people, but they are often mixed with alcohol or become a binge-drink, in which case they may lead to adverse effects. Athletes should avoid them, especially any time during or either side of training; they can cause irritability, increase blood pressure and dehydration, and the effects of long-term use have not been established. Those on medication or with any medical conditions, especially cardiac-related, should seek the advice of a physician before using them; however, since they are expensive, have no ergogenic benefits, and are potentially harmful, it would seem wiser to simply avoid them altogether.

Though labelled as 'energy' drinks, they rarely contain more than 200kcal a can (most are about 100kcal), and most of these calories come from carbohydrates in the form of sugar. Stranger still are the sugar-free energy drinks - with most not offering more than 20kcal a can (and typically about 10kcal), the term 'energy drink' is a misnomer if ever there were one.

8.5 Supplements and banned substances

It is not uncommon for supplements to contain greater levels of substances than those claimed on the ingredients label; but perhaps more alarmingly, there are many that contain ingredients not on the label at all. These include weight loss supplements, as well as ergogenic aids. A 2006 study of 103 supplements available on the Internet found one creatine product and three 'mental enhancers' that contained traces of hormones and pro-hormones not stated on the label; they also found 14 pro-hormone products that included several more ingredients than indicated on the labels.

Athletes may unwittingly ingest a banned substance that will cause them to fail a urine or blood test, and sometimes these are substances given to them by their nutrition advisor. So if you are involved in competition (professional or amateur), extra care must be taken before ingesting anything; a second opinion is advisable. There is no list of illegal or banned substances to which every country or every sporting body agrees, so no attempt has been made to include one in this text. In any case, things may change, so it is better to check with your sporting organisation; they are not all the same.

8.6 The placebo

During drug trials the subjects are usually given either the real drug or a placebo; the placebo is nothing more than a sugar pill that appears exactly the same as the actual drug on trial, and neither the subjects nor the administrators are aware of which is which. This is known as the 'double-blind' method, and the idea is to eliminate any influence on the results by either the administrator or the subject. On the face of it, such a method might seem a good idea, but there is a strange phenomenon known as the 'placebo effect'; a beneficial effect produced by the placebo, but caused by the subjects 'belief' rather than the properties of the placebo itself. It is so powerful that in medical and psychological trials, two placebos have shown to work better than one, and four better than two. Different coloured placebos, including striped ones, and even package-design have also shown to have different effects, depending on the condition being tested. The placebo is a problem in the medical world, and unfortunately things are no different in the sport-medicine world. Research has shown that motivation and expectancy are greater in many subjects who are on sport-supplement trials, and consequently the results are often significantly affected by unusually enhanced performances by those on placebos.

Any trial results, positive or negative, are always open to the suspicion of the placebo effect - which is one of the many reasons that repeated trials are so important - and there seems to be no easy (or affordable) solution. Some trials are a comparison of two drugs that are already known to have positive effects, and such trials may or may not include a placebo. However, it may not matter, as the placebo effect can occur even in trials that do not use a placebo; the mere fact of being tested may cause a placebo effect in some people. In our view, the placebo effect may run far deeper than just being on a trial or taking a pill.

People may react differently, depending on the administrator; some prefer those of the same or even different nationality, or those with a particular accent. Age, gender, attire and appearance, personality, tone - and even odour - may also be factors. The equipment, environment and general ambience may also affect the subjects performance; newly decorated places, colour schemes, new, old or modern equipment or venues, cleanliness, size, shape, airiness, odour, and location may all have hidden but significant effects on trial results.

With so many variables to consider, it is clearly an impractical task, but that does not mean improvements cannot be made. It might be an idea to administer placebos and the real drug intermittently on the same subjects. For example, a subject on a 12-week trial might take a placebo for week one, the trial drug during weeks two and three, a placebo for the next two weeks, and so on, with each subject on a unique placebo-drug schedule. The drug-placebos sets can be arranged in advance for each subject and delivered by a neutral party; the administrator's job is no different from usual trials.

Another, similar, idea might be for the subjects to administer the drugs for themselves; they have to collect their daily doses from a designated pigeon-hole and each administration is *knowingly* observed on camera by unseen nurses or doctors. Such methods might be better than those already in place, but they will inevitably cost more money. Unfortunately, it seems that profit is taking precedence over anything else by those with the capital and the means to fund such projects.

8.7 Buying supplements

Sport supplements is big business and there are now more sport shops on the high streets and on the Internet than ever before. This certainly makes purchasing supplements convenient, but there are a number of things that need to be borne in mind before doing so. We have already mentioned the problem of supplements containing banned substances and/or substances that are not listed amongst the ingredients, and supplements that contain so many different substances that it becomes difficult to manage intakes, but the concerns do not end here.

Supplements are often sold in large quantities that make them expensive if you want to try them for a short time, and so may turn out to be a complete waste of money if you find that they do not work. They are often sold by unqualified or poorly trained staff who will merrily make unfounded claims for their products, and many such products are tested by the company that is selling them. Furthermore, the claims made for many or all of the individual components may have some authority, but this has no bearing on how such substances would work in combination; comparatively few have been tested properly in this regard, and most combinations have not been tested at all.

Some products do not have any ingredients listed on their labelling, even though they should, which is a particular problem with some herbal products. In such cases you are strongly advised to avoid them, even if offered a free trial sample. Over the years, many conventional medicines have had to be withdrawn owing to later-discovered severe side-effects - even fatalities - despite the years and hundreds of millions of pounds that go in to *each* drug before it is deemed safe for marketing.

Yet, the drug trials of sport supplements are not nearly as rigorous and well-regulated, so be sure to do your own research on any supplement and its supplier before taking them - or better still, consult a qualified sport physician for advice on supplementation and suppliers *(see the **Useful websites for sports nutrition**, page 326).*

Perhaps every athlete wants a magic pill that will increase speed, strength and endurance by a large percentage in a short time and with little or no extra effort in the gym. Yet if such things do exist they may do more harm than good, and they will almost certainly be illegal or banned by sport organisations. Ergogenic aids must be treated as just that, an 'aid', something that helps rather than something that does all the work. In any case, even if some of the available sport supplements do cause significant changes in a short time, these rapid advances will not last; as you improve the changes become far more subtle, and in many cases the gains may eventually cease altogether or even reverse if you overdo it.

9 UPPING THE MASS

In the world of sport, there is as a much a need to increase body mass as there is to decrease it; perhaps more. Some athletes choose to increase their BM, such as boxers who want to fight in higher-weight divisions, whilst others might need to because success in their sport demands it - such as body builders and certain types of rugby player. However, there is also a natural increase in BM that happens as we get older; this is of course safest and easiest, though care needs to be taken to prevent too much of the increase coming by way of excess fat. Many athletes spend too much time and energy fighting with their BM, whether it be increasing or decreasing it, and this can drain athletes to the point that it will affect their performance come the day of the event. There are two other ways of improving your body mass other than the natural increase:

- increasing your fat percentage (not normally a good way)
- increasing your muscle mass (normally the better way)

9.1 Training and increasing BM

Resistance training is considered the most efficient way to stimulate muscle growth. Research has shown that the fastest gains in size and strength seem to be from lifting heavy weights - perhaps between 70 and 80 per cent of your maximum - though a very recent paper suggests that even lifting 30 per cent of your maximum has the same results when lifting until your willpower is exhausted.

A weight might be considered as 'heavy' if you can perform about six to ten repetitions; if you can perform more than this - say ten to twelve repetitions, then your size gains will be less, though still significant.

In weight training there are generally two types of movement regarding the ratio of the muscles involved; the isolated movements and the compound movements. **Isolated movements** concentrate more on one muscle or muscle group, such that about 80 per cent (or more) of the movement targets that muscle; leg extensions and kickbacks for instance. **Compound movements** are those that include at least two highly involved muscle groups with typical ratios of 50:50 and 60:40; for example, the bench press is generally considered a chest exercise, but it has a high proportion of shoulder muscle activity too; perhaps a ratio of 60-40 or 70:30 (depending on the position of the hands on the barbell) in favour of the chest muscles.

To increase your body mass you should concentrate on compound movements that target the bigger muscle groups, such as the quadriceps (thigh muscles) and pectorals (chest muscles). Some examples are:

1. bench press
2. lat pull down
3. dead lifts (lifting a barbell from the floor until standing upright; arms straight throughout)
4. clean and jerks (barbell raised from the floor to overhead in two movements)
5. snatches (as above but in one movement)
6. semi-squats

Items *4.*, *5.* and *6.* need particular care as they require proper training and special equipment; they can also be very dangerous, so supervision is advisable during all such movements. In any case, be sure that you really do need to increase your muscle mass, as there is a fine line between muscle mass increasing your speed and power, and muscle mass slowing you down.

If you exercise a muscle group to exhaustion you need seven days recovery before repeating the same workout or before exercising that same muscle group. So it is better to exercise each muscle group once a week: chest to exhaustion on one day, legs to exhaustion on another, shoulders to exhaustion on yet another day and so on. The pace of your muscle gains depends on the individual, but in general, muscle and strength gains are normally faster in the early stages.

Always aim for a gradual increase in body mass, so do not be tempted to overeat to quicken the increase; it is very important to keep an eye on your composition, as gains of more than 1kg a month could mean the increase is owing to fat as well as muscle, or perhaps just fat. After the initial fast gains, expect body mass increases of no more than half to one kilogramme a month, or about 0.25-1.0 per cent of your body mass a week. If you find that all your efforts are in vain, you may have to graciously concede to nature by accepting that you are genetically unsuitable for a large muscle mass, and continuing the fight may cause more harm than good *(see **9.2, Body types**, below).*

9.2 Expected gain

Apart from your hormone balance, the two main influences on your potential to increase body mass are your genetics and body type. Genetics determine your proportion of fast twitch (type II) and slow twitch (type I) muscle fibres. Fast twitch fibres generate power and increase in mass more readily than slow twitch fibres, so those with a greater amount of fast twitch fibres respond far better and quicker to strength- and muscle-building exercises. Slow twitch cannot be converted into fast twitch, and vice versa; we have what we are born with, which is why some can never become lean heavyweight boxers, and others cannot become long-distance runners.

Body types

There are three body types but we all primarily belong to just one of these: ectomorph, mesomorph and endomorph.

- **Ectomorphs** are naturally slim with long limbs, narrow shoulders and narrow hips, and they tend to have difficulty building muscle mass or storing fat.
- **Mesomorphs** have naturally athletic builds, with wide shoulders and narrow hips, and they normally gain muscle mass easily but not fat.
- **Endomorphs** are naturally stocky, have a rounded build with wide shoulders and hips, and an even distribution of fat; they tend to gain both fat and muscle easily.

9.3 Diet for BM increase

To increase your body mass you will need to consume more calories than you burn. You may either consume an additional fixed number of calories or an additional fixed percentage of your TDEE; the suggestions below are not the only 'figures' used, but most will not deviate too much from them:

1. your TDEE plus an extra 500kcal, or
2. your TDEE plus an extra 20 per cent.

The first suggestions is often favoured owing to its simplicity, but the second suggestion might be preferable as it is more finely tuned to individuals, and as your body mass increases it will change accordingly. In either case, it is probably better to build up to your new intake by daily increases in increments of about 100kcal until you reach your requirement. It might be easier if you eat three substantial meals a day as well as two or three well-chosen snacks.

Wholemeal bread, potatoes, bananas, cream-soups, oils (such as olive, coconut and palm), nuts and seeds are all wholesome foods, particularly for fats and carbohydrates, and useful for increasing body mass. The time between meals and snacks should not exceed three or four hours as this might encourage the breakdown of protein, and slow down glycogen storage; in any case, be sure to avoid large and infrequent meals, as this will produce fluctuations in blood sugar and insulin that will almost certainly result in a reduction of much-needed glycogen stores.

Dietetic method for BM increase

1. Find your TDEE plus 20 per cent.
2. Find your minimum essential carbohydrates intake.
3. Then adjust your protein intake to 1.8-2.0g per kg body mass. The normal strength-training intake is 1.4-1.8g per kg of body mass, but remember that your calories have increased, and therefore your protein needs to increase proportionally.
4. The fat intake should be between 15 and 30 per cent of your new intake (TDEE+20%); there are no generally recommended intakes in terms of g/kg/BM.
5. Sum items 2-4 and subtract the result from the figure obtained at item *1*.
6. Any leftover calories should be made up with good quality carbohydrates, fats or both.

Example

Let's assume that a 70kg, male athlete has a TDEE of about 3000kcal a day, including exercise, and requires a minimum of 5g of carbohydrates per kg of body mass for his sport.

1. TDEE = 3000, so 20 per cent is another 3000 × 0.2 = 600kcal. Summing these gives a total of 3600kcal a day.
2. Minimum essential carbohydrate intake is 5g × 70 = 350g (1400kcal).
3. The protein intake range is 1.8g × 70 and 2.0g × 70 - i.e. 126g to 140g (or 504kcal to 560kcal).
4. The fat intake range is: [0.15 × 3600 = 540kcal] to [0.30 × 3600 = 1080kcal].
5. Items *2.* to *4.* sum to:
   a) 1400 + 504 + 540 = 2444kcal (using the lower values in the ranges).
   b) 1400 + 560 + 1080 = 3040kcal (using the higher values in the ranges)
6. From *5a)* we have 3600 - 2444 = 1156kcal to make up with good quality carbohydrates, fats or both, and from *5b)* we have 3600 - 3040 = 560kcal.

Note: Referring to steps *5a)* and *5b)*, you are not limited to using the two lower values in the range, or the two higher values; these were chosen for simplicity and convenience. You may just as well use any permutation: protein (lower) with fat (lower), protein (lower) with fat (higher), protein (higher) with fat (lower), or protein (higher) with fat (lower). These options are included in the **Excel program**.

As mentioned at the end of *Chapter 5.5.5*, **your TDEE and each of your macronutrient intakes are entirely dependent on your body mass**, so as this changes (increases in this case), it is important to review them regularly, at least until you reach your desired body mass.

9.4 Weight-gain supplements

There are many supplements specifically concerned with 'weight gain', and many are labelled as such so that consumers know they are different from just the usual protein supplements. The problem with weight-gain products is that they are often extremely high in calories - so much so that it may make it difficult to avoid excessive and unwanted fat increases; a single serving could easily constitute over 1200kcal, which would already be way over 20 per cent of a massive 5000kcal.

Furthermore, weight-gain products tend to include many ingredients, including large amounts of vitamins and minerals, and muscle-building substances such as creatine; thus making your intakes all the more difficult to refine, whilst also increasing the risk of adverse effects from hard-to-pinpoint substances.

So if you think you need to supplement your diet whilst trying to increase your body mass, it would be better to choose a suitable protein type and perhaps certain other supplements that have been well-tested for increasing muscle mass, such as creatine. If your protein requirement is too difficult to meet through your diet alone - a common problem for vegans and vegetarians - then you might have little choice but to use a supplement.

10 Women in Training

Despite the chapter title, '*Women* in Training', much of it applies to men as well, especially *Eating disorders*. In general though, this chapter is a compendious look at some of the unique, or more common, issues that affect women athletes: female athlete triad (eating disorders, amenorrhoea and osteoporosis), iron deficiency anaemia, sport anaemia and training when with child.

10.1 Eating disorders

An eating disorder is a distorted pattern of thinking and behaviour about food, and includes a range of clinical conditions that affect people physically, psychologically and socially; they are very much about attitude and behaviour towards food as well as the more obvious consumption of food. The three more common ones are:

- **Anorexia nervosa**: a condition in which individuals employ an extremely restrictive diet often coupled with excessive exercise.
- **Bulimia nervosa**: a condition in which individuals binge-eat and then fast or purge what they have eaten by using laxatives and/or forcing themselves to be sick before the food has been fully digested.
- **Compulsive eating**: a condition in which individuals feel compelled to overeat.

10.1.1 Anorexia nervosa

In the UK, **anorexia nervosa** affects about one in every 250 women and about one in every 2000 men, and it usually develops at around the age of 16 or 17. It commonly leads to osteoporosis, kidney disease and heart failure, and since about 20-30 per cent of people do not respond to treatment, and about five per cent die from malnutrition caused by it, anorexia nervosa is certainly the most serious of the eating disorders. Those who suffer with it are often very difficult to persuade to receive help, or even to admit that they have a problem.

Even when treatment begins, it may take five to six years before they completely recover, and relapses are common. Treatment will include **cognitive behavioural therapy (CBT)**, which aims to rectify a person's attitude and behaviour towards food and eating, but also includes nutritional support and advice with the intention of helping the patient to reach a suitable body mass safely. There is no single cause for anorexia nervosa, but most experts agree that the condition is probably caused by a combination of factors, including psychological, biological and cultural ones. Some individuals have distinct personality traits that may make them more prone to the disease, and certain cultures promote very slim women as an ideal that puts pressure on many young girls (in particular), who may aspire to be such women.

However, 'cultural differences' does not necessarily mean different countries. Anorexia seems to be the least common eating disorder amongst African American adults and adolescents, and in one recent 12-month study, not a single case of anorexia was found among black Caribbean adults. Another study, in 2003, in which nearly 2000 subjects took part in a telephone screening and an in-person diagnostic interview, showed distinct differences between black women's and white women's susceptibility to eating disorders. Fifteen of the white women met the criteria for anorexia nervosa, but not a single black women; 23 white women met the criteria for bulimia nervosa against only four black women, and 27 white women met the criteria for binge-eating against 15 black women.

Other cultural differences have been shown between Japanese women and American women; Japanese women with anorexia, bulimia, or both, appear to have lower levels of drive for thinness and perfectionism than American women. The problem of anorexia is greatly aggravated by malnutrition, as this has a biological effect that causes obsessive behaviour and thinking, which is linked with anorexia nervosa. This creates a vicious cycle; the individual's poor diet continues, thus making these biological effects worse.

10.1.2 Bulimia nervosa

Bulimia nervosa is far more common than anorexia nervosa, and may occur at any age, but usually affects women between the ages of 16 and 40 - though on average it develops at about the age of 18 or 19. There are about 1.6 million people who suffer from bulimia nervosa in the UK, most of whom are women - though a substantial 80,000 of these are men. Although it is very unusual to die from bulimia nervosa, it should still be taken very seriously and professional help should be sought.

Treatment may include CBT, or other psychological treatments, and medication. There are many factors that may cause bulimia nervosa, including a low self-esteem, depression, stress, psychological problems, and even genetics. Some become bulimic because they have a low opinion of themselves and think that becoming slim will lift this. Many binge-eat to make themselves happy, but then guilt and/or fear of becoming fat causes them to regurgitate, so a cycle begins.

Bulimia also seems to be more common in those who have anxiety disorders such as obsessive compulsive disorder and post-traumatic stress disorder. As with anorexia, bulimia may also be caused by cultural pressure, but it may also be linked to genetics; those who have a close relative who has (or had) bulimia seem to be four times more likely to develop it than those who do not.

10.1.3 Binge-eating

Binge-eating is difficult to define, so it is not clear how prevalent it is; however, it seems that it affects men and women equally and that it normally occurs between the ages of 30 and 40. Those who binge-eat regularly often fall into a pattern called the **binge-eating cycle**. Consuming large amounts of high-sugar foods may cause a rise in blood sugar, which will in turn cause the pancreas to release insulin (a hormone that regulates the amount of glucose in the blood), which will cause the blood sugar levels to drop rapidly.

This results in a false message being sent to the brain that more glucose is required; a binge-eater will typically answer this call with more high-sugar foods, and so the cycle begins again. If a binge-eater ingests far more calories than are burned - and this is mostly the case - fat levels will increase, and obesity often results. Obesity may seriously affect health by leading to a number of chronic conditions, including hypertension (high blood pressure), high cholesterol, type 2 diabetes, and heart disease, and it can also shorten your life expectancy by a number of years.

Treatment for binge-eating may include self-help programmes, CBT and medication. There are many factors that may lead to binge-eating, such as depression, stress, anger, boredom, sadness, low self-esteem, skipping meals, and avoiding certain foods.

10.2 Amenorrhoea

Amenorrhoea refers to an abnormal absence of menstruation, whilst **oligomenor-rhoea** refers to abnormally infrequent menstruation. Either of these is cause for concern in girls and women who have gone through puberty, are not pregnant, have not had a hysterectomy or who have not gone through the menopause, and so might be a sign of an underlying health problem.

If you have not had your first period by the age of 14 then you may have **primary amenorrhoea**; if you have ceased having them regularly, then you may have **secondary amenorrhoea**. In either case, you would be well advised to see your doctor. Another type of amenorrhoea, and of particular interest to athletes, is called **hypothalamic amenorrhoea**, which is caused when the part of the brain that regulates the menstrual cycle stops working as it should; it is thought to be prompted by stress and excessive weight loss (often triggered in those with a BMI = 19) or training.

Amenorrhoea is more common in teenage girls and young women, especially those involved in sport, gymnastics and dance; approximately one in 25 women will be affected by amenorrhoea at some point in their lives.

10.3 Osteoporosis

Osteoporosis is a medical condition in which the bones become brittle (hard but liable to fracture or shatter) and fragile (easily fractured or damaged) from loss of density, and typically as a result of hormonal changes or deficiency of calcium or vitamin D. During childhood our bones grow (and repair) very quickly, but as we age, this process slows significantly. In terms of length, bones stop growing between the ages of 16 and 18, but the density continues to increase into our late 20s; from about 35 onwards our density gradually decreases.

Women are more susceptible to osteoporosis than men, largely owing to hormonal changes that affect bone density. Oestrogen is any of a group of steroidal hormones that promote the development and maintenance of female characteristics of the body, and it is essential for healthy bones. After the menopause the levels of oestrogen fall, which may lead to a sudden decrease in bone density; the risk is even higher for those who have gone through the menopause or had a hysterectomy before the age of 45.

The risk is also increased in those who have amenorrhoea for over six months caused by excessive dieting or training. Men may also develop osteoporosis, but the cause is unclear; however, the link might again be hormonal. Testosterone helps to keep bones healthy, and those with low levels of it are at an increased risk of osteoporosis. Not all the causes of osteoporosis are known, but the risk is known to be increased by things such as a low BMI, a family history of it, long periods of inactivity (especially long-term bed rest) and a host of medications and other diseases.

The symptoms are difficult to spot, but common injuries amongst those with osteoporosis are wrist, hip and spinal fractures. If your doctor suspects that you have osteoporosis, or that you might develop it, he may refer you for a bone density scan called a DEXA (dual energy X-ray absorptiometry) scan; a short and painless procedure that measures bone density. The treatment depends on several factors, but it may include medication to strengthen your bones. Some preventative measures include regular exercise, wholesome eating, controlled alcohol intake and not smoking.

10.4 Female athlete triad

The female athlete triad refers to energy availability, menstrual function and bone mineral density (BMD), and the interrelationships amongst them that may lead to eating disorders, functional hypothalamic amenorrhea, and osteoporosis. Each of energy availability, menstruation and BMD is regarded as a continuum of severity from normal/healthy to disease. At the normal end we have optimum bone density and energy availability, and normal menstrual cycle (eumenorrhoea). As this goes from healthy towards the unhealthy end, we have energy deficiency (with or without disordered eating), functional hypothalamic amenorrhoea, and bone density loss, with severe cases known as osteoporosis.

A female athlete can have one, two, or all three parts of the triad. Since the numbers of female athletes have increased, so has the number of incidences of the triad increased, and even though it is more common in athletes, it also occurs in non-athletes. The triad was first mentioned in 1993 by the American College of Sports Medicine, but associations between the three conditions have been observed amongst female athletes long before this. The syndrome is often difficult to recognise, and thus often goes unnoticed until it reaches a more severe stage.

It is important for athletes, parents and coaches to be made aware of female athlete triad for the sake of prevention and suitable intervention. Many researchers strongly suggest that unhealthy weight loss practices be discouraged via rule changes, and that athletes be assessed for the Triad, via annual physical examinations and screening examinations, before any participation in sporting events. It is often suggested that the first aim of any treatment for the Triad is to correct the 'energy availability' component by increasing the energy intake, and reducing and/or ceasing exercise.

However, whilst this might be true, it is also a very specialised area of medicine, and any attempt at self-correction of such a serious condition might be extremely dangerous or even fatal. Regardless of what you might read on the Internet, it is vital that you seek the advice of a doctor or other medical professional before you do anything else - even if you are enquiring on behalf of someone else.

Triad: eating disorders

Many female athletes desperately try to lose weight as a way to improve their athletic performance or appearance, especially for aesthetic or weight-dependent sports, which may lead to an eating disorder. Recent research suggests that females athletes are at least equally at risk from eating disorders as non-athletes, but others suggest it is higher. Anorexics are able to push themselves to exercise, despite feeling exhausted, and they are often very strong-willed and highly driven to succeed; their bodies may adapt by becoming more energy-efficient by metabolism reduction.

However, for all their efforts, performance will eventually fall, owing to continued glycogen and nutrient depletion, and the longer it goes unattended the more serious these health effects will become - they may even be fatal. Eating disorders are higher in female athletes than in male athletes; so much so, that eating disorders in male athletes are in danger of being overlooked. Male athletes at high risk are also those involved in aesthetic or weight-dependent sports; for both genders these are sports that require low body weight, low fat levels, a thin appearance, or a combination of these. Some such sports are:

- ballet
- body building
- cycling
- distance running
- fighting sports
- gymnastics
- horse racing
- ice skating

Research has found that athletes, male and female, have similar characteristics to those with eating disorders:

- obsession
- competitiveness
- perfectionism
- compulsiveness

Warning signs: anorexia nervosa

Physical signs:
- severe weight loss*
- well below average weight*
- periods irregular or stopped completely*
- excess hair on face and arms
- always cold
- sleeping problems
- dry/yellow skin

Psychological signs:
- obsession with food, diet and thinness
- claiming to be fat when clearly thin*
- very scared of weight gain
- low self-esteem
- depression and anxiety

Behavioural signs:
- eating very little
- relentless exercise*
- over-keen interest in calories
- arguing about food*
- refusal to eat in company*
- lying about eating*
- obsessive weighing

Warning signs: bulimia nervosa

Physical signs:
- tooth decay, enamel erosion
- puffy face
- normal weight, then extreme fluctuations*
- abrasions on knuckles, perhaps from self-induced vomiting*
- irregular periods
- muscle cramps/weakness
- frequently dehydrated

Psychological signs:
- low self-esteem
- impulsiveness
- depression and anxiety
- anger
- body dissatisfaction
- fanatical about body image, weight and food*

Behavioural signs:
- bingeing on food, up to 5000kcal (or even more)*
- comfort eating
- withdrawal and guilt after eating
- purging - vomiting and laxative abuse*
- frequent weighing
- disappearing after meals, perhaps to regurgitate food*
- eating in secret*
- may steal food or laxatives

*These are perhaps the stronger of the signs.

Triad: amenorrhoea

Intense exercise and not eating enough calories can lead to a reduction in levels of oestrogen - the hormone that helps to regulate the menstrual cycle - so this may result in amenorrhoea or oligomenorrhoea. Some girls may experience amenorrhoea if they greatly increase their training intensity, and some young girls may never even get their first period if they train very hard. Most studies have shown that amenorrhoea is higher in athletes than in non-athletes. The causes are unclear, though it is believed to be a combination of things:

- low calorie intake
- disordered eating
- intense training before menarche (the first menstrual period)
- high intensity training and volume in general
- low fat levels
- physical and emotional stress

One severe side-effect from amenorrhoea is that it causes a reduction in BMD, which increases risk of early osteoporosis and stress fractures. This is partly owing to low oestrogen and progesterone levels, both of which act directly on bone cells to maintain bone turnover. When hormone levels drop, the breakdown of old bone exceeds the speed of new bone formation, which results in a loss of bone minerals and a loss of BMD. Training therefore, no longer has a positive effect on bone density: it cannot compensate for the negative effects of low oestrogen and progesterone. However, high hydrocortisone levels (cortisol) and poor nutrition may also contribute to a loss in BMD. Hydrocortisone is a steroid hormone released in response to stress; it increases blood sugar, aids in the metabolism of the macronutrients, suppresses the immune system and decreases bone formation. Amenorrhoea has many effects on performance, all of which are linked to low oestrogen levels. These include:

- soft tissue injuries
- stress fractures
- prolonged healing of injuries
- reduced ability to recover from hard training

Triad: osteoporosis

Studies have shown that female elite athletes have a higher BDM than female non-athletes, from as little as three per cent more to over 20 per cent more. However, a combination of low fat, low calories, low calcium and immense training and stress can result in bone thinning, stress fractures and ultimately premature osteoporosis. Gastrointestinal (stomach and intestinal) problems, electrolyte imbalances, kidney and bowel disorders, and depression are also common. Low oestrogen levels and poor nutrition, especially low calcium intake, can lead to osteoporosis, so not getting enough calcium at an early age can have a lasting effect on a woman's BDM later in life.

10.5 Iron deficiency anaemia

There are several types of anaemia, including pernicious anaemia (lack of vitamin B$_{12}$) and folate deficiency anaemia, but the most common type is iron deficiency anaemia (IDA), and is the one we shall be focusing on. IDA is a condition in which there is a deficiency of red cells in the blood caused by a lack of iron, to the extent that haemoglobin levels fall, resulting in pallor (an unhealthy pale appearance) and weariness.

Blood contains a fluid called plasma, which includes three types of cells: white blood cells, which are part of the immune system, red blood cells, which carry oxygen around the body in haemoglobin (a red protein), and platelets that help the blood to clot. Red blood cells are produced in the bone marrow - a soft fatty substance found inside the larger bones - in which millions of new blood cells are produced every day to replace old cells that break down. If there is a lack of red blood cells, then there is necessarily a lack of haemoglobin, so the organs and tissues may not get as much oxygen as they should.

IDA is distinct from **non-anaemic iron deficiency** (sometimes termed **latent iron deficiency**), which refers to depleted iron stores but not a lowering of haemoglobin levels; however, non-anaemic iron deficiency often leads to IDA if left untreated. The most common symptoms of IDA are:

- weariness
- lethargy (lack of energy)
- dyspnoea (shortness of breath)
- palpitations (irregular heartbeats)
- pallor
- mouth ulcers
- dry, flaking nails

Less common symptoms include:

- headaches
- itchiness
- sore tongue
- pica (a desire to eat non-food items such as ice, paper or clay)

The most common cause of IDA in men is bleeding in the stomach or intestines; it is also the most common cause in women who have been through the menopause. The acid in your stomach usually aids digestion, but if there is too much it can damage your stomach lining and cause stomach ulcers; these are open sores that may occasionally bleed, and in some cases the blood from the ulcers will appear in vomit or stools.

The most common cause of IDA in pre-menopausal women is menstruation and pregnancy. In most cases, only those with particularly heavy menstruation (menorrhagia) will develop IDA, but it is very common in pregnant women. During pregnancy a woman's body needs extra iron so that her baby will have a sufficient blood supply and adequate oxygen and nutrients.

This is why many pregnant women require iron supplements, especially from the 20th week of pregnancy. There are many other conditions or situations that may cause IDA, including inflammatory bowel disease, oesophagitis (inflammation of the gullet), blood donations, excessive nose bleeds, haematuria (blood in the urine), mal-absorption of iron, coeliac disease (chronic failure to digest) and certain cancers.

Athletes and IDA

Iron is vital to the athlete as it plays an important role in energy utilisation and the delivery of oxygen to muscles, so inadequate levels will affect performance because the maximum oxygen intake will be less. Since the body has no natural way to replace iron that is lost owing to exertion, it is important that dietary intakes complement the intensity of training.

Such loses may be great, for example; during exertion an athlete's visceral blood flow (the blood flow in the internal organs) may be reduced by more than 50 per cent, and continued training may aggravate these losses to the extent that iron deficiency anaemia occurs. There are many contributors to an athlete's iron losses, but the main ones seem to be gastrointestinal bleeding, haematuria, perspiration and haemolysis.

Iron loss and exercise

IDA will, by definition, mean a reduction in the amount of oxygen being carried to the muscles, thus lowering endurance and increasing fatigue; however, it remains inconclusive as to whether latent iron deficiency will limit exercise capacity. It is not unusual for an athlete to incur **gastrointestinal bleeding** from strenuous exercise, as even minor damage to the stomach and intestinal lining may cause this, but such bleeding may also occur from regular use of anti-inflammatory drugs, such as ibuprofen. These days, many athletes use anti-inflammatory drugs for pain relief, especially before and during endurance events, and after exercise in general.

Haematuria may occur from exercise-induced trauma in the glomerulus (a cluster of nerve endings or blood vessels, especially of the kidney) or of **haemolysis** (the rupture or destruction of red blood cells); for this condition the urine will have a cloudy appearance. Iron is also lost through **perspiration**, and athletes with high perspiration rates may consequently have higher iron losses; furthermore, such losses may also be cumulative if the training is prolonged or if multiple sessions are involved. **Haemolysis** has been observed in a variety of exercises, including swimming, cycling, running and weight training; for this condition the urine will have a light-pink appearance.

Any form of training that includes strong muscle contractions may cause compression in the blood vessels, which may result in haemolysis. But it seems that haemolysis is usually caused by hard and repeated pounding of the feet on hard surfaces, often coupled with a poor running gait and unsuitable footwear. However, foot-strike haemolysis has very recently been contested. In 2012, a study of foot-strike haemolysis on 60-km ultra-marathon runners concluded that running does not change levels of haemoglobin, haematocrit (a measure of the percentage of red blood cells against the total blood volume), red blood cell count or even potassium concentration.

Other causes of iron loss or iron deficiency that are peculiar to athletes are **bladder movement** caused by exercise, low calorific intakes, vegetarian diets, diarrhoea, and exercise in general. Excessive bladder movement caused by pounding-type exercise, such as running or jumping, may result in bleeding of the bladder's interior wall. The recommended 14.8mg of iron a day for women is difficult to attain on a so-called **average 2000kcal**; female athletes may need nearer 3000kcal a day to meet the necessary intake, especially if their diet does not include any of the richer sources of iron.

Moreover, the problem is even harder for female vegetarians since their diet will be typically low in iron and/or may contain iron that is difficult for the digestive system to absorb. It may seem that those with **amenorrhoea** should have a lower chance of iron deficiency, but studies show that this is not the case. Indeed, those with amenorrhoea actually have a greater risk, perhaps owing to their typically low calorie diets. Up to 85 per cent of **endurance runners have blood in their faeces** after an event, resulting in a fairly significant amount of iron loss - women that run even as little as eight to ten kilometres a day lose twice as much blood in their stools as do non-exercising women.

The very act of **exercising seems to impair the absorption of iron**; for example, iron-deficient runners may absorb only 16 per cent of dietary iron, whereas iron-deficient sedentary people may absorb 30 per cent. Since iron deficiency is so common amongst female athletes (and women in general), it is advisable that they have their iron levels checked at least once a year, and in good time before any major sporting event.

Dilutive pseudo-anaemia (sport anaemia)

An athlete's iron status should not be judged by one-off blood tests, especially if taken soon after hard training as this results in a significant increase in the volume of plasma in the blood, which dilutes the concentration of haemoglobin and red blood cells. Consequently, the subject may be wrongly diagnosed as anaemic even though the iron levels are normal. This occurrence is called dilutive 'pseudo-anaemia' in the medical field, but is commonly referred to as sport-anaemia (or sports anaemia) amongst athletes; it is usually short-term, often occurring in those new to training or in those involved in heavy training.

Pseudo-anaemia does not require or respond to iron supplementation, and is unlikely to affect performance; only those who actually have IDA (not pseudo-anaemia) need and respond to iron supplementation. If anything, the raised blood plasma levels are a sign of increased fitness, since the blood will be flowing more easily and thus increasing the efficiency of the heart. Even moderate, regular jogging may increase blood plasma by five per cent, and elite endurance athletes may have an increase of a massive 20 per cent.

Iron supplements

There seems to be no evidence to suggest that iron supplementation will improve performance in those with normal iron levels, so it is inadvisable to take them without having first consulted a sport physician or other suitably qualified professional. In a recent 2010 study, 170 marathon runners were observed for iron levels; 28 per cent of the female runners were iron deficient, but over 16 per cent of the male runners had signs of iron overload. This highlights a common difference between male and female athletes; male athletes often think more is better, whereas female athletes often limit daily calorie intakes (and consequently nutrient intakes) because of weight concerns.

Iron in foods

The most abundant sources of iron are found in dried herbs, particularly thyme (124mg per 100g) and parsley (98mg per 100g), and both are also very high in fibre, protein and most vitamins and minerals - but notably in vitamin C; dried thyme contains about 50mg per 100g, and dried parsley contains about 122mg per 100g. Dried cocoa powder also contains very high levels of iron - about 36mg per 100g, though it is much lower in a typical bar of dark chocolate.

Nonetheless, there is a distinct lack of research into how well these sources of iron are absorbed by people; having a high content is pointless if it is not readily absorbed. Studies that included herbal infusions and plant drugs have not shown good absorption rates, so until there is further research, it is the iron found in liver and other ferrous (animal sources) forms that will continue to be considered as the richest and most easily absorbed.

The most abundant ferrous form of iron is found in duck liver, at about 30mg per 100g, followed by pork liver at about 18mg per 100g, and chicken liver at about 13mg per 100g. However, pork liver may be the best of these, as it contains the most vitamin C and protein (though only slightly more protein than chicken liver), and the least amount of sodium, cholesterol and saturated fat. Meat, fish and poultry are also generally rich and easily absorbed sources of iron.

There are, of course, iron supplements, though these are less easily absorbed, and ferric forms (plant sources), which contain much lower levels and are also less easily absorbed. Iron is far better absorbed if taken with a rich source of vitamin C, which is why it is often recommended that iron supplementation be complemented with vitamin C supplementation - usually on an empty stomach, as this will further enhance absorption. However, supplementing in this way seems pointless unless you have a particular reason why you cannot meet the daily iron requirements through food sources that will, if chosen with care, include many other important nutrients.

If you are a vegetarian, some iron-rich comestibles include: wholegrain (such as brown rice), dried fruits (especially tomatoes and apricots), sesame and sunflower seeds, beans and most dark-green leafy vegetables such as curly kale and watercress. Many believe that spinach is a good source of iron, but it contains substances that inhibit iron absorption so it is not a good source, even though its iron content is quite high. There are several known inhibitors of iron absorption, including tannins (bitter-tasting substances found in some foods and drinks, such as berries, chocolate, tea and wine), bran and high-calcium products.

Since tea is drunk so frequently and in so many countries, and is where much research has been focussed, it is well to concentrate here. The idea that tea inhibits iron absorption is not new, though it has fairly recently become contentious. In a 2008-study, a group of young Indian women were observed for the effects of tea-drinking in relation to iron absorption. The results in both the control subjects and those with IDA showed that two cups of tea decreased iron absorption more than just one cup, though both showed significant decreases. In the same study, iron absorption increased proportionally and significantly, according to the ratio of vitamin C to iron ingested.

However, in the same year, a study of black South African women showed that black tea consumption did not affect iron status; the same results were obtained from other studies in western populations that had adequate iron stores. The relationship between tea-drinking and iron absorption may be cultural or related to different ethnic groups; in the UK, for example, many of those with Indian or Indian sub-continental backgrounds have shown to have higher rates of iron deficiency.

However, it may simply be down to the timing of when tea (and perhaps other inhibitors) is consumed, and with what. A 2004 review suggested that those at risk of iron deficiency should drink tea between meals, and should wait at least one hour after eating to drink tea, rather than unnecessarily omitting tea entirely from their diet. Those who do not have a risk of iron deficiency need no such restrictions on tea drinking.

Cooking food in iron pans is another way to significantly increase the iron content of your food - as much as 44 times more than food cooked in aluminium utensils. In one study, the iron content of spaghetti sauce increased from less than 1mg per serving to nearly 6mg, and apple sauce went from 0.35mg to about 7.3mg per serving. Therefore, care should be taken if the food is going to be served to very young children, as their iron needs are much lower than adults, and consequently their risk of overdosing is far higher. Apart from vitamin C, other enhancers of iron absorption include fructose, and the amino acids cysteine, lysine and histidine.

10.6 Training and pregnancy

Many female athletes suffer a loss of normal menstrual function, which in turn may affect their fertility, especially those involved in hard training. However, normal menstrual function and fertility can usually be corrected by simply adopting a more appropriate, less intense, training programme, and by consuming a balanced energy intake. Dieting or even strict control of your weight gain during pregnancy is not recommended unless on the advice of your doctor.

During pregnancy you will need extra nutrients to ensure the health of you and your baby. At the other extreme, obesity might hinder fertility or cause other health problems during pregnancy. A BMI of more than 30 increases the health risks to both you and your baby, including miscarriage, high blood pressure, blood clots and genital and urine infection. It can also cause haemorrhage after the birth, as well as problems with breast-feeding, babies born with high birth weights, premature births, and stillbirths. Furthermore, more than half of the women who die during pregnancy are overweight or obese.

Continued training during pregnancy is fine (indeed, advisable), but depending on your particular training programme, you will probably need to gradually reduce the frequency and intensity, especially during the final trimester, as this is when your weight increase is highest, and of course there will be other physiological changes to consider. Active and fit women cope better with their changing weight, and seem better able to deal with giving birth and getting back into shape afterwards.

Some exercises to avoid, though, are those that include high trauma to the body or high risks of falling, such as horse riding, gymnastics, contact sports and cycling. Any activities that include high pressure to the body, such as scuba diving, and those at high altitudes (more than 2500 metres), must also be avoided. Exercise that includes lying on your back, especially after the 16th week of pregnancy, is also inadvisable because this may cause you to feel faint.

Some good exercises include yoga, light weight training, swimming, stretching, walking and the more gentle aspects of t'ai chi ch'uan. Training should be further reduced and then completely ceased (gradually) during the last few weeks of pregnancy, as advised by your doctor.

The total weight gained during pregnancy depends on your body mass before pregnancy, though as an idea, those of normal BMI (less than 25 and more than or equal to 18.5) should put on a total of between 11kg and 16kg, including about 0.4-0.5kg a week during the second and third trimesters. However, there are no such official figures in the UK, and there are many factors involved, so the best advice is to consult your obstetrician.

Calorie intake during pregnancy

The Department of Health (DoH) recommends no change during the first two trimesters for the general population, but athletes may need to adjust their intakes during these times if training is being reduced substantially. During the third trimester the DoH recommends an extra 200 calories be consumed a day, but this applies only to those who are not under-eating or over-eating.

That apart, some sports nutritionists question whether this is necessary, since as an athlete you should have already taken into account the changing needs of calorie intakes, so simply adding on a fixed amount may not apply. Once again, such advice should come only from a sport physician, especially if are involved in very demanding activities.

General dietary advice

Consume:
- foods rich in omega-3 and omega-6
- daily folic acid supplements of 400 mcg, as it reduces the risk of neural tube defects - these should be taken from the time you stop contraception until the 12th week of pregnancy
- foods rich in fibre
- replace high-fat foods with 'five-a-day' fruit and vegetables
- eat a wholesome breakfast
- monitor your portion sizes and meal frequency with care

Avoid consumption of:

- alcohol, especially during the first trimester
- fried foods
- comestibles high in sugars and fats
- vitamin A supplements
- any fish liver oil supplements
- liver (including liver pâté)
- mould-ripened soft cheeses such a brie and camembert, and blue-veined cheese to reduce the risk of listeria poisoning (a type of bacteria that makes people sick if they eat infected food)
- eggs, or at least make sure they are not raw or lightly cooked, to reduce the risk of salmonella poisoning

Care must also be taken with many other supplements and herbal foodstuffs, as many carry warnings against consumption for those who are pregnant, so make sure you read the label thoroughly. However, the simplest and safest thing to do is to seek professional medical advice before consuming anything you are unsure about.

11 Competition Fuel

This short summary chapter covers all the essential intakes for a variety of events - from one week before, to the moments just after the occasion. It is very important to have read all the preceding chapters before this one, as the information herein is extremely vague, and could so easily be misunderstood.

11.1 The week before

The main aims one week before are to:

- fill muscles and the liver with glycogen stores so you can compete with a full supply
- keep adequately hydrated

11.1.1 Short duration events: four minutes or less

Such events are fuelled by ATP-PC and muscle glycogen. Training that might cause muscle-fibre damage should be scheduled earlier in the week, and at a lower-than-normal intensity, or avoided altogether. Such training includes:

- hard running
- sparring/bag work
- weight training

Make sure you consume your required daily carbohydrate intakes (*see 2.3*).

11.1.2 Endurance events: lasting longer than 90 minutes

Your carbohydrate intake should be moderate:

- 8-12g per kg of BM, 36-72 hours before the event

11.1.3 Endurance events: up to 90 minutes, or multiple heats

Taper your training in the final week so that the intensity decreases as you approach the competition day. Make sure you maintain (or increase to):

- 8-12g of CHO per kg of BM during the final three days

11.1.4 Weekly events

Lower the intensity during the two days before the event, and taper your training prior only to the most important competition, such as a cup final. Increase, or maintain, your carbohydrate intake during the final two days to:

- 8-12g of CHO per kg of BM during the final three days

11.1.5 All events in general

Your total calorie intake should remain the same as normal during the pre-competition week, unless your pre-competition week is tapered or is training-free. In this case, match your energy requirements by lowering your intake accordingly. In any case, whether your calorie intakes remain the same or not, the proportions of carbohydrates, protein and fat are likely to change. Make sure you do not leave a gap of more than three hours between each meal/snack.

11.2 The day before

During your pre-competition week you should have adequately filled your liver and muscles with glycogen stores if that was what the event required, and you should also have adequately hydrated. All you now have to do is maintain these; so remain adequately hydrated and ensure that your glycogen stores are topped up by consuming high-carbohydrate foods:

- Keep to low-GL meals throughout the day.
- Do not skip your evening meal or snack (even if you are having pre-competition nerves), as this is an important time for topping up muscle glycogen stores.
- Keep to simple and familiar foods.
- Avoid all fatty or oily foods.
- Absolutely no alcohol.

11.2.1 Pre-competition nerves

This often occurs and can reduce the appetite and also cause nausea, diarrhoea and stomach cramps. If solid food is impossible, try light meals, MRP, sport drinks, smoothies or similar. Avoid any unfamiliar foods or anything that you know may aggravated anxiety, and **do not eat high-fibre foods, any flatulence-causing vegetables or other foods such as:**

- cabbage
- cauliflower
- sprouts
- broccoli
- diet products

11.3 On the day

Have your pre-competition meal one-to-four hours prior to the event if possible.

- **1-4g of carbohydrates per kg of BM**

This will allow time for the stomach to empty and for blood sugar levels to normalise, and it will also top up liver glycogen stores. If you are quite nervous, then perhaps your pre-competition meal should be consumed nearer four hours prior to the event, because nerves can hinder digestion. The exact timing is an individual thing; you will have to find this out for yourself. Aim to:

- keep your liver and muscle glycogen stores topped up
- maintain blood-sugar levels
- keep hunger at bay
- keep adequately hydrated

11.3.1 Meal on the day

Observe the following as general advice throughout the day:

- low GL
- low fat, low protein and low-to-moderate fibre
- high carbohydrates
- eat little and eat slowly
- avoid anything salty or spicy
- keep to familiar foods
- keep to easily digestible foods
- adequate and appropriate fluids

11.3.2 Just before competition time

Suitable time just before the event (depends on the individual):

- 1-4g of carbohydrates per kg of BM
- about 5-7ml of appropriate fluid per kg of BM in temperate conditions

11.4 During events

Avoid high-fructose drinks, as they are not absorbed as fast as sucrose, glucose or glucose polymers, and have been known to cause stomach upsets.

For events lasting longer than 60 minutes:

- consume 30-60g of CHO per kg of BM per hour (depending on intensity).
- drink *ad libitum.*

11.4.1 Between events

Intake as follows:

- Take 50-75g of carbohydrates as soon as possible, certainly within the 45 minutes immediately after the event.
- Continue at a rate of 1-1.5g per kg BM for the next few hours or until your next event.
- Drink appropriate fluids *ad libitum.*

11.5 Post competition

Ensure that you replenish your fluid losses, and your muscle and liver glycogen stores:

- Take 50-75g of carbohydrates as soon as possible, certainly within the 45 minutes immediately after the event.
- Continue at a rate of 1-1.5g per kg BM for the next few hours or until your next meal.

After a competition, especially a successful one, athletes tend to feel hyperactive. There will have been much build-up and then… it is suddenly all over! So it is always a good idea to relax completely for a few days after an event… *if you can?*

Appendix A - Alternative RMR calculations

Harris-Benedict BMR

Male BMR = 66 + (13.7 × BM in kg) + (5 × height in cm) - (6.8 × age in years*)

Female BMR = 665 + (9.6 × BM in kg) + (1.8 × height in cm) - (4.7 × age in years*)

*Age in years is normally whole number years, but using decimal numbers (e.g., 27.5 years old) is also acceptable, and a little more accurate.

Simple RMR method

Male: (BM in kg) × 24 = kcal a day.

Female: (BM in kg) × 23 = kcal a day.

Total energy expenditure calculation

Multiply your RMR (using the standard calculation) by the appropriate factor (see table below)

		Activity factors	
Level	Activity intensity	Male	Female
1	**very light**: mainly sitting and standing activities	1.3	1.3
2	**light**: walking 5 km an hour, golf, child care, house cleaning	1.6	1.3
3	**moderate**: walking 5.5-6.5 km an hour, cycling, tennis, dance	1.7	1.6
4	**heavy**: manual digging, football, climbing, squash	2.1	1.9
5	**exceptional**: competing in professional athletic activities	2.4	2.2

Example:

Consider a 24-year-old female who has a BM of 54kg and plays football regularly. Her total daily energy expenditure would be:

(14.7 × 54 + 496) × 1.9 = 2451kcal.

Appendix B - Cardiac Output (CO)

The cardiac output is the volume of blood pumped by the heart, in a particular ventricle, per minute. It is the product of the **stroke volume** (SV) and the resting heart rate (HR):

$$CO = SV \times HR$$

Where the stroke volume is the difference of the end-diastolic volume (EDV) and the end-systolic volume (ESV):

$$SV = (EDV) - (ESV)$$

Systolic refers to the contraction of the heart when blood is pumped into the arteries. Diastolic refers to the period between two contractions of the heart, when the heart relaxes and allows the chambers to fill with blood. Men normally have higher stroke volumes because they have larger hearts in general, but there are many other factors too. Certainly an active female could have a higher stroke volume than a sedentary male, for instance. An average healthy adult male who weighs 70kg will typically have an EDV = 120ml, and an ESV = 50ml, so his stroke volume would be:

$$SV = 120 - 50 = 70ml$$

With 70ml of blood ejected with each heartbeat at 70 bpm, we get a cardiac output of:

$$CO = 70 \times 70 = 4900ml/min$$

This is typical for an average adult male, but the CO could go up to and above 30,000ml per minute (30 litres) during extreme aerobic exercise.

In healthy, but non-exercising people, a cardiac increase will normally be due to an increase in heart rate, which typically ranges from 50-100 bmp (athletes will have a different range, perhaps 30-60 bmp). However, the stroke volume can also vary, the normal range is from 70-120ml. Aerobic exercise may increase stroke volume, which results in a lower resting heart rate and therefore an improved RMR.

Recommended Reading

1 Human Energy

Energy storage

http://www.ncbi.nlm.nih.gov/pubmed/22253914 (2012)

Increasing dietary fat elicits similar changes in fat oxidation and markers of muscle oxidative capacity in lean and obese humans

In lean humans, increasing dietary fat intake causes an increase in whole-body fat oxidation and changes in genes that regulate fat oxidation in skeletal muscle, but whether this occurs in obese humans isnot known... In response to an isoenergetic increase in dietary fat, whole-body fat oxidation similarly increases in LN and OB, in association with a shift towards oxidative metabolism in skeletal muscle, suggesting that the ability to adapt to an acute increase in dietary fat is not impaired in obesity.

http://www.ncbi.nlm.nih.gov/pubmed/16725163 (2006)

Effects of (-)-hydroxycitrate on net fat synthesis as de novo lipogenesis

We conclude that an experimental condition resulting in DNL in humans was created and that treatment with HCA during overfeeding with carbohydrates may reduce DNL.

http://www.ncbi.nlm.nih.gov/pubmed/15592484 (2004)

Concept of fat balance in human obesity revisited with particular reference to de novo lipogenesis

Although the numerous factors (mostly exogenous) influencing DNL have been studied, in particular the effect of CHO overfeeding, there is little information on the rate of DNL in habitual conditions of life, that is, large day-to-day fluctuations of CHO intakes, different types of CHO ingested with different glycemic indexes, alcohol combined with excess CHO intakes, etc.

http://www.ncbi.nlm.nih.gov/pubmed/10919929 (2000)

Macronutrient disposal during controlled overfeeding with glucose, fructose, sucrose, or fat in lean and obese women

Of the excess carbohydrate, 74% was oxidized; there were no significant differences between the various O(cho) treatments. O(fat) stimulated fat oxidation by 18% and suppressed carbohydrate oxidation. On average, 12% of the excess energy was stored as glycogen and 88% as fat; there was no significant difference between overfeeding treatments.

http://www.ncbi.nlm.nih.gov/pubmed/7598063 (1995)

Fat and carbohydrate overfeeding in humans: different effects on energy storage

Carbohydrate overfeeding produced progressive increases in carbohydrate oxidation and total energy expenditure resulting in 75-85% of excess energy being stored. Alternatively, fat overfeeding had minimal effects on fat oxidation and total energy expenditure, leading to storage of 90-95% of excess energy. Excess dietary fat leads to greater fat accumulation than does excess dietary carbohydrate, and the difference was greatest early in the overfeeding period.

Alcohol

http://www.ncbi.nlm.nih.gov/pubmed/15730339 (2012)

Interaction between alcohol and exercise: physiological and haematological implications

Although the effects of alcohol consumption on the rheological properties of the blood are not known, recent experimental evidence suggests that alcohol use following exercise is associated with unfavourable changes in the main determinants of blood viscosity. It is well documented that alcohol use modulates the immune system and impairs host defence. Compelling evidence is also mounting to suggest that chronic alcohol use is linked with adverse effects on the body systems and organs including the brain, the cardiovascular system and the liver.

http://www.ncbi.nlm.nih.gov/pubmed/18369928 (2008)

Assessing effects of alcohol consumption on protein synthesis in striated muscles

The dynamic balance of proteins in striated muscle is dependent upon rates of protein synthesis and protein degradation. We have shown that protein synthesis is depressed in striated muscle after either acute alcohol intoxication or chronic alcohol ingestion.

http://www.ncbi.nlm.nih.gov/pubmed/18334613 (2008)

Acute and chronic ethanol consumption differentially impact pathways limiting hepatic protein synthesis

Ethanol-induced inhibition of hepatic protein synthesis is not rapidly reversed by cessation of ethanol consumption. In conclusion, sustained eIF2alpha phosphorylation is a hallmark of excessive alcohol intake leading to inhibition of protein synthesis. Enhanced phosphorylation of eIF2alpha represents a unique response of liver to alcohol intoxication, because the ethanol-induced elevation of eIF2alpha(P) is not observed in skeletal muscle or heart.

http://www.ncbi.nlm.nih.gov/pubmed/17602031 (2007)

The athlete with muscular cramps: clinical approach

Cramps also may occur as a side effect of certain drugs (e.g., lipid-lowering agents, antihypertensives, beta-agonists, insulin, oral contraceptives, alcohol).

http://www.ncbi.nlm.nih.gov/pubmed/15730339 (2005)

Interaction between alcohol and exercise: physiological and haematological implications

It is well documented that alcohol use modulates the immune system and impairs host defence. Compelling evidence is also mounting to suggest that chronic alcohol use is linked with adverse effects on the body systems and organs including the brain, the cardiovascular system and the liver.

Energy systems

http://www.ncbi.nlm.nih.gov/pubmed/16138786 (2005)

Multiple sprint work : physiological responses, mechanisms of fatigue and the influence of aerobic fitness

Despite years of investigation, limitations in analytical techniques combined with methodological differences between studies have left many issues regarding the physiological response to multiple sprint work unresolved. As such, multiple sprint work provides a rich area for future applied sports science research.

http://www.ncbi.nlm.nih.gov/pubmed/12238940 (2002)

Factors affecting the rate of phosphocreatine resynthesis following intense exercise

Within the skeletal muscle cell at the onset of muscular contraction, phosphocreatine (PCr) represents the most immediate reserve for the rephosphorylation of adenosine triphosphate (ATP). As a result, its concentration can be reduced to less than 30% of resting levels during intense exercise. As a fall in the level of PCr appears to adversely affect muscle contraction, and therefore power output in a subsequent bout, maximising the rate of PCr resynthesis during a brief recovery period will be of benefit to an athlete involved in activities which demand intermittent exercise.... results from studies...have been somewhat inconsistent with respect to the relationship between aerobic power and PCr recovery following intense exercise.

http://www.ncbi.nlm.nih.gov/pubmed/11219498 (2001)

The relationship between aerobic fitness and recovery from high intensity intermittent exercise

In summary, the literature suggests that aerobic fitness enhances recovery from high intensity intermittent exercise through increased aerobic response, improved lactate removal and enhanced PCr regeneration.

http://www.ncbi.nlm.nih.gov/pubmed/8964751 (1996)

Contribution of phosphocreatine and aerobic metabolism to energy supply during repeated sprint exercise

These data suggest that aerobic metabolism provides a significant part (approximately 49%) of the energy during the second sprint, whereas PCr availability is important for high power output during the initial 10 s.

http://www.ncbi.nlm.nih.gov/pubmed/1324108 (1992)

Fatigue and changes of ATP, creatine phosphate, and lactate during the 400-m sprint

It was concluded that after 200 m the speed of running decreased, although CP was not depleted and lactate concentration was not at maximum level. Complete fatigue occurred when CP stores were depleted and B-La and M-La attained an individual maximum.

http://www.ncbi.nlm.nih.gov/pubmed/3471061 (1986)

Muscle fatigue and lactic acid accumulation

Lactic acid is formed and accumulated in the muscle under conditions of high energy demand, rapid fluctuations of the energy requirement and insufficient supply of O_2. During intense exercise sustained to fatigue muscle pH decreases to about 6.4-6.6… Muscle fatigue is thus considered to be due to an insufficient rate of ADP rephosphorylation resulting in a block in the activation process or in the excitation/contraction coupling.

VO2 Max

http://www.ncbi.nlm.nih.gov/pubmed/22262016 (2012)

Evaluation of the American College of Sports Medicine submaximal treadmill running test for predicting Vo2 max

In conclusion, the ACSM equation provides a reasonably good estimation of Vo2 max with no difference in predictive accuracy between P Vo2 max-2 and P Vo2 max-All, and hence, either approach may be equally useful in tracking an individual's aerobic fitness over time. However, if a precise knowledge of Vo2 max is required, then it is recommended that this be measured directly.

http://www.ncbi.nlm.nih.gov/pubmed/18390918 (2008)

How did A V Hill understand the Vo2 max and the 'plateau phenomenon'? Still no clarity?

A recent editorial in Medicine and Science in Sports and Exercise concludes that the study of Hawkins and colleagues confirms 'beyond any doubt the proposition of Hill and Lupton'. It is not clear which of Hill and Lupton's propositions have been proved 'beyond any doubt'.

http://www.ncbi.nlm.nih.gov/pubmed?term=Limiting%20factors%20for%20 maximum%20oxygen%20uptake%20and%20determinants%20of%20endurance%20performance (2000)

Limiting factors for maximum oxygen uptake and determinants ofendurance performance

In the exercising human, maximal oxygen uptake (Vo2 max) is limited by the ability of the cardiorespiratory system to deliver oxygen to the exercising muscles.

http://www.ncbi.nlm.nih.gov/pubmed?term=Familial%20aggregation%20
ofV%CB%99O2%20max%20response%20to%20exercise%20training%3A%20
results%20from%20the%20HERITAGE%20Family%20Study (1999)

Familial aggregation of VO(2max) response to exercise training: results from the HERITAGE Family Study

We conclude that the trainability of VO(2max) is highly familial and includes a significant genetic component.

http://www.ncbi.nlm.nih.gov/pubmed/9140894 (1997)

Maximal oxygen uptake: 'classical' versus 'contemporary' viewpoints

The traditional view of Vo2 max owes a great deal to the work of A V Hill, who conducted experiments on exercising man in Manchester, England, in the 1920s... After carefully reviewing the evidence on both sides of the issue, we conclude that the older 'classical' Vo2 max paradigm of A V Hill is the correct one.

Muscle types

http://www.ncbi.nlm.nih.gov/pubmed/21760934 (2011)

A new method for non-invasive estimation of human muscle fiber type composition

This quick method provides a valid alternative for the muscle biopsy method. In addition, this technique may also contribute to the diagnosis and monitoring of many conditions and diseases that are characterized by an altered muscle fiber type composition.

http://www.ncbi.nlm.nih.gov/pubmed/21936292 (2011)

Common errors in textbook descriptions of muscle fiber size in nontrained humans

Exercise science and human anatomy and physiology textbooks commonly report that type IIB muscle fibers have the largest cross-sectional area of the three fiber types. These descriptions of muscle fiber sizes do not match with the research literature examining muscle fibers in young adult nontrained humans. For men, most commonly type IIA fibers were significantly larger than other fiber types (six out of 10 cases across six different muscles). For women, either type I, or both I and IIA muscle fibers were usually significantly the largest (five out of six cases across four different muscles).

http://www.ncbi.nlm.nih.gov/pubmed/21362056 (2011)

Effects of resistance training on endurance capacity and muscle fiber composition in young top-level cyclists

In conclusion, concurrent strength/endurance training in young elite competitive cyclists led to an improved 45-min time-trial endurance capacity that was accompanied by an increased proportion of type IIA muscle fibers and gains in MVC and RFD, while capillarization remained unaffected.

http://www.ncbi.nlm.nih.gov/pubmed/18535124 (2008)

Single muscle fiber contractile properties of young competitive distance runners

These data indicate that highly trained endurance runners have elevated contraction velocity in both slow and fast twitch myofibers. These characteristics of the fast twitch muscle fibers have not been previously reported in competitive endurance athletes and may contribute to the high level of running performance in these athletes.

http://www.ncbi.nlm.nih.gov/pubmed/10769046 (2000)

Fiber type composition of the vastus lateralis muscle of young men and women

Six fiber types (I, IC, IIC, IIA, IIAB, and IIB) were classified... for the major fiber types (I, IIA, and IIB)... With the exception of fiber Type IC, no significant differences were found between men and women for muscle fiber type distribution... the cross-sectional area of all three major fiber types was larger for the men compared to the women. In addition, the Type IIA fibers were the largest for the men, whereas the Type I fibers tended to be the largest for the women.

http://www.ncbi.nlm.nih.gov/pubmed/7493202 (1995)

Human aging, muscle mass, and fiber type composition

These results indicate a gradual decrease in size/volume with advancing age, accompanied by a replacement by fat and connective tissue. This aging atrophy seems to be due to a reduction in both number and size of muscle fibers, mainly of type 2, and is to some extent caused by a slowly progressive neurogenic process.

Fatigue

http://www.ncbi.nlm.nih.gov/pubmed/22514538 (2012)

Fatigue is a Brain-Derived Emotion that Regulates the Exercise Behavior to Ensure the Protection of Whole Body Homeostasis

The fatigue increasing more rapidly than the amount of work done saves us from the injury which lesser sensibility would involve for the organism so that 'muscular fatigue also is at bottom an exhaustion of the nervous system'. It has taken more than a century to confirm Mosso's idea that both the brain and the muscles alter their function during exercise and that fatigue is predominantly an emotion, part of a complex regulation, the goal of which is to protect the body from harm.

http://www.ncbi.nlm.nih.gov/pubmed/21425889 (2011)

Interactive processes link the multiple symptoms of fatigue in sport competition

Based on this understanding, we reinforce the proposal that fatigue is best described globally as an exercise-induced decline of performance as this is inclusive of all view-points.

http://www.ncbi.nlm.nih.gov/pubmed/21425886 (2011)

Is it time to retire the A V Hill Model?: A rebuttal to the article by Professor Roy Shephard

I now include evidence from more than 30 studies, which, in my opinion, can only be interpreted according to a model of exercise regulation where the CNS, acting in an anticipatory manner, regulates the exercise behaviour by altering skeletal muscle recruitment, specifically to ensure that homeostasis is maintained during exercise. Since few, if any, of those studies can be explained by the 'brainless' A V Hill Cardio-vascular Model on which Professor Shephard bases his arguments, I argue that it is now the appropriate time to retire that model.

http://www.ncbi.nlm.nih.gov/pubmed/15388560 (2004)

Logical limitations to the 'catastrophe' models of fatigue during exercise in humans

It is concluded that there is little published evidence supporting the theory that fatigue occurs only after physiological homeostasis fails according to the prediction of these catastrophe models. Rather, it is proposed that fatigue in any form of exercise may form part of a regulated, anticipatory response co-ordinated in the subconscious brain. The ultimate goal of this regulation is to preserve homeostasis in all physiological systems during exercise, regardless of intensity or duration or the environmental conditions in which it is undertaken.

2 Carbohydrates

Carbohydrate loading

http://www.ncbi.nlm.nih.gov/pubmed/20975938 (2010)

Metabolic factors limiting performance in marathon runners

Carbohydrate loading prior to marathon running influences performance because it permits a runner of a given aerobic capacity (VO_2 max) and leg muscle distribution to run at greater speeds without 'hitting the wall', succumbing to the failure mode associated with the exhaustion of glycogen reserves.

http://www.ncbi.nlm.nih.gov/pubmed/18049981 (2009)

Nutrition for distance events

Race preparation strategies should include preparation of adequate fuel stores, including carbohydrate loading for prolonged events such as the marathon or 50-km walk. Fluid and carbohydrate intake during races lasting an hour or more should also be considered.

http://www.ncbi.nlm.nih.gov/pubmed/17465604 (2007)

Nutrition strategies for the marathon: fuel for training and racing

Muscle glycogen provides a key fuel for training and racing a marathon. Carbohydrate 'loading' can enhance marathon performance by allowing the competitor to run at their optimal pace for a longer period before fatiguing. For the well-trained runner, this may be achieved by tapering exercise over the final days before the marathon and ensuring carbohydrate intakes of 10-12g/kg/day over the 36-48 hours prior to the race

http://www.ncbi.nlm.nih.gov/pubmed/17507743 (2007)

Carbohydrate loading and female endurance athletes: effect of menstrual-cycle phase

These data support previous observations of greater resting [glyc] in the ML than the MF phase of the menstrual cycle and suggest that lower glycogen storage in the MF phase can be overcome by carbohydrate loading.

http://jap.physiology.org/content/91/1/225.abstract (2001)

Gender differences in carbohydrate loading are related to energy intake

There were no gender differences in the proportion of pro- and macroglycogen or hexokinase activity. A low energy intake may explain the previously reported lower capacity for women to glycogen load compared with men.

Pre-exercise carbohydrates

http://content.karger.com/ProdukteDB/produkte.asp?Doi=322698 (2011)

The Myths Surrounding Pre-Exercise Carbohydrate Feeding

It can be concluded that advice to avoid carbohydrate feeding in the hour before exercise is unfounded. Nevertheless athletes may develop symptoms similar to those of hypoglycaemia, even though they are rarely linked to actual low glucose concentrations. An individual approach may therefore be necessary to minimize these symptoms even though they do not appear to be related to exercise performance.

http://journals.cambridge.org/action/displayAbstract?fromPage=online&aid=2688328 (2008)

The effect of a pre-exercise carbohydrate meal on immune responses to an endurance performance run

The amount of carbohydrate consumed in the pre-exercise meal may be the most important influencing factor rather than the type of carbohydrate in modifying the immunoendocrine response to prolonged exercise.

Carbohydrates during exercise

http://www.ncbi.nlm.nih.gov/pubmed/20683237 (2011)

Effects of ingesting protein in combination with carbohydrate during exercise on endurance performance: a systematic review with meta-analysis.

We conclude that compared to carbohydrate alone, coingestion of protein and carbohydrate during exercise demonstrated an ergogenic effect on endurance performance when assessed by time to exhaustion and also where supplements were matched for carbohydrate (isocarbohydrate).

http://www.ncbi.nlm.nih.gov/pubmed/21411610 (2011)

Carbohydrate ingestion during endurance exercise improves performance in adults.

The data support that ingestion of CHO between 30g/h and 80g/h enhances endurance exercise performance in adults.

http://www.ncbi.nlm.nih.gov/pubmed/18091017 (2008)

Carbohydrate availability and muscle energy metabolism during intermittent running

These results suggest that CHO-E ingestion improves endurance capacity during intermittent high-intensity running in subjects with high pre-exercise muscle glycogen concentrations.

http://ajpendo.physiology.org/content/295/1/E70.short (2007)

Protein coingestion stimulates muscle protein synthesis during resistance-type exercise

We conclude that, even in a fed state, protein coingestion stimulates whole body and muscle protein synthesis rates during resistance-type exercise.

http://jap.physiology.org/cgi/content/abstract/96/4/1331 (2003)

Higher dietary carbohydrate content during intensified running training results in better maintenance of performance and mood state

Comparison of 5.4 to 8.5g CHO·kg-1·day - 1 showed better performance.

Post-exercise carbohydrates

http://jap.physiology.org/content/105/1/7.abstract (2007)

High rates of muscle glycogen resynthesis after exhaustive exercise when carbohydrate is coingested with caffeine

We provide the first evidence that in trained subjects, coingestion of large amounts of Caff (8mg/kg BM) with CHO has an additive effect on rates of postexercise muscle glycogen accumulation compared with consumption of CHO alone.

http://www.ncbi.nlm.nih.gov/pubmed/16775553 (2006)

Post-exercise muscle glycogen recovery enhanced with a carbohydrate-protein supplement.

C+P supplements, given early after exercise, enhance glycogen resynthesis relative to CHO and PLB. However, this does not influence performance in this type of exercise bout.

http://www.ncbi.nlm.nih.gov/pubmed?term=Determinants%20of%20Post-Exercise%20Glycogen%20Synthesis%20During%20Short-Term%20Recovery.%20 (2003)

Determinants of post-exercise glycogen synthesis during short-term recovery

Thus, when carbohydrate intake is insufficient (<1.2g/kg/h), the addition of certain amino acids and/or proteins may be beneficial for muscle glycogen synthesis. Furthermore, ingestion of insulinotropic protein and/or amino acid mixtures might stimulate post-exercise net muscle protein anabolism.

http://jap.physiology.org/cgi/content/abstract/95/3/983 (2003)

Effect of alcohol intake on muscle glycogen storage after prolonged exercise

We conclude that 1) the direct effect of alcohol on postexercise glycogen synthesis is unclear, and 2) the main effect of alcohol intake is indirect, by displacing CHO intake from optimal recovery nutrition practices.

http://jap.physiology.org/cgi/content/abstract/93/4/1337 (2002)

CHO-pro supplement early post exercise (10 min) is better for muscle glycogen replenishment than CHO alone.

Note that each supplement included 6g fat. (80g CHO, 28g Pro, 6g fat), LCHO (80g CHO, 6g fat), or HCHO (108g CHO, 6g fat).

Glycaemic index/load

http://www.ncbi.nlm.nih.gov/pubmed/20479489 (2010)

Glycemic index and endurance performance.

Despite the fact that the relationship between GI and sporting performance has been a topic of research for more than 15 yr, there is no consensus on whether consuming CHO of differing GI improves endurance performance. Until further well-designed research is carried out, athletes are encouraged to follow standard recommendations for CHO consumption and let practical issues and individual experience dictate the use of HGI or LGI meals and supplements before, during, and after exercise.

http://www.ncbi.nlm.nih.gov/pubmed/20020785 (2010)

Glycaemic index, glycaemic load and exercise performance

The claims for GL have been disputed by a number of sports nutrition specialists, and have gone largely unrecognized by professional and scientific bodies. Research on the effect of the GL on exercise performance and capacity is still at an early stage, but recent studies have shown that the concept may have some merit as far as sports nutrition is concerned. It has been suggested that the GL may be a better predictor of glycaemic responses than the GI alone.

http://www.ncbi.nlm.nih.gov/pubmed/19230767 (2010)

Effect of the glycaemic index of a pre-exercise meal on metabolism and cycling time trial performance.

The low GI meal led to an increase in the availability of carbohydrate and a greater carbohydrate oxidation throughout the exercise period, which may have sustained energy production towards the end of exercise and led to the improved TT performance observed.

http://www.ncbi.nlm.nih.gov/pubmed/17992183 (2007)

Glycemic index and glycemic load: measurement issues and their effect on diet-disease relationships.

Most studies, which have demonstrated health benefits of low GI or GL involved naturally occurring and minimally processed carbohydrate containing cereals, vegetables and fruit. These foods have qualities other than their immediate impact on postprandial glycemia as a basis to recommend their consumption.

http://www.ajcn.org/content/76/1/5.full (2002)

International table of glycemic index and glycemic load values: 2002

This revised table contains almost three times the number of foods listed in the original table... and contains nearly 1300 data entries derived from published and unpublished verified sources.... The revised table also lists the glycemic load associated with the consumption of specified serving sizes of different foods.

http://www.glycemicindex.com/

My note: University of Sydney GI and GL website and database

General

http://www.ncbi.nlm.nih.gov/pubmed/22394348 (2012)

The ingestion of combined carbohydrates does not alter metabolic responses or performance capacity during soccer-specific exercise in the heat compared to ingestion of a single carbohydrate.

These results suggest that when ingested in moderate amounts, the type of carbohydrate does not influence metabolism during soccer-specific intermittent exercise or affect performance capacity after exercise in the heat.

http://www.ncbi.nlm.nih.gov/pubmed/21846165 (2011)

Effects of acute carbohydrate supplementation on endurance performance: a meta-analysis.

Carbohydrate supplements with an appropriate composition and administration regimen can have large benefits on endurance performance. More research and better reporting are required to investigate the moderating effects of gender and salt.

http://adisonline.com/sportsmedicine/pages/articleviewer.aspx?year=2001&issue=3 1040&article=00003&type=abstract (2001)

Guidelines for Daily Carbohydrate Intake: Do Athletes Achieve Them?

CHO intake ranges of 5 to 7g/kg/day for general training needs and 7 to 10g/kg/day for the increased needs of endurance athletes are suggested.

3 Protein

Note: many links related to Chapter 3: Protein are covered in the recommended reading for Chapter 8: Supplements.

http://www.ncbi.nlm.nih.gov/pubmed/22139562 (2011)

Role of dietary proteins in sports

The previously separate dietary protein recommendations for strength and endurance athletes are no longer supported, and the daily intake for adult athletes suggested by most of the entities is about 1.5g · kg(-1) body mass with a range of perhaps 1.0 to 2.0g · kg(-1) body mass. This recommendation is a broad landmark that needs to be adapted to the individual circumstances of the athlete.

http://www.ncbi.nlm.nih.gov/pubmed/22150425 (2011)

Dietary protein for athletes: from requirements to optimum adaptation

Our consensus opinion is that leucine, and possibly the other branched-chain amino acids, occupy a position of prominence in stimulating muscle protein synthesis; that protein intakes in the range of $1.3\text{-}1.8g \cdot kg(-1) \cdot day(-1)$... will maximize muscle protein synthesis... Elevated protein consumption, as high as $1.8\text{-}2.0g \cdot kg(-1) \cdot day(-1)$ depending on the caloric deficit, may be advantageous in preventing lean mass losses during periods of energy restriction to promote fat loss.

http://www.ncbi.nlm.nih.gov/pubmed/20048505 (2009)

Protein for exercise and recovery

There is a significant body of evidence to indicate that individuals who are engaged in intense training require more dietary protein than sedentary counterparts (i.e., 1.4-2g/kg/day). For most individuals, this level of protein intake can be obtained from a regular and varied diet. However, recent evidence indicates that ingesting protein and/or amino acids prior to, during, and/or following exercise can enhance recovery, immune function, and growth and maintenance of lean body mass.

http://www.ncbi.nlm.nih.gov/pubmed/19699838 (2009)

A moderate serving of high-quality protein maximally stimulates skeletal muscle protein synthesis in young and elderly subjects.

A 113-g serving of lean beef increased muscle protein synthesis by approximately 50% in both young and older volunteers. Despite a threefold increase in protein and energy content, there was no further increase in protein synthesis after ingestion of 340g lean beef in either age group. Ingestion of more than 30g protein in a single meal does not further enhance the stimulation of muscle protein synthesis in young and elderly.

http://www.ncbi.nlm.nih.gov/pubmed/20368372 (2009)

The role of milk- and soy-based protein in support of muscle protein synthesis and muscle protein accretion in young and elderly persons

Milk proteins, specifically casein and whey, are the highest quality proteins and are quite different in terms of their rates of digestion and absorption. New data suggest that whey protein is better able to support MPS than is soy protein, a finding that may explain the greater ability of whey protein to support greater net muscle mass gains with resistance exercise

http://www.ncbi.nlm.nih.gov/pubmed/19057193 (2009)

Dietary protein recommendations and the prevention of sarcopenia.

To maximize muscle protein synthesis while being cognizant of total energy intake, we propose a dietary plan that includes 25-30g of high quality protein per meal.

http://www.pubmedcentral.nih.gov/articlerender.fcgi?artid=2117006 (2007)

International Society of Sports Nutrition position stand: protein and exercise

In summary, exercising individuals need more dietary protein than their sedentary counterparts, which can be obtained from whole foods as well as from high quality supplemental protein sources such as whey and casein protein.

http://www.ncbi.nlm.nih.gov/pubmed/17241913 (2007)

Protein requirements and recommendations for athletes: relevance of ivory tower arguments for practical recommendations

In general, scientific opinion on this controversy seems to divide itself into two camps - those who believe participation in exercise and sport increases the nutritional requirement forprotein and those who believe protein requirements for athletes and exercising individuals are no different from the requirements for sedentary individuals.

http://www.ncbi.nlm.nih.gov/pubmed/18187436 (2007)

Dietary protein and resistance training effects on muscle and body composition in older persons

Findings from controlled feeding studies show that older persons retain the capacity to metabolically adjust to lower protein intakes by increasing the efficiency of nitrogen retention and amino acid utilization. However, they also suggest that the recommended dietary allowance of 0.8g protein $\times$ kg(-1) $\times$ d(-1) might not be sufficient to prevent subtle accommodations and blunt desired changes in body composition and muscle size with resistance training.

http://www.ncbi.nlm.nih.gov/pubmed/17413102 (2007)

Consumption of fluid skim milk promotes greater muscle protein accretion after resistance exercise than does consumption of an isonitrogenous and isoenergetic soy-protein beverage

Milk-based proteins promote muscle protein accretion to a greater extent than do soy-based proteins when consumed after resistance exercise. The consumption of either milk or soy protein with resistance training promotes muscle mass maintenance and gains, but chronic consumption of milk proteins after resistance exercise likely supports a more rapid lean mass accrual.

http://www.ncbi.nlm.nih.gov/pubmed/15798080 (2005)

Dietary protein to support anabolism with resistance exercise in young men.

In young men... we observed a tendency (P = 0.11) for greater gains in whole body lean mass... with consumption of milk. While strength gains were not different between the soy and milk-supplemented groups...

http://www.ncbi.nlm.nih.gov/pubmed/16001875 (2005)

The Protein Digestibility-Corrected Amino Acid Score (PDCAAS)--a concept for describing protein quality in foods and food ingredients: a critical review.

Although PDCAAS is a rapid and useful method, it often shows discrepancies when compared to PER values.

http://www.ncbi.nlm.nih.gov/pubmed/14971434 (2004)

Protein and amino acids for athletes

Current literature suggests that it may be too simplistic to rely on recommendations of a particular amount of protein per day. Acute studies suggest that for any given amount of protein, the metabolic response is dependent on other factors, including the timing of ingestion in relation to exercise and/or other nutrients, the composition of ingested amino acids and the type of protein.

http://www.ncbi.nlm.nih.gov/pubmed/11255140 (2001)

Exercise, protein metabolism, and muscle growth

The response of muscle protein metabolism to a resistance exercise bout lasts for 24-48 hours; thus, the interaction between protein metabolism and any meals consumed in this period will determine the impact of the diet on muscle hypertrophy.

4 Fat

Body mass index (BMI) and body fat

http://www.ncbi.nlm.nih.gov/pubmed/22089480 (2012)

Are under- and overweight female elite athletes thin and fat? A controlled study

Our data show that BMI is not a valid measure for assessing or monitoring body composition in female elite athletes, and it should be used carefully in female non-athletes.

http://www.ncbi.nlm.nih.gov/pmc/articles/PMC3302984/?tool=pubmed (2012)

The obesity paradox in chronic disease: facts and numbers

For patients with established chronic disease, there is sufficient evidence to support the benefits of large body size - i.e., the obesity paradox. This uniform finding is shared over a variety of cardiovascular, pulmonary, and renal diseases and is counterintuitive to the current concepts on ideal body mass.

http://www.ncbi.nlm.nih.gov/pubmed/20737611 (2010)

The role of fat mass index in determining obesity

The discrepancy observed between BMI and PBF reflects a limitation of BMI. Conversely, FMI accurately assessed obesity in our study of Mexican Americans, but further studies are necessary to confirm our findings in different ethnic groups.

http://www.ncbi.nlm.nih.gov/pubmed/20130075 (2010)

The predictive value of different measures of obesity for incident cardiovascular events and mortality.

We measured body mass index (BMI), waist circumference (WC), waist-to-height ratio (WHtR), and waist-to-hip ratio (WHR) and assessed cardiovascular and all-cause mortality and the composite endpoint of incident stroke, myocardial infarction, or cardiovascular death…WHtR represents the best predictor of cardiovascular risk and mortality, followed by WC and WHR. Our results discourage the use of the BMI.

http://www.ncbi.nlm.nih.gov/pubmed/21509084 (2010)

Optimum anthropometric criteria for ideal body composition related fitness

The three aims of this study were to establish equations for ideal body composition related fitness to be used by adults willing to gain optimum body composition related fitness; to predict the possible symmetrical major muscle circumference, and to compute the ideal body fat percentage (BFP) with ideal body mass (IBW) based on the body mass index (BMI).

http://www.ncbi.nlm.nih.gov/pubmed/19672278 (2010)

Appropriateness of waist circumference and waist-to-hip ratio cutoffs for different ethnic groups

There is possible evidence that Asians should have a lower WC cutoff than Europeans.

The evidence is insufficient for specific cutoffs for African-American, Hispanic and Middle Eastern populations but some studies indicate current cutoffs for Europeans may be appropriate, whereas there is insufficient evidence for the other ethnic groups. Future studies are needed to address the methodological limitations of the current literature.

http://www.ncbi.nlm.nih.gov/pubmed/19893101 (2009)

Overweight in trained subjects - are we looking at wrong numbers? (Body mass index compared with body fat percentage in estimating overweight in athletes.)

Eighty-five trained subjects had a BMI of 25 or higher, indicating overweight. Of these, only three individuals had excess BF%. The results of the present study suggest that a BMI > or = 25kg.m(-2) is not an accurate predictor of overweight in trained subjects.

http://www.nutritionj.com/content/7/1/5 (2008)

To treat or not to treat: comparison of different criteria used to determine whether weight loss is to be recommended

The use of the BMI alone, as opposed to an assessment based on body composition, to identify individuals needing lifestyle intervention may lead to unfortunate misclassifications.

http://www.ncbi.nlm.nih.gov/pubmed/17890752 (2008)

Adolphe Quetelet (1796-1874)--the average man and indices of obesity

Adolphe Quetelet (1796-1874) was a Belgian mathematician, astronomer and statistician, who developed... the Quetelet Index until it was termed the Body Mass Index in 1972 by Ancel Keys (1904-2004).

http://www.ncbi.nlm.nih.gov/pubmed/18419029 (2008)

Evaluation of body fat estimated from body mass index and impedance in Belgian male military candidates: comparing two methods for estimating body composition

To limit false-negative classifications, additional impedance measurements in the BMI category between 25.0 and 27.0kg/m^2 is mandatory to determine whether there is really an excess fat mass.

http://www.ncbi.nlm.nih.gov/pubmed/18283284 (2008)

Accuracy of body mass index in diagnosing obesity in the adult general population

The accuracy of BMI in diagnosing obesity is limited, particularly for individuals in the intermediate BMI ranges, in men and in the elderly. A BMI cutoff of> or =30kg m(-2) has good specificity but misses more than half of people with excess fat. These results may help to explain the unexpected better survival in overweight/mild obese patients.

http://www.ncbi.nlm.nih.gov/pmc/articles/PMC2164947/?tool=pubmed (2007)

Measurement and Definitions of Obesity In Childhood and Adolescence: A field guide for the uninitiated

Decisions in respect of children are even more complex. As with adults, the relationships between BMI and levels of fat, and between levels of fat and associated morbidities, differ between ethnic groups. In addition, BMI levels, and their relationship with levels of fat vary according to sex, age and maturity.

http://www.ncbi.nlm.nih.gov/pubmed/16920472 (2006)

Association of bodyweight with total mortality and with cardiovascular events in coronary artery disease: a systematic review of cohort studies.

We found 40 studies with 250,152 patients that had a mean follow-up of 3.8 years. Patients with a low body-mass index (BMI) (i.e., <20) had an increased relative risk (RR) for total mortality (RR=1.37 [95% CI 1.32-1.43), and cardiovascular mortality (1.45 [1.16-1.81]), overweight (BMI 25-29.9) had the lowest risk for total mortality (0.87 [0.81-0.94]) and cardiovascular mortality (0.88 [0.75-1.02]) compared with those for people with a normal BMI. Obese patients (BMI 30-35) had no increased risk for total mortality (0.93 [0.85-1.03]) or cardiovascular mortality (0.97 [0.82-1.15]). Patients with severe obesity (> or =35) did not have increased total mortality (1.10 [0.87-1.41]) but they had the highest risk for cardiovascular mortality (1.88 [1.05-3.34]).

http://www.ncbi.nlm.nih.gov/pubmed/14557832 (2004)

Overweight Japanese with body mass indexes of 23.0-24.9 have higher risks for obesity-associated disorders: a comparison of Japanese and Mongolians

Since the relationship between abdominal fat mass and BMI is ethnic-specific, a universal BMI cutoff point is inappropriate for Asian populations such as the Japanese and Mongolians.

http://www.ncbi.nlm.nih.gov/pubmed/12164465 (2002)

Asians are different from Caucasians and from each other in their body mass index/body fat per cent relationship

All Asian populations studied had a higher BF% at a lower BMI compared to Caucasians. Generally, for the same BMI their BF% was 3-5% points higher compared to Caucasians.

http://www.ncbi.nlm.nih.gov/pubmed/12164474 (2002)

Elevated body fat percentage and cardiovascular risks at low body mass index levels among Singaporean Chinese, Malays and Indians

The data from the current study, which includes evidence that not only risk factors, but also BF% are elevated at low BMI values, presents a strong case for lowering the BMI cut-off value for overweight and obesity among Singaporeans, from 25kg m(-2) and 30kg m(-2) to 23kg m(-2) and 27kg m(-2), respectively.

http://www.ncbi.nlm.nih.gov/pubmed?term=Healthy percentage body fat ranges%3A an approach for developing guidelines based on body mass index
http://www.ncbi.nlm.nih.gov/pubmed/10966886 (2000)

Healthy percentage body fat ranges: an approach for developing guidelines based on body mass index

The approach taken was to link healthy body mass index (BMI; in kg/m(2)) guidelines established by the National Institutes of Health and the World Health Organization with predicted percentage body fat.

Fat percentage measuring equipment
http://www.ncbi.nlm.nih.gov/pubmed/18723322 (2009)

Validity of segmental multiple-frequency bioelectrical impedance analysis to estimate body composition of adults across a range of body mass indexes

Eight-electrode, segmental MF-BIA is a valid method to estimate %BF in adults with BMI classified as N and OW, but not as OB. Estimation of trunk resistance with current segmental MF-BIA devices may explain the underestimation of %BF in the adults with OB BMI. Further examination of the effect of waist circumference and body fat distribution on the accuracy of BIA measurements is warranted.

http://www.ajcn.org/cgi/content/full/81/1/74 (2005)

Comparison of multifrequency bioelectrical impedance analysis with dual-energy X-ray absorptiometry for assessment of percentage body fat in a large, healthy population

BIA is a good alternative for estimating %BF when subjects are within a normal body fat range. BIA tends to overestimate %BF in lean subjects and underestimate %BF in obese subjects.

http://www.springerlink.com/content/61na4091mp8pw0l1/ (2001)

Evaluation of the BOD POD for estimating percentage body fat in a heterogeneous group of adult humans.

The primary purpose of this investigation was to compare estimations of percentage body fat (%fat) using air displacement plethysmography (ADP) and hydrostatic weighing (HW) in a heterogeneous (age and %fat) sample of the population.

Fish oils and fats

http://journals.lww.com/cardiovascularpharm/pages/articleviewer.aspx?year=2008 &issue=12000&article=00010&type=abstract (2008)

Fish Oil Reduces Heart Rate and Oxygen Consumption During Exercise

This study indicates that FOs may act within the healthy heart and skeletal muscle to reduce both whole-body and myocardial O_2 demand during exercise, without a decrement in performance.

http://journals.lww.com/cardiovascularpharm/pages/articleviewer.aspx?year=2008 &issue=12000&article=00010&type=abstract (2008)

Fish Oil Reduces Heart Rate and Oxygen Consumption During Exercise

This study indicates that FOs may act within the healthy heart and skeletal muscle to reduce both whole-body and myocardial O_2 demand during exercise, without a decrement in performance.

http://www.ncbi.nlm.nih.gov/pubmed/16365076 (2006)

Dietary saturated fat intake is inversely associated with bone density in humans: analysis of NHANES III

These data indicate that BMD is negatively associated with saturated fat intake, and that men may be particularly vulnerable to these effects.

http://www.ncbi.nlm.nih.gov/pubmed/9089901 (1997)

Omega-3 fatty acid supplementation does not improve maximal aerobic power, anaerobic threshold and running performance in well-trained soccer players

In conclusion, the results do not support the hypothesis that endurance athletes can improve maximal aerobic performance by omega-3 fatty acid supplementation.

http://www.nhs.uk/conditions/cholesterol/Pages/Introduction.aspx
My note: an easy-to-read NHS article about cholesterol, includes a short video.

5 Losing the fat

RMR

http://www.ncbi.nlm.nih.gov/pubmed/16720129 (2006)

Best practice methods to apply to measurement of resting metabolic rate in adults: systematic review

http://www.ajcn.org/content/84/3/475.full (2006)

The underappreciated role of muscle in health and disease

The importance of maintaining muscle mass and physical and metabolic functions in the elderly is well-recognized. Less appreciated are the diverse roles of muscle throughout life and the importance of muscle in preventing some of the most common and increasingly prevalent clinical conditions, such as obesity and diabetes.

http://www.ncbi.nlm.nih.gov/pubmed/15883556 (2005)

Comparison of predictive equations for resting metabolic rate in healthy nonobese and obese adults: a systematic review

The Mifflin-St Jeor equation is more likely than the other equations tested to estimate RMR to within 10% of that measured, but noteworthy errors and limitations exist when it is applied to individuals and possibly when it is generalized to certain age and ethnic groups.

http://jap.physiology.org/content/89/3/977.abstract (2000)

Resistance training increases total energy expenditure and free-living physical activity in older adults

These results suggest that resistance training may have value in increasing energy expenditure and lipid oxidation rates in older adults, thereby improving their metabolic profiles.

http://jap.physiology.org/cgi/content/full/82/1/298 (1996)

Effect of an 18-wk weight-training program on energy expenditure and physical activity

In conclusion, although of modest energy cost, weight-training induces a significant increase in [average daily metabolic rate] ADMR.

http://jap.physiology.org/cgi/content/abstract/76/1/133 (1994)

Strength training increases resting metabolic rate and norepinephrine levels in healthy 50- to 65-yr-old men

RMR, measured by indirect calorimetry, increased 7.7% with strength training... These results indicate that a heavy-resistance strength-training program increases RMR in healthy older men, perhaps by increasing FFM and sympathetic nervous system activity.

HIIT

http://www.ncbi.nlm.nih.gov/pubmed/21113312 (2011)

High-intensity intermittent exercise and fat loss

The effect of regular aerobic exercise on body fat is negligible; however, other forms of exercise may have a greater impact on body composition. For example, emerging research examining high-intensity intermittent exercise (HIIE) indicates that it may be more effective at reducing subcutaneous and abdominal body fat than other types of exercise.

http://www.ncbi.nlm.nih.gov/pubmed/18197184 (2008)

The effects of high-intensity intermittent exercise training on fat loss and fasting insulin levels of young women.

HIIE three times per week for 15 weeks compared to the same frequency of [steady-state exercise] SSE exercise was associated with significant reductions in total body fat, subcutaneous leg and trunk fat, and insulin resistance in young women.

Thermogenesis

http://www.ncbi.nlm.nih.gov/pubmed/21276644 (2011)

Diet induced thermogenesis, fat oxidation and food intake following sequential meals: influence of calcium and Vitamin D

Higher calcium and Vitamin D intake at a breakfast meal acutely increased postprandial FOR and DIT over two successive meals, and reduced spontaneous energy intake in the subsequent 24-hour period.

http://jasn.asnjournals.org/content/19/6/1041.full (2008)

Just Add Water

My note: general ideas, and many misconceptions addressed, about water. A good, clear and short paper which references many very recent articles.

http://jap.physiology.org/content/103/2/616.abstract (2007)

Thermic effect of food and β-adrenergic thermogenic responsiveness in habitually exercising and sedentary healthy adult humans

The increase in [energy expenditure] EE during incremental isoproterenol administration was greater… in habitual exercisers… than in sedentary adults…

http://arno.unimaas.nl/show.cgi?fid=9176 (2007)

THE BATTLE AGAINST OBESITY - A ROLE FOR THERMOGENIC AND SATIATING FOOD INGREDIENTS

My note: an eight-chapter, easy-to-read pdf.

http://jcem.endojournals.org/content/91/9/3598.abstract (2006)

Water-Induced Thermogenesis Reconsidered: The Effects of Osmolality and Water Temperature on Energy Expenditure after Drinking

Drinking distilled water at room temperature did not increase energy expenditure. Cooling the water before drinking only stimulated a small thermogenic response, well below the theoretical energy cost of warming the water to body temperature. These results cast doubt on water as a thermogenic agent for the management of obesity.

http://www.jacn.org/cgi/reprint/23/5/373 (2004)

The Effects of High Protein Diets on Thermogenesis, Satiety and Weight Loss: A Critical Review

My note: a pdf on thermogenesis, fat loss, weight loss, and satiety; Harvard School of Public Health. Includes an e-mail address and 83 references.

http://www.nutritionandmetabolism.com/content/1/1/5#B6 (2004)

Diet induced thermogenesis

A mixed diet consumed at energy balance results in a diet induced energy expenditure of 5 to 15 % of daily energy expenditure… In conclusion, the main determinants of diet-induced thermogenesis are the energy content and the protein- and alcohol fraction of the diet. Protein plays a key role in body weight regulation through satiety related to diet-induced thermogenesis.

Fat loss

http://womenshealth.about.com/od/gynecologicalhealthissues/a/leptinstudy.htm (2010)

Study Finds Leptin Restores Reproductive Function in Women (updated 2010)

An easy-read article discussing the findings of a study of 14 competitive, female athletes described in the September 2, 2004 issue of The New England Journal.

http://www.nature.com/oby/journal/v19/n4/full/oby2010203a.html (2010)

The Effects of Consuming Frequent, Higher Protein Meals on Appetite and Satiety During Weight Loss in Overweight/Obese Men

Collectively, these data support the consumption of HP intake, but not greater eating frequency, for improved appetite control and satiety in overweight/obese men during energy restriction-induced weight loss.

http://www.pnas.org/content/107/42/18226 (2010)

Regional differences in cellular mechanisms of adipose tissue gain with overfeeding

Inherent differences in preadipocyte cell dynamics may contribute to the distinct responses of different fat depots to overfeeding, and fat-cell number increases in certain depots in adults after only 8 weeks of increased food intake.

http://www.fasebj.org/cgi/content/meeting_abstract/23/1_MeetingAbstracts/101.4 (2009)

Effect of viscosity, protein and dietary fibre in beverages on perceived satiety

Dietary fibre and whey protein increased perceived satiety significantly and independently. The sample containing both dietary fibre and whey protein had the greatest effect on perceived satiety. Higher viscosity showed a tendency to increase satiety compared to the samples with lower viscosity (p=0.091). Dietary fibre and protein in beverages have thus potential to affect weight management.

http://www.plosone.org/article/info:doi/10.1371/journal.pone.0004377 (2009)

Metabolic and Behavioral Compensations in Response to Caloric Restriction: Implications for the Maintenance of Weight Loss

For the first time we show that in free-living conditions, CR results in a metabolic adaptation and a behavioral adaptation with decreased physical activity levels. These data also suggest potential mechanisms by which CR causes large inter-individual variability in the rates of weight loss and how exercise may influence weight loss and weight loss maintenance.

http://journals.lww.com/acsm-essr/pages/articleviewer.aspx?year=2009&issue=040 00&article=00008&type=abstract (2009)

Exercise Improves Fat Metabolism in Muscle But Does Not Increase 24-h Fat Oxidation

Although exercise improves the capacity of muscle to oxidize fat, our studies suggest that moderate duration exercise ($\leq$1 h) has little impact on 24-h fat oxidation.

http://journals.lww.com/acsm-msse/pages/articleviewer.aspx?year=2008&issue=110 00&article=00001&type=abstract (2008)

Effect of Exercise Training Intensity on Abdominal Visceral Fat and Body Composition

The present data indicate that body composition changes are affected by the intensity of exercise training with HIET more effectively for reducing total abdominal fat, subcutaneous abdominal fat, and AVF in obese women with the metabolic syndrome.

http://jap.physiology.org/cgi/content/abstract/106/1/5 (2008)

Aerobic exercise training reduces epicardial fat in obese men

These results suggest that aerobic exercise training may be an effective nonpharmacological strategy for decreasing the ventricular epicardial fat thickness and visceral fat area in obese middle-aged men.

http://arno.unimaas.nl/show.cgi?fid=11858 (2008)

TRIGGERS FOR FOOD INTAKE REGULATION - Sensory and metabolic effects of specific food Components.

My note: an 10-chapter, easy-to-read pdf.

http://www.pmc.ps/pdf/Handbook of Obesity Clinical Applications, 3rd edition.pdf

Handbook of Obesity: Clinical applications, 3rd edition. 2008.

My note: A 674-page pdf, including hundreds of references.

http://www.ncbi.nlm.nih.gov/pubmed/18454136 (2008)

Dynamics of fat cell turnover in humans

Approximately 10% of fat cells are renewed annually at all adult ages and levels of body mass index. Neither adipocyte death nor generation rate is altered in early onset obesity, suggesting a tight regulation of fat cell number in this condition during adulthood.

My note: contradicts the 'Handbook of obesity' above, which states that the number of fat cells can increase in extreme cases.

http://www.nature.com/nrendo/journal/v3/n7/full/ncpendmet0554.html (2007)

The role of physical activity in producing and maintaining weight loss

This article reviews the role of physical activity in producing and maintaining weight loss.

http://aje.oxfordjournals.org/content/167/2/188.full (2007)

Energy Intake at Breakfast and Weight Change: Prospective Study of 6,764 Middle-aged Men and Women

Redistribution of daily energy intake, so that more energy is consumed at breakfast and less energy is consumed later in the day, may help to reduce weight gain in middle-aged adults.

http://jap.physiology.org/content/102/4/1341.abstract?ijkey=8d68eeb230083bfca7b8 0b4dae3a34d65c303353&keytype2=tf_ipsecsha (2006)

Inactivity induces increases in abdominal fat

Thus two important findings have been elucidated: 1) increases in measured abdominal fat masses occur in both AL and PF groups at WL173, and 2) adipocyte expansion via hyperplasia occurred with an ad libitum diet following cessation of voluntary running.

http://jap.physiology.org/cgi/content/full/102/4/1308 (2006)
Inactivity and fat cell hyperplasia: fat chance?
My note: some interesting results about fat cell hyperplasia (increase in number) and hypertrophy (increase in mass).

http://www.ncbi.nlm.nih.gov/pubmed/12037652 (2002)
The influence of the type of dietary fat on postprandial fat oxidation rates: monounsaturated (olive oil) vs saturated fat (cream)
If postprandial fat oxidation rates are higher after high [monounsaturated fat] MUFA, rather than [saturated fat] SFA meals, then a simple change to the type of dietary fat consumed might have beneficial effects in curbing weight gain in men consuming a relatively high-fat diet. This may be particularly evident in men with a large waist circumference.

6 Fluid Essentials

Electrolytes
http://www.ncbi.nlm.nih.gov/pmc/articles/PMC1978469/ (2007)
Validity of Devices That Assess Body Temperature During Outdoor Exercise in the Heat
Compared with rectal temperature (the criterion standard), gastrointestinal temperature was the only measurement that accurately assessed core body temperature. Oral, axillary, aural, temporal, and field forehead temperatures were significantly different from rectal temperature and, therefore, are considered invalid for assessing hyperthermia in individuals exercising outdoors in the heat.

http://www.ncbi.nlm.nih.gov/pubmed/18156662 (2007)
Sweat mineral-element responses during 7 h of exercise-heat stress
Sweat sodium, potassium, and calcium losses during multiple hours of sustained sweating can be predicted from initial sweat composition. Estimates of sweat zinc losses, however, will be overestimated if sweat zinc conservation is not accounted for in sweat zinc-lossestimates.

My note: A small study (six males, one female) of mineral and trace element losses through perspiration.

http://journals.lww.com/acsm-essr/Abstract/2007/07000/Caffeine,_Fluid_Electro-lyte_Balance,_Temperature.8.aspx (2007)

Caffeine, Fluid-Electrolyte Balance, Temperature Regulation, and Exercise-Heat Tolerance

This review, contrary to popular beliefs, proposes that caffeine consumption does not result in the following: (a) water-electrolyte imbalances or hyperthermia and (b) reduced exercise-heat tolerance.

http://bjsm.bmj.com/content/40/2/98.abstract (2005)

Exercise associated hyponatraemia: quantitative analysis to understand the aetiology

Actions to prevent hyponatraemia should focus on minimising over drinking relative to sweating rate and attenuating salt depletion in those who excrete salty sweat. This simulation demonstrates the complexity of defining fluid and electrolyte consumption rates during athletic competition.

http://www.ncbi.nlm.nih.gov/pubmed/15256693 (2004)

Fluid and electrolyte intake and loss in elite soccer players during training.

These data indicate that sweat losses of water and solute in football players in training can be substantial but vary greatly between players even with the same exercise and environmental conditions. Voluntary fluid intake also shows wide inter-individual variability and is generally insufficient to match fluid losses.

http://www.ncbi.nlm.nih.gov/pubmed/11547892 (2001)

Fluid and electrolyte balance in ultra-endurance sport.

School of Physical Education and Department of Human Nutrition, Otago University, Dunedin, New Zealand.

Sport and fluids

http://www.tandfonline.com/doi/abs/10.1080/17461391.2010.487115 (2011)

Effects of ingesting a sports drink during exercise and recovery on subsequent endurance capacity

Ingestion of the sports drink during and after moderate-intensity exercise replaces fluids and energy lost more effectively than water and a placebo, leading to an improvement in subsequent endurance capacity.

http://onlinelibrary.wiley.com/doi/10.1111/j.1467-3010.2011.01897.x/full (2011)

Potential role for protein in assisting post-exercise rehydration

… Emerging research looking into milk proteins, whey and casein, points to a role for protein in assisting post-exercise fluid retention. The most obvious mechanisms are enhanced sodium and water absorption from the gut, and increased plasma protein synthesis resulting in higher osmotic pressure exerted by plasma proteins. This article reviews current strategies to enhance post-exercise recovery of fluid balance, with a focus on protein.

http://bjsm.bmj.com/content/early/2010/11/01/bjsm.2010.075507.abstract (2010)

Protection of total body water content and absence of hyperthermia despite 2% body mass loss ('voluntary dehydration') in soldiers drinking ad libitum during prolonged exercise in cool environmental conditions

The finding that TBW was protected by ad libitum drinking despite ~2% body mass loss suggests that the concept of 'voluntary dehydration' may require revision.

http://versita.metapress.com/index/Y4VH46K41T1K7M13.pdf (2010)

POST-EXERCISE REHYDRATION: NO CHANGE IN DIURESIS FROM WATER INGESTED AT DIFFERENT TEMPERATURES

Conclusion: when men are rehydrated with a volume of water equivalent to 120% of weight loss, after dehydration to 2% BM, water temperature (within this range) has no effect on diuresis or fluid retention.

http://onlinelibrary.wiley.com/doi/10.1111/j.1467-3010.2009.01790.x/abstract (2009)

Hydration in sport and exercise: water, sports drinks and other drinks

The current generation of commercially available sports drinks are generally formulated to meet the needs of many athletes in many different situations.

http://www.sciencedirect.com/science/article/pii/S0899900709001130 (2008)

Postexercise rehydration in man: The effects of osmolality and carbohydrate content of ingested drinks

This study suggests that, following the rehydration protocol used, hypertonic glucose-sodium drinks may be more effective at restoring and maintaining hydration status after sweat loss than more dilute solutions when the sodium concentration is comparable

http://journals.lww.com/acsm-msse/pages/articleviewer.aspx?year=2008&issue=090 00&article=00012&type=abstract (2008)

Cold Drink Ingestion Improves Exercise Endurance Capacity in the Heat

Compared with a drink at 37°C, the ingestion of a cold drink before and during exercise in the heat reduced physiological strain (reduced heat accumulation) during exercise, leading to an improved endurance capacity (23 ± 6%).

http://www.ku.ac.ke/images/stories/docs/publications/enviromental_human/Elite-Kenyan-Endurance-Runners.pdf (2008)

Elite Kenyan Endurance Runners are Hydrated Day-To-Day with Ad Libitum Fluid Intake

The main finding of the present investigation is that despite low daily fluid intake, elite Kenyan endurance runners remain well hydrated day-to-day during an important training period.

http://walking.about.com/od/fluids/f/coldwatermyth.htm (2008)

Is Drinking Cold Water During or After Exercise Good or Bad?

http://journals.lww.com/acsm-csmr/Abstract/2008/07000/Sports_Drinks,_Exercise_Training,_and_Competition.8.aspx (2008)

Sports Drinks, Exercise Training, and Competition

http://bjsm.bmj.com/content/42/10/796.abstract (2008)

Drinking policies and exercise-associated hyponatraemia: is anyone still promoting overdrinking?

Drinking policies during exercise have changed substantially throughout history. Since the mid-1990s, however, there has been an increase in the promotion of over drinking by athletes.

http://journals.cambridge.org/action/displayAbstract?fromPage=online& aid=1057236 (2007)

Milk as an effective post-exercise rehydration drink

The results of the present study suggest that milk can be an effective post-exercise rehydration drink and can be considered for use after exercise by everyone except those individuals who have lactose intolerance.

http://www.informaworld.com/smpp/content~db=all~content=a778567937 (2007)

The influence of drink temperature on thermoregulatory responses during prolonged exercise in a moderate environment

These results suggest that there may be a role for drink temperature in influencing thermoregulation during exercise.

http://www.ingentaconnect.com/content/adis/smd/2007/00000037/00000010/ art00006 (2007)

Hydration and Muscular Performance: Does Fluid Balance Affect Strength, Power and High-Intensity Endurance?

A critical review of the available literature suggests hypohydration limits strength, power and high-intensity endurance and, therefore, is an important factor to consider when attempting to maximise muscular performance in athletic, military and industrial settings.

http://www.jacn.org/cgi/content/abstract/26/suppl_5/575S (2007)

Assessing Hydration Status: The Elusive Gold Standard

Acknowledging that total body water (TBW) turnover is complex, and that no measurement is valid for all situations, this review evaluates 13 hydration assessment techniques.

http://jcem.endojournals.org/cgi/content/abstract/91/9/3598 (2006)

Water-Induced Thermogenesis Reconsidered: The Effects of Osmolality and Water Temperature on Energy Expenditure after Drinking

Drinking distilled water at room temperature did not increase energy expenditure. Cooling the water before drinking only stimulated a small thermogenic response, well below the theoretical energy cost of warming the water to body temperature. These results cast doubt on water as a thermogenic agent for the management of obesity.

http://walking.about.com/gi/o.htm?zi=1/XJ&zTi=1&sdn=walking&cdn=health&tm=570&f=10&tt=12&bt=1&bts=1&zu=http://www.aims-association.org/guidelines_fluid_replacement.htm (2006)

IMMDA's REVISED FLUID RECOMMENDATIONS FOR RUNNERS & WALKERS

Interesting ideas on water intake (actually recommends drinking once thirsty!) and includes a fluid intake calculation guide.

http://bjsm.bmj.com/content/40/5/406.abstract (2005)

Voluntary fluid intake and core temperature responses in adolescent tennis players: sports beverage versus water

Ad libitum consumption of a CHO-E drink may be more effective than water in minimising fluid deficits and mean core temperature responses during tennis and other similar training in adolescent athletes.

http://www.runcim.org/data/ProperHydrationForDistanceRunning.pdf (2004)

Proper Hydration for Distance Running-Identifying Individual Fluid Needs

http://www.uni.edu/dolgener/Advanced_Sport_Nutrition/fluid_intake.pdf (2003)

Fluid and fuel intake during exercise

My note: A 12-page pdf offering general fluid intake advice and other related information. (Include nearly five pages of references)

http://www.scienceblog.com/community/older/2003/D/20031325.html (2003)

How much should athletes drink during exercise?

… Until the late 1960s, athletes were advised not to drink during exercise…

http://www.usatf.org/groups/coaches/library/2007/hydration/IMMDAAdvisoryStatement.pdf (2002)

IMMDA ADVISORY STATEMENT ON GUIDELINES FOR FLUID REPLACEMENT DURING MARATHON RUNNING

A more reasonable approach is to urge these participants not to drink as much as possible but to drink *ad libitum* (according to the dictates of thirst) no more than 400-800ml/hour.

http://www.ingentaconnect.com/content/adis/smd/2000/00000029/00000003/art00004 (2000)

The Effectiveness of Commercially Available Sports Drinks

Our conclusions are three-fold. First, because of variations in drink composition and research design, much of the sports drinks research from the past cannot be applied directly to the effectiveness of currently available sports drinks. Secondly, in studies where a practical protocol has been used along with a currently available sports beverage, there is evidence to suggest that consuming a sports drinks will improve performance compared with consuming a placebo beverage. Finally, there is little evidence that any one sports drink is superior to any of the other beverages on the market.

Glycerol

http://www.ingentaconnect.com/content/adis/smd/2010/00000040/00000002/art00002 (2010)

Guidelines for Glycerol Use in Hyperhydration and Rehydration Associated with Exercise

… glycerol ingestion before, during or following exercise is likely to improve the hydration state of the endurance athlete.

http://www.springerlink.com/content/w121h3620uj5m181/ (2007)

Hyperhydrating with glycerol: effects on thermoregulation, hydration and athletic performance during specific exergonic exercise in a warm-humid environment

http://www.ncbi.nlm.nih.gov/pubmed?term=Effect of glycerol-induced hyperhydration on thermoregulatory and cardiovascular functions and endurance performance during prolonged cycling in a 25 %5Bdegrees%5DC environment (2006)

Effect of glycerol-induced hyperhydration on thermoregulatory and cardiovascular functions and endurance performance during prolonged cycling in a 25 [degrees]C environment

It is concluded that, compared with WIH, GIH decreases urine production, but does not improve cardiovascular or thermoregulatory functions, nor does it improve EP during 2 h of cycling in a 25 [degrees] C environment in trained athletes consuming 500ml/h of fluid during exercise.

http://jap.physiology.org/content/63/6/2262.short (1987)

Hyperhydration with glycerol solutions

My note: the first paper to demonstrate the benefits of glycerol regarding water retention

Water in general

http://www.sciencedirect.com/science/article/pii/S0738081X10000465 (2010)

Nutrition and water: drinking eight glasses of water a day ensures proper skin hydration - myth or reality?

We have found no scientific proof for this recommendation; nor is there proof, we must admit, that drinking less water does absolutely no harm. The only certainty about this issue is that, at the end of the day, we still await scientific evidence to validate what we know instinctively to be true.

http://jasn.asnjournals.org/cgi/content/full/19/6/1041 (2008)

Just Add Water

My note: General ideas, many misconceptions addressed, about water. A good, clear and short paper which references many very recent articles.

http://ajpregu.physiology.org/content/283/5/R993.short (2002)

'Drink at least eight glasses of water a day.' Really? Is there scientific evidence for '8 × 8'?

Despite the seemingly ubiquitous admonition to 'drink at least eight 8-oz glasses of water a day' (with an accompanying reminder that beverages containing caffeine and alcohol do not count), rigorous proof for this counsel appears to be lacking.

http://www.mineralwaters.org/index.php

Mineral Waters of the World

My note: a website that includes the information on over 3500 brands of mineral water from more than 135 countries.

http://www.ccwater.org.uk/upload/pdf/why_tap_water_winner.pdf

Why tap water is a winner

My note: a short, easy to read pdf document that addresses some of the misconceptions about tap water in the UK.

Alcohol

http://www.ncbi.nlm.nih.gov/pubmed/20878178 (2011)

A low dose of alcohol does not impact skeletal muscle performance after exercise-induced muscle damage

Significant decreases in all measures of muscular performance were observed over time under both conditions (all $P < 0.05$); however, no difference between treatments was evident at any of the measured time points (all $P > 0.05$). Therefore, consumption of a low dose of alcohol after damaging exercise appears to have no effect on the loss of force associated with strenuous eccentric exercise.

http://www.ncbi.nlm.nih.gov/pmc/articles/PMC3257708/?tool=pubmed (2010)

Alcohol, Athletic Performance and Recovery

A significant body of literature has established an array of adverse symptoms caused by acute alcohol ingestion. However the notion that alcohol consumption effects performance has not received enough consistent validation to advance beyond being anecdotal. Nevertheless, just because alcohol is not yet comprehensively shown to have a negative influence on performance, does not imply this review advocates its use prior to, or following competition. Indeed, the data demonstrates a severe lack of analysis on the possible detrimental action of alcohol in the recovering athlete.

http://www.ncbi.nlm.nih.gov/pubmed/19230764 (2010)

Acute alcohol consumption aggravates the decline in muscle performance following strenuous eccentric exercise.

These results indicate that consumption of even moderate amounts of alcohol following eccentric-based exercise magnifies the normally observed losses in dynamic and static strength. Therefore, to minimise exercise related losses in muscle function and expedite recovery, participants in sports involving eccentric muscle work should avoid alcohol-containing beverages in the post-event period.

http://www.ncbi.nlm.nih.gov/pubmed/20012446 (2010)

Post-exercise alcohol ingestion exacerbates eccentric-exercise induced losses in performance

… consumption of moderate amounts of alcohol after damaging exercise magnifies the loss of force associated with strenuous eccentric exercise. This weakness appears to be due to an interaction between muscle damage and alcohol rather than the systemic effects of acute alcohol consumption.

http://www.ncbi.nlm.nih.gov/pubmed/16822341 (2006)

The effect of alcohol on athletic performance

Central nervous system function is impaired at high doses, resulting in decrements in cognitive function and motor skill, as well as behavioral changes that may have adverse effects on performance. Effects may persist for hours after intoxication.

Other

http://www.uptodate.com/contents/cold-stimulus-headache (last updated: 2012)

Cold stimulus headache

http://jat.oxfordjournals.org/content/27/7/520.full.pdf (2003)

Caffeine Content of Specialty Coffees

7 Micronutrients

Vitamins, minerals and supplements

http://ajl.sagepub.com/content/early/2012/01/19/1559827611431541.abstract (2012)

Iron Deficiency in Athletes: An Update

Routine screening is advocated for at-risk athletes, particularly elite-level female competitors in distance sports, and, although controversial, many authorities recommend iron treatment for athletes with hypoferritemia (ferritin <12-20 ng/ml), even without overt anemia. However, 'blind' supplementation with oral iron by athletes is not recommended.

http://summaries.cochrane.org/CD007176/antioxidant-supplements-for-prevention-of-mortality-in-healthy-participants-and-patients-with-various-diseases (2012)

Antioxidant supplements for prevention of mortality in healthy participants and patients with various diseases

The present systematic review included 78 randomised clinical trials. In total, 296,707 participants were randomised to antioxidant supplements (beta-carotene, Vitamin A, Vitamin C, Vitamin E, and selenium) versus placebo or no intervention… The current evidence does not support the use of antioxidant supplements in the general population or in patients with various diseases.

http://www.ncbi.nlm.nih.gov/pubmed/21951331 (2011)

Fat burners: nutrition supplements that increase fat metabolism.

In this review the evidence for some of these supplements is briefly summarized. Based on the available literature, caffeine and green tea have data to back up its fat metabolism-enhancing properties. For many other supplements, although some show some promise, evidence is lacking.

http://www.ncbi.nlm.nih.gov/pubmed/22060178 (2011)

Antioxidant supplementation during exercise training: beneficial or detrimental?

We recommend that an adequate intake of vitamins and minerals through a varied and balanced diet remains the best approach to maintain the optimal antioxidant status in exercising individuals.

http://www.ncbi.nlm.nih.gov/pubmed/22150424 (2011)

Nutrition for winter sports.

Winter sports are played in cold conditions on ice or snow and often at moderate to high altitude… winter sport athletes may benefit from dietary and sport supplements; however, attention should be paid to safety and efficacy if supplementation is considered.

http://www.jssm.org/vol8/n4/15/v8n4-15text.php (2009)

EFFECTS OF SODIUM PHOSPHATE LOADING ON AEROBIC POWER AND CAPACITY IN OFF ROAD CYCLISTS

The main aim of this paper was to evaluate the effects of short-term (6 days) phosphate loading, as well as prolonged (21 days) intake of sodium phosphate on aerobic capacity in off-road cyclists… The results indicate a significant ($p < 0.05$) increase in Vo2 max…

http://www.ncbi.nlm.nih.gov/pubmed/18427858 (2008)

Current micronutrient recommendations in Europe: towards understanding their differences and similarities

The large variation in current micronutrient recommendations for population groups as illustrated for Vitamin A and Vitamin D strengthens the need for guidance on setting evidence based, up-to-date European recommendations.

http://content.karger.com/ProdukteDB/produkte.asp?Aktion=ShowAbstract&ArtikelNr=000140515&Ausgabe=238713&ProduktNr=223977 (2008)

Influence of an Antioxidant Vitamin-Enriched Drink on Pre- and Post-Exercise Lymphocyte Antioxidant System

Supplementation with moderate levels of antioxidant vitamins reduces exercise-induced oxidative damage, but without blocking the cellular adaptation to exercise.

http://www.sciencedirect.com/science/article/pii/S0891584907001086 (2007)

Moderate exercise is an antioxidant: Upregulation of antioxidant genes by training

Because these signals result in an upregulation of powerful antioxidant enzymes, exercise itself can be considered an antioxidant. We have found that interfering with free radical metabolism with antioxidants may hamper useful adaptations to training.

http://jama.ama-assn.org/content/297/8/842 (2007)

Mortality in Randomized Trials of Antioxidant Supplements for Primary and Secondary Prevention

Objective: To assess the effect of antioxidant supplements on mortality in randomized primary and secondary prevention trials.

Data Extraction: We included 68 randomized trials with 232 606 participants (385 publications).

Conclusions: Treatment with beta carotene, Vitamin A, and Vitamin E may increase mortality. The potential roles of Vitamin C and selenium on mortality need further study.

Letters

There were several responses (*some* of these are below) to the editor that took issue with much of the above meta-analysis.

http://jama.ama-assn.org/content/298/4/401.2.extrac (2007)

To the Editor: We believe that the approach used in the meta-analysis of mortality in randomized trials of antioxidant supplements by Dr Bjelakovic and colleagues1 erred in several important ways, probably resulting in biased conclusions.

http://jama.ama-assn.org/content/298/4/400.1.extract (2007)

http://www.ncbi.nlm.nih.gov/pubmed/17240780/ (2006)

B-vitamins and exercise: does exercise alter requirements?

… Current research suggests that exercise may increase the requirements for riboflavin and Vitamin B_6, while data for folate and Vitamin B_{12} are limited. Athletes who have poor diets, especially those restricting energy intakes or eliminating food groups from the diet, should consider supplementing with a multivitamin/mineral supplement.

http://www.ncbi.nlm.nih.gov/pubmed/18500950 (2005)

Dietary supplements and sports performance: minerals.

The two major classes of minerals are the macrominerals and the trace elements. The scope of this article will focus on the ergogenic theory and the efficacy of such mineral supplementation.

http://www.ncbi.nlm.nih.gov/pubmed/15212745 (2004)

Vitamin and mineral status: effects on physical performance.

Use of vitamin and mineral supplements does not improve measures of performance in people consuming adequate diets. Young girls and individuals participating in activities with weight classifications or aesthetic components are prone to nutrient deficiencies because they restrict food intake and specific micronutrient-rich foods.

http://www.ncbi.nlm.nih.gov/pmc/articles/PMC2129136/ (2004)

Dietary Supplements and Sports Performance: Introduction and Vitamins

Obtaining adequate vitamins, including use of supplements, may also be prudent behavior for some athletes.

http://www.ncbi.nlm.nih.gov/pubmed/10919964 (2000)

Magnesium, zinc, and chromium nutriture and physical activity.

Physically active individuals with concerns about meeting guidelines for nutrient intake should be counseled to select and consume foods with high nutrient densities rather than to rely on nutritional supplements. The indiscriminate use of mineral supplements can adversely affect physiologic function and impair health.

http://www.sciencedirect.com/science/article/pii/0165799295900357 (1995)

Vitamin E prevents exercise-induced DNA damage

Our results demonstrate that Vitamin E prevents exercise-induced DNA damage and indicate that DNA breakage occurs in WBC after exhaustive exercise as a consequence of oxidative stress.

Dietary advice and general information

http://www.ncbi.nlm.nih.gov/pmc/articles/PMC3070624/?tool=pubmed (2011)

International Society of Sports Nutrition position stand: meal frequency

My note: A comprehensive and easy-to-read report about meal frequency, including 88 references.

http://www.ncbi.nlm.nih.gov/pubmed/19225360 (2009)

American College of Sports Medicine position stand. Nutrition and athletic performance.

Vitamin and mineral supplements are not needed if adequate energy to maintain body weight is consumed from a variety of foods. However, athletes who restrict energy intake, use severe weight-loss practices, eliminate one or more food groups from their diet, or consume unbalanced diets with low micronutrient density may require supplements.

http://www.dh.gov.uk/en/index.htm

Department of Health: public health, adult social care and the NHS

http://www.defra.gov.uk/

Department for Environment Food and Rural Affairs (Defra)

The UK government department responsible for food standards and production, agriculture, fisheries and rural communities.

http://ods.od.nih.gov/ (USA)

Office of Dietary Supplements - National Institutes of Health

http://www.nhs.uk/LiveWell/5ADAY/Pages/5ADAYhome.aspx

NHS Choices, your health, your choices - 5 A Day

My note: part of the National Health Service website; plenty of clear and concise advice about your 'five-a-day' fruit and vegetables.

http://www.nhs.uk/Livewell/loseweight/Pages/Healthybreakfasts.aspx

NHS Choices, your health, your choices - Five healthy Breakfasts

Part of the National Health Service website; five easy-to-make wholesome breakfast ideas.

http://www.nice.org.uk/nicemedia/documents/scientificbas_nutreduc.pdf

The Scientific Basis of Nutrition Information - A Synopsys of Dietary Reference Values

A briefing paper prepared for the Health Education Authority...

Cooking methods

http://www.sciencedirect.com/science/article/pii/S0963996910001286 (2010)

Cooking methods of Brassica rapa affect the preservation of glucosinolates, phenolics and Vitamin C

... results showed high retentions of individual compounds in steaming, and the lowest retentions were obtained in the traditional high-pressure cooking. High retention of health-promoting compounds in the cooking water should be considered for increasing the intake of properties of B.

http://www.sciencedirect.com/science/article/pii/S0308814608014684 (2008)

The effect of cooking methods on mineral and vitamin contents of African catfish

Proximate composition, mineral and vitamin contents (A, E, B_1, B_2, niacin and B_6) were investigated in cooked African catfish. Different cooking treatments were used...

http://onlinelibrary.wiley.com/doi/10.1002/1521-3803(20001201)44:6%3C451::AID-FOOD451%3E3.0.CO;2-5/abstract (2000)

Vitamin C losses in some frozen vegetables due to various cooking methods

... According to the results, it was found that thawing before cooking is useless and causes more Vitamin C loss. Therefore, frozen vegetables must not be thawed before cooking. In order to prevent Vitamin C from destruction, using double based stainless steel pan, minimum amount of water and cooking of frozen vegetables are recommended.

http://www.sciencedirect.com/science/article/pii/S0308814698001800 [1998]

Vitamin C in frozen, fresh squeezed, unpasteurized, polyethylene-bottled orange juice: a storage study

'... over a period of 24 months. Vitamin C content declined from an initial value of 40.6mg/100ml to 32.8mg/100ml...'

Haemolysis

http://www.ncbi.nlm.nih.gov/pubmed/21751854 (2011)

Intravascular haemolysis during prolonged running on asphalt and natural grass in long and middle distance runners.

Our findings indicate that intravascular haemolysis occurs significantly after prolonged running. Furthermore, we conclude that uneven grass surface results in greater haemolysis compared to asphalt road.

http://journals.lww.com/acsm-msse/Abstract/2009/05000/Training_Surface_and_ Intensity__Inflammation,.21.aspx (2009)

Training Surface and Intensity: Inflammation, Hemolysis, and Hepcidin Expression

Conclusion: Greater running intensities incur more inflammation and hemolysis, but these variables were not affected by the surface type trained upon.

http://jap.physiology.org/content/94/1/38.full.html#ref-list-1 (2002)

Footstrike is the major cause of hemolysis during running

The present data indicate that, whereas general circulatory trauma to the red blood cells associated with 1 hour of exercise at 75% maximal oxygen uptake may result in some exercise-induced hemolysis, footstrike is the major contributor to hemolysis during running.

8 Sport Supplements

General information: supplements and ergogenic aids

http://sph.sagepub.com/content/4/2/142.short (2012)

Emerging Supplements in Sports

An Internet search of common fitness and bodybuilding sites... of... the most commonly identified supplements, including glutamine, choline, methoxyisoflavone, quercetin, zinc/magnesium aspartate, and nitric oxide... Scientific evidence is not available to support the use of these supplements for performance enhancement.

http://www.nhs.uk/news/2011/05May/Documents/BtH_supplements.pdf (2011)

Supplements - Who needs them?

My note: An easy-to-read special NHS report (pdf) on supplements. It references 53 recent papers, most of which were published in 2010 and 2011.

http://www.ncbi.nlm.nih.gov/pmc/articles/PMC2853497/?tool=pubmed (2010)

ISSN exercise & sports nutrition review: research & recommendations

This paper is a five-year update of the sports nutrition review article published as the lead paper to launch the JISSN in 2004 and presents a well-referenced overview of the current state of the science related to how to optimize training and athletic performance through nutrition.

My note: this clear and easy-to-read paper covers all the common ergogenic aids, macronutrients and micronutrients.

http://www.springerlink.com/content/v31p781583p07667/ (2007)

Performance enhancement with supplements: incongruence between rationale and practice

This study provided a platform for assessing congruence between athletes' reasons for supplement use and their actual use. These results suggest that a lack of understanding exists in supplement use.

http://ajs.sagepub.com/content/32/6/1543.short (2004)

Ergogenic Aids: A Review of Basic Science, Performance, Side Effects, and Status in Sports

ß-alanine

http://www.ncbi.nlm.nih.gov/pubmed/20479615 (2010)

Role of beta-alanine supplementation on muscle carnitine and exercise performance

In conclusion, beta-alanine supplementation seems to be a safe nutritional strategy capable of improving high-intensity anaerobic performance.

http://www.ncbi.nlm.nih.gov/pubmed/22253993 (2010)

Effects of beta-alanine on muscle carnosine and exercise performance: a review of the current literature

This paper overviews the theoretical rationale and potential ergogenic value of β-ALA supplementation with or without creatine as well as provides future research recommendations.

http://www.ncbi.nlm.nih.gov/pubmed/20199122 (2010)

Muscle carnosine metabolism and beta-alanine supplementation in relation to exercise and training

Beta-Alanine is rapidly developing as a popular ergogenic nutritional supplement for athletes worldwide, and the currently available scientific literature suggests that its use is evidence based. However, many aspects of the supplement, such as the potential side effects and the mechanism of action, require additional and thorough investigation by the sports science community.

http://www.ncbi.nlm.nih.gov/pubmed/19214556 (2009)

The effect of 4 weeks beta-alanine supplementation and isokinetic training on carnosine concentrations in type I and II human skeletal muscle fibres

The results indicate that 4 weeks' training has no effect on the muscle carnosine content. Whilst an increase was seen with beta-alanine supplementation, this was not further influenced by training. These findings suggest that beta-alanine availability is the main factor regulating muscle carnosine synthesis.

BCAA

http://www.ncbi.nlm.nih.gov/pubmed/22050133 (2011)

The effect of branched chain amino acids on psychomotor performance during treadmill exercise of changing intensity simulating a soccer game

It is concluded that BCAA supplementation might be recommended in sport activities that change in intensity and require quick responses to external signals (eg, soccer and other team games).

http://www.ncbi.nlm.nih.gov/pubmed/22168756 (2011)

Potential therapeutic effects of branched-chain amino acids supplementation on resistance exercise-based muscle damage in humans

The main point is that BCAA supplementation may decrease some biochemical markers related with muscle soreness but this does not necessarily reflect on muscle functionality.

http://www.ncbi.nlm.nih.gov/pubmed/21297567 (2011)

"branched-chain amino acids supplementation enhances exercise capacity and lipid oxidation during endurance exercise after muscle glycogen depletion

In conclusion, BCAA supplementation increases resistance to fatigue and enhances lipid oxidation during exercise in glycogen-depleted subjects.

http://www.ncbi.nlm.nih.gov/pubmed/20601741 (2010)

Branched-chain amino acid supplementation before squat exercise and delayed-onset muscle soreness

These results suggest that muscle damage may be suppressed by BCAA supplementation.

http://www.ncbi.nlm.nih.gov/pubmed/20300014 (2010)

Amino acid supplements and recovery from high-intensity resistance training

These findings suggest that short-term amino acid supplementation, which is high in BCAA, may produce a net anabolic hormonal profile while attenuating training-induced increases in muscle tissue damage.

http://www.springerlink.com/content/l43v022r415t2065/ (2009)

Consuming a supplement containing branched-chain amino acids during a resistance-training program increases lean mass, muscle strength and fat loss

Ingestion of a supplement containing BCAAs while following an 8-week resistance training program resulted in a greater decrease in percent body fat, an increase in lean mass, and 10-RM [repetition maximum] strength...

http://www.ncbi.nlm.nih.gov/pubmed/15173434 (2004)

Exercise promotes BCAA catabolism: effects of BCAA supplementation on skeletal muscle during exercise

These findings suggest that fatty acids may be one of the regulators of BCAA catabolism and that the BCAA requirement is increased by exercise. Furthermore, BCAA supplementation before and after exercise has beneficial effects for decreasing exercise-induced muscle damage and promoting muscle-protein synthesis; this suggests the possibility that BCAAs are a useful supplement in relation to exercise and sports.

Caffeine

http://content.karger.com/produktedb/produkte.asp?doi=322696 (2011)

Caffeine and Creatine Use in Sport

The purpose of this paper is to review the pharmacology and potential mechanism(s) of action of caffeine and creatine as they pertain to possible use as an ergogenic aid in sport.... Results: Caffeine taken before (3-6mg/kg) or during (1-2mg/kg) endurance exercise enhances performance, through central nervous system and direct muscle effects. Creatine monohydrate supplementation at higher (approx. 20g/day × 3-5 days) or lower (approx. 5g/day × 30 days) doses increases skeletal muscle total and phospho-creatine by 10-20%.

http://www.ncbi.nlm.nih.gov/pmc/articles/PMC2824625/?tool=pubmed (2010)

International society of sports nutrition position stand: caffeine and performance

My note: *A comprehensive and easy-to-read report in favour of caffeine, including 97 references.*

http://findarticles.com/p/articles/mi_qa3867/is_1_132/ai_n55242012/ (2010)

Myth buster: caffeine does not exhibit a diuretic effect during exercise performance

Because of its diuretic potential, nutrition experts, exercise physiologists and clinicians often advise athletes to abstain from ingesting caffeine or caffeinated beverages prior to exercise... In a well-designed study, they reported a significant increase in run time to exhaustion at 70 per cent VO_2 max following acute caffeine ingestion compared to the placebo trial... All six investigations, including the present one, concur that caffeine intake, when compared to a control condition, does not increase heat storage during exercise, nor does it adversely affect performance in a hot and/or humid environment.

http://www.ncbi.nlm.nih.gov/pubmed/19757860 (2009)

Caffeine and anaerobic performance: ergogenic value and mechanisms of action

The effect caffeine elicits on endurance performance is well founded. However, comparatively less research has been conducted on the ergogenic potential of anaerobic performance...

http://journals.lww.com/acsm-csmr/Abstract/2003/08000/Caffeine_and_Exercise.8.aspx (2003)

Caffeine and Exercise

It improves performance and endurance during prolonged, exhaustive exercise. To a lesser degree it also enhances short-term, high-intensity athletic performance.

http://www.ingentaconnect.com/content/adis/smd/2001/00000031/00000011/art00002 (2001)

Caffeine and Exercise: Metabolism, Endurance and Performance

It has also been shown to increase speed and/or power output in simulated race conditions. These effects have been found in activities that last as little as 60 seconds or as long as 2 hours. There is less information about the effects of caffeine on strength...

Creatine

http://www.ncbi.nlm.nih.gov/pubmed/20591625 (2011)

Low-dose creatine supplementation enhances fatigue resistance in the absence of weight gain

Ingesting a low dose ($\approx$2.3g/d) of creatine for six weeks significantly increased plasma creatine concentration and enhanced resistance to fatigue during repeated bouts of high-intensity contractions.

http://www.ncbi.nlm.nih.gov/pubmed/22131203 (2011)

Ergolytic/ergogenic effects of creatine on aerobic power

The results indicated that Cr loading did not positively or negatively influence VO_2 max, CV, time to exhaustion or body mass ($p > 0.05$). These results suggest Cr supplementation may be used in aerobic running activities without detriments to performance.

http://www.ncbi.nlm.nih.gov/pubmed/21399917 (2011)

Studies on the safety of creatine supplementation

We advise that high-dose (>3-5g/day) creatine supplementation should not be used by individuals with pre-existing renal disease or those with a potential risk for renal dysfunction (diabetes, hypertension, reduced glomerular filtration rate). A pre-supplementation investigation of kidney function might be considered for reasons of safety, but in normal healthy subjects appears unnecessary.

http://www.ncbi.nlm.nih.gov/pubmed/21424716 (2011)

Analysis of the efficacy, safety, and regulatory status of novel forms of creatine

… there is little to no evidence that any of the newer forms of creatine are more effective and/or safer than CM [creatine monohydrate] whether ingested alone and/or in combination with other nutrients… the safety, efficacy, and regulatory status of CM is clearly defined… other forms of creatine present in today's marketplace as a dietary or food supplement is less clear.

http://www.ncbi.nlm.nih.gov/pubmed/19387397 (2009)

Effects of creatine monohydrate and polyethylene glycosylated creatine supplementation on muscular strength, endurance, and power output

The purpose of this study was to examine the effects of a moderate dose of creatine monohydrate (CM) and two smaller doses of polyethylene glycosylated (PEG) creatine on muscular strength, endurance, and power output… PEG creatine may have ergogenic effects that are comparable to those of CM, but with a smaller dose of creatine.

http://www.ncbi.nlm.nih.gov/pubmed/18708688 (2008)

Effect of creatine supplementation and resistance-exercise training on muscle insulin-like growth factor in young adults

Results showed that RET [resistance exercise training] increased intramuscular IGF-I content by 67%, with greater accumulation from CR (+78%) than PL (+54%; p=.06). There were no differences in IGF-I between vegetarians and nonvegetarians. These findings indicate that creatine supplementation during resistance-exercise training increases intramuscular IGF-I concentration in healthy men and women, independent of habitual dietary routine.

http://www.ncbi.nlm.nih.gov/pubmed/17985060 (2007)

Effects of creatine supplementation on the onset of neuromuscular fatigue threshold and muscle strength in elderly men and women (64-86 years)

While more research is needed, CR supplementation may improve upper body grip strength and lower body muscle endurance which may be important for maintaining health and independent living in elderly men and women.

http://www.ncbi.nlm.nih.gov/pmc/articles/PMC2048496/?tool=pubmed (2007)

International Society of Sports Nutrition position stand: creatine supplementation and exercise

My note: *A comprehensive and easy-to-read report in favour of creatine, including 100 references.*

http://www.ncbi.nlm.nih.gov/pubmed/19124889 (2006)

Side effects of creatine supplementation in athletes

Even if there is a slight increase in mutagenic agents (methylamine and formaldehyde) in urine after a heavy load of creatine (20g/day), their excretion remains within a normal range... In summary, the major risk for health is probably associated with the purity of commercially available creatine.

Ephedrine

http://www.ncbi.nlm.nih.gov/pubmed/20479486 (2010)

Pseudoephedrine ingestion and cycling time-trial performance

PSE improved cycling TT performance by 5.1%... The ingestion of 180mg of PSE 60 minutes before the onset of high-intensity exercise improved cycling TT performance in well-trained athletes.

http://www.ncbi.nlm.nih.gov/pubmed/16531903 (2007)

Pseudoephedrine enhances performance in 1500-m runners

Pseudoephedrine significantly decreased time to completion of 1500-m time trials in the present study by 2.1%... with no reported side-effects. The finding was that 2.5mg. kg(-1) bw pseudoephedrine ingested 90 minutes pre-exercise improves 1500-m running performance.

http://www.ncbi.nlm.nih.gov/pubmed/15625222 (2005)

Psychiatric effects of ephedra use: an analysis of Food and Drug Administration reports of adverseevents

The authors reviewed all 1820 adverse event reports related to dietary supplements containing herbal ephedra... Of importance, two-thirds of all cases involved patients with pre-existing psychiatric conditions and /or use of other medications or illicit substances.

http://www.ncbi.nlm.nih.gov/pubmed/12672771 (2003)

Efficacy and safety of ephedra and ephedrine for weight loss and athletic performance: a meta-analysis

Ephedrine and ephedra promote modest short-term weight loss (approximately 0.9kg/mo more than placebo) in clinical trials. There are no data regarding long-term weight loss, and evidence to support use of ephedra for athletic performance is insufficient. Use of ephedra or ephedrine and caffeine is associated with increased risk of psychiatric, autonomic, or gastrointestinal symptoms, and heart palpitations.

http://www.ncbi.nlm.nih.gov/pubmed/12900684 (2003)

Effects of pseudoephedrine on maximal cycling power and submaximal cycling efficiency

A therapeutic dose of pseudoephedrine hydrochloride does not affect anaerobic cycling performance or aerobic cycling efficiency.

My note: the dosage of ephedrine was 60mg.

http://www.ncbi.nlm.nih.gov/pubmed/12466695 (2002)

A moderate dose of pseudoephedrine does not alter muscle contraction strength or anaerobic power

These results demonstrated that a 120mg dose of PSE did not enhance force production, time to fatigue, fatigue index, or power output in young men or women. Therefore, there does not appear to be an ergogenic benefit from the ingestion of 120mg PSE in high-intensity exercise performance.

http://www.ncbi.nlm.nih.gov/pubmed/10971304 (2000)

Muscular and cardiorespiratory effects of pseudoephedrine in human athletes

The administration of a 180mg dose of PSE increased maximum torque, produced in an isometric knee extension and produced an improvement in peak power during maximal cycle performance, as well as improving lung function.

Fat burners

http://www.ncbi.nlm.nih.gov/pubmed/21951331 (2011)

Fat burners: nutrition supplements that increase fat metabolism

Based on the available literature, caffeine and green tea have data to back up its fat metabolism-enhancing properties. For many other supplements, although some show some promise, evidence is lacking.

http://www.pubmedcentral.nih.gov/articlerender.fcgi?artid=2621121 (2009)

Thermogenic effect of an acute ingestion of a weight loss supplement

Results indicate a significant increase in energy expenditure in young, healthy individuals following an acute ingestion of a weight loss supplement.

My note: another 'Meltdown'' paper, but this time using five male and five female subjects.

http://www.pubmedcentral.nih.gov/articlerender.fcgi?artid=2637826 (2008)

The acute effects of the thermogenic supplement Meltdown on energy expenditure, fat oxidation, and hemodynamic responses in young, healthy males

In conclusion, these data presented herein suggest that Meltdown enhances fat oxidation and REE more than placebo for up to 60 min and 120 min, respectively...

My note: a small trial (10 male subjects) for Meltdown, a commercial weight-loss supplement (fat burner).*

http://www.ncbi.nlm.nih.gov/pmc/articles/PMC2276475/ (2008)

Acute effects of ingesting a commercial thermogenic drink on changes in energy expenditure and markers of lipolysis

Acute TD ingestion appears to stimulate significant increases in energy expenditure and circulating levels of FFA while substrate oxidation and circulating levels of glycerol experienced non-significant decreases across time. Additional research needs to further examine the impact of prolonged daily ingestion of TD on energy expenditure, changes in body composition and efficacy of daily ingestion of TD. These studies will provide additional evidence for any role TD may play at promoting weight loss and/or achieving weight maintenance.

http://www.ncbi.nlm.nih.gov/pubmed/16840650 (2007)

Obesity and thermogenesis related to the consumption of caffeine, ephedrine, capsaicin, and green tea

A combination of caffeine and ephedrine has shown to be effective in long-term weight management… However, adverse effects of ephedrine prevent the feasibility of this approach. Capsaicin has been shown to be effective, yet when it is used clinically it requires a strong compliance to a certain dosage, that has not been shown to be feasible yet. Also positive effects on body-weight management have been shown using green tea mixtures… In addition, tea catechins have antiangiogenic properties that may prevent development of overweight and obesity.

http://www.nature.com/oby/journal/v13/n7/abs/oby2005142a.html (2005)

Body Weight Loss and Weight Maintenance in Relation to Habitual Caffeine Intake and Green Tea Supplementation

Investigation of the effect of a green tea-caffeine mixture on weight maintenance after body weight loss in moderately obese subjects in relation to habitual caffeine intake… High caffeine intake was associated with weight loss through thermogenesis and fat oxidation and with suppressed leptin in women. In habitual low caffeine consumers, the green tea-caffeine mixture improved WM, partly through thermogenesis and fat oxidation.

http://www.ncbi.nlm.nih.gov/pubmed/15051593 (2004)

Dietary supplements for body-weight reduction: a systematic review

Data on the following dietary supplements were identified: chitosan, chromium picolinate, Ephedra sinica, Garcinia cambogia, glucomannan, guar gum, hydroxy-methylbutyrate, plantago psyllium, pyruvate, yerba maté, and yohimbe. The reviewed studies provide some encouraging data but no evidence beyond a reasonable doubt that any specific dietary supplement is effective for reducing body weight. The only exceptions are E. sinica- and ephedrine-containing supplements, which have been associated with an increased risk of adverse events.

The evidence for most dietary supplements as aids in reducing body weight is not convincing. None of the reviewed dietary supplements can be recommended for over-the-counter use.

http://www.ncbi.nlm.nih.gov/pubmed/15292480 (2004)

Effect of a dietary herbal supplement containing caffeine and ephedra on weight, metabolic rate, and body composition

… weight loss at 12 weeks was 3.5 +/- 0.6kg with C&E compared with 0.8 +/- 0.5kg with placebo ($p < 0.02$)… C&E increased RMR significantly by 8% compared with placebo, promoted more weight and fat loss than placebo, and was well tolerated.

Glutamine

http://www.ncbi.nlm.nih.gov/pubmed/22397703 (2012)

L-alanyl-L-glutamine ingestion maintains performance during a competitive basketball game

Rehydration with AG appears to maintain basketball skill performance and visual reaction time to a greater extent than water only.

http://www.ncbi.nlm.nih.gov/pubmed/20181080 (2010)

Examination of the efficacy of acute L-alanyl-L-glutamine ingestion during hydration stress in endurance exercise

Results demonstrate that AG supplementation provided a significant ergogenic benefit by increasing time to exhaustion during a mild hydration stress. This ergogenic effect was likely mediated by an enhanced fluid and electrolyte uptake.

http://www.ncbi.nlm.nih.gov/pubmed/18806122 (2008)

Dosing and efficacy of glutamine supplementation in human exercise and sport training

… the suggested reasons for taking glutamine supplements (support for immune system, increased glycogen synthesis, anticatabolic effect) have received little support from well-controlled scientific studies in healthy, well-nourished humans.

http://www.ncbi.nlm.nih.gov/pubmed/11822473 (2001)

Effect of glutamine supplementation combined with resistance training in young adults

We conclude that glutamine supplementation during resistance training has no significant effect on muscle performance, body composition or muscle protein degradation in young healthy adults.

Herbal supplements

http://www.ncbi.nlm.nih.gov/pubmed/22738038 (2012)

Effect of Spirulina maxima on postprandial lipemia in young runners: a preliminary report

Forty-one runners (10-26 years old; 21 men and 20 women) volunteered to participate in the study. All of them were physically active for at least 1 year before the study and were not undergoing training during the study. The subjects consumed 5 g of Spirulina during 15 days…Sixty-two percent of the youngest runners (10-16 years) studied exhibited the best response to the treatment. Orally administered S. maxima decreased postprandial lipemia in sporting teenagers. The youngest people were the most responsive to the beneficial effects of Spirulina on postprandial lipemia.

http://www.nlm.nih.gov/medlineplus/druginfo/natural/923.html (2012)

MedlinePlus - Blue-green algae

My note: an easy-to-read page of information on blue-green algae, with 24 references,

http://www.ncbi.nlm.nih.gov/pubmed/21115335 (2011)

Antiobesity effects of green tea catechins: a mechanistic review

Green tea catechins (GTC)… Results from a number of randomized, controlled intervention trials have shown that consumption of GTC (270mg to 1200mg/day) may reduce body weight and fat.

http://www.ncbi.nlm.nih.gov/pubmed/21480414 (2011)

The safety of Citrus aurantium (bitter orange) and its primary protoalkaloid p-synephrine

The data indicate that based on current knowledge, the use of bitter orange extract and p-synephrine appears to be exceedingly safe, with no serious adverse effects being directly attributable to these ingredients.

http://www.ncbi.nlm.nih.gov/pubmed/21804969 (2011)

Safety assessment of plant food supplements (PFS)

… PFS may contain compounds of concern at levels far above those found in the regular diet. In addition, the traditional use of a PFS compound as a herb or tea does not guarantee its safety when used as a supplement. This points at a need for stricter regulation and control of botanical containing products, especially given their expanding market volume.

http://www.ncbi.nlm.nih.gov/pubmed/21321426 (2011)

Effects of acute supplementation of Panax ginseng on endurance running in a hot & humid environment

We conclude that acute supplementation of 200mg of PG did not affect the endurance running performance of the heat-adapted male recreational runners in the heat.

http://www.ncbi.nlm.nih.gov/pubmed/20010119 (2010)

Ergogenic and antioxidant effects of spirulina supplementation in humans.

Nine moderately trained males took part in a double-blind, placebo-controlled, counterbalanced crossover study. Each subject received either spirulina (6g × d(-1))or placebo for 4 wk. Spirulina supplementation induced a significant increase in exercise performance, fat oxidation, and GSH concentration and attenuated the exercise-induced increase in lipid peroxidation.

http://www.ncbi.nlm.nih.gov/pubmed/20682072 (2010)

Effects of capsinoid ingestion on energy expenditure and lipid oxidation at rest and during exercise

The changes we observed confirm previous data on the thermogenic and metabolic effects of capsinoids at rest and further promote its potential role as an adjunct weight loss aid, in addition to diet and exercise.

http://www.ncbi.nlm.nih.gov/pubmed/19680234 (2010)

Effects of catechin enriched green tea on body composition.

We conclude that consumption of two servings of an extra high-catechin GT leads to improvements in body composition and reduces abdominal fatness in moderately overweight Chinese subjects.

http://www.ncbi.nlm.nih.gov/pubmed/19574616 (2009)

Is ginseng an ergogenic aid?

The purpose of this review is to provide an update on published empirical research focusing primarily on the efficacy of ginseng with respect to physical and athletic performance. Despite attempts in recent investigations to improve on the scientific rigor used in examining the ergogenic properties of ginseng, the authors conclude that many of the same methodological shortcomings observed in earlier studies persist. Enhanced physical performance after ginseng administration in well-designed investigations remains to be demonstrated.

http://www.ncbi.nlm.nih.gov/pubmed/19736596 (2009)

A novel green tea meal replacement formula for weight loss among obese individuals: a randomized controlled clinical trial

… 120 (25 male, 95 female) healthy, overweight and obese persons were included (each of them occupy one-third of the whole population)… This green tea meal replacement formula contributes to the lower body weight and reduced low-density lipoprotein cholesterol level.

http://www.ncbi.nlm.nih.gov/pubmed/19685436 (2008)

Health potential for functional green teas?

… green tea may also have measurable acute effects on energy metabolism and fat oxidation and in particular during physical activity…

http://www.ncbi.nlm.nih.gov/pubmed/17618964 (2007)

Effect of adding exercise to a diet containing glucomannan

… exercise appeared to augment the reduction in fat mass (by 63% and 50%; men and women, respectively) and waist circumference…

http://www.ncbi.nlm.nih.gov/pubmed/17214405 (2006)

Yohimbine: the effects on body composition and exercise performance in soccer players

The results of the current study indicate that supplementation with yohimbine combined with resistance training does not significantly alter the body mass, muscle mass, or performance indicators in professional soccer players. Nonetheless, yohimbine supplementation appears to be suitable as a fat loss strategy in elite athletes.

http://www.ncbi.nlm.nih.gov/pubmed/16944194 (2006)

Preventive effects of Spirulina platensis on skeletal muscle damage under exercise-induced oxidative stress

The effects of spirulina supplementation on preventing skeletal muscle damage on untrained human beings were examined. Sixteen students volunteered to take Spirulina platensis in addition to their normal diet for 3-weeks…These results suggest that ingestion of S. platensis showed preventive effect of the skeletal muscle damage and that probably led to postponement of the time of exhaustion during the all-out exercise.

http://www.ncbi.nlm.nih.gov/pmc/articles/PMC2129138/?tool=pubmed (2006)

Dietary Supplements and Sports Performance: Herbals

My note: a report on selected herbal supplements with regards to sport performance, including ginseng, kava kava and ginko biloba.

http://www.ncbi.nlm.nih.gov/pubmed/16320857 (2005)

Glucomannan and obesity: a critical review

At doses of 2-4g per day, GM was well-tolerated and resulted in significant weight loss in overweight and obese individuals.

http://www.ncbi.nlm.nih.gov/pubmed/15836459 (2005)

Adverse events of herbal food supplements for body weight reduction: systematic review

In conclusion, adverse events are reported for a number of herbal food supplements, which are used for reducing bodyweight... the reported risks are sufficient to shift the risk-benefit balance against the use of most of the reviewed herbal weight-loss supplements. Exceptions are Garcinia cambogia and yerba mate, which merit further investigation.

http://www.ncbi.nlm.nih.gov/pubmed/15614200 (2005)

Experiences with three different fiber supplements in weight reduction.

Glucomannan induced body weight reduction in healthy overweight subjects, whereas the addition of guar gum and alginate did not seem to cause additional loss of weight.

http://www.ncbi.nlm.nih.gov/pubmed/15902991 (2005)

Assessment of the effects of eleutherococcus senticosus on endurance performance

This article reviews the studies that evaluated the effects of ES during endurance exercise... However, each of these reports contains severe methodological flaws, which seriously threaten their internal validity, thereby rendering hazardous the generalization of the results. On the other hand, five studies that used rigorous research protocols show no benefit of ES on CF, FAM, and EP. It is therefore concluded that ES supplementation (up to 1000 to 1200mg/d for 1 to 6 wk) offers no advantage during exercise ranging in duration from 6 to 120 min.

http://journals.cambridge.org/action/displayAbstract?fromPage=online&aid=913084 (2004)

Effects of green tea on weight maintenance after body-weight loss

The present study was conducted to investigate whether green tea may improve weight maintenance by preventing or limiting weight regain after weight loss of 5-10% in overweight and moderately obese subjects… We conclude that weight maintenance after 7·5% body-weight loss was not affected by green tea treatment and that habitual caffeine consumption affected weight maintenance in the green tea treatment.

http://www.ncbi.nlm.nih.gov/pubmed/11099371 (2000)

The effect of siberian ginseng (Eleutherococcus senticosus) on substrate utilization and performance

In contrast with previous reports, the results of this study suggest that ES supplementation does not alter steady-state substrate utilization or 10-km cycling performance time.

HMB

http://www.ncbi.nlm.nih.gov/pubmed/20857835 (2010)

Effect of HMB supplementation on body composition, fitness, hormonal profile and muscle damage indices

There is a huge market for ergogenic supplements for athletes. However, only a few products have been proven to have ergogenic effects… One such supplement is beta-hydroxy beta-methylbutyrate (HMB)… Several studies have shown that combining exercise training with HMB supplementation leads to increased muscle mass and strength…

http://www.ncbi.nlm.nih.gov/pubmed/19387395 (2009)

Effects of beta-hydroxy-beta-methylbutyrate supplementation during resistance training on strength, body composition, and muscle damage in trained and untrained young men: a meta-analysis

Supplementation with HMB during resistance training incurs small but clear overall and leg strength gains in previously untrained men, but effects in trained lifters are trivial. The HMB effect on body composition is inconsequential.

http://www.ncbi.nlm.nih.gov/pubmed/19387396 (2009)

Effects of nine weeks of beta-hydroxy-beta- methylbutyrate supplementation on strength and body composition in resistance trained men

In previously trained men, supplementation of HMB in conjunction with resistance training provides a substantial benefit to lower-body strength, but it has negligible effects on body composition.

http://www.ncbi.nlm.nih.gov/pubmed/17530933 (2007)

Effects of six weeks of beta-hydroxy-beta-methylbutyrate (HMB) and HMB/creatine supplementation on strength, power, and anthropometry of highly trained athletes

HMB and HMBCr were concluded to have no ergogenic effect on muscular strength and endurance, leg power, or anthropometry when taken orally by highly trained male athletes over six weeks.

http://www.ncbi.nlm.nih.gov/pubmed/14632320 (2002)

Supplementing with beta-hydroxy-beta-methylbutyrate (HMB) to build and maintain muscle mass: a review

In several studies combining HMB supplementation and resistance exercise, researchers have concluded that HMB may play an important role in reducing protein degradation and/or increasing recovery of damaged muscle cells.

http://www.ncbi.nlm.nih.gov/sites/entrez/11128859?dopt=Abstract&holding=f1000, f1000m,isrctn (2000)

Beta-hydroxy-beta-methylbutyrate ingestion, Part I: effects on strength and fat free mass

… it appears that higher doses of HMB (i.e., $> 38mg \times kg(-1) \times d(-1)$) do not promote strength or FFM gains.

Meal replacement products

http://www.ncbi.nlm.nih.gov/pubmed/21616195 (2011)

A structured diet and exercise program promotes favorable changes in weight loss, body composition, and weight maintenance

In sedentary and obese women, an SDE-based program appears to be more efficacious in promoting and maintaining weight loss and improvements in markers of health and fitness compared to an MRP type program with encouragement to increase physical activity.

http://www.ncbi.nlm.nih.gov/pubmed/20222968 (2010)

Efficacy of a meal replacement diet plan compared to a food-based diet plan after a period of weight loss and weight maintenance: a randomized controlled trial

Our data suggest that the meal replacement diet plan evaluated was an effective strategy for producing robust initial weight loss and for achieving improvements in a number of health-related parameters during weight maintenance, including inflammation and oxidative stress, two key factors more recently shown to underlie our most common chronic diseases.

http://www.ncbi.nlm.nih.gov/pubmed/18752682 (2008)

A controlled trial of protein enrichment of meal replacements for weight reduction with retention of lean body mass

Higher protein MR within a higher protein diet resulted in similar overall weight loss as the standard protein MR plan over 12 weeks. However, there was significantly more fat loss in the HP group but no significant difference in lean body mass.

Nitric oxide and L-arginine

http://www.ncbi.nlm.nih.gov/pubmed/22260513 (2012)

The effect of nitric-oxide-related supplements on human performance.

Studies involving untrained or moderately trained healthy subjects showed that NO donors could improve tolerance to aerobic and anaerobic exercise. However, when highly trained subjects were supplemented, no positive effect on performance was indicated. In addition, all this evidence is mainly based on a young male population.

http://www.ncbi.nlm.nih.gov/pubmed/22251130 (2012)

Acute l-arginine supplementation increases muscle blood volume but not strength performance

It is still premature to recommend nutritional supplements containing L-arg as an ergogenic aid to increase muscle strength during resistance training in healthy subjects.

http://www.ncbi.nlm.nih.gov/pubmed/21395365 (2011)

L-Arginine as a potential ergogenic aid in healthy subjects

In summary, it is still premature to recommend dietary supplements containing L-arginine as an ergogenic aid for healthy physically active subjects.

Pro-hormones

http://www.ncbi.nlm.nih.gov/pubmed/21649617 (2011)

Effect of dehydroepiandrosterone [DHEA] on muscle strength and physical function in older adults: a systematic review

Overall, the benefit of DHEA on muscle strength and physical function in older adults remains inconclusive. Some measures of muscle strength may improve, although consensus was not reached. DHEA does not appear to routinely benefit measures of physical function or performance.

http://www.ncbi.nlm.nih.gov/pubmed/20863330 (2010)

Dehydroepiandrosterone combined with exercise improves muscle strength and physical function in frail older women

DHEA supplementation improved lower extremity strength and function in older, frail women involved in a gentle exercise program of chair aerobics or yoga. No changes were found in BMD either due to small sample size, short duration of study or no effect. The physical function findings are promising and require further evaluation as frail women are at high risk for falls and fracture.

http://www.ncbi.nlm.nih.gov/pubmed/20122454 (2010)

Dehydroepiandrosterone to enhance physical performance: myth and reality

However, evidence for an ergogenic activity of DHEA is still largely nonexistent. Randomized trials in elderly subjects with an age-dependent decrease in DHEA have provided little or no evidence for enhanced physical performance after long-term administration of DHEA, 50mg/d, and smaller short-term studies in healthy male athletes using higher doses were completely negative. Thus the widely perceived performance-enhancing activity of DHEA is still more myth than reality.

http://www.ncbi.nlm.nih.gov/pubmed/21789881 (2010)

Effects of short-term dehydroepiandrosterone supplementation on body composition in young athletes

Results of this study suggest that DHEA supplementation has no beneficial effects on body composition in young competitive athletes.

http://www.ncbi.nlm.nih.gov/pubmed/17723877 (2007)

Testosterone precursors: use and abuse in pediatric athletes

The dietary supplements androstenedione, dehydroepiandrosterone, and androstenediol are precursors in the endogenous production of testosterone. Studies have demonstrated repeatedly that acute and long-term administration of these oral testosterone precursors does not effectively increase serum testosterone levels and fails to produce any significant changes in lean body mass, muscle strength, or performance improvement compared with placebo.

http://www.ncbi.nlm.nih.gov/pubmed/16888459 (2006)

Testosterone prohormone supplements

We focus primarily on androstenedione, but we also discuss DHEA, androstenediol, 19-nor androstenedione, and 19-nor androstenediol supplements. Contrary to marketing claims, research to date indicates that the use of prohormone nutritional supplements (DHEA, androstenedione, androstenediol, and other steroid hormone supplements) does not produce either anabolic or ergogenic effects in men. Moreover, the use of prohormone nutritional supplements may raise the risk for negative health consequences.

http://www.ncbi.nlm.nih.gov/pubmed?term=meal replacements for athletes (2004)

Dietary supplements

There is no evidence that prohormones such as androstenedione are effective in enhancing muscle mass or strength, and these prohormones may result in negative health consequences, as well as positive drug tests. Contamination of supplements that may cause an athlete to fail a doping test is widespread.

http://www.ncbi.nlm.nih.gov/pubmed/10589853 (1999)

Effects of anabolic steroids on the muscle cells of strength-trained athletes

Intake of anabolic steroids and strength-training induce an increase in muscle size by both hypertrophy and the formation of new muscle fibers.

Protein

http://www.ncbi.nlm.nih.gov/pubmed/19284589 (2009)

Resistance training with soy vs whey protein supplements in hyperlipidemic males

Twenty-eight overweight, male subjects (BMI 25-30) with serum cholesterol >200mg/dl were randomly divided into 3 groups (placebo (n = 9), and soy (n = 9) or whey (n = 10) supplementation)… Participation in a 12-week resistance exercise training program significantly increased strength and improved both body composition and serum cholesterol in overweight, hypercholesterolemic men with no added benefit from protein supplementation.

http://www.ncbi.nlm.nih.gov/pubmed/20048505 (2009)

Protein for exercise and recovery

However, recent evidence indicates that ingesting protein and/or amino acids prior to, during, and/or following exercise can enhance recovery, immune function, and growth and maintenance of lean body mass. Consequently, protein and amino acid supplements can serve as a convenient way to ensure a timely and/or adequate intake for athletes. Finally, adequate intake and appropriate timing of protein ingestion has been shown to be beneficial in multiple exercise modes, including endurance, anaerobic, and strength exercise.

http://www.ncbi.nlm.nih.gov/pubmed/17908291/ (2007)

International Society of Sports Nutrition position stand: protein and exercise

The superiority of one protein type over another in terms of optimizing recovery and/or training adaptations remains to be convincingly demonstrated.

http://www.ncbi.nlm.nih.gov/pubmed/15798080 (2005)

Dietary protein to support anabolism with resistance exercise in young men

While strength gains were not different between the soy and milk-supplemented groups we would argue that the true significance of a greater increase in lean mass that we observed with milk consumption may be more important in groups of persons with lower initial lean mass and strength such as the elderly.

http://www.ncbi.nlm.nih.gov/pubmed/15909468 (2005)

Proteins and amino acid supplementation in sports: are they truly necessary?

The use of supplements for the healthy, non-competitive adult engaged in recreational sports is usually not warranted.

Ubiquinone (Q10)

http://www.ncbi.nlm.nih.gov/pubmed/22079391 (2012)

Coenzyme Q10 supplementation and exercise-induced oxidative stress in humans.
The theoretically beneficial effects of coenzyme Q10 (Q10) on exercise-related oxidative stress and physical capacity have not been confirmed to our knowledge by interventional supplementation studies. Our aim was to investigate further whether Q10 supplementation at a dose recommended by manufacturers influences these factors. Although in theory Q10 could be beneficial for exercise capacity and in decreasing oxidative stress, the present study could not demonstrate that such effects exist after supplementation with a recommended dose.

http://www.ncbi.nlm.nih.gov/pubmed/20669312 (2010)

Safety and tolerability of high-dosage coenzyme Q10 in Huntington's disease and healthy subjects
Subjects started on 1200mg/day of CoQ(10), increasing every 4 weeks by 1200mg to a maximum dosage of 3600mg/day... Dosages of 2400mg/day may provide the best balance between tolerability and blood level achieved. Further studies examining the efficacy of 2400mg/day are planned.

http://www.ncbi.nlm.nih.gov/pubmed/18318910 (2008)

Effects of acute and 14-day coenzyme Q10 supplementation on exercise performance in both trained and untrained individuals.
To determine whether acute (single dose) and/or chronic (14-days) supplementation of CoQ10 will improve anaerobic and/or aerobic exercise performance by increasing plasma and muscle CoQ10 concentrations within trained and untrained individuals... Subjects consumed twice daily (morning and night), 100mg.
Results indicate that acute and chronic supplementation of CoQ10 may affect acute and/or chronic responses to various types of exercise.

ZMA

http://www.nature.com/ejcn/journal/v63/n1/abs/1602899a.html (2007)

Serum testosterone and urinary excretion of steroid hormone metabolites after administration of a high-dose zinc supplement

The present data suggest that the use of ZMA has no significant effects regarding serum testosterone levels and the metabolism of testosterone in subjects who consume a zinc-sufficient diet.

http://www.ncbi.nlm.nih.gov/pubmed/18500945 (2004)

Effects of Zinc Magnesium Aspartate (ZMA) Supplementation on Training Adaptations and Markers of Anabolism and Catabolism

Results indicate that ZMA supplementation during training does not appear to enhance training adaptations in resistance trained populations.

Combined supplements

http://www.ncbi.nlm.nih.gov/pubmed/21553504 (2011)

Whey protein and creatine as nutritional supplements

Whey protein and creatine seem to have positive effects on muscle size, strength and athletic performance without major adverse effects and high costs. Most studies have shown that supplementation of whey protein can enhance muscle growth in response to resistance training. Some studies also suggest that whey may enhance recovery from heavy exercise and possibly decrease muscle damage and soreness. Creatine supplementation increases the intracellular pool of phosphocreatine in skeletal muscle. Phosphocreatine provides a reserve of energy to rapidly regenerate ATP, which is consumed as a result of muscle contraction. Creatine has been studied in hundreds of clinical trials and has shown benefits including increased muscle strength, power and size…

http://www.ncbi.nlm.nih.gov/pubmed/22107883 (2011)

Effects of carbohydrate, branched-chain amino acids, and arginine in recovery period on the subsequent performance in wrestlers

There was no significant difference in these biochemical parameters between the CHO and CHO+AA trials. Supplementation of carbohydrate with or without BCAA and arginine during the post-match period had no effect on the performance in the following simulated match in wrestlers. In addition, BCAA and arginine did not provide additional insulinemic effect.

http://www.ncbi.nlm.nih.gov/pubmed/21207054 (2011)

Effect of caffeine ingestion after creatine supplementation on intermittent high-intensity sprint performance

The present study determined that caffeine ingestion after creatine supplements augmented intermittent high-intensity sprint performance.

http://www.ncbi.nlm.nih.gov/pubmed/20156347 (2010)

The effects of a pre-workout supplement containing caffeine, creatine, and amino acids during three weeks of high-intensity exercise on aerobic and anaerobic performance

These results demonstrated improvements in Vo2 max, CV [critical velocity], and LBM [lean body mass] when GT [Game Time*] is combined with HIIT [high-intensity intermittent training]. Three weeks of HIIT alone also augmented anaerobic running performance, Vo2 max and body composition.

http://www.ncbi.nlm.nih.gov/pubmed/20126965 (2010)

The effects of supplementation with creatine and protein on muscle strength following a traditional resistance training program in middle-aged and older men

Resistance training in middle-aged and older men significantly increased muscular strength and added muscle mass with no additional benefits from creatine and/or protein supplementation.

http://www.ncbi.nlm.nih.gov/pubmed/18550961 (2008)

The effect of ephedra and caffeine on maximal strength and power in resistance-trained athletes

Our results do not support the contention that supplementation with ephedra or caffeine will enhance either muscle strength or anaerobic exercise performance.

http://www.ncbi.nlm.nih.gov/pubmed/17277594 (2007)

Effects of whey isolate, creatine, and resistance training on muscle hypertrophy

Although WP and/or CrM seem to promote greater strength gains and muscle morphology during RE training, the hypertrophy responses within the groups varied. These differences in skeletal muscle morphology may have important implications for various populations and, therefore, warrant further investigation.

http://www.ncbi.nlm.nih.gov/pubmed/15487903 (2004)

Caffeine and ephedrine: physiological, metabolic and performance-enhancing effects

Caffeine-ephedrine mixtures, however, have been reported in several instances to confer a greater ergogenic benefit than either drug by itself... Caffeine-ephedra mixtures may thus become one of most popular ergogenic aids in the years to come and while they may indeed prove to be one of the most effective ones.

http://www.ncbi.nlm.nih.gov/pubmed/11448573 (2001)

Creatine and beta-hydroxy-beta-methylbutyrate (HMB) additively increase lean body mass and muscle strength during a weight-training program

In summary, CR and HMB can increase LBM and strength, and the effects are additive. Although not definitive, these results suggest that CR and HMB act by different mechanisms.

http://www.ncbi.nlm.nih.gov/pubmed/10584049 (1999)

Efficacy of a green tea extract rich in catechin polyphenols and caffeine in increasing 24-h energy expenditure and fat oxidation in humans.

Green tea has thermogenic properties and promotes fat oxidation beyond that explained by its caffeine content per se. The green tea extract may play a role in the control of body composition via sympathetic activation of thermogenesis, fat oxidation, or both.

Energy drinks

http://www.ncbi.nlm.nih.gov/pmc/articles/PMC2966367/?tool=pubmed (2010)

Energy Beverages: Content and Safety

The main ingredients of energy/power drinks are caffeine, taurine, glucuronolactone, B vitamins, guarana, ginseng, ginkgo biloba, l-carnitine, sugars, antioxidants, and trace minerals... Ingestion of EBs before an event or during training can have serious adverse effects, most notably restlessness and irritability; can increase blood pressure; and may result in dehydration. The long-term effects of EBs on the human body have not been established. Limited ingestion of EBs by healthy people is not likely to cause major adverse effects, but binge consumption or consumption with alcohol may lead to adverse events. Individuals with medical illnesses, especially underlying heart disease, should check with their physician before using EBs, because they may exacerbate their condition.

Supplements and banned substances

http://www.ncbi.nlm.nih.gov/pubmed/18563865 (2008)

Nutritional supplements cross-contaminated and faked with doping substances

Recently a nutritional supplement for weight loss was found to contain the beta2-agonist clenbuterol. The application of such nutritional supplements is connected with a high risk of inadvertent doping cases and a health risk.

http://www.ncbi.nlm.nih.gov/pubmed/18049988 (2007)

The use of dietary supplements by athletes

There are well-documented roles for creatine, caffeine, and alkalinizing agents in enhancing performance in high-intensity exercise, although much of the evidence does not relate to specific athletic events. There are potential costs associated with all dietary supplements, including the risk of a positive doping result as a consequence of the presence of prohibited substances that are not declared on the label.

http://www.ncbi.nlm.nih.gov/pubmed/16430680 (2006)

Research of stimulants and anabolic steroids in dietary supplements

The results have also shown that one creatine product and three 'mental enhancers' contained traces of hormones or prohormones not claimed on the labels and 14 prohormone products contained substances other than those indicated by the manufacturer. The oral intake of the creatine product revealed the presence of the two main nandrolone metabolites (19-norandrosterone and 19-noretiocholanolone) in urine.

http://www.ncbi.nlm.nih.gov/pubmed/16195040 (2005)

Contamination of dietary supplements and positive drug tests in sport

Although it is undoubtedly the case that some athletes are guilty of deliberate cheating, some positive tests are likely to be the result of inadvertent ingestion of prohibited substances present in otherwise innocuous dietary supplements.

http://www.ncbi.nlm.nih.gov/pubmed/12131059 (2002)

Nutritional supplements and doping.

It is known that many supplement products contain substances that are prohibited in sport-typically stimulants or anabolic steroid precursors.

Placebo

http://www.ncbi.nlm.nih.gov/pubmed/19317519 (2009)

The placebo effect in sports performance: a brief review

Findings suggest that psychological variables such as motivation, expectancy and conditioning, and the interaction of these variables with physiological variables, might be significant factors in driving both positive and negative outcomes.

http://www.ncbi.nlm.nih.gov/pubmed/17876973 (2007)

'Because I know it will!': placebo effects of an ergogenic aid on athletic performance.

Results showed that believing one had taken the substance resulted in times almost as fast as those associated with consuming the drug itself. In contrast, taking the drug without knowledge yielded no significant performance increment.

http://ukpmc.ac.uk/abstract/MED/17693687/reload=0;jsessionid=0JNKSTE504zyi0l1U05E.80 (2007)

Positive and negative placebo effects resulting from the deceptive administration of an ergogenic aid.

Collectively, data suggest that subjects' belief in the efficacy or otherwise of a placebo treatment might significantly influence findings in experimental research.

9 Upping the Mass

Note: many links related to Chapter 9: Upping the Mass are covered in the recommended reading for Chapter 8: Supplements.

http://www.ncbi.nlm.nih.gov/pubmed/22215165 (2012)

Effect of dietary protein content on weight gain, energy expenditure, and body composition during overeating: a randomized controlled trial

To evaluate the effects of overconsumption of low, normal, and high protein diets on weight gain, energy expenditure, and body composition.

Among persons living in a controlled setting, calories alone account for the increase in fat; protein affected energy expenditure and storage of lean body mass, but not body fat storage.

http://www.nrcresearchpress.com/doi/abs/10.1139/H2012-022 (2012)

Bigger weights may not beget bigger muscles: evidence from acute muscle protein synthetic responses after resistance exercise

It is often recommended that heavier training intensities (~70%-80% of maximal strength) be lifted to maximize muscle growth. However, we have reported that intensities as low as 30% of maximum strength, when lifted to volitional fatigue, are equally effective at stimulating muscle protein synthesis rates during resistance exercise recovery. This paper discusses the idea that high-intensity contractions are not the exclusive driver of resistance exercise-induced changes in muscle protein synthesis rates.

http://www.ncbi.nlm.nih.gov/pubmed/22142410 (2012)

Effects of exercise and amino acid supplementation on body composition and physical function in community-dwelling elderly Japanese sarcopenic women: a randomized controlled trial

The data suggest that exercise and AAS together may be effective in enhancing not only muscle strength, but also combined variables of muscle mass and walking speed and of muscle mass and strength in sarcopenic women.

http://www.ncbi.nlm.nih.gov/pubmed/21775530 (2011)

Increased consumption of dairy foods and protein during diet- and exercise-induced weight loss promotes fat mass loss and lean mass gain in overweight and obese premenopausal women.

Therefore, diet- and exercise-induced weight loss with higher protein and increased dairy product intakes promotes more favorable body composition changes in women characterized by greater total and visceral fat loss and lean mass gain.

http://www.ncbi.nlm.nih.gov/pubmed/16373953 (2008)

The role of dairy foods in weight management

These concepts are confirmed by epidemiological data as well as recent clinical trials which demonstrate that diets which include at least three daily servings of dairy products result in significant reductions in body fat mass in obese humans in the absence of caloric restriction and markedly accelerates the weight and body fat loss secondary to caloric restriction compared to low dairy diets. These data indicate an important role for dairy products in both the ability to maintain a healthy weight and the management of overweight and obesity.

http://www.ncbi.nlm.nih.gov/pubmed/12433852 (2003)

Effect of dietary supplements on lean mass and strength gains with resistance exercise: a meta-analysis

In conclusion, two supplements, creatine and HMB, have data supporting their use to augment lean mass and strength gains with resistance training.

10 Women in Training

The Female Athlete Triad

http://www.ncbi.nlm.nih.gov/pubmed/22341014 (2012)

The female athlete triad

With the surge of females participating in athletics within the past 10-15 years, it is both conceivable and likely that the prevalence of this syndrome will continue to grow. Therefore, it is imperative that appropriate screening and diagnostic measures are enacted by a multidisciplinary team of health care providers, counselors, teachers, and dietitians in order to provide the proper care to affected athletes... Treatment for each component of the triad includes both pharmacological and nonpharmacological measures, with emphasis placed upon increased energy availability and overall improved nutritional health. Using this all-encompassing type of approach, sports medicine practitioners should feel empowered to continue to promote the lifelong well-being of female athletes in the years to come.

http://www.ncbi.nlm.nih.gov/pubmed/22019502 (2012)

Can we reduce eating disorder risk factors in female college athletes? A randomized exploratory investigation of two peer-led interventions.

Female athletes are at least as at risk as other women for eating disorders (EDs) and at risk for the female athlete triad (i.e., inadequate energy availability, menstrual disorders, and osteoporosis). This study investigated whether two evidence-based programs appear promising for future study if modified to address the unique needs of female athletes.

http://www.ncbi.nlm.nih.gov/pubmed/22177389 (2012)

Eating psychopathology amongst athletes: links to current attachment styles.

The current findings provide evidence to suggest that insecure attachment styles influence athletes' eating psychopathology via their impact on self-esteem, depression, and self-critical perfectionism. Moreover, self-esteem and depression may play more significant role in transferring the impact of insecure attachment styles on elevated eating.

http://www.ncbi.nlm.nih.gov/pubmed/22379716 (2012)

Aesthetic sports as high-risk contexts for eating disorders--young elite dancers and gymnasts perspectives.

This is the first study developed in Portugal which investigates specific characteristics of dance and gymnastics environments that make them high-risk contexts for the development of eating disorders.

http://www.ncbi.nlm.nih.gov/pubmed/21774749 (2011)

Anorexia athletica in pre-professional ballet dancers.

We conclude that more sensitive tools to differentiate between sport-specific (eating) patterns, anorexia athletica and clinically relevant eating disorders are needed, especially for aesthetic sports such as ballet. It remains an important goal to identify athletes with symptoms of anorexia athletica irrespective of their physique and/or sport.

http://www.ncbi.nlm.nih.gov/pubmed/19642982 (2011)

The relation between athletic sports and prevalence of amenorrhea and oligomenorrhea in Iranian female athletes

This study performed as a cross-sectional study. All élite Iranian female athletes of 34 sports federations, including female athletes in national teams and medalists of Tehran were invited to participate. A total of 788 (95% response rate) returned the questionnaires and were examined... These findings support the previous findings in the literature that the prevalence of amenorrhea/oligomenorrhea is high in athletes.

http://www.ncbi.nlm.nih.gov/pubmed/21484043 (2011)

Negative addiction to exercise: are there differences between genders?

No differences were seen in the development of negative addiction exercise symptoms in males and females and there were no changes in the quality of life and mood of these athletes.

http://www.ncbi.nlm.nih.gov/pubmed/20709126 (2010)

Are female athletes at increased risk for disordered eating and its complications?

The purpose of the study was to make a systematic review and describe and confront recent studies that compare the presence of disordered eating and its complications in young female athletes and controls subject.

http://www.ncbi.nlm.nih.gov/pubmed/20446837 (2010)

Relationships among injury and disordered eating, menstrual dysfunction, and low bone mineral density in high school athletes: a prospective study.

These findings indicate that disordered eating, oligomenorrhea/amenorrhea, and low BMD were associated with musculoskeletal injuries in these female high school athletes.

http://www.ncbi.nlm.nih.gov/pubmed/20840569 (2010)

Aspects of disordered eating continuum in elite high-intensity sports.

The prevalence of eating disorders is increased in elite athletes and for this group the cause of starting to diet is related to (a) perception of the paradigm of appearance in the specific sport, (b) perceived performance improvements, and (c) socio-cultural pressures for thinness or an 'ideal' body.

http://www.ncbi.nlm.nih.gov/pubmed/17490455 (2008)

Prevalence of eating disorders and the predictive power of risk models in female elite athletes: a controlled study.

The purposes of this study were to examine the percentage of female elite athletes and controls with disordered eating (DE) behavior and clinical eating disorders (EDs), to investigate what characterize the athletes with EDs, and to evaluate whether a proposed method of screening for EDs in elite athletes does not falsely classify sport-specific behaviors as indicators of EDs.

http://www.ncbi.nlm.nih.gov/pubmed/17909417 (2007)

American College of Sports Medicine position stand. The female athlete triad.

The female athlete triad (Triad) refers to the interrelationships among energy availability, menstrual function, and bone mineral density, which may have clinical manifestations including eating disorders, functional hypothalamic amenorrhea, and osteoporosis.

http://www.ncbi.nlm.nih.gov/pubmed/17879287 (2007)

Prevalence of eating disorders among Blacks in the National Survey of American Life.

Anorexia was the rarest eating disorder among African American adults and adolescents, with age of onset for adults in mid adolescence. No 12-month case of anorexia was found among Caribbean Black adults. Binge eating was the most prevalent eating disorder among adults and adolescents.

http://www.ncbi.nlm.nih.gov/pubmed/17905685 (2007)

Eating disorders in sports - sport in eating disorders

The strong correlation of eating disorders with excessive physical activity and sport underlines the significant role of the weight loss method among diagnostical criteria of eating disorders. Among sportsmen, eating disorders have a higher prevalence (23-25%).

http://www.ncbi.nlm.nih.gov/pubmed/16445307 (2006)

Eating disorders in the male athlete.

Eating disorders do occur in male athletes. They are less prominent than in female athletes, and therefore in danger of being missed. The high-risk sports fall into the same categories as with females: aesthetic sports, sports in which low body fat is advantageous, such as cross-country and marathon running, and sports in which there is a need to 'make weight', including wrestling and horse racing.

http://www.ncbi.nlm.nih.gov/pubmed/15690462 (2005)

The clinical presentation of Japanese women with anorexia nervosa and bulimia nervosa: a study of the Eating Disorders Inventory-2.

Compared with the standardization sample, all the Japanese groups reported significantly greater maturity fears, the Japanese AN-restricting subtype group (AN-R) reported lower levels of drive for thinness and perfectionism, the Japanese BN group reported lower levels of drive for thinness, and the Japanese NonED Group reported lower levels of drive for thinness and perfectionism but higher rates of ineffectiveness.

http://www.ncbi.nlm.nih.gov/pubmed/15849292 (2005)

Low bone mineral density is two to three times more prevalent in non-athletic pre-menopausal women than in elite athletes: a comprehensive controlled study.

Female elite athletes have 3-20% higher BMD than non-athletic controls and HI sports athletes have 3-22% higher BMD compared with MI and LI sports athletes. Low BMD is two to three times more common in non-athletic premenopausal women than in elite athletes.

http://www.ncbi.nlm.nih.gov/pubmed/15334132 (2004)

Eating disorders among athletes

Over the past 20 years, a number of studies have been published that generally suggest a higher frequency of eating disorders among athletes than among non-athletes. Participation in competitive sport has also been considered an important factor related to the development of eating disorders.

http://www.ncbi.nlm.nih.gov/pubmed/14712163 (2004)

Prevalence of eating disorders in elite athletes is higher than in the general population.

The prevalence of EDs is higher in athletes than in controls, higher in female athletes than in male athletes, and more common among those competing in leanness-dependent and weight-dependent sports than in other sports. A collaborative effort among coaches, athletic trainers, parents, physicians, and athletes is optimal for recognizing, preventing, and treating EDs in athletes.

http://www.ncbi.nlm.nih.gov/pubmed/12856447 (2003)

A true picture of eating disorders among African American women: a review of literature.

Sufficient examination of the relationship of familial roles, cultural influences, and unique stressors to African American women are not prevalent in the available studies and are not evaluated as substantial influences on maladaptive eating regulation responses.

http://www.ncbi.nlm.nih.gov/pubmed/12832249 (2003)

Eating disorders in white and black women.

Fifteen white (1.5%) and no black women met lifetime criteria for anorexia nervosa; more white women (N=23, 2.3%) than black women (N=4, 0.4%) met criteria for bulimia nervosa; binge eating disorder also was more common among white women (N=27, 2.7%) than black women (N=15, 1.4%). Few women (white: N=16, 28.1%; black: N=1, 5.3%) ever had received treatment for an eating disorder.

Anaemia Iron Deficiency

http://www.ncbi.nlm.nih.gov/pubmed/22682343 (2012)

Foot-strike haemolysis after a 60-km ultramarathon

This is the first study demonstrating that long-distance running does not induce clinically significant changes in haemoglobin, haematocrit, RBC count or potassium concentration.

http://www.ncbi.nlm.nih.gov/pubmed/22382172 (2012)

Iron Status Is Associated With Endurance Performance and Training in Female Rowers.

Less highly-trained rowers with poor iron status had a lower VO_2peak (-0.32 L/min, p=0.02), and were less energetically-efficient (-1.7%, p=0.09) compared to more highly-trained rowers with poor iron status.

http://www.bloodtransfusion.it/articolosing.aspx?id=000283 (2012)

Sports anaemia: facts or fiction?

There is an ongoing, unsolved debate as to whether iron supplementation, often used by elite athletes, is really necessary or not. A preliminary question that needs an answer is whether the existence of sports anaemia is supported by facts or whether it is fiction.

http://www.ncbi.nlm.nih.gov/pubmed/21751854 (2011)

Intravascular haemolysis during prolonged running on asphalt and natural grass in long and middle distance runners.

Our findings indicate that intravascular haemolysis occurs significantly after prolonged running. Furthermore, we conclude that uneven grass surface results in greater haemolysis compared to asphalt road.

http://www.ncbi.nlm.nih.gov/pubmed/20197784 (2010)

Iron excess in recreational marathon runners.

We investigated the iron status of 170 male and female recreational runners participating in the Zürich marathon... Iron depletion was present in 28% of female runners but in <2% of males, whereas one in six male runners had signs of iron overload. Although iron supplements are widely used by athletes in an effort to increase performance, our findings indicate excess body iron may be common in male recreational runners and suggest supplements should only be used if tests of iron status indicate deficiency.

http://www.ncbi.nlm.nih.gov/pubmed/22628339 (2009)

Haematological and iron metabolism parameters in professional cyclists during the Giro d'Italia 3-weeks stage race

Haematological assessment is crucial for evaluating athletes healthy status. Professional athletes experience physiological modifications during competitions and over a season: the risk of sports anaemia is high. Few descriptions of haematological parameters behaviour during a 3-weeks' cycling stage race have been published.

http://www.ncbi.nlm.nih.gov/pubmed/18641987 (2008)

Prepartum anaemia: prevention and treatment.

His review focuses on the occurrence, prevention and treatment of anaemia during pregnancy in Western societies. Iron deficiency anaemia (IDA) is the most prevalent deficiency disorder and the most frequent form of anaemia in pregnant women.

http://www.ncbi.nlm.nih.gov/pubmed/18092176 (2008)

Anemia and iron status in young fertile non-professional female athletes.

Nearly one fifth of recreational athletes have anemia and a third have iron deficit, these conditions can decrease their physical performance.

http://onlinelibrary.wiley.com/doi/10.1111/j.1365-2621.2002.tb09582.x/abstract (2002)

Release of Iron into Foods Cooked in an Iron Pot: Effect of pH, Salt, and Organic Acids

Salt had no effect, but acidic pH or organic acids (citrate > lactate) significantly increased iron amount, from 1.7mg to 26.8mg Fe per 100g. The amounts released could be important in the treatment and prevention of iron deficiency.

Iron absorption

http://www.ncbi.nlm.nih.gov/pubmed/21916535 (2012)

Herbal infusions as a source of calcium, magnesium, iron, zinc and copper in human nutrition

It is felt that in average consumption the herbal infusions are not important as calcium, magnesium, iron, zinc and copper sources in human nutrition.

http://www.ncbi.nlm.nih.gov/pubmed/21795430 (2011)

Calcium does not inhibit the absorption of 5 milligrams of nonheme or heme iron at doses less than 800 milligrams in nonpregnant women

In conclusion, we demonstrated an isolated effect of calcium (as chloride) on absorption of 5mg of iron provided as nonheme (as sulfate) and heme (as CRBC) iron. This effect was observed at doses higher than previously reported from single-meal studies, starting at ~800mg of calcium.

http://www.ncbi.nlm.nih.gov/pubmed/18666620 (2008)

The content of Ca, Mg, Fe and Cu in selected species of herbs and herb infusions

The values of extractions in the infusions of herb were as follows: 16.1-73.8% Ca, 14.4-37.3% Mg, 5.1-9.7% Fe, 13.1-21.8% Cu. This indicates that a very small part of the ironcan be potentially treated as a bioavailable fraction for persons, using plant drugs as infusions.

http://www.ncbi.nlm.nih.gov/pubmed/18400710 (2008)

Iron absorption in young Indian women: the interaction of iron status with the influence of tea and ascorbic acid.

Mean fractional iron absorption from the reference rice meal was approximately 2.5 times as great in the IDA group as in the control group ($P < 0.05$). The consumption of 1 or 2 cups of tea decreased iron absorption in the control subjects by 49% ($P < 0.05$) or 66% ($P < 0.01$), respectively, and in the IDA group by 59% or 67% ($P < 0.001$ for both), respectively. AA (molar ratio to iron, 2:1 or 4:1) increased iron absorption by 270% or 343%, respectively, in control subjects and by 291% or 350%, respectively, in subjects with IDA ($P < 0.001$).

http://www.ncbi.nlm.nih.gov/pubmed/18275622 (2008)

Association between consumption of black tea and iron status in adult Africans in the North West Province: the THUSA study

Our findings demonstrate that iron deficiency and iron deficiency anaemia is not significantly explained by black tea consumption in a black adult population in South Africa. Tea intake was also not shown to be related to iron status in several sub-populations at risk for iron deficiency.

http://www.ncbi.nlm.nih.gov/pubmed/17249489 (2006)

Mineral migration from stainless steel, cast iron and soapstone (steatite) Brazilian pans to food preparations

We conclude that while cast iron and glass could be best for the consumer's nutritional health, stainless steel and steatite can be used with relatively low risk, provided acid foods are not routinely prepared in those materials.

http://www.ncbi.nlm.nih.gov/pubmed/16155272 (2005)

Inhibitory effects of dietary calcium on the initial uptake and subsequent retention of heme and nonheme iron in humans: comparisons using an intestinal lavage method.

Calcium supplementation reduced heme and total iron without significantly affecting nonheme-iron absorption, regardless of meal bioavailability.

http://www.ncbi.nlm.nih.gov/pubmed/15743017 (2004)

Enhancers of iron absorption: ascorbic acid and other organic acids.

Based on the limited data available, other organic acids may only be effective at ratios of acid to iron in excess of 100 molar. This would translate into the minimum presence/addition of 1g citric acid to a meal containing 3mg iron.

http://www.ncbi.nlm.nih.gov/pubmed/14718031 (2004)

Impact of tea drinking on iron status in the UK: a review.

From the available evidence there is no need to advise any restriction on tea drinking in healthy people with no risk of iron deficiency. In groups at risk of iron deficiency the advice should be to drink tea between meals and to wait at least 1 hour after eating before drinking tea.

http://www.ncbi.nlm.nih.gov/pubmed/12001007 (2002)

Tea consumption and iron status.

This overview shows that tea consumption does not influence iron status in Western populations in which most people have adequateiron stores as determined by serum ferritin concentrations. Only in populations of individuals with marginal iron status does there seem to be a negative association between tea consumption and iron status.

http://www.ncbi.nlm.nih.gov/pubmed/11029010 (2000)

Effect of tea and other dietary factors on iron absorption

Recommendations with respect to tea consumption (when in a critical group) include: consume tea between meals instead of during the meal; simultaneously consume ascorbic acid and/or meat, fish and poultry.

http://www.ncbi.nlm.nih.gov/pubmed/9336558 (1997)

Twelve weeks of endurance exercise training does not affect iron status measures in women.

Results of this study suggest that participation in 12 weeks of moderate-intensity endurance exercise training (walking/running or cycling) is not associated with negative effects on selected measures of iron status in healthy, previously untrained women with normal iron stores (serum ferritin > or = 20 micrograms/L).

http://www.ncbi.nlm.nih.gov/pubmed/9406897 (1997)

Determination of iron content in different parts of herbs used traditionally for anaemia treatment in East Africa

The prominent iron contents of 35.69 and 35.21mg/100g were found in the rootbark of Bridelia cathartica and Lannea stuhlmannii, respectively. The iron content of the decoctions prepared in the traditional way was low. However, the therapeutic potential of the herbs cannot be established on the basis of available iron content alone as other factors play a role in the absorption of iron in the body.

Pregnancy

http://www.nice.org.uk/nicemedia/live/13056/49926/49926.pdf (2010)

National Institute for Health and Clinical Excellence (NICE) -

Dietary interventions and physical activity interventions for weight management before, during and after pregnancy.

My note: an easy-to-read 60-page pdf by the National Health Service, though only 29 pages of core reading., with direct links to other useful online publications by NICE.

USEFUL WEBSITES FOR SPORTS NUTRITION

Australia

http://www.glycemicindex.com/
University of Sydney GI and GL website and database

http://www.ausport.gov.au/ais/
Australian Institute of Sport

http://www.ausport.gov.au/ais/nutrition/recipes/
Recipes

http://sma.org.au/
Sports medicine Australia

Canada

http://www.casm-acms.org/
Canadian Academy of Sport and Exercise Medicine

United Kingdom

http://www.basem.co.uk/
British Association of Sport and Exercise Medicine

http://www.basem.co.uk/index.php?Page=index&PageID=1097
Categories of sports medicine qualification

http://bjsm.bmj.com/
British Journal of Sport Medicine

http://www.bda.uk.com/foodfacts/index.html
The British Dietetic Association

http://www.gmc-uk.org/doctors/register/LRMP.asp
General Medical Council - List of Registered medical Practitioners

http://www.food.gov.uk/

Food Standards Agency

http://www.dh.gov.uk/en/index.htm
Department of Health

United States of America
http://www.acsm.org/
American College of Sports Medicine

http://aoasm.org/
American Osteopathic Association of Sports Medicine

http://ajs.sagepub.com/
American Journal of Sports Medicine

Research papers and other useful links
http://www.cochrane.org/
The Cochrane Collaboration
An international collaboration that prepares and updates healthcare reviews, and also arranges the largest collection of records of randomised controlled trials in the world.

http://www.ncbi.nlm.nih.gov/pubmed/
PubMed
A free database that allows access to over 21 million citations on biomedical literature.

Google scholar UK
http://scholar.google.co.uk/schhp?hl=en

BMI
http://www.bbc.co.uk/news/health-18770328#G1A24H1.58W42C167 (2012)
Where are you on the global fat scale?
My note: a BBC webpage that allows you to enter your age, height, weight, gender and country (includes 177 countries) for a better tailored BMI.

SUGGESTED REFERENCE GUIDES

Manual of nutrition (Reference Book 342) (Paperback) by Food Standards Agency. Only 205 pages and therefore very expensive at about £83 at the time of writing, but it is easy to read and contains a wealth of useful information on nutrition, including nutrients and their roles in the body (and the foods that provide them), the effects of cooking, DRVs, diet planning and much more. ISBN-13: 978-0112431169

Dietary Reference Values of Food Energy and Nutrients for the United Kingdom (Report on Health & Social Subjects) [Paperback] by the Department of Health.
This is the latest publication by the DoH on DRVs. It has 235 pages of useful and easy-to-find information. At the time of writing it retailed at £19.50. ISBN-13: 978-0113213979

Manual of Dietetic Practice [Hardcover], Fourth Edition. Edited by Briony Thomas of The British Dietetic Association, and Jacki Bishop, formerly senior lecturer in Nutrition and Dietetics at the University of Surrey.
A massive 952-page reference book put together by over 60 very highly qualified professionals in dietetics and human nutrition. About £75 at the time of writing. ISBN-13: 978-1405135252.

Excel download and programs

Link for free download: https://drive.google.com/folderview?id=0B0oVUwyLmK 33YXlpUEYtVkJHSjQ&usp=sharing

Fuel for Sport Excel Programs

All the Excel folders, workbooks and sheets are listed below exactly as they appear in the program.

Workbooks only

Workbook: Excel program information (read this first)

- Sheet: Information

Workbook: Conversions

- Sheet: Conversions

Workbook: Personal data sheets

- Sheet: Blank
- Sheet: Example

Folders and workbooks

Folder: Fuel for Sport Excel Chapter **1 Human Energy**

➢ Workbook: Fat loss & exercise

- Sheet: Fat loss & exercise

Folder: Fuel for Sport Excel Chapter **2 Carbohydrates**

➢ Workbook: CHO intakes, GI and GL

- Sheet: CHO intakes
- Sheet: GI and GL

Folder: Fuel for Sport Excel Chapter **3 Protein**

➢ Workbook: Protein intakes

- Sheet: Protein

Folder: Fuel for Sport Excel Chapter **4 Fat**

➢ Workbook: Fat % and predictions, waist and hip ratios, and BMI

- Sheet: Fat % prediction
- Sheet: Waist-hip ratios

- Sheet: BMI
- Sheet: Fat % and true fat loss

Folder: Fuel for Sport Excel Chapter **5 Losing the Fat**

- ➤ Workbook: DIT
  - Sheet: DIT
- ➤ Workbook: Food guide analysis
  - Sheet: Food guide analysis
- ➤ Workbook: RMR, TDEE, fat loss and fat cells
  - Sheet: RMR methods
  - Sheet: TDEE
  - Sheet: Fixed kcal reduction
  - Sheet: Fat loss methods
  - Sheet: Recom. Fat loss mtd.
  - Fat cells and fat loss

Folder: Fuel for Sport Excel Chapter **6 Fluid Essentials**

- ➤ Workbook: Fluid Essentials all-in-one
  - Sheet: Salt and sodium
  - Fluid loss and perspiration rates
  - Sheet: Glycerol and fluids
  - Sheet: Homemade fluids
  - Sheet: Units of alcohol

Folder: Fuel for Sport Excel Chapter **8 Supplements**

- ➤ Workbook: Caffeine and creatine
  - Sheet: Caffeine and creatine

Folder: Fuel for Sport Excel Chapter **9 Upping the Mass**

- ➤ Workbook: Dietetic method for BM increase
  - Sheet: BM increase
  - Sheet: BM %-age gains

INDEX

β

β-alanine   182, 183, 287, 288

A

adenosine diphosphate (ADP)   19, 247, 264

adenosine monophosphate (AMP)   19

adenosine triphosphate (ATP)   19-22, 27, 28, 31, 51, 118, 175, 204,
                                            246, 309

adipose tissue   28, 29, 69, 268

aerobic exercise   21-23, 31, 52, 87, 190, 242, 266, 269,
                                            308

aerobic lipolytic system   31

aerobic system   21, 23, 28, 29, 31

after burn   87

air displacement plethysmography method   74

alanine   52, , 182, 183, 287, 288

albumen (egg protein)   53, 203

alcohol   8, 17-19, 89, 90, 93, 118, 123, 125,
                                            148, 149, 154, 156-161, 168, 208, 222,
                                            236, 238, 243-245, 254, 268, 278-280,
                                            311, 330

alkaloids   200

amenorrhoea   64, 218, 221, 222, 226, 230

American College of Sports Medicine   222, 247, 284, 318, 327

amino acids   8, 20, 32, 51-55, 58, 92, 173, 181-183,
                                            185, 187, 196, 202-205, 233, 254, 257,
                                            259, 288, 289, 307, 309, 310

amylopectin   34

amylose   34

anabolic steroids   200, 201, 306, 312,

anaemia   162, 179, 180, 208, 227, 229, 231, 320,
                                            321, 323, 324

anaerobic exercise   20, 26, 31, 82, 87, 184, 185, 204, 206,
                                            304, 310

anaerobic glycolytic system   20

androgen   200

androstenedione	201, 306
anorexia nervosa	162, 218, 219, 224, 318, 320
appetite suppressers	191
apricots	232
Archimedes's principle	72
arginine	20, 52, 187, 207, 304, 309
asparagine	52
aspartic acid	52
aspirin	132, 191, 207
ATP phosphocreatine (ATP-PC) system	19, 21, 23, 28, 237

B

bad cholesterol	65, 79, 82
ballet	105, 224, 316
banned substances	195, 208, 209, 211, 312
basal body temperature	123
basal metabolic rate (BMR)	83, 84, 241
beats per minute (bpm)	24, 242
bioelectrical impedance analysis (BIA)	71, 73, 263, 264
biological value (BV)	56, 57, 203, 204
binge-eating	219, 220
Bod Pod	74, 264
body builders	198, 212
body building	162, 224
body composition	59, 69-71, 74, 84-86, 116, 184, 194, 197, 201, 206, 258-261, 263, 266, 269, 295, 297, 299, 300, 302, 303, 305, 307, 310, 311, 313, 314
body fat	61- 64, 67, 69, 75, 93, 116, 184, 195, 243, 259- 261, 263, 264, 266, 289, 313, 314, 318
body mass index (BMI)	9, 14, 59, 61, 66-71, 85, 86, 114, 221, 222, 234, 235, 259-263, 270, 307, 327, 329, 330
body types	67, 214
bone density	64, 67, 106, 221, 222, 226, 264
bone loss	64
branched-chain amino acids (BCAA),	52, 182-185, 257, 288, 289, 309
breakfast	112, 168, 199, 235, 267, 270, 285

bulimia nervosa	162, 218-220, 225, 318, 320

C

caffeinated drinks	148, 135, 156, 182, 186
calcium	118, 121, 133, 151, 171, 175, 206, 221, 227, 232, 266, 267, 271, 322, 323
calorie counting	113, 114
capsaicin	91, 193, 194, 295, 296
capsinoids	193, 194, 299
carbohydrates	8, 11, 17, 18, 20-22, 26, 33-37, 40-47, 49, 51, 57, 81, 89-93, 96, 97, 99-105, 134-136, 139, 144, 152, 154-156, 172, 173, 181, 198, 199, 202, 205, 207, 208, 215, 216, 238-240, 243, 251-253, 256, 329
carbohydrate cycle	41, 144, 145, 150, 202, 207
carbohydrate loading	36, 43, 49, 50, 251, 252
carbohydrate storage	33
cardiovascular disease	200
casein	53, 55, 57, 203, 257, 258, 273
catechins	195, 296, 298
cell damage	163, 180, 198
cellulose	34
cheese	79, 171, 172, 175, 177, 236
chicken liver	232
chitosan	206, 296
chlorine	118, 119, 133, 151, 175
chocolate	13, 14, 38, 79, 125, 155, 167, 231, 232
cholesterol	41, 48, 59, 64-66, 79, 80, 82, 194, 199, 200, 220, 232, 265, 300, 307
choline	12, 286
chromium	176, 206, 283, 296
coffee	90, 154-156, 186, 196, 280
cognitive behavioural therapy (CBT)	218, 220
conjugated linoleic acid (CLA)	206
contact sports	234
convulsions	132
copper	176, 205, 322
cramps	18, 132, 136, 189, 225, 238, 245

crash diets	113
creatine	19, 20, 182, 187-189, 190, 202, 207, 209, 216, 217, 246, 289-293, 303, 309-312, 315, 330
creatinine	20
cycling	43, 94, 145, 167, 190, 224, 229, 234, 241, 255, 277, 278, 293, 294, 302, 321
cysteine	52, 233

D

dairy products	33, 55, 57, 58, 109, 110, 172, 173, 183, 185, 193, 314
dance	105, 221, 241, 316
dehydration	106, 113, 117, 118, 125-128, 130, 132, 136, 138, 140, 143, 144, 157, 189, 208, 273, 311
delaying fatigue	32
Department of Health (DoH)	41, 82, 163, 164, 166, 235, 284, 327, 328,
dehydroepiandrosterone (DHEA)	201, 305, 306
dextrin	34, 35
diarrhoea	204, 230, 238
dieresis	137
diet and metabolism	111
dietary-induced thermogenesis (DIT)	83, 89, 90, 142, 267, 330
dietary reference values (DRVs)	163, 170, 328
dieting	105, 106, 112, 121, 222, 234
disaccharides	33, 34
dispensable amino acids (DAA)	51, 183, 192, 202, 207
distance running	224, 276, 320,
diuresis	136, 138, 147, 156, 273
dizziness	41, 126, 132
docosahexanoic acid (DHA)	80
docosapentanoic acid (DPA)	80, 81
dried herbs	231
dual energy x-ray absorptiometry (DEXA)	71, 72, 74, 222, 264

E

eating disorders	63, 93, 105, 106, 162, 192, 218, 219, 222-224, 315-320
ectomorphs	214
eggs	53, 55, 171-174, 177, 183, 185, 236
eicosapentanoic acid (EPA)	80
electrolytes	118, 131-135, 139, 148, 149, 152- 156, 160, 271
endomorphs	214
endurance athletes	13, 14, 22, 129, 131, 143, 145, 187, 192, 231, 249, 251, 256, 265
energy drinks	186, 208, 311
energy in use	24
energy replacement drinks	134
ephedrine	91, 182, 190, 191, 207, 293-296, 311
essential fat	59, 79, 80
estimated average requirement (EAR)	164
ethnicity	68, 85, 87
exercise duration	26, 129, 141

F

famine response	111, 113
fast twitch	23, 87, 214, 249
fasting	66, 83, 84, 92, 111, 121, 266
fasting mode	111
fat-burning foods	83, 91
fat cell hypertrophy	114
fat distribution	70, 72, 76, 263
fatigue	17, 21, 23, 27, 29-32, 41, 42, 44, 48, 49, 78, 124, 130, 144, 179, 183, 184, 187, 190, 229, 245-247, 250, 289, 291, 292, 294, 314
fatigue during aerobic exercise	31
fatigue during anaerobic exercise	31
fat loss	42, 54, 74-76, 81, 83, 87-89, 91, 96, 97, 99, 100-106, 112, 113, 114, 190, 191, 193, 194, 197, 199, 206, 207, 257, 266-268, 289, 297, 300, 304, 314, 329, 330

fat loss/weight loss predictions	76
fat oxidation	91, 191, 195, 196, 243, 244, 266, 269, 271, 295, 296, 299, 300, 311
fat percentage	59-64, 69-76, 78, 85, 86, 99, 100, 104, 128, 167, 195, 212, 260, 261, 263
fat percentage ratings	61, 62
female athlete triad	218, 222, 223, 315, 318
fibre	17, 23, 24, 33, 34, 36, 40, 41, 47, 166, 194, 198-200, 214, 231, 235, 237, 239, 268, 269, 288
fighting sports	224
fish	20, 55, 57, 58, 80, 93, 109, 110, 171, 173, 176, 177, 183, 187, 190, 193, 198, 232, 236, 264, 284, 285, 324
fixed calorie reduction	97, 98
fixed-percentage reduction method	99
fluid balance	117, 118, 273, 275
fluid cycle	118, 136, 142, 148, 157
fluid deficit	118, 128, 129, 130, 141, 146, 276
fluid intake	58, 117, 118, 126, 128, 131, 137, 140, 141, 143, 146-149, 272, 274, 276
fluid replacement drinks	134
fluids	45, 49, 58, 76, 112, 118, 125, 128, 132, 134-136, 139, 142, 144, 147, 149, 152, 154, 155, 159, 160, 193, 200, 239, 240, 272-274, 330
folic acid	173, 235
Food and Drug Administration (FDA)	57, 190, 293
food labelling	119, 170
food plate	83, 107-109, 111
food pyramid/triangle	83, 107-109, 111, 165, 168
forskolin	194
free radicals	163
fructose	33, 34, 233, 240, 243
fast twitch (FT)	23, 87, 214, 249

G

gamma-linoleic acid	80
gastrointestinal bleeding	229
ginkgo biloba	208, 301, 311

ginseng	197, 208, 299, 301, 302, 311
glycaemic load (GL)	33, 37-40, 42, 43, 47, 91, 112, 238, 239, 255, 326, 329
glucomannan	194, 296, 300, 301
glucose	20-22, 26, 29, 31, 33, 34, 36-38, 40, 41, 43, 44, 47, 53, 57, 91-93, 113, 136, 139, 144, 145, 148, 150, 152-155, 176, 220, 240, 243, 252, 274
glutamic acid	52
glutamine	192, 193, 202, 203, 286, 297
glycaemic index (GI)	33, 36, 37, 40, 254, 255
glycerine	136
glycerol	136, 138, 139, 143-145, 147, 149, 150, 153, 154, 185, 277, 278, 295, 330
glycine	20, 52, 187
glycogen	19-22, 24-29, 31, 32, 34, 35, 40-49, 51, 52, 54, 57, 87, 91-93, 97, 111, 113, 135, 148, 156, 168, 192, 194, 215, 223, 237- 240, 244, 251, 252-254, 289, 297
glycolysis	21, 22, 28
green tea	91, 155, 191, 195, 207, 281, 295, 296, 298-300, 302, 311
growth hormones	200
guarana	196, 208, 311
guideline daily amounts (GDA)	119, 121, 170
gymnastics	63, 135, 221, 224, 234, 316

H

haematuria	228, 229
haemoglobin	176, 227, 230, 231, 320
haemolysis	180, 229, 230, 286, 320, 321
headaches	9, 126, 132, 142, 186, 197, 228
heart rate (HR)	24, 48, 242, 264
heat exhaustion	124, 126
heat stroke	124, 191
hemp seed protein	203
herbal infusions	232, 322
high-density lipoprotein (HDL)	65, 66, 79, 82
high-intensity intermittent exercise (HIIE)	88, 266

high-intensity interval training (HIIT)	21, 88, 187, 266, 310
histidine acids	52, 183, 233
HMB	182, 197, 198, 302, 303, 311, 315
homemade sport fluids	135, 149, 156
hormones	48, 64, 123, 182, 200, 201, 209, 221, 305, 306, 312
horse racing	135, 224, 318
hydrogenated fat	82
hydrostatic weighing	71, 72, 266
hydroxycitric acid	206
hyperthermia	118, 124, 271-273
hypertonic drinks	135, 148
hypoglycaemia	31, 41, 42, 44, 252
hyponatraemia	117, 128, 131, 132, 134, 140, 145, 272, 274
hypothermia	118, 124, 125, 128
hypotonic sports drinks	148

I

ibuprofen	132, 229
ice skating	224
inflammatory drugs	229
insensible fluid losses	117
insoluble fibre (dietary fibre)	34, 40, 41, 194, 268, 269
insulin	40, 42, 91, 92, 205, 215, 220, 245, 266, 292
International Society of Sports Nutrition	12, 258, 284, 290, 293, 307
intra-abdominal fat	60, 77
iodine	176
iron	174, 176, 179, 180, 196, 205, 218, 227-231, 233, 280, 320-322, 324, 325
iron deficiency	179, 180, 218, 227, 229, 230, 233, 280, 320, 321-324
iron-deficiency anaemia (IDA)	179, 180, 218, 227-229, 231, 233, 321, 323
isoflavones	206
isoleucine	52, 183, 184
isotonic drinks	135, 135, 144
isotonic sport drink	145

J

jogging   25, 94, 144, 231

K

kava kava   197, 301
kidneys   20, 58, 91, 118, 131, 149, 160, 204

L

lactic acid   20, 21, 29-31, 247
lactic acid system   20
lactose   34, 203, 275
l-arginine   207, 304
leptin   92, 93, 268, 296
leucine   52, 183, 184, 197, 257
lipolysis   21, 295
lipolytic glycolysis   22
lipoprotein profile   65, 66
liposuction   114
low-density lipoprotein (LDL)   65, 79, 80, 82, 194, 199, 300
lower reference nutrient intake (LRNI)   164
lysine   52, 233

M

macronutrients   18, 89, 90, 96, 98, 102, 105, 117, 180, 226, 287
macrophages   48
magnesium   12, 118, 121, 133, 175, 179, 182, 205, 283, 286, 309, 322
maltodextrin   35
manganese   177
marathon runners   8, 129, 140, 230, 231, 251, 321
meal frequency   12, 235, 284
meal replacement products (MRPs)   35, 198, 199, 302
meat   8, 20, 55, 57, 58, 79, 107, 109, 110, 170, 175, 177, 183, 185, 187, 190, 196, 232, 324
mesomorphs   214

metabolic rate	57, 83, 84, 87, 91, 97, 265, 266, 297
methionine	20, 52, 187, 205
methoxyisoflavone	12, 286
maximum heart rate (MHR)	24
micronutrients	162, 170, 178, 280, 287
Mifflin-St Jeor method	83
milk	13, 14, 34, 47, 53, 55, 57, 79, 121, 135, 148, 152, 171-173, 175-177, 185, 193, 196, 198, 203, 257-259, 273, 275, 307
minerals	119, 134, 151, 152, 162-164, 174, 176-179, 181, 196, 198, 199, 203, 205, 208, 216, 226, 231, 280, 281, 283, 311
monosaccharaides	33, 34
monounsaturated fat	79-81, 271
muscle anabolism	200, 205
muscle fibres	17, 23, 24, 200, 214, 288
muscle loss	54, 87, 97
muscle spasms	132

N

National Institutes of Health (NIH)	61, 62, 263, 284
near infrared interactance (NIR)	74
negative calories	90
net protein utilization (NPU)	56
nitric oxide	12, 206, 207, 286, 304
non-essential fats	79
Nutrition Society	15
nuts	47, 55, 57, 58, 79, 80, 168, 172-175, 177, 215

O

oats	41, 72, 79, 121, 168
obesity	9, 67, 68, 114, 191, 220, 234, 243, 260-263, 265, 267, 270, 276, 295, 296, 298, 301, 314
oestrogen	64, 221, 226, 227
oily fish	80, 171
oligomenorrhoea	221, 226
oligosaccharide	35

omega-3	79-82, 235, 265
omega-6	79-81, 235
omega-9	79
osteoporosis	206, 218, 221, 222, 226, 227, 315, 318
oxygen debt	29, 30, 87

P

palpitations	186, 191, 195, 228, 294
parsley	193, 231
pasta	41, 58, 169
pectin	34
perspiration	18, 117, 118, 125, 130, 131, 133, 140, 141, 229, 272, 330
phenylalanine	52
phosphocreatine (PC)	19-21, 23, 27, 28, 187, 237, 246, 290, 309
phosphorus	175
placebo	201, 209, 210, 273, 277, 281, 290, 294, 295, 297, 299, 306, 307, 313
plasma	113, 135, 137, 147, 227, 231, 273, 291, 308
polysaccharides	34, 35, 170
polyunsaturated fat	79, 80
pork liver	232
potassium	118, 121, 133, 134, 175, 230, 271, 320
post-training fluid	135, 146, 147, 152, 153
pregnancy	134, 173, 176, 228, 234, 235, 321, 325
pre-training fluid	137-139, 143
pre-training hydration	137
pro-hormones	138, 200, 201, 209, 305
proline	52
protein	8, 17, 18, 24, 26, 36, 39-42, 45, 47, 51-58, 81, 89, 90, 92, 93, 96, 97, 99, 100-105, 111, 113, 135, 153-156, 168, 172, 177, 181-185, 192, 193, 196, 198, 199, 201-205, 207, 215-217, 227, 231, 232, 238, 239, 244, 245, 252-254, 256, 257, 259, 267-269, 273, 289, 297, 300, 303, 304, 307, 309, 310, 313, 314, 329

protein digestibility correct amino acid score (PDCAAS)	55, 57, 203, 204, 259
protein efficiency ratio (PER)	56, 259
protein powder	153, 154, 199, 202, 204

Q

quercetin	12, 286
Quetelet Index	66, 261
Adolphe Quetelet	66, 261

R

recommended daily allowance (RDA)	8, 170
reference nutrient intake (RNI)	164, 167, 170-172, 174-177
relative protein	56
resistance training	43, 47, 86, 94, 187, 192, 212, 249, 258, 268, 289, 297, 300, 302-304, 307, 309, 310, 315
respiration	117, 125, 140
resting metabolic rate (RMR)	83-87, 94, 95, 241, 242, 265, 266, 297, 330

S

salt	117-121, 132, 134, 150, 152-154, 166, 168, 170, 175, 176, 239, 256, 272, 322, 330
salt tablets	134
saturated fat	64, 79, 81, 96, 168, 232, 264, 271
scuba diving	234
selenium	177, 281, 282
serine	52
serotonin	32
skin-fold callipers	72
slow twitch (ST)	23, 87, 214
snacking	167
sodium	118-121, 131, 133, 134, 147, 152, 153, 166, 175, 176, 180, 199, 232, 271, 273, 274, 281, 330
sodium chloride	118, 134, 152, 175, 176
soluble fibre (roughage)	36, 40, 41

soy protein	53, 55, 203, 204, 257, 258
spinach	171, 173, 193, 196, 232
spirulina	196, 298, 299, 300
starch	33, 34, 36, 170
starvation mode	84, 111
steroids	200, 201, 306, 312
St John's wort	197
stomach cramps	136, 238
storage fat	60, 63
stress	48, 49, 58, 64, 78, 85, 220, 221, 226, 227, 271, 300, 304, 308, 320
subcutaneous fat	60
sucrose	34, 35, 240, 243
supplements	53, 54, 126, 156, 163, 170, 176-182, 186-188, 190, 191, 193-195, 199, 200, 202-211, 216, 217, 228, 231, 232, 235, 236, 252, 254, 256, 280-284, 286, 287, 289, 293-298, 301, 302, 304, 306, 307, 309, 310, 312, 313, 315, 321, 330

T

tea	90, 91, 154-156, 191, 195, 207, 232, 233, 281, 295, 296, 298-300, 302, 311, 322-324
temperature	17, 59, 72, 79, 84, 85, 89, 90, 117, 118, 121-125, 127-130, 142, 147, 157, 186, 190, 267, 271-273, 275, 276
testosterone	64, 78, 200, 201, 205, 222, 306, 308, 309
thermogenesis	83, 88-90, 142, 266-268, 275, 295, 296, 311
threonine	52
thyme	231
thyroxin	85
tomatoes	196, 232
total daily energy expenditure (TDEE)	83, 94-96, 99, 100-103, 105, 112, 214-216, 241, 330
trace elements	174, 176, 283
trans-fatty acids	82
triglyceride (level)	65

| tryptophan | 32, 52 |
| tyrosine | 52 |

U

ubiquinone	204, 308
University of Sydney	40, 255, 326
unsaturated fat	79, 96
urine/urination	18, 20, 53, 92, 117, 118, 126, 129, 131, 137, 141, 146, 147, 149, 157, 163, 171, 186, 189, 198, 209, 228, 229, 234, 278, 293, 312

V

valine	52, 183, 184
vegetables	34, 41, 55, 80, 90, 93, 109, 110, 121, 165, 166, 169, 171-173, 175-177, 232, 235, 239, 255, 284, 285
vegetarian	58, 230, 232
vegetarians	20, 107, 171, 187, 190, 203, 204, 217, 230, 292
visceral fat	60, 269, 314
vitamin A (retinal)	163, 171, 236, 281, 282
vitamin B_1 (thiamine)	172
vitamin B_2 (riboflavin)	126, 171, 172, 283
vitamin B_3 (niacin)	173, 285
vitamin B_4	171
vitamin B_5 (pantothenic acid)	173
vitamin B_6 (pyridoxine)	173, 205, 283
vitamin B_9 (folic acid)	173, 235
vitamin B_{12} (cobalamin)	162, 173, 196, 227, 283
vitamin C (ascorbic acid)	151, 164, 166, 169, 171, 174, 231-233, 281, 282, 285, 286, 322-324
vitamin D	171, 221, 266, 267, 282
vitamin E	163, 172, 177, 281, 282, 284
vitamin G	170
vitamin H or B_7 (biotin)	174
VO_2 max	247, 248, 281, 310
vomiting	132, 205, 225

W

waist-to-hip ratio 77, 260

walking 25, 94, 95, 144, 167, 234, 241, 274, 276, 314, 324

weight training 212, 229, 234, 237, 266, 311

weight-gain supplements 54, 216

whey protein 53, 56, 57, 203, 257, 268, 307, 309

World Health Organization (WHO) 57

X

xylose 33

Y

yoga 234, 305

yohimbine 196, 197, 207, 300

Z

zinc 177, 179, 205, 271, 283, 308, 309, 322

zinc methionine and magnesium aspartate (ZMA) 182, 205, 286, 308, 309